Alpha Development Team

Publisher
Kathy Nebenhaus

Editorial Director
Gary M. Krebs

Managing Editor
Bob Shuman

Marketing Brand Manager
Felice Primeau

Acquisitions Editor
Jessica Faust

Development Editors
Phil Kitchel
Amy Zavatto

Assistant Editor
Georgette Blau

Production Team

Development Editor
Al McDermid

Production Editor
Robyn Burnett

Copy Editor
Susan Aufheimer

Cover Designer
Mike Freeland

Photo Editor
Richard H. Fox

Illustrator
Jody Schaeffer

Book Designers
Scott Cook and Amy Adams of DesignLab

Indexer
Angie Bess

Layout/Proofreading
Carrie Allen, John Bitter, Pete Lippincott

Contents at a Glance

Contents

Foreword

Everyone wants to know what their handwriting says about them, but so often they are afraid that they will come off poorly and it will be a hurtful experience. Actually, it is just the opposite because there are so many more positive qualities to be found in a handwriting than there are problems. We look at our handwriting and think that it doesn't look neat enough or it doesn't look like what we were taught in school. These things are not that important to the handwriting analyst who is looking for the basic personality and character of the writer. And, the handwriting analyst is in the happy position of revealing some very astonishingly supportive qualities in each of us.

All of us have been intrigued by the many *Idiot's Guides* that have helped us around the complexities of a variety of subjects. This new book, *The Complete Idiot's Guide to Handwriting Analysis*, opens the door to handwriting terms and tools in a light-hearted, down-to-earth, humorous way that will appeal to the general public as they pursue what might otherwise be a task, rather than an adventure.

Sheila Lowe comes to us with a 30-year background of teaching handwriting, and of operating a thriving business known as Sheila Lowe & Associates, the Write Choice. She was certified by the American Handwriting Analysis Foundation in Campbell, California. Well-known and admired for her outstanding Vanguard Conferences for graphologists in business across the United States, her computer program, *Sheila Lowe's Handwriting Analyzer*, has brought handwriting analysis into the 21st century.

Through her creation of the Vanguard Conferences, Sheila has worked tirelessly to help graphologists adopt and maintain ethical standards of practice. In order to raise the standards of graphology, she sponsors a certification program, not only of those entering the profession, but also those who are already graphologists and want to assure themselves that they are, as she puts it, "top of their field."

Sheila has been on the lecture, radio, and television talk show circuit across the country. She is always championing the merits of handwriting analysis as a personnel management tool—part of a company's testing package, where the analyst, as part of the testing team, helps the client select the best applicant for the job description according to the guidelines of the EEOC. In a one-on-one personal assessment, the analyst helps the client come to a fuller realization of personal gifts with information as to how to overcome any soft areas that might be holding back the client from realizing his full potential. Sheila's philosophy is, "It is always worthwhile to make others aware of their own worth!"

Sheila has included all these facets of her education and living into the *The Complete Idiot's Guide to Handwriting Analysis*. The reader will quickly realize that handwriting is not only "brain writing" in expressive movement, but behavior manifested nonverbally on paper. It is where the conscious and the unconscious meet.

June Canoles, SND

Introduction

Is something blocking you from getting what you want, socially, financially, in your marriage? Your career? Sometimes we don't know the answer ourselves, but the causes appear in our handwriting. The fact that you've picked up this book shows that you are interested in learning more about yourself or someone you care about.

Handwriting analysis can provide the kind of information you need to improve your self-image and all your relationships. Like a mirror image of who you really are inside, handwriting reflects your strengths and potentials, your fears and dreams, thinking style and social style, and helps identify areas you might like to develop further.

When I began studying handwriting in 1967, I felt frustrated by the vagueness in the explanations for different parts of handwriting. Even worse were the contradictory definitions between books. How do you know which one to believe?

The Complete Idiot's Guide to Handwriting Analysis teaches the *theory* behind handwriting analysis. Rather than making lists of letters and their supposed meanings, understand why certain strokes are formed the way they are.

Maybe you've studied handwriting before, but found the method you learned didn't quite "click" for you; or maybe this is your very first exposure to handwriting analysis personality this way. Either way, you're about to get an entirely different perspective on those squiggles and lines we leave on paper. So get ready to change the way you look at other people, yourself, and, most assuredly, handwriting!

How to Use This Book

An old Chinese proverb says "A journey of a thousand miles begins with the first step." Learning to analyze handwriting may seem like an impossible task, but if we break it into manageable parts, you'll be surprised at how easy it can be. This book has six sections, each one designed to lead you step-by-step though the process.

Part 1, Read My Loops, Lays a foundation of solid research. We'll discuss what you can learn from handwriting, and the tools you'll need.

Part 2, This Is Your Life: The Page, shows a whole new way to look at handwriting and the paper it's written on. You'll learn about time and space in handwriting before dipping your toes into the complexities of personality development.

Part 3, Let's Dance: Movement, introduces the more advanced concepts of rhythm, speed, and pressure. Then we'll learn how connections between letters and slant reveal emotional responsiveness.

Part 4, Just My Style: Form, moves into the outer self, and explores the masks people wear in public.

Part 5, Sweating the Small Stuff, gets into some of the details of writing on envelops, individual letter forms, beginning and ending strokes. You'll also learn about red flags for some very nasty behavior, including substance abuse.

Part 6, The Last Word, teaches you how to write a handwriting analysis and shows how to make your education pay off. Finally, we'll discuss the role computers play.

Scattered throughout each chapter are boxes of useful and interesting "extra" information.

Fine Points

These are the nitty-gritty, down-and-dirty tips and tricks that give you that little something extra.

Chicken Scratch

Pay attention to these warnings. They'll help you avoid the mistakes and pitfalls that could end up hurting the people you want to help.

Write Words

Graphology has some words you've probably never heard of before. Here's where you'll find out what they mean.

Tales from the Quill

Graphologists have some fascinating stories to tell. Here's where you'll find them.

Acknowledgments

In the beginning was Roland Sparks, without whose kicks in the butt, this book would never have been possible. He got me going in the right direction; Billie Talley, who showed me the way through quicksand when there seemed no hope; Si Cohen, mentor, past partner, friend, whose example (good and bad!) has been a learning experience. Then, that listening ear, shoulder to cry on, and generally good bud, Linda Larson, who generously shares whatever she has; and Roger Rubin, graphologist extraordinaire, who's always ready with a second opinion, advice, or a bawdy joke.

Without Bob Joseph's unbounded kindness, patience, and direction, I might have abandoned this challenging field altogether. I thank him for that, and for hanging in through countless phone calls, day and night, from all over the country. My deep appreciation to Edi Steele (who earned $400 a week as a graphologist during the depression) for her wonderful stories, instruction, and friendship. Many thanks, also, to Tam Deachman, who has made many important contributions to my progress, and whose feedback on this project has been invaluable; and thanks to David Karpeles, who made available a never-before published handwriting sample of Adolph Hitler.

And, finally, extra special thanks and appreciation to my second and third husband Bill McElroy, who so often literally footed the bill to allow me to do my work. His pride in what I do and his support have gotten me through. This book is dedicated to him.

Special Thanks to the Technical Reviewer

The Complete Idiot's Guide to Handwriting Analysis was reviewed by an expert who double-checked the accuracy of what you'll learn here, to help us ensure that this book gives you everything you need to know about handwriting analysis. Special thanks are extended to Tricia Clapp.

Part 1
Read My Loops

Before you get started studying for your new career or hobby as a handwriting analyst, there are a few things you'll need to know. Things such as, where it all got started, who the Masters were, and the feud that's been waged between the two main schools of thought for most of this century.

Then, there's the stuff you'll need to outfit your graphologist's toolkit. It's not a lot, but it is important. I'll also get you prepared to head out in search of those all-important handwriting samples. Suitably outfitted, you'll soon be on your way to looking at handwriting up-close and personal.

Chapter 1

Your Handwriting Is You

In This Chapter

- Who is this person, anyway?
- Historically speaking
- How the French and Germans see it
- Everybody else gets into the act

Have you ever looked at your doctor and wondered if the sloppy handwriting on his prescription pad reflects the way he diagnoses his patients? Or have you seen a neat, pretty handwriting and thought, "that looks like a friendly person"? If you're reading this book you've probably looked at many handwritings and connected what you saw with some personality trait that you know fits the writer to a tee.

The study of personality is as intriguing as a hall of mirrors—just when you think you've got it figured out, another side emerges to mystify and confound you. Long before Sigmund Freud, who brought new meaning to the word "complex," man sought answers to the question of why we feel and act as we do.

Researchers have developed a wide array of personality tests to help psychologists understand what makes people tick. If you've ever faced a psychological test battery, you know it can be an intimidating way to spend a day: There you are, sweating the 550 items on the widely used *MMPI,* wondering whether you've answered "correctly." You're trying to decide whether that *ink blot* is a sheep in wolf's clothing or merely a flower; and you're making up stories that you hope will properly fit the *TAT,* all the while wondering if the results will make you look like an axe murderer. And by the time you've finished, you're beginning to *feel* like an axe murderer!

Write Words

MMPI (Minnesota Multiphasic Personality Inventory) is a psychological test developed during World War II and still widely used in personality assessment today. Like handwriting analysis, it addresses matters such as moods, fears, and general preferences. **Ink blot** (or Rorschach test) is a test for which there are no right or wrong answers, but the psychologist interprets a person's view of a series of inkblots. In the **TAT** (or Thematic Apperception Test) the subject is shown a series of pictures and is asked to tell a story about what is happening in each one.

There is an easier way to learn the truth about who someone really is on the inside, and that person doesn't have to answer even one question: handwriting analysis. Handwriting is a projection of personality in the truest sense of the word. Just like the movie you see projected onto the silver screen, the trail of ink someone leaves behind on a sheet of paper vividly tells a story—his or her story.

Behind Every Handwriting Is a Human Being

From the moment of birth, an infant's tiny brain begins to record every experience, every sight, every sound. Billions of life events are stored in that miraculous computer in his head, waiting for the moment when a fact or event needs to be called up and remembered. No amount of gigabytes or RAM could match the memory functions of this computer as its highly complex system of programming keeps track of every single piece of information.

Of course, most experiences are not important enough to keep in the foreground of our daily life, and some are just too embarrassing or too painful to *want* to remember them. Freud recognized that far too many things happen for us to be able to remember them all, so most memories are archived or stored in the unconscious mind, waiting to be recalled when we need them.

Like an iceberg with most of its mass hidden beneath the surface, most of the experiences that make us who we are remain unseen yet ever present. When a certain event or sound or a particular scent jogs your memory, you might suddenly recall something that happened when you were only three years old. Wow! You had totally forgotten, but there it is again, as clear as if it had just happened this morning. And it doesn't have to be anything important.

Handwriting as Body Language

Handwriting is a "psychic photograph" of the larger part of the iceberg. It is a written record of how the writer has processed all the experiences she has amassed in her lifetime. You might think of it as a sort of *EEG* (brain wave recording) of personality. In fact, some handwriting analysts say it should be called "brainwriting," rather than handwriting. Why is that?

When you pick up a pen and begin to write, everything that ever happened to you coalesces and travels down the nerves from your brain, through your arm, into your hand and out onto the paper in the flow of ink from your pen.

Body language, tone of voice, and facial expressions tell a lot about someone, and handwriting is just one more piece of the puzzle. The difference is, you may be able to consciously change the way you walk, your facial expression, or how you speak, but your handwriting will tell the truth about who you are inside.

Write Words

EEG (electroencephalogram) is a device used to record brainwaves.

Whether your analysis uncovers a sweet-natured, generous person, or an uptight, angry one, never forget, there is a human being behind every handwriting. The Golden Rule you learned in grade school still applies: Treat others as you want to be treated. In this case that could mean having your own handwriting analyzed; it's a very humbling experience. You'll find that giving someone else the power to know so much about you can leave you feeling quite naked and vulnerable! Remember that feeling each time you pick up someone else's writing and start to talk about it.

Serious Fun

Handwriting analysis is a wide-open field with a wide variety of helpful applications. Couples who want to get along better have their handwriting analyzed to learn more about each other's needs and motivations. Teachers often find they can bring out better behavior in problem students after they have the students' handwriting examined. Therapists use it to track their clients' progress in therapy, and law enforcement officials use it to determine dangerousness in suspects.

Tales from the Quill

In *United States v. Mara.* 410 U.S. 19, 41 LW 4185 (1973), the Supreme Court stated: "Handwriting, like speech, is repeatedly shown to the public and there is no more expectation of privacy in the physical characteristics of a person's script than there is in the tone of his voice." Although the *United States v. Mara* case dealt with whether or not a person can be compelled to produce an example of her own handwriting for examination, it can also be applied to handwriting analysis for personality assessment. It demonstrates that handwriting is an individual characteristic.

People wanting to change careers have discovered their dream job after having their handwriting analyzed. And companies interested in building an excellent team have their employees' handwriting analyzed to see how they can be more productive and get along better as team members. Analysis of new applicants' handwriting will show their potential for being a good fit on the existing team.

Besides all these serious uses of graphology, some people simply think it's fun to have their handwriting analyzed to see what it can tell about them. They already know their personal faults and foibles, but are often surprised to learn from someone else about all the good qualities that they take for granted in themselves. After all, who doesn't like to hear how noble, pure, and virtuous they are! Okay, so that's exaggerating, but it doesn't hurt anyone's ego to hear the positives once in a while.

You'll probably be surprised to learn how long graphology has been around and what a distinguished history it has. Let's pull out our time machine and take a brief trip into the olden days to unearth some highlights of a fascinating past.

In the Beginning: The Origins of Graphology

Handwriting analysis (the technical term is "graphology") isn't as new as you might think. It was born after long labor, and with contributions from many countries. The first recorded remarks about handwriting being related to personality appeared in 330 B.C. and are attributed to that great teacher, Aristotle. He wrote:

> "Speech is the expression of ideas or thoughts or desires. *Handwriting is the visible form of speech.* Just as speech can have inflections of emotions, somewhere in handwriting is an expression of the emotions underlying the writer's thoughts, ideas, or desires."

Perhaps Aristotle was the very first handwriting analyst!

The earliest published work on the study of handwriting appeared in the 17th century (1621), when Camillo Baldi, an Italian doctor, wrote his treatise on handwriting and character. He maintained that, "Handwriting, being a manifestation of the one who writes, somehow reproduces something of its writer's temperament, personality, or character." No surprise to learn that Dr. Baldi taught Aristotle's theories at university.

Long after Baldi, many famous writers continued to acknowledge the role that handwriting plays in demonstrating personality. Shakespeare was one, as was Goethe. Others include Edgar Allan Poe, George Sand (do you suppose she analyzed the handwriting of her lover, Chopin?), Dumas, Zola, Chekhov, C.G. Jung, and Albert Einstein.

Chicken Scratch

Along with the writing sample, you hold the writer's psyche in your hands, which gives you tremendous power. That power may be wielded delicately like a surgeon's scalpel, or carelessly, like a chainsaw. Use your power with great care. A good maxim for the beginning handwriting analyst is, "with great power comes great responsibility."

The Granddaddy of Graphology

After Baldi not much was recorded for 200 years as far as serious studies in graphology go. It was late in the 1800s when a French monk, Jean Hippolyte Michon, considered the grandfather of modern *graphology*, created the first formal system to study handwriting. All modern graphological thought has its foundations in Michon's research. In fact, he is the one who coined the French term, "graphologie."

Abbé Michon was a man of varied interests. Besides his work in the priesthood he was a writer, botanist, geologist, historian, archeologist, and architect. Among his many contributions was a complex system of classifying plants; he also applied a similar system to handwriting and called it "the study of fixed signs."

Write Words

graph-o-lo-gy, n. the study of handwriting, and the inferring of character or aptitude from it [fr. Gk graphein, writing + logos, discourse]. *The New Lexicon Webster's Dictionary.*

That is, Michon broke handwriting down into a series of strokes (signs), each of which he gave a personality trait name. His method looked at handwriting as if it were a jigsaw puzzle. The analyst would break the writing apart, interpret what each piece meant, then build the results into a picture that would describe the writer's personality. Even back then, before scientists knew much about the workings of the mind, Michon recognized that the brain, rather than the hand, controlled handwriting.

In 1875 Abbé Michon founded the still-active *Société de Graphologie*, one of the leading institutions for studying graphology at the university level. For Michon, graphology was the sister of psychology and he spoke of the importance of balancing all the various signs in the writing to make as detailed an analysis as possible, to understand the complexity of a human being.

The next major scholar of graphology was a student of Michon, Jules Crepieux-Jamin (try saying that five times fast!). Crepieux-Jamin recognized the importance of examining handwriting as a whole, rather than simply as a collection of individual fixed signs. He taught that "the study of the school of fixed signs is to graphology as the study of alphabet is to reading prose." He was responsible for persuading Alfred Binet (developer of the Stanford-Binet I.Q. test) to test the reliability of handwriting analysis, with outstanding results.

For many years the study of graphology remained alive and well in the universities of Europe. There was a time when graphology was a required subject for a psychology or a teaching degree, and most companies insisted upon a graphological profile before they would hire a job applicant. All that changed, however, during World War II, as we'll shortly see.

Fine Points

In some graphology books you will find our Italian graphological forebear's name spelled as "Baldo," rather than Baldi. Robert Backman, of the Handwriting Analysis Research Library tracked down the correct spelling, as you see it here.

Spreading It Around

Towards the end of the 19th century, a German professor of psychology, Wilhelm Preyer, conducted experiments on people who had lost an arm and had to write holding a pen in their mouths or between their toes. He found that the handwriting characteristics didn't change, which confirmed the handwriting/brainwriting link: Regardless of the organ used to hold the writing instrument, the result was the same because handwriting reflects the personality. Preyer's findings were published in *Psychology of Handwriting.*

Have you noticed a difference in your handwriting when you are feeling upbeat, compared to those days when you wish you had stayed in bed? A German psychiatrist, Georg Meyer, experimented with patients who experienced both manic and depressed states. He wanted to find out whether there was a relationship between mood and handwriting. What Dr. Meyer discovered was that when the patients were in a manic state, their handwritings were startlingly different from when they were depressed (Just like yours!).

The first German graphological society was founded by Ludwig Klages, the acknowledged leader of the German school, which is also called the Gestalt Method. Klages made quite a name for himself, publishing textbooks for European graphological institutes and universities. One problem with Klages's method was that he based his graphological laws and principles on his own personal philosophies, rather than on a more objective standard.

Basically, if Klages thought the writing was good-looking, all interpretations would be positive, but if he didn't like the way it looked, the interpretation would be negative—a pretty simplistic view. Because his system was mainly intuitive (and, therefore, subjective), no one else could do it quite the same way he could.

Tales from the Quill

Despite Klages's efforts to wipe out other systems of graphology, a small band of graphologists continued to practice behind closed doors. Happily, handwriting analysis is now beginning to make a comeback all over the Continent. Encouraging reports about the growth of graphology as a serious field of study have arrived from Hungary, Czechoslovakia, Poland, Iceland, Italy, Spain and other nations through Internet graphology discussion groups. Ironically, graphology seems to be in a decline in France and Germany.

Furthermore, Klages, as it turns out, was chummy with Adolph Hitler (who, by the way, had very nasty handwriting). When Hitler came to power, Klages persuaded him to outlaw all other systems of handwriting analysis. So graphology, which had been thriving in Europe, more or less died out for the next 40 or 50 years, as far as the public was concerned.

While Klages and Hitler were enjoying each other's company and dodging bombs in Germany, Dr. Max Pulver was busy at the University of Zurich, applying the basic principles of Klages's system to the field of psychoanalysis and Jung's depth psychology. Pulver's greatest contribution to the field was in identifying that handwriting could be classified into three zones that paralleled Freud's concepts of personality structure (id, ego, and superego). We'll cover this parallel in detail in Chapter 9.

Tales from the Quill

The late, great graphologist, Felix Klein, learned graphology in Vienna at the age of 13. He was in his mid twenties when World War II broke out and he was arrested and sent to concentration camps at Dachau and Buchenwald. There he used his graphology skills to survive. As Felix himself told it, one freezing winter day, a German officer who had heard he analyzed handwriting demanded an analysis for himself. Felix was escorted into the cozy warmth of the officer's quarters where he managed to stretch the analysis into an all day event. When Felix was finished, the officer was so delighted with the results that he asked him what he wanted in return. He got his answer quickly—a cheese sandwich. That night, the sandwich was divided into 17 pieces and relished by everyone in the barracks.

Graphology Finally Crosses the Pond

The United States got into the act around the turn of the century. Louise Rice, an American newspaperwoman, brought graphology back home with her when she returned from being on assignment in Europe. Her 1927 book, *Character Reading From Handwriting* (Newcastle Publishing Co. Inc., 1996), has recently been reprinted and is available commercially once again.

Some of the early graphology research in the U.S. was lead by June Downey at the University of Iowa. Her work culminated in the publication of *Graphology and the Psychology of Handwriting* in 1919.

We're going to do some geographical switching back and forth here, so you may need a scorecard to keep up!

Another important name to remember is Robert Saudek, a Czech graphologist who emigrated to England. His experiments centered on examining speed. He wanted to see whether certain aspects of writing could be mechanically measured for consistency. They could! Saudek's books *Experiments With Handwriting* (Reprinted: Books for Professionals, 1978) and *The Psychology of Handwriting* (Reprinted: Books for Professionals, 1978) remain on every graphologists recommended reading list today (and they're better than counting sheep when you have insomnia!).

The most basic element of handwriting is the stroke. It's really very simple. The stroke is what you see when you look at a line of ink under a microscope. The technical term is "*ductus*." Doctor Rudolf Pophal, a professor of neurology in Hamburg, Germany, introduced a concept he called *stroke picture*. He showed how the effects of activity in different areas of the brain influenced the stroke. Pophal identified three different varieties of stroke which can be seen only through high power magnification. Each type of stroke characterizes different personality types.

Write Words

Ductus refers to the actual writing stroke, the line of ink left by the pen. **Stroke Picture** is the quality of the stroke, whether it looks grainy (granular), stringy (striated) or smooth (homogenous). **Rhythm** is the ebb and flow of movement as the pen travels across the paper.

Other German contributors include Professor Robert Heiss at Freiburg University, who combined psychology with graphology. His work became a standard text in European universities; and Roda Wieser, who studied the handwritings of criminals. She made the historic discovery that the handwritings of criminals had a very different type of *rhythm* than noncriminals: The criminals' writing lacked the elasticity found in writings of noncriminals.

Meanwhile, back in France, Ania Teillard introduced into graphology Jung's philosophies of conscious/unconscious, extroversion/introversion, persona/shadow. She also addressed the psychic function types of thinking, feeling, sensation, and intuition, as well as the different complexes and the way they are expressed in writing. Teillard's *The Soul and Handwriting* (Reprint: Scriptor Books, 1993) is a beautiful composite of her theories and a personal favorite of mine.

Not one to be left on the sidelines, the Harvard Psychological Clinic jumped in around 1930. Internationally recognized researchers, Gordon Allport and Philip E. Vernon developed a set of measuring scales to experiment on speed, size of writing, and pressure. They were able to successfully replicate their findings several times over, which was a victory for reliability and validity of graphological theory. They published their findings in *Studies in Expressive Movement* (Macmillan, 1933).

Hungarian psychologist Dr. Klara Roman, who helped establish courses for credit in handwriting studies at the New School for Social Research in New York, made several very important contributions. While working for the Hungarian government, Dr. Roman created a special circular measuring chart she called the Graphological

Psychogram. You'll get a sneak peek at this chart in Chapter 4. The Psychogram shows at a glance how the writer's energy is distributed in his personality.

Doctor Roman also invented the Graphodyne, which was an instrument used to measure pressure, and she wrote the *Encyclopedia of the Written Word* (Frederick Ungar Publishing Co., 1968). Another of her books, *Handwriting, Key to Personality* (The Noonday Press, 1962), is still considered the bible of holistic graphologists today.

In 1939 Rose Wolfson wrote *Study in Handwriting Analysis.* She examined groups of delinquents and nondelinquents and reported that their handwritings showed some significant differences. And, in 1942 Thea Stein Lewinson and Joseph Zubin used scientific research principles to develop a system of rating scales and applied them to the writings of both normal and abnormal people. Their findings also confirmed that there were significant differences in the handwritings of the two groups.

Diagrams of the Unconscious (Grune & Stratton, 1948), written by Werner Wolff in 1948, is still viewed as a major classical text. The culmination of Wolff's 20 years of research and observation, *Diagrams* isn't easy reading, but most graphologists would kill to get a copy, as they are extremely scarce. I bought mine from a colleague who was selling her library and retiring.

In 1950, Doctor Ulrich Sonnemann, associate professor at the New School for Social Research in New York, made one of the last major contributions to the early development of professional graphology in the U.S. His book, *Handwriting Analysis As a Psychodiagnostic Tool* (Grune & Stratton, 1950), includes a series of tables that illustrate how the same trait in a handwriting could be interpreted negatively or positively, depending upon what other factors surround it. This was a big step beyond Klages's system (remember—if the writing looked good the person was deemed good, and if it looked bad...well, you know).

We've only scratched the surface of graphological history. As you can see, in the early days, graphology was taken very seriously in Europe. Yet, despite all the research and evidence to show that it is based on sound psychological and scientific principles, there followed a long period when graphology was viewed as little better than tea leaf reading. Graphologists were feeling like Rodney Dangerfield. Lately though, they've begun to get more respect.

Research continues, but most of it is being done by individual graphologists. More formal studies will have to be conducted at university level before the scientific community as a whole accepts graphology as a legitimate practice in the helping professions.

Two Schools of Thought

Now we know some of the foundations of graphological research it's time to explore the two major schools of thought. In this section we'll look at how the French did it first, and then how the Germans took graphology in an entirely new direction.

Mais Oui! The French Approach

Earlier, you met Abbé Michon, on whose work all graphological systems are based. Let's now take a closer look at how the French school analyzes handwriting.

Since Abbé Michon used a classification system to study handwriting, the tendency is to take the handwriting apart and examine it piece by piece. For this reason, the French method is sometimes referred to as "atomistic."

The Categories

The French divide handwriting into several categories. The main ones are:

1. *Layout:* how the writing is organized on the page
2. *Dimension:* how much space the writing takes up (size of letters)
3. *Pressure:* the depth component
4. *Form:* writing style
5. *Speed:* writing tempo
6. *Continuity:* types and degree of connections within and between letters
7. *Direction:* which way the writing is moving

Fine Points

The French method of graphology is also called atomistic (consisting of many separate, often disparate elements) because it examines handwriting bit by bit. Using Crepieux-Jamin's system of categories, the handwriting is broken down into its various components and examined separately, as if through a microscope.

In 1930's Chicago, a man named Milton Bunker founded a school based on Abbé Michon's method (although Michon was not given credit) and coined the term, "Graphoanalysis." Only graduates of Bunker's school, the International Graphoanalysis Society (IGAS) can legally use the trademarked name. Similar to Michon's original method, the IGAS system assigns a personality trait to each stroke of handwriting and is thus known as the trait-stroke approach. Although the school is responsible for spreading the word about handwriting analysis to a wide audience, its code of ethics, which forbids students to associate with graphologists who learned other methods, has long been a sore point for those wanting to branch out and learn other methods. Members who attended meetings of other organizations were summarily expelled from the society. Late word is that the society has recently begun loosening up its policy.

Achtung! The German School

As you might guess, the Germans approach handwriting analysis quite differently from the French. The German method is also known as holistic or *gestalt.* This means that the whole is greater than the sum of its parts, and that no one element of handwriting

Tales from the Quill

The French method is the basis for what is known in the United States as "Graphoanalysis." Graphoanalysis is a trademarked name that can be used only by graduates of that school. The German method is used by a comparatively small but dedicated group of graphologists in the United States. Bitter rivalry exists between the proponents of the two schools of thought, because each believes its method is "the only one."

means anything outside the context of the whole handwriting. German or gestalt graphology argues that handwriting is made up of three types of pictures, each having its own special rhythm:

1. *The picture of space:* how the writer sees the world
2. *The picture of movement:* how the writer acts in the world
3. *The picture of form:* how the writer sees himself

Write Words

Gestalt is a pattern of unified elements that cannot be interpreted outside of the whole. The sum is greater than its parts.

The way these three pictures fit together forms the basis for understanding the core personality. If there is disturbance in any of the pictures, it tells the handwriting analyst where in the personality there are problems. All this will make more sense as we go further in depth into each of the three pictures in later chapters.

For the serious graphologist, getting a grasp of the whole picture is vital to a good understanding of the basic personality. Without it, all that's left is a list of personality traits, which mean little by themselves. Most agree, however, that neither the trait nor the holistic method is the "best," but when used in combination, provides the most complete picture of the person's disposition.

The Least You Need to Know

- ➤ A vast body of formal research has been done in the field of graphology, which supports its validity and reliability.
- ➤ All graphology methods begin with Abbe Michon's system but they don't end there.
- ➤ There are two basic schools of graphology, holistic and atomistic.
- ➤ Much more needs to be done to replicate early validity and reliability studies before graphology will be accepted into the mainstream.

Chapter 2

Dead Men Tell No Tales, but Handwriting Does

In This Chapter

- Handwriting expresses needs
- Signatures can be symbolic
- We may be different but we're all alike
- Recognizing what graphologists can and can't do

Long after you have gone on to that big ink well in the sky, your handwriting will still be around to tell others about what made you who you were. Imagine your great-great grandchildren bringing a letter you wrote to a 21st century graphologist and asking, "What was she like?" The words you put on paper today just may tell on you tomorrow!

Analyzing the handwriting of someone's ancestors is one very rewarding way to use graphology. For a son whose father died while he was too young to remember him, a handwriting analysis can bring his father back to life and help the son get to know what he was like.

Frequently, an adult child will produce a handwriting sample of a parent he didn't get along with who has died. The son or daughter is looking for answers to why there was so much friction and conflict between them. He feels hurt that he was never able to develop a good relationship with the parent, no matter how much or how hard he tried. A graphological autopsy, as some call it, allows people to feel a connection to their forebears that may not have been present in life, and can bring a sense of closure where before there were only questions.

Tales from the Quill

A woman who heard me lecture spoke of losing her father when she was a small child. All she had to remember him by was a small sample of his handwriting, which she wanted analyzed. She knew there had been friction between her parents and remembered feeling frightened by their loud arguments. Her mother's negative comments about him left her with a burning desire to know the truth. The analysis gave my client a sense of closure, because she found that at last, she could understand things about herself that had also been part of her father.

Graphology is a unique way to learn about people in all areas of your life and improve the way you deal with them. Graphic expressions of all kinds can help add the pieces needed to complete the puzzle that is the human being.

Symbols Etched in Ink

Everyone living has needs—from the most basic biological, instinctual needs for food, safety, and reproduction, to the need for belonging and love, to the need to express one's creative urges. All humans share similar needs, but not all humans express them in exactly the same way.

Some psychologists say that unless the most basic needs of life are met, the person doesn't progress to the next level. You know that when you're really hungry, you don't much care about your creative needs or going to a movie. All you can think about is meeting that most basic need for food. If you don't eat, you'll die. When a child learns at a very young age that getting enough food to eat from one day to the next is a struggle, it's extremely difficult for him to progress to the next stage of emotional growth.

In handwriting, we can see at which level the writer is. If she has had trouble getting the lowest needs on the ladder taken care of (that is, food, warmth, and security,) her handwriting will be stuck at a very undeveloped stage. The writer has had to concentrate on keeping herself alive rather than worrying about how mature her handwriting looks.

If she has moved up a few rungs on the needs ladder, but hasn't gotten her need for love properly satisfied, it will be manifested in the overly rounded forms of one who depends on others for emotional nurturing and love. She hasn't yet learned to love herself.

We see a broad spectrum of development in the people who bring their handwriting for analysis. Relatively few have reached the top of the ladder and achieved what some psychologists call self-actualization. That's a fancy way of saying he's done what he wants to in life and feels good about it.

Some needs are conscious and others are unconscious (particularly the lower level, physiological ones). The need for intellectual stimulation, for instance, is a conscious need, and is different from the unconscious need for food, water, and air. Handwriting is a demonstration, a manifest symbol, of those needs that the writer feels compelled to express, whether the need is conscious or not. Learning to measure and weigh the written line in all its many expressions is the key that unlocks the door to personality.

Fine Points

Carl Jung said, "A true symbol appears only when there is a need to express what thought cannot think or what is only divined or felt."

The forms created in ink and the spaces around them reveal to the trained eye what motivates a particular type of behavior. Similar to the way an artist uses line, color, and texture in his brush strokes, every movement of the pen uncovers something of the writer's temperament.

As in other fields, artists come in a variety of styles and types. I don't pretend to know anything about art, but even I am aware that there's a big difference between Rembrandt and Peter Max.

Visualize a painting by French Impressionist Claude Monet. He often chose as his subject outdoor scenes, daubing vivid colors on the canvas in thick, sensuous brush strokes. His style creates a blurry picture that suggests a love of natural beauty, color, and texture.

Contrast Monet with a stark Dali scene, its sharp edges, strong colors, and clearly defined objects often depicting disturbing subject matter.

Each artist and his works evoke distinct and very different sensations because each creation was produced by a very different type of personality. Their work projects something that is symbolic of the artist's nature. Not surprisingly, an artist's handwriting generally has very similar qualities to her artwork. The same is true of musicians. A tempestuous musical score by Beethoven closely resembles his stormy handwriting.

In handwriting as in art, even subtle changes in the line of ink demonstrate different aspects of the writer's character. It is as if in guiding the pen across the page the writer is drawing the observer a picture of what is going on inside him from moment to moment.

Observing someone's facial expressions, body language, and tone of voice makes it pretty easy to figure out how they are feeling. When someone is unhappy or depressed her shoulders tend to droop, the spring goes out of her step, her voice sounds heavy, and her eyes are lackluster. On the other hand, when things are going well and the same person is having a good day, you'll see her throw her shoulders back, put a smile on her face, and you'll hear a definite lilt in her voice.

Tales from the Quill

When the famous English painter Thomas Gainsborough painted a portrait he would place the handwriting of his subject on his easel, next to his painting. He felt that seeing the handwriting helped him to understand the subject better. By studying the way the person wrote, it was as if he could glimpse inside her soul and know his subject on a level that was not accessible just from studying her as a model. The handwriting rounded out his artistic sense.

The thousands of pen strokes crisscrossing a sheet of paper symbolize the writer's feelings *at the time of writing* and often parallel his or her facial expression, tone of voice, body language. From one writing impulse to the next, a change of direction, a retrograde movement, a sharp break, speaks volumes about the way the writer experiences the world and how he functions in it.

What type of person might have penned the slashing, heavy strokes that we see in the following handwriting sample? Is this the sort of graphic expression you would expect from a sweet, retiring, little old grandma? Even if you know nothing at all about handwriting, the hostility in the writing leaps off the page. It gets in your face and throws down a challenge.

Coarse, heavy writing.

What about the soft, neat forms in the next sample? Somehow it's obvious that the writer is, well, nice. There's no other way to describe it. The handwriting gives the impression of someone who wants to be helpful, to get along, someone who would prefer to avoid conflict and confrontation in any way she can.

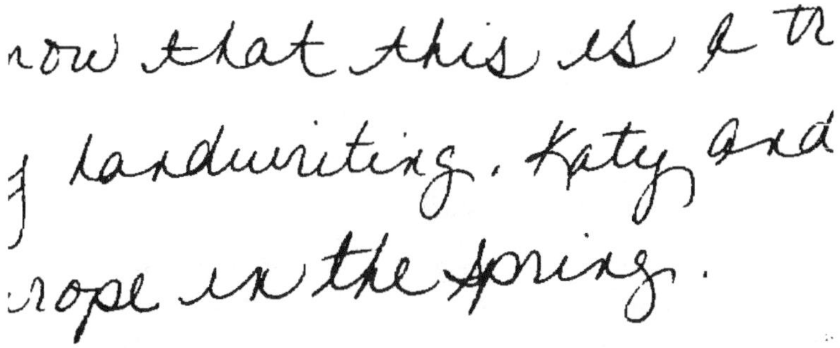

Rounded writing.

Would you be surprised to learn that the first sample was written by a killer who slashed his victims to death with a knife? Or that the second one is a nurse whose emotions get very involved with the patients she cares for? Their handwriting speaks for them, if only we listen.

Looking for Symbols

Sometimes we see in signatures symbols that represent the writer's profession. Liberace drew a little piano in his signature; a ship's captain unconsciously forms his ship sailing on the water; golfer Greg Norman, known as "the Great White Shark," clearly draws—guess what?—yes, a shark, in his signature, as you can see in the next sample.

A symbolic signature.

A wealth of celebrity handwriting samples are reproduced in a handy little book called *The Most Important Thing I Know* (Cader Books, 1997). In their own handwriting, one hundred famous people tell what they've learned in life. Some wonderful examples of symbols include the signature of sports figure Magic Johnson—it has a definite basketball hoop incorporated in it!

Symbols can also appear in some unexpected places. People in prison regularly use symbols such as happy faces and hearts in their letters, perhaps as a metaphor for false bravado, a pitiful attempt to lighten their awful situation. In a later chapter we'll consider the symbolism in doodles, which can be analyzed in much the same way as handwriting can.

The following illustrations show the handwriting of two famous people who were accused of murder. Notice the happy symbols that show their profound denial.

Tales from the Quill

Handwriting is filled with unconscious symbols. The infamous Susan Smith, known as "Killer Mom," chose to replace the word "heart" with pictures of hearts in the letter in which she confessed to drowning her two little boys in the family car that she had pushed into a lake. Perhaps she couldn't bear to use the word "heart," considering the enormity of what she had done to her children. O.J. Simpson, in his so-called suicide letter, signed with a happy face—a written form of whistling by the graveyard?

Susan Smith who killed her two sons.

couldn't believe wh
children w/ all my ♥.
prayed to them for
will find it in their ♥

O.J. Simpson who was accused of murdering his wife.

We May Be Different But We're All Alike

In his classic book, *Diagrams of the Unconscious* (Grune & Stratton, 1948) (an oldie but a goody), Dr. Werner Wolff describes a series of experiments he conducted where he asked a group of subjects to write the letter *g* as an aggressive person would, and then write it as a submissive person would. Every person in the group wrote the submissive *g* small and the aggressive *g* larger.

Wolff further discovered that other types of graphic forms have similar associations for different people. He asked several groups to match a set of figures, one angular, one rounded (see the next illustration) with groups of concepts that included words, tastes, smells, feelings, elements, colors, and music. The consistency between the matches was an amazing 80 percent.

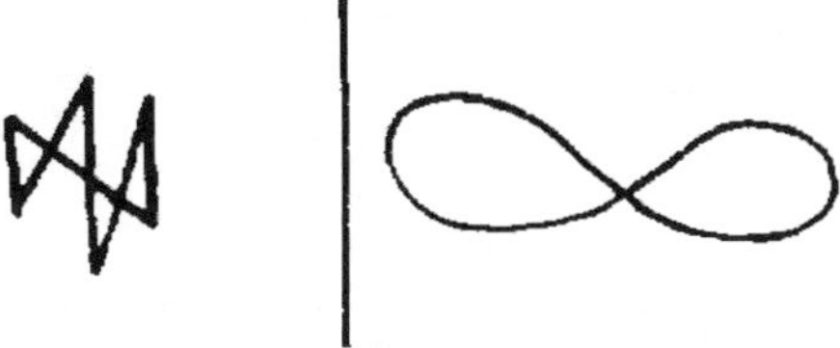

Wolff's graphic forms.

These experiments were important because they demonstrated that samples of writing show a consistent, recognizable expressive style. People are instinctively able to identify the symbolic meanings, whether it is in actual handwriting or simply the way a line is formed.

Researchers discovered that in every part of the world the scribbles made by very young children follow a particular pattern according to their ages. Regardless of whether the child lives in the United States or Uganda, at age three what a child draws is essentially going to be the same. Transferring this knowledge to handwriting, it's easy to see why graphic forms can be analyzed to reveal personality.

Next time you're with a group of friends, try an experiment that I do with every class I teach: Ask them to use line to express certain emotions. They are not to draw pictures or use words, but they can use straight lines, rounded lines, heavy or light lines, any kind of line. The emotions their lines are to represent could be anger, love, happiness, sadness. Instruct them not to compare notes or look at each other's representations.

You will find that in most cases the lines people draw, even though they do them independently, are very similar. Anger is almost always drawn as heavy, straight lines. Love is drawn with curved, lighter pressured lines, sadness produces lines that point downward with very light pressure, but happy lines point up. All this tells us that handwriting analysis isn't magic. It is based on common sense and the ability to understand the symbols that are an innate part of all of us.

Handwriting samples can be matched with other expressive behaviors. Doodles, musical scores, posture, gait when walking, and voice, all tend to share similar characteristics, which shows that all expressive behavior is consistent. A person who walks with a bounce in his step is likely to have a bouncy looking handwriting. Someone who seems to be marching to an inner drummer has handwriting with a very definite march tempo. These are behaviors that we don't have to think about as we do them. They just come naturally.

Fine Points

When you want to do a handwriting experiment, be very specific in your instructions. Let the subjects know exactly what you want them to do. Otherwise, you will likely get a lot of interesting, but not too helpful results.

John may not have been taught that an outgoing, forceful personality is reflected in large, heavy-pressured, right-slanted writing; yet, he associates those traits with Tom, a big, beefy football player whose handwriting is large, heavy-pressured, and right-slanted. Mother's writing on the other hand, is smaller, more precise, rounded.

We know by her behavior that Mother is gentle and passive, rather shy and willing to let others take the lead, but without some knowledge of graphology we wouldn't know that her handwriting demonstrates those particular personality traits. If Mother and Tom are so different in character, their differences must be symbolized in their behaviors, including their handwriting.

Tales from the Quill

Graphologist Marlene Vallen is frequently called on to work in a group setting, perhaps at a corporate event or conference. She notes that many of the handwritings are very similar. Just as people who hang out together or work together often are alike in their personalities, their handwriting also shares corresponding characteristics. This makes it hard on the handwriting analyst, who has to come up with different ways of describing the same thing!

The fact is, handwriting is as individual as a fingerprint and in many subtle ways unique to the writer. If it were not true that parts of one's personality are manifest in handwriting, everyone would write alike, just the way they learned in school. But there are as many different writing styles as there are writers. When a letter arrives in the mail, the writing on the envelope can usually be readily identified as Cousin Ted, or Jenny's boyfriend Mark, or Mom because the familiar script symbolizes the individual personality of the writer.

Will Handwriting Reveal My Deepest, Darkest Secrets?

Some people wonder if handwriting can reveal deeply hidden secrets. The answer is, yes! If you had a very difficult childhood and are still troubled by traumatic events, your handwriting will reflect it. On the other hand, if you have been able to work through the difficulties, your handwriting will show your emotional growth. In Part 2, we'll explore some of the ways to determine whether old memories are still hanging on and impacting emotional growth.

If the writer is living a lifestyle that feels uncomfortable, signs of guilt are likely to appear in her handwriting. The same is true of someone behaving dishonestly in any area of his or her life. If someone feels guilty about his behavior, it will be evident in some very subtle ways that only a professionally trained handwriting analyst will be able to detect.

He Wrote, She Wrote: Sex in Handwriting

One of the things that cannot be conclusively determined from handwriting is gender. You may be surprised if you assume that a pretty, rounded script was written by a woman, only to find out that the author was a 45-year-old man. The reverse is also true. An aggressive-looking, energetic handwriting could easily be penned by a petite 25-year-old woman.

Instead of gender, what we can infer is the degree of masculinity/femininity, or sensitivity in the script. Another way to look at it is to seek a balance between yin and yang energies. In Asian cultures, yin is associated with the softer, more delicate (feminine) characteristics, while yang relates to more robust (male) energy, which is directed outwards.

A writing may be strongly masculine or strongly feminine, or somewhere along the spectrum between the two. Handwriting characteristics that are associated with male energy would include heavier pressure, movement to the right (long t-crossings, for instance), and a dynamic style. Curved forms, medium pressure, and pretty writing are generally associated with femininity.

Some graphologists claim they can tell a writer's sexual preference. The experts, however, do not. The best we can do is point out some indications of discomfort in sexual functioning, but not the specific source of the discomfort.

In other words, if someone is comfortable with his or her lifestyle there will be nothing to indicate that person's sexual orientation. If, however, a person feels guilty about how he or she is living, there will likely be signs pointing to it.

Fine Points

Marie Bernard's book, *Sexual Deviations As Seen in Handwriting* (The Whitston Publishing Company, 1985), contains many interesting samples of famous people, including Oscar Wilde. What she labels as "deviations" includes homosexuality, which is no longer considered abnormal by psychologists, but the samples are worth the price of the book.

What Can Handwriting Analysis Tell?

Handwriting reveals potentials at the time of writing. Whether the writer will act on those potentials or not is a question the analyst cannot answer. We'd have to be God to do that, and that's one responsibility I can do without.

A handwriting may look more like a serial killer than a serial killer's, but that doesn't mean the writer is positively going to act out his hostile or aggressive emotions. All it does mean is that certain characteristics exist in his personality that are similar to characteristics found in someone who has acted on them. Handwriting shows potential, only. Having an emotion is not the same as acting on it.

Unless he has a crystal ball, it is impossible for the handwriting analyst to know whether exactly the right set of circumstances will come together at exactly the right time to arouse someone to act on his *potential* for violence.

Here are some of the things that handwriting reveals:

- Handwriting provides information about how the writer relates to other people: Is he friendly or reserved, sociable or antisocial, aggressive or submissive?
- Handwriting reveals how the writer thinks: Is he logical or intuitive? Does he create entirely new ideas or is he stuck in the mud of convention, afraid to move out and generate his own ideas?
- Handwriting indicates the state of the ego, whether it is strong and well-developed, or weak and battered.
- Handwriting reveals how the writer uses his energy: Does he conserve it carefully or spread it around with wild abandon? Does he tire easily, have low vitality and stamina, or can he work all day and party all night without feeling the strain?
- Handwriting tells about the writer's fears and inhibitions, what she has learned from past experiences and how she uses that knowledge: Will she learn from painful experiences and put the lesson to use the next time, or repress it and pretend it never happened, repeating the same mistakes over and over again?
- Handwriting demonstrates how one controls oneself. Is he controlled by the past? Does she still carry old childhood messages in her head, feeling as if someone were peering over her shoulder, telling her what to do every minute? Has he learned self-discipline, understanding the difference between what is right and wrong in a mature, adult fashion?

What Can't Handwriting Analysis Tell?

Some handwriting analysts have been heard to brag, "I can tell you *everything* from your handwriting!" They are either lying, ignorant, or, to give them the benefit of the doubt, maybe they're psychic.

Handwriting does uncover a tremendous amount of helpful and important information, but it certainly doesn't tell *everything*. People are just too complex for one tool to be able to reveal 100 percent of their personalities.

Knowing what handwriting can't do is just as important as knowing what it can. By recognizing your limitations as a handwriting analyst you can avoid creating unrealistic expectations in yourself and your clients.

Tales from the Quill

I once asked a client how she felt about the handwriting analysis report I had prepared for her. She said, "I thought it was great! It was really me!" Then she hesitated before continuing, "...But it wasn't all of me." This was a humbling reminder of my own limitations as an analyst: Handwriting does not show all about the writer, just as no psychological test shows all.

We've already discussed how handwriting doesn't tell you about the writer's sex or sexual preference. Age is another factor that can't be determined through handwriting analysis. Not conclusively, anyway. You may be handed a writing sample which you're sure was written by a young girl, only to learn that the writer is a woman in her mid 30s. Or, you are surprised at the vitality in the writing of someone who, as it turns out, is in his 80s.

When doing an analysis, it's important to get at least a ballpark idea of the writer's chronological age. Without it you won't be able to gauge his or her emotional maturity. A 20-year old who writes with the graphic maturity of a 30-year old will have a different analysis than if the situation were reversed.

The following handwriting sample is a good example of not being able to tell age from the script.

The writing looks like that of a 16-year-old, but the writer is 35.

Another "can't do" is handedness. Handwriting doesn't reveal which hand the writer uses. Many non-graphologists believe it's possible to tell by checking the slant. Contrary to popular belief, however, left-slanted writing is not necessarily preferred by left-handed people. We do make some allowances for lefties though. Left-handers get a little bit of extra credit for having adapted to a right-handed world.

Some types of movement in handwriting are easier for a left-hander to make than others. For instance, *angles* and *arcades* are more natural for a lefty to form than are *garlands*. You'll be reading more about those forms later in the book.

Write Words

In handwriting, **angles** refer to straight strokes. Sometimes a straight stroke is appropriate, but at other times a stroke may be made straight when it should have been curved. An **arcade** is a rounded form, like an arch; and a **garland** is a rounded form, like a cup.

The lefty's instincts tell him to move from right to left, just the opposite of the right-hander. Since we live in pretty much of a right-handed world, Mr. or Ms. Lefty has to twist into some pretty uncomfortable positions just to write in notebooks made with the spiral binding on the left.

It's for this reason that there may be more of a tendency for certain features of the left-hander's writing to move leftward. Lower loops may pull to the left for instance, and the margins may drift leftwards. When we see these things, knowing the person is a southpaw, the interpretation is somewhat different than if the same characteristics appear in a right-hander's script.

It seems to make left-handers feel better when they hear that left-handedness is a sign of someone driven more by the right side of the brain—the creative side. Besides, you can tell them, "Only lefties are in their right mind!"

The list of famous left-handed people is quite astounding. Here are just a few:

- Buzz Aldrin
- Carol Burnett
- Charlie Chaplin
- Bill Clinton
- Benjamin Franklin
- Joan of Arc
- John F. Kennedy
- Paul McCartney
- Don Rickles
- General Norman Schwarzkopf
- Queen Victoria

Although some *cultural* features can be identified with training, handwriting doesn't reveal racial characteristics. As we'll see in Part 4, handwriting from different countries does have some conspicuous national differences, but much depends on whether the writer writes in the copybook model, which is the style he was taught in school.

Tales from the Quill

Several years ago, my colleague Pauline Clapp and I undertook a research project on left-handedness. We studied 132 handwritings, half-lefties and half-righties, with half males and half females in each group. The results were not surprising to those who believe that handwriting comes from the brain, not just the hand: It was not possible to conclusively determine, just from the handwriting, which group was which.

It was interesting to note that the group with the poorest form development was the left-handed males (medical research has suggested that left-handedness in boys is often the result of a difficult birth). The only two writers who adopted a left slant in the group we studied turned out to be right-handed.

You may be able to tell what general part of the world the writer hails from, but in American writings, race cannot be distinguished with any certainty—another piece of evidence for using graphology as a nondiscriminatory hiring tool.

Handwriting cannot tell what religion the writer is. It may suggest that she has religious leanings, and it can give some indications about spiritual and philosophical attitudes, but certainly not which church she attends or if she attends one at all. What handwriting can show is whether the writer had a very strict upbringing and if she learned to fear authority.

Handwriting cannot foretell the future, but it does give a lot of helpful information about the past. Even when handwriting analysis is used to base some predictions of future performance on the job, it definitely is not like a crystal ball. Any prognostications a graphologist makes are based on how the writer has assimilated his past experiences, the effects of which are evident in the writing in a very general way.

The written word provides the means to gather information that provides an excellent overview of personality and gives insights into how the writer functions. Yet, what makes handwriting analysis such a great tool for personality assessment in the corporate world is its nondiscriminatory aspects: the areas of personality which it cannot reveal—age, sex, race, religion.

The Least You Need to Know

- Handwriting is symbolic of behavior and attitudes.
- You can learn a lot from handwriting, but it doesn't reveal *everything* about you.
- Handwriting cannot reveal the future, but it tells a lot about the past.
- Handwriting tells a lot about how the writer thinks, feels, and behaves.
- Handwriting analysis is a nondiscriminatory tool for hiring.

Chapter 3

The Preliminaries

In This Chapter

- Everyone wants to be analyzed
- Responsibility or liability
- Signatures don't count
- If it's in ink, it can be analyzed
- Sometimes the handwriting is on the wall

You're at a cocktail party and the host introduces you to a fellow guest who, it turns out, is a dentist. What's your first thought? If you answer truthfully, you're probably tempted to tell the dentist about your gum problem, or maybe that story about the time your kid's front teeth got knocked out on a Saturday night and you had to assist the dentist. Or, you're flying to Miami, you find yourself seated next to a lawyer, and you're just itching to ask him how to draft your will.

Professionals of all varieties become accustomed to finding themselves faced with people seeking advice who would never dream of making an appointment and paying to have their questions answered. I know a psychologist who, when introduced to someone socially, tells them he's a trash collector to avoid being forced into explaining why he isn't going to do instant therapy with them.

Tales from the Quill

Like many professionals, 1930s humorist Will Rogers was expected to be "on" all the time. As the story goes, he was invited to Hearst Castle as a weekend guest. During the visit, William Randolph Hearst asked Rogers to entertain the other guests with a few jokes, which Rogers graciously did. A few days later, Mr. Hearst received a hefty bill in the mail. At his protest, "But you were here as a guest!" Rogers replied (I'm paraphrasing here), "When Mrs. Rogers accompanies me I'm a guest. When I'm asked to entertain, I get paid."

I Should Let You See My Handwriting

When you first learn how to analyze handwriting you can expect to be bombarded with requests for free advice. You'll be amazed at the number of people who pop out of the woodwork, bringing with them handwriting samples of their friends, relatives, and neighbors. They'll want to know what secrets you can uncover to confirm that their boss is a jerk, their grandson is on drugs, or that their neighbor is a gossiping busybody. And they'll be thrilled with anything you can tell them, especially if it's juicy. Soon, you'll have a boundless supply of handwritings to use for practice.

Be Kind

Be sure to tell the people you analyze the good stuff about them. For some reason, negative traits are easier to see quickly, and, let's face it, they're more fun to talk about! Even experienced analysts tend to focus on the down side of personality. Maybe we pick out the less flattering parts of their nature to make people realize that we really do know what we're talking about and that handwriting analysis "works"! Just make sure to sandwich the bad stuff between some positives.

Unfortunately, in some cases finding the positives is not always so easy. If you're looking at the writing of a bad-tempered, narrow-minded know-it-all, uncovering his higher self can be a big challenge. At the very least, look for some signs of how the person manages to cope in the world. He can't be *all* bad...can he?

Think of it this way: If he's asking for an analysis of his writing, he is most likely experiencing major problems in his life and is, at the very least, beginning to question whether some of them might be caused by his own behavior. He recognizes that some aspects of his personality could use developing (that's a nice way of saying "improvement"). So look hard until you find some redeeming qualities and talk about them.

Euphemisms help. If, instead of using words like "angry" you substitute "frustrated," the client usually accepts it much more gracefully. After all, who wants to be thought of as a nasty S.O.B.? It's much nicer to be viewed as frustrated and misunderstood.

"Scary" is a word often used by those who have their handwriting analyzed: "It's scary that a stranger can know that much about me," they say. They will marvel at how awesome you are, to be able to get so much information "just from my handwriting!" People seem to believe that by looking at their handwriting you instantly know every evil thought that ever passed through their heads. That's what scares them!

Fine Points

"Saying it Softly" is a monograph by Sister June Canoles (the most dynamic nun you'll ever meet!), which offers kinder, gentler ways of handling some of the more troublesome personality traits. Order it directly from Sr. June at (408) 252-9696.

This is where Responsibility comes in, with a very large R. Before beginning to analyze anyone's handwriting, please make it abundantly clear that you are still a student. For now, any analyses you do are purely for practice and you should check your conclusions with a handwriting professional whenever possible.

When Three's a Crowd

You can have fun with graphology, but it's definitely not a party gag or parlor game. It is a helpful tool to understand other people better, and I'm about to give you a piece of serious advice: Be very careful about analyzing the writing of anyone who is not present or doesn't know your client is requesting an analysis of his or her handwriting. This is called *third-party analysis.*

Third-party analysis is a very controversial practice, even among handwriting professionals. There are some ethical considerations that need to be addressed before preparing an analysis for one who brings you someone else's writing to be analyzed.

Let's say someone brings you the handwriting of her boss, and wants to know what you can see there. The employee is convinced that the boss is a closet maniac and wants you to verify her feelings. She has some Post-it notes with some scribbled words. Of course, the boss doesn't know that her employee has snagged this sample of her handwriting for you to look at. Should you comment on it?

Write Words

It's called a **third-party** report when you are asked to analyze the handwriting of someone who hasn't given his or her permission for the analysis.

Think of it this way: How would it feel to discover that your friend, mother, husband, or wife had secretly taken a personal letter or maybe a Valentine card you'd sent that person and had it analyzed to find something out about you (sorta like Linda Tripp taping Monica Lewinsky)? Personally, I would not be happy about it and I don't know many people who would. Unless there is a compelling *need to know* (not just a *want* to know), it's a very good idea to steer clear of discussing the handwriting of someone who isn't present. You don't want to be guilty of invasion of privacy.

But who might have a genuine need to know? Parents who suspect their teenager is suicidal or on drugs; a person who is thinking of getting married but has concerns about his fiancée's honesty; an employer investigating a sexual harassment case. Situations like these could provide a legitimate reason for investigating whether these tendencies appear in the third party's handwriting. However, when faced with such difficult questions, it would be best to refer the client to an experienced professional who is equipped to properly handle them.

Chicken Scratch

More than one handwriting professional has reported taking on a third-party analysis without the permission of the writer, only to later be threatened with a lawsuit for invasion of privacy when the third party got his hands on the report. Insisting on the writer's permission will protect you.

But What Should I Write?

Okay, you've got someone who wants her handwriting analyzed and you've laid a good foundation for doing the analysis. The client will ask, "What should I write?"

The most desirable sample is written unselfconsciously, which usually means not written specifically for analysis. If the client has some previously written handwriting samples, they are probably better representations of her natural handwriting style.

One notable exception to be aware of is notes written in haste, such as personal reminders or class notes, which could skew the analysis. If someone analyzed my handwriting using the scribbles on my notepad I'm sure a padded cell would be reserved in my name.

If the client has nothing appropriate on hand for analysis, the next best thing is to ask him to write a letter to you or anyone else, even himself. Most importantly, the specimen should be long enough to allow for a thorough analysis. That means at least one full page, and preferably two. Without an adequate sample the results are quite likely to be skewed or just plain wrong.

Frequently, a very short writing sample will be missing some aspect that would show up in a longer one. In some cases, even a very small item that appears only once could be significant. If something appears just once, the behavior that it symbolizes may occur only occasionally. But if the symbol indicates a potential for violence, for example, this would be a critical part of the analysis that you wouldn't want to overlook. When an indicator appears a few times (say, less than five times), it is considered a trend. But when it appears regularly, you can be sure it's a habit.

You aren't going to analyze content, spelling, or grammar, so the subject matter of the sample is unimportant. Any topic will do, but no fair copying from a book or writing poetry or song lyrics, because these force the writer to follow an unnatural pattern of spacing.

What we're looking for is a free-flowing specimen, like a letter or an essay. Asking your client to write about what she did last weekend or what her goals are for the future will help her get going. If the client draws a complete blank, you can suggest she write about her earliest childhood memory.

Some clients are concerned that what they write about will influence your report. In that case you can explain that the analysis would be the same even if they wrote in a language that you don't speak, since the analysis is based on thousands more factors than the individual letters or words. But if they're still worried, let them choose some neutral content that won't give anything away.

Fine Points

Charlie Cole, founder of the American Handwriting Analysis Foundation, often told his students, "If you want to learn how to analyze handwriting, you must do analyses!" To hone your skills, practice, practice, practice.

Some graphologists believe that if you know anything about the client at all it nullifies the report. That's a bit extreme, but we do try to stay as objective as possible. If you want to read what the client wrote, wait until after you've done the analysis.

Here's My Signature, What Can You Tell Me?

People frequently like to scribble their signature and wave it under your nose, asking for an analysis. Without a body of writing to compare to, a signature is usually not suitable for comment. If you fall into the trap of basing an analysis on a signature alone, you'll put yourself at risk of making some major mistakes. The signature is the person's outer image only, and may not reveal the truth about her inner self.

Comparing the signature to the text reveals how open and candid the writer is about who he really is. If there is a wide disparity between signature and text, you'll know right away that what you see is not what you get. (Chapter 18 will tell you why!)

When someone asks for a signature analysis, I ask him to imagine a photograph of my nose and from that tell me what my face looks like. Putting a nose into the perspective of the whole face can create a very different picture than trying to figure out what someone looks like based on one small piece of evidence. Analyzing a signature outside the context of the whole writing is like looking at someone's nose and trying to describe her face.

It's a good idea to get a signature along with the rest of the writing, but don't analyze it by itself.

Tales from the Quill

Handwriting is such a personal thing that when someone discovers that his script reveals his true personality, he immediately either feels defensive or wants to share himself with you. About 95 percent of people who learn about your graphology skills will offer one of four stock responses: 1) "I should let you see my handwriting!" 2) "You don't want to see my handwriting!" 3) "I wouldn't want to know what you would find out!" 4) "I hate my handwriting."

You Can't Analyze My Writing, I Only Print

Those of us baby boomers who learned to write in the 1950s and earlier remember the drudgery of being forced to do handwriting exercises, day after day. Handwriting then was viewed more as an art form that needed to be developed and handled with care.

In today's world printing rather than writing in cursive (connected writing) is becoming more and more common. In some states, such as California, cursive writing is no longer taught after the fourth grade as a result of budget cuts. Teachers simply don't have the time to spend instructing the students how to connect their letters. The computer keyboard is also used with much greater frequency and writing less so. The bad news is, we can't analyze keyboard printing, but the good news is, we *can* analyze handprinting.

Some handwriting analysts refuse to examine printing. These are generally people trained only in the trait-stroke method of analysis, which doesn't address printing at all (we'll talk more about the trait-stroke method in Chapter 20). However, using the principles of gestalt graphology as taught in these pages, any kind of graphic expression is open for analysis, including printing, drawings, and even childhood scribbles.

In printed writing people still have to choose how they are going to arrange the space on the page. You can evaluate the margins, space between lines and words, alignment of the baseline, pressure, and many other elements important for analysis. Think of printing as simply another form of writing with many of the same elements to be examined as in cursive script.

True, printing breaks the connections between letters, but some printers continue to connect parts of words, and some letters get close enough to bump up against each other even though they don't actually connect. This is very significant and will be covered in Chapter 14 where we'll discuss connectedness.

Some generalities can be made about printers as a group: Those who adopt printed writing generally do so because they want to be crystal clear about what they are saying. They tend to be less emotional and more analytical and logical than some cursive writers.

Chicken Scratch

Never toss out a handwriting sample. You never know when you might need to study a particular handwriting style. Build a collection of samples right from the beginning.

I Learned to Write in Timbuktu

People of all nationalities are fascinated by handwriting analysis. You may be handed a sample written in French, German, or Russian Cyrillic; not to mention Arabic, Hebrew, or Japanese. Being at least passingly familiar with the copybook style of the particular language will be especially helpful if you don't speak it. Some of the more common copybook models taught in schools are included in Chapter 4.

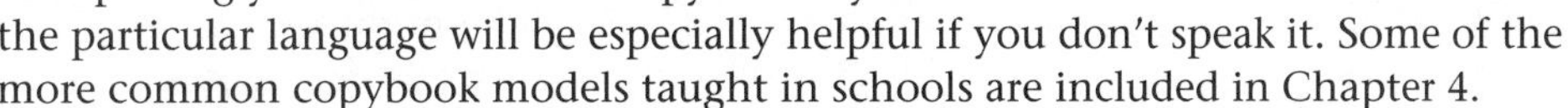

Comparing the writing specimen to the copybook model from which the person learned to write gives you a point of departure. You'll know how far she's departed from what she originally learned, which will give some clues about how original she is compared to how close she sticks to convention. If your client learned to write outside the United States, ask where she went to school.

Tales from the Quill

When I arrived in the United States from England I was in the fifth grade. My teacher, Mr. Sturm, required that I practice page after page of the Palmer Method school model. Nearly 40 years later, as a handwriting professional, I firmly believe that forcing a child to change his or her natural writing style (like switching a left-hander to his right hand) can have a damaging effect on the self-image. We write the way we do for a reason. The notable exception is when the child is working with a handwriting professional, using specific therapeutic techniques (see Chapter 25).

There are substantial differences in writing styles taught in various countries around the world. You need to be aware of cultural variations in order to produce an accurate report.

Scripts such as Hebrew and Arabic or Asian languages need some special consideration because the direction is different from what English-style writings follow, but they can still be analyzed accurately.

If all you learned was what it means to cross your t's or dot your i's in a particular way, you wouldn't be able to analyze foreign languages. Using the gestalt principles presented later in this book will make analyzing any handwriting, even in a language you don't know, much easier. Being knowledgeable about page layout, writing style, and writing movement will allow you to analyze in any language as accurately as you can in English.

As Good As It Gets: The Ideal Sample

The computer adage, "garbage in, garbage out," can easily be applied to the sample you work from. The best sample will produce the best report. On the other hand, working with a scrap of writing, a few words on a greeting card, or a torn-off piece of notebook paper can't be expected to yield the same high-quality results as a well-prepared, adequate sample.

The ideal sample is a rare find indeed. Most of the time graphologists have to be content to work with specimens that are far from perfect. However, the well-trained graphologist learns how to make adjustments to compensate for what is lacking and still come up with accurate results. Bottom line: The best sample produces the best report.

Now it's time to talk about what you should ask for when a client orders a handwriting analysis report.

The Pen's the Point

Entire organizations exist for pen collectors, and choice of writing instrument can be quite telling. Even before you begin analyzing the writing it produces, the choice of writing instrument may reveal important information. For instance, the person who prefers a pen that produces a thick line of ink but doesn't require a lot of pressure may enjoy sensual experiences without putting much effort into obtaining them.

The fountain pen is the pen of choice for many executives these days, though often just for signing important documents. The choice of a fountain pen may provide insight about the writer's socioeconomic status or attitudes about money and beautiful things.

A calligraphy pen yields an interesting line, and is often employed by people who are creative, but in a conventional way. If the client claims to always use this type of pen, allow him to use it to prepare his sample. However, if he does calligraphy as an art form only—say, to address invitations—he should use a regular pen for his handwriting sample.

The client should use her favorite writing instrument to prepare the handwriting specimen (except for pencil, which doesn't allow for as rich a variety of strokes as a pen does). Ask her to make a note of what type of pen she used, whether it was ballpoint, razor-point, felt- or chisel-tip, or, more rarely, a fountain pen.

Fine Points

The National Writing Instrument Manufacturer's Association sponsors National Handwriting Day each year on January 23. The date is significant for being John Hancock's birthday. His bold signature stands out on the Declaration of Independence.

Don't Rush It

The client should prepare the sample when she feels relaxed, not rushed or stressed. Some soft background music can help. She should be seated at a table or desk where there is plenty of elbowroom and a smooth writing surface.

One note of caution: If the client generally has a cocktail or a couple of beers after work, or a glass of wine with dinner, she should prepare her writing sample at some other time. Even one alcoholic beverage will have an effect on the writing sample.

Bonding with Paper

Photocopy paper is excellent for our purposes, and 20-pound bond is the best. Heavier stock, such as vellum or parchment, makes it more difficult to determine pen pressure, which is an important part of the analysis. Heavily textured paper causes the ink to bleed and distort the edges of the stroke, which could affect the analysis. So pilfer a piece from your computer printer or fax machine and you'll be all set.

Tales from the Quill

As a graphologist you'll learn that handwriting samples come in many shapes and sizes. In my 30-plus years in the field I've been asked to analyze handwriting on an assortment of media from cocktail napkins, photographs, sports balls, and plaster casts, to spray painting on a wall. Richard Kokochak, a handwriting analyst in Michigan, analyzed the petroglyphs he found in a cave. On a trip to Egypt, Ruth Holmes, a well-known graphologist, found that, just like handwriting, even the hieroglyphics in the pharaoh's tombs could be analyzed. Ruth was featured in many national newspapers when she successfully helped select several juries for Dr. Jack Kevorkian (also known as "Dr. Death" for his determination to help terminally ill patients end their lives), using handwriting analysis.

Letter-sized paper, 8 $^1/_2 \times 11$ inches, allows plenty of room to write. Smaller sizes can alter the way the writer uses the space. Last time you were on vacation, remember how cramped the space was on the postcards? You can't help but notice how much less room there is to write "Having a wonderful time, wish you were here" on a postcard than on a full sheet, so the tendency is to squeeze things together much more than you normally might.

The paper should be unlined, which makes some people cringe in horror. The more structured person feels threatened by that big blank space confronting him. Of course, the person who protests having to forego the ruled line has already told you something about himself. Unlined paper tells us about the writer's ability to create his own structure. Don't let him cheat by putting a ruled surface under the unlined paper! Using pre-printed lines creates a false baseline (see Chapter 8), which may affect the way the writer moves his pen across the paper.

No Fair Copying!

An original sample is always best. There are times, however, when only a photocopy is available, but this usually comes up only in a third-party analysis. You can always return the original if the client wants it back.

Tales from the Quill

There are some good reasons why you should stay away from writing samples that have been reproduced. Photocopies make it impossible for you to properly determine pressure, a very important element in handwriting. However, a photocopy, if it's good quality, *can* give you a good idea about the pressure pattern (the light/dark pattern). A faxed sample should be analyzed only by a highly experienced graphologist, because compensation must be made for some important factors such as pressure and line quality. Also, some faxes distort size and margins, which could skew the analysis. The same is generally true of writing that has been scanned into a computer, although properly scanned writing is closer to the original than a photocopy or fax.

Ask for the sample to be signed so you can compare the signature with the body of text. You'll want to check to see whether the signature and the text match, or if there are major differences. If the signature is very different from the text, the writer has different public and private selves (see Chapter 18).

If the client learned to write in a country other than the United States, the sample should state where he learned to write and how long he has been writing in English. Someone who has written in English for 20 years can naturally be expected to be more comfortable with the written word than someone who began writing in a second language only a couple of years earlier. It is helpful for the client to include a sample in both English and his native language.

Okay to Print

If the client says he only prints, let him prepare his sample the way he normally does. Printing is a little more difficult to analyze, but forcing someone to write cursive when he is more comfortable with printing is akin to forcing a left-hander to write right-handed—a definite no-no!

Chicken Scratch

If you absolutely must analyze a faxed sample, ask the person faxing it to set the sending machine on the finest resolution possible. It makes a difference in the quality of the writing that prints out at the receiving end.

Ask the person who prints to include a few lines of cursive as well, even if he tells you he never, ever writes in cursive. It will be hard for him to remember how to form the letters, but the style will tell something about his emotional state when he began printing.

You might also ask at what age he started printing, and whether his line of work requires printing. Engineers, architects, draftspersons, and law enforcement personnel are just a few examples of people whose careers require printed writing. Next time you get a speeding ticket, look at the highway patrol officer's writing—it will be block printed, guaranteed!

Getting Personal

Some medications influence handwriting, and certainly some medical conditions do. Parkinson's disease and other illnesses that affect muscle functioning can cause shakiness that an inexperienced person wouldn't know how to interpret.

Fine Points

When analyzing printing, don't be thrown off because the letters are not connected. The basic elements of the page are still there for you to draw upon: margins, baseline, size, slant, general organization, and many other important factors. In fact, the only thing that is missing *is* the connections. See Chapter 14 for further discussion of printing.

Someone might produce a very shaky handwriting sample, but if you didn't know he was writing in a helicopter you could misinterpret the shakiness and assume he was ill. So if you receive a shaky-looking sample ask if the writer is using any prescription medications or recreational drugs which might have an effect on the writing.

The same is true of health problems or recent emotional trauma that might cause temporary changes in the handwriting. When a client has gone through a divorce, job change, or other major life crisis, her handwriting will quite likely show some significant changes, though temporarily. Handwriting changes in some ways that reflect what is going on at the time of writing. Even though it still tells the truth about the basic personality, your present mood will influence the size and slant. When you are excited and happy or excited and angry, your writing gets larger and slants more to the right.

The other personal information that is helpful, though not absolutely essential, is the writer's approximate age, sex, and which hand she writes with (remember, these things can't be determined with any certainty from the handwriting).

It all boils down to this: Ask for at least a full page on unlined paper, in ink. Then work with what you get.

The Least You Need to Know

- People will start asking you to analyze their handwriting "just for fun." That means "for free."
- Signatures are not adequate for analysis by themselves.
- Printed writing and foreign writing are appropriate for analysis.
- You won't always get an ideal sample, so there are certain things you'll need to ask for.

Chapter 4

Tools of the Trade

In This Chapter

- What you'll need to get started
- Measuring and charting
- Extras that make things easier
- School models from around the world
- Recommended reading for the new graphologist

Looking for a great new career, but don't want to make a big financial investment? Love helping people? Want to work independently at home? Have I got a job for you!

Handwriting analysis fits the criteria very nicely for many people who are starting a study of graphology after retiring from some other lifelong career. Nurses, schoolteachers, human resource managers, and a myriad of other professionals are attracted to this helping occupation.

Psychologists, priests, and guidance counselors frequently choose graphology as an avocation or sideline to help in their present calling. People who suffer some physical disability that keeps them from going outside the home to a regular 9 to 5 job find graphology perfect for their needs. For some it is simply an interesting hobby to help them improve their day-to-day relationships.

Embarking on a study of handwriting analysis couldn't be easier. No state licensing is currently required and, for the moment at least, no college degree is required to practice (some handwriting professionals feel that changes need to be made to upgrade the status of the profession).

Tales from the Quill

Few colleges offer courses for credit in handwriting analysis. Fort Lewis College in Durango, Colorado, is one which lists a program that gives students credit toward a psychology degree (see Chapter 26). Other colleges sponsor periodic weekend or short-term classes. For those who have the self-discipline to follow a home-study program, several good correspondence schools are available. Appendix A in the back of this book lists the ones I personally recommend. The book you are now reading provides a solid foundation to pursue more serious study, if that's where your interest takes you.

The Absolute Necessities

A basic understanding of personality development is an integral part of studying graphology. Without it, putting together all the various indicators and traits that you find in a handwriting sample and turning them into a meaningful analysis would be a tall order. Handwriting analysis is, after all, about understanding personality!

Brushing up on what you learned in Psych. 101 in high school or college is a good place to start. Any basic psychology book will do, as long as it covers the main schools of thought—psychoanalytic, neo-Freudian, humanistic, behaviorism, and learning theories—and supplies an overview of each one.

After that comes the really interesting stuff—a smattering of abnormal psychology. To understand what's normal, you have to know something about what's not. Again, a good basic college text will furnish the essentials. If abnormal psychology is an area that attracts you, there are plenty of examples of pathology in handwriting to hold your attention. You'll find some of them in Appendix E in the back of this book.

More Than You Ever Wanted to Know About Magnifying Glasses

A good magnifying glass is first and foremost in the graphologist's toolbox. Look in the drafting section of your favorite office supply store or check the Internet. Magnifying glasses come in many shapes and sizes with all sorts of handles and stands. A plain, hand-held type may be priced under $5 and is perfectly adequate.

The magnification should be between 2× and 5×. Stronger than 5× isn't necessary for our purposes. Some magnifiers have a small inset with a higher power than the main part of the lens. The Bausch and Lomb magnifier that I use cost $12 at Staples. Shape is irrelevant. It can be round, square, or rectangular, so long as you can see through it clearly.

Why magnify? Under magnification, handwriting sometimes exposes otherwise hidden features that may affect the analysis. Little dots or blebs in the writing line might point to a physical problem; there may be angles where rounded forms should be; and, after forming an opinion about the writing as a whole, magnifying parts of it may give the analyst a different view that adds helpful information.

Some analysts like to work with a magnifying glass that hangs around their necks; others prefer the type that fits on their heads like a visor. But use the visor-type only if you don't mind your family making fun of you. It tends to make the wearer look like a miner.

Fine Points

A lighted magnifier attached to the desk lets you work with your hands free. It's easy to move the handwriting around under the lens and a larger area is visible than with the small, hand-held type of magnifying glass. You can find one in your local office supply or home improvement store.

Bookstores sell flat magnifiers that can be overlaid on a whole page. These also come in a variety of smaller sizes, some in a plastic case that fits nicely into a pocket or purse. The drawback is that the magnification usually is not very strong.

If you're wondering whether you should buy a microscope, don't bother. That is, unless you want to get into forgery examination, but that's a whole different story with an entirely different focus. For graphology, an ordinary magnifying glass will do just fine.

Let's Get This Straight

An ordinary 12-inch wooden, metal or plastic ruler comes in handy for measuring baselines and margins. In fact, anything that can be used to draw a straight line will do. See-through plastic rulers with squares printed in millimeters are especially helpful for measuring letter height and width.

Measuring Slant

A protractor is helpful for measuring slant. Again, you can pick plastic or metal, whichever you prefer. As long as you can get a good ideas of the degree of slant, from 120° to 40°. Don't worry, if it sounds complicated, it will become clear in Chapter 16 where we talk about slant and get into the details of how to measure various parts of handwriting.

Plotting the Mind: Charts, Diagrams, and Graphs

Long ago, in a galaxy far, far away… Where was I? Oh! When I began reading books about graphology I found the references to "long lower loops" or "tall upper loops" puzzling. How are you to know what's long or short or tall, I wondered. Since I didn't know anyone

Tales from the Quill

At a recent American Association of Handwriting Analysts conference, each registrant received a pocket-size lighted magnifying glass. It's a good idea to have one of these handy little items for your briefcase or purse. You never know when someone is going to thrust his handwriting under your nose and ask for your opinion. I recommend against doing quickies, but if you just can't resist, you'll get a better look through a lighted magnifier.

knowledgeable about graphology at the time, I had to do a lot of guesswork, never knowing whether I was on the mark or way off base. It was pretty frustrating.

After 10 years of struggling on my own, I discovered that, in an effort to objectify graphology, several charts and graphs had been developed. By measuring certain aspects of handwriting, the analyst didn't have to guess at whether a loop was long or extra long, whether small letter height was small, medium, or tall, or a multitude of other items. There were absolutes and guidelines. What a relief!

For each area of handwriting where taking measurements is appropriate (and there are about 12 of them), there are some simple standards to follow. Even graphologists more comfortable with an intuitive approach should be aware of what these basic measurements are, since they provide a "jumping off" point or a basis for comparison.

Experienced graphologists don't rely on measurements, but in the beginning they are important. In each section of the book where I explain an aspect of handwriting that can be measured, I'll tell you what the comparison standards are.

Fine Points

You can buy a Psychogram Guide, a special plastic guide for measuring handwriting slant and other aspects. It has the protractor degrees (some types show a number score instead) printed right on it. It can be ordered from Graphex (614) 457-9034.

Some schools actually require their students to measure 100 slants on a page! The mere thought curls my toes! I've found that taking random measurements from a few places on the page is adequate. That is, with one caveat: When you're just starting out, you need lots of practice.

Beyond taking the basic measurements, some systems offer charts on which to plot dozens of handwriting characteristics. Two of these, the Roman-Staempfli Psychogram and the Wittlich Diagram are circular. Klara Roman called the Psychogram a "profile in a circle," because it indicated, at a glance, how the energy in the personality is distributed.

The following figure is the Psychogram, which Dr. Klara Roman created for the Hungarian Government in the 1930s. Forty points are plotted around the circle and divided into eight sections or syndromes. So, if you want to know how the client's ego looks, you just check the scores in the Ego section. Or, if you want to know how her social attitudes compare to her inhibitions, you can check those areas.

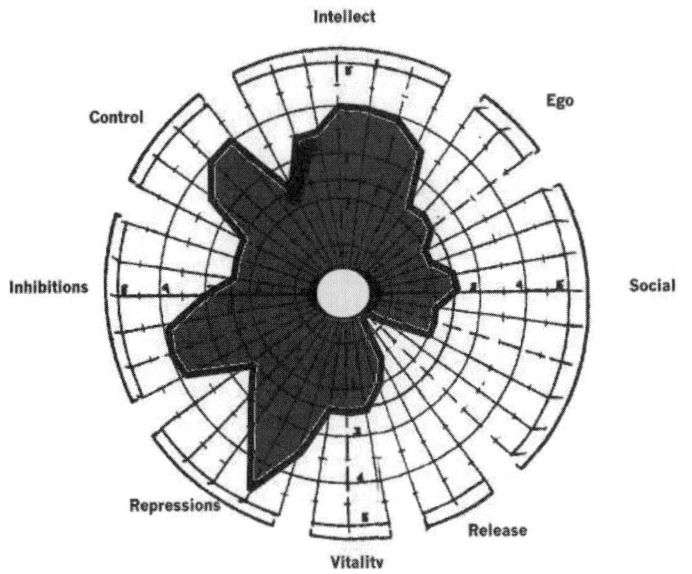

The Roman-Staempfli Psychogram.

The Psychogram can also be divided into quadrants. The upper half represents the conscious aspects of personality—the intellectual, ego, and self-control. The lower half represents the unconscious: emotional release, vitality, and defenses. The left half of the circle depicts the introverted side of the personality, which includes inhibitions and over-control, and the right side, you guessed it, is the extroverted side, the ego and social functions.

When all the points are plotted around the circle and the resulting graph is filled in, the basic personality becomes evident. The Psychogram is a wonderful tool for requiring the graphologist to look at hundreds of features they might otherwise miss. By measuring and weighing all of these items, you can feel comfortable that you aren't going to miss anything vital in your analysis. Learning the Psychogram is a whole course in itself, but we will explore many of the items found on it.

Chicken Scratch

Don't get so caught up in taking measurements that you forget to keep the whole picture in mind. Measurements are handy for objectifying the handwriting when you are a beginner, but only to provide a frame of reference.

Nice, but Not Essential

In the high-tech world of the 90s and beyond, all manner of sophisticated equipment is available to help us do our work, whatever it may be. Apart from the normal business equipment essential to any career—telephone, fax, computer—you may want to add a scanner.

Many new computers come with scanners, and inexpensive scanners abound on the market. You don't have to spend a lot of money to get good quality results with a scanner, but I've found that sticking with name brands, such as Hewlett Packard, Kodak, and Canon has saved me time. Twice now, I've bought off-brands and had to return them. You'd think I would learn!

Scanning handwritings and saving them to the hard disk is an excellent way to archive samples. But make sure you keep the hard copy somewhere safe, in case you experience a hard-drive crash and lose everything you've saved.

One of the benefits to scanning handwriting samples is that each one can be named and placed in a folder according to the classification you choose. You could have a folder of handwritings within a particular profession—schoolteachers, nurses, or plumbers. Or, you might prefer to file according to handwriting style or feature. Whatever you find easiest to work with.

When looking for a particular sample, simply do a search on the name or type of writing and have it pop up almost instantaneously. It's so much easier than wading through boxes of handwritings in your closets or garage, assuming you haven't come up with a more brilliant filing system than I have. If you start a good filing system when you begin collecting writing samples, it will be easy. Waiting for 30 years and thousands of samples, makes it a daunting task! I've just begun filing my collection of samples in plastic covers, in four-inch, three-ring binders. Ten binders are now sitting on top of my husband's computer hutch, and that's only the beginning!

One drawback to scanning handwritings is that they take up an incredible amount of disk space. On the positive side, the quality is better than a photocopy if you do it right. The key is not to scan at a higher resolution than your printer can output. I've found 300 dpi optimal (if this is all Greek to you, just move on to the next section). After you've scanned the sample, export it to your favorite image editing software and reduce the size to 50 percent and 72 dpi. The quality will still be good but the size saved on disk will be much smaller.

What about computer programs for graphology? Well, that's another subject, and we'll go into detail about the program I've developed in Chapter 26.

School Models You Need to Know

The absolute measures mentioned earlier in this chapter are based on school models or copybooks. The copybook is the standard by which the student learns to write in cursive script. Graphologists learn what the school model, or copybook (abbreviated "CB") requires, and compares the writing sample to determine how far the writer deviated from what he learned in school.

Writing just the way you learned in school isn't necessarily a good thing. In general, those who adhere to the school model are most comfortable following rules and sticking to a familiar structure. They don't like to strike out on their own or make things up as they go along.

Life would get pretty chaotic without at least some who enjoy setting and following rules and regulations, so the rest of us can be grateful that there are those who are willing to be the administrators. The types of people who feel most comfortable with school model writing are secretaries, grade school teachers, and nurses.

Chicken Scratch

Back up your computer files regularly! There's no reason to lose work that has taken many hours of preparation. This advice is offered from the school of painful personal experience.

There is a big "however" here. Another group who also tend to be school model writers are those in prison. The difference is, they follow a different set of rules. They have followed the wrong crowd. Still, like their law-abiding counterparts, they need structure. The lesson is, just because someone writes just like they learned in school, doesn't make them a better person. As in all other aspects of handwriting analysis, you have to look at the whole picture.

On the following pages you'll find some school models for the United States and some of the more common nationalities you may run into.

The Palmer Copybook, commonly used in the United States prior to 1980.

The D'Nealian Copybook, commonly used in the United States since 1980.

A B C D E F G H I
J K L M N O P Q R
S T U V W X Y Z

a b c d e f g h i
j k l m n o p q r
s t u v w x y z

a b c d e f g
h i j k l m n
o p q r s t u
v w x y z

The British Copybook.

I J L · T F Z · H
K · A M N · B P
R · S · C G E · O Q
D X U V W Y

Type d'écriture..

i, u, n, m, r, v, w, o, a, c, e, x, s.
t, d, l, b, h, k, f,
q, g, y, p, j, z.
1, 2, 3, 4, 5, 6, 7, 8, 9, 0.
I F H K T P W Z J
L S C E G O A M N
P B R D U X Y Q

The French Copybook.

a b c d e (e) f g h
i j k l m n o p qu
r s ß (ß) t u v w x y z
ä ö ü (. , ; : „ " - ! ?)
A B C D E F G H I J
K L M N O P Qu R
S T U V W X Y Z
12345 Ä Ö Ü 67890

The German Copybook.

Books for the Budding Analyst

If I had a dollar for everyone who has called or e-mailed me and complained about the contradictions they've found in the many graphology books they've read, I could buy a new computer. They usually want me to explain the inconsistencies. Hmmm, maybe I should charge a dollar before I answer. . .

The trouble is, most of the commercially available books get on the market because they're sexy. Not sexy like Madonna, but sexy in that they get the consumer's attention. Let's face it folks, it's easier to sell a book about love and relationships than it is to sell an encyclopedia. Unfortunately, the person who wants to learn good graphology is the one who suffers.

Books that promise quick and easy shortcuts to ferreting out your friend's and neighbor's secrets aren't doing anyone any favors. They'll feed you nonsense like "a large lower loop means the one who makes it is promiscuous." Wouldn't it be nice if you could go down a list of "this means that," and every time you saw a particular indicator it would mean the same thing? It would make everything so simple. But handwriting analysis doesn't work that way.

The truth is, meaning depends on context. Yes, a big lower loop in one handwriting could mean the writer was promiscuous. But in another writing, depending on other surrounding factors, it could mean that the writer likes to brag about his sexual prowess, but when he gets into the clinch, can't perform. Quite a difference!

The books I'm about to recommend are my own personal favorites. I know several of the authors and can vouch for them supplying good, accurate information. The one and only area of disagreement is noted.

- *Handwriting Analysis, the Complete Basic Book* (Newcastle Publishing Company, 1980) by Karen Amend and Mary Ruiz. Here's that one disagreement: In the section dealing with the capital I, the authors offer an interpretation opposite everyone else's in the field. They later adjusted their position. Karen and Mary (Mary passed away several years ago) are excellent analysts and I recommend this extremely helpful book more than any other to beginners.

Fine Points

Some of the best material you can buy comes in the form of unpublished monographs. Information on some of the deeper aspects of personality in handwriting is available from Mostly Books 877-90BOOKS (877-902-6657) (**http://www.tucson.com/mostlybooks**).

- *Achieving Compatibility through Handwriting Analysis,* Volume 1 and 2 (Newcastle Publishing Company, 1992) by Karen Amend and Mary Ruiz. This two-volume set offers a wealth of basic information plus couples case histories.
- *The Art of Graphology* (The Whitston Publishing Company, 1985) by Marie Bernard. An excellent introduction to European gestalt graphology with many fine samples of famous people. By the way,

Marie, who passed away in the mid 1990s, was a very colorful character, by all accounts.

- *You and Your Private I* (Llewellyn, 1998) by Jane Nugent Green. Recently reprinted, this in-depth exploration of the capital I should be on every graphologist's bookshelf.
- *You Are What You Write* (Macmillan, 1973) by Huntington Hartford. Heir to the A&P grocery chain fortune, Hartford made a great contribution with this publication. He compiled the opinions of many classical authors on different aspects of handwriting. Hartford saved you the trouble by pulling together many resources into this one book. This book can sometimes be found in catalogs that advertise deeply discounted books.
- *Handwriting Analysis, A Guide to Understanding Personality* (Whitford Press, 1990) by Baruch Lazewnik. Lazewnik, an Israeli graphologist, guides you through a series of handwriting analyses done in the gestalt manner.
- *Personality in Handwriting* (reprinted by Graphex, 1997) by Klara Roman. The "bible" of gestalt graphology. No serious graphologist should be without it.
- *Handwriting, A Personality Projection* (reprinted by Fern Ridge Press, 1989) by Frank Victor. Another must-read because it doesn't settle for the simplistic trait lists that so many do.

Tales from the Quill

When you find graphology books in the New Age or Occult section at your favorite bookstore, do everyone in the field a favor and ask the manager to put them where they belong—in the Psychology section. The Library of Congress (**http://www.loc.gov**) changed graphology's classification in 1980, from Occult to three different listings: Documentary Evidence Selection of Personnel by Management, Personnel Selection, and Diagnostic Graphology.

You won't find many of these books at your local Barnes & Noble or Borders. However, they aren't hard to come by. Mostly Books, a delightful store in Tucson, Arizona, carries an extensive selection of handwriting analysis volumes. That's because one of the owners, Tricia Clapp, is herself, a skilled handwriting analyst. In fact, graphology classes are conducted in the store on a weekly basis.

Next time you're in Tucson, stop by the store. Tricia and her sister, Bobbe, would be thrilled to show you their collection. The address is 6208 Speedway. In the meantime, check out their Web site at **http://tucson.com/mostlybooks/** (e-mail: *MostlyBook@tucson.com*) where you can peruse the covers of the many handwriting (and other) books they have available, and order them online or over the phone. They also offer many worthwhile privately published papers that you won't find anywhere else.

The Least You Need to Know

- Basic psychology is an indispensable part of graphology.
- A handwriting analyst needs a good magnifying glass and slant-measuring tool.
- Learning to measure is important for beginners. It teaches them to pay attention to elements of handwriting they might otherwise overlook.
- Being familiar with copybooks is helpful to the beginning analyst.
- Read lots of other books to augment the information you learn from this one.

Part 2

This Is Your Life: The Page

Okay, you've got a handwriting sample in front of you—what now? What do all those squiggles and lines mean, anyway? Part 2 takes you through the basic principles of handwriting analysis, and shows you how to see handwriting differently.

We'll go to the very heart of handwriting—space, form, and movement—and learn how each part impacts all the rest. This is like no other book you'll read on this subject, anywhere.

Chapter 5

Looking at the Big Picture

In This Chapter

- Looking at handwriting in a whole new way
- What environment means in handwriting
- How to find a balance between writing and paper
- Putting yourself in someone else's space

Handwriting is rich with symbolism that is not readily apparent to the untrained eye. For the graphologist, an empty sheet of paper waiting to be filled with writing takes on a special significance that might astonish the casual observer.

The way the handwriting is arranged on the page is a metaphor for how the writer organizes his daily affairs; his perspective on life; how he expresses his emotions, and much more. Handwriting clearly demonstrates the writer's behavior within his or her environment, and you are about to learn how to unravel the mysteries found there.

First, though, let's clarify what *environment* means in this context. To the average person the word environment means something quite different from what it means to the handwriting analyst. In fact, these days, it can be an emotionally charged word. The spotted owl and its vanishing habitat might leap to mind, or maybe the rain forests of Brazil; the ozone layer; the need to protect our environment, the earth, our home. It is, after all, the human environment. But one's own environment needn't be so grand. It might simply be your living room, the office, or your car. Essentially, it is wherever you are at the moment.

Write Words

According to *Webster's Revised Unabridged Dictionary*, **environment** means that which environs or surrounds; or refers to surrounding conditions, influences, or forces, by which living forms are influenced and modified in their growth and development.

An environment may be natural or unnatural. A lion's natural environment is the jungle where he can roam free, doing what lions do best. The zoo is an unnatural environment for a lion. Yet, while he is probably not as happy in the zoo as he would be in the jungle, he can live a long life there. A dolphin's natural environment is the ocean. Put her in a tank of sea water and she will know the difference; yet, she can adapt and exist in an environment that is not completely natural to her way of life.

Humans, too, have natural and unnatural environments. Someone raised in the inner city, or a sophisticated cosmopolite, might feel strange and uncomfortable if he were suddenly transported to the Appalachian Mountains. Yet, both can adapt to the new environment and learn to live in it, if necessary.

By now you're probably scratching your head wondering, "What does all this have to do with handwriting?" The answer is, everything, because your handwriting depicts how you behave within your environment, natural or unnatural, physical or emotional. And handwriting analysis helps us determine how well you have made the necessary adaptations to that milieu.

A Room with a View

The paper on which you write represents your personal environment. The handwriting you place upon it illustrates how you behave there. It doesn't matter whether you use a piece of lowly notebook paper or expensive watermarked vellum. You can turn it into a jungle, a desert, a cozy den, or a sophisticated drawing room. It's entirely up to you.

Let's visualize a piece of paper as a room. Until you begin laying ink on the paper, the "room" remains empty, a background waiting to be filled with the furnishings you choose. Begin mentally planning the decor of your imaginary room. Pick out the color and style carpeting and paint or wallpaper that appeals to you, the type of furniture you prefer; consider where you might hang the artwork, the personal knickknacks and ornaments that make it yours and no one else's. You can have whatever you want in this room. After all, it's just a mental exercise, so live a little! Be as extravagant as you like.

Just as your personal style and taste determine the design and final look of a literal room, your past experiences and relationships will influence how your handwriting appears in your symbolic room. But in this room, no architect, designer, or painter can be blamed when things don't go as planned. In the final analysis (pun intended) you, the writer, get to take full responsibility for what appears there.

It's All in How You See It

Analyzing handwriting is a way of exploring someone else's reality. Doing it successfully is a matter of learning how to see handwriting in an entirely new way, and that requires a change in your frame of reference. This section is all about *eye training,* or how to change your frame of reference.

Write Words

The most important lesson for beginning handwriting-analysis students is **eye training,** learning how to look at handwriting in a whole new way.

Changing your frame of reference can be as easy as turning out a light. Things look very different in the dark, even though they are the same objects you saw with the lights on. Or, you could look at an object from a different perspective. As a kid you may have laid on your back and hung your head off the end of your bed to find that the floor and ceiling look completely different from that angle.

Changing one's frame of reference means scrapping what you think you know about something and looking at it from a different point of view. Let's say I show you a table and ask you to draw it. Tables come in all shapes, sizes, materials, styles, so how will you draw one? No offense, but unless you are naturally artistic, your drawing probably won't look a whole lot like the model.

Why not? Because you drew your preconceived idea of a table—four legs and a top, which may bear little resemblance to the actual piece of furniture. You were not really seeing the table as it is. In order to draw it accurately, you must look at the table in a way that will fool your brain into disregarding what you already know about tables, and make it see the real thing.

So, to change your frame of reference you could dim the lights or hang a gauzy curtain in front of the table, or lie on the floor and look at it from a different direction. Anything to make you lose touch with what you think tables look like. From your new frame of reference, and seeing through new eyes, you are forced to simply draw a series of lines, not what you always thought of as a table, and, voila! You are amazed to find that your drawing turns out looking much more like the real thing than your first effort.

Fine Points

Betty Edwards' book, *Drawing on the Artist Within* (J.P. Tarcher, Inc., 1979), offers some exercises to help get in touch with your creative side. These are helpful in training your eyes to look at handwriting in a new way.

Your First How-To Exercise

To get you looking at the writing in a new way, rather than seeing it as a collection of words, we'll apply a very simple technique. This is similar to the way we changed our view of the table.

You'll need a full-size sheet of paper covered with writing—your own or someone else's—any old page of writing will do. Take a good look at it. What do you see? Okay, at this point it's just a bunch of words. Now let's change your perspective.

Tales from the Quill

Getting into your right brain helps with this exercise. You can automatically switch over from the left-brain to right-brain functioning with a handwriting movement. Take a sheet of lined paper and make several rows of infinity signs, turned on their sides. Focus on the movement until you feel the perceptual shift. You'll know it when you feel sort of dreamy, which means your conceptual self—the right brain—has taken over.

We can do this by propping the paper up on a stand on the desk or table, or taping it to the wall and standing back several feet so you cannot clearly read the content. Stare at it for awhile. Try to see the page as if it were a painting, your own personal Picasso or Rembrandt, if you prefer.

Force yourself to look past what you think you know about handwriting and see the lines produced by the ink. See the shapes, the colors produced by the flow of ink, the textures, the area between the shapes, the white space that creates a border around the whole picture.

Let your eyes relax and become unfocussed for a moment (If you've ever been frustrated by one of those posters where you stare at the picture until a new and different picture emerges, you'll know what I mean). There is an Aha! moment where the marks on the paper seem to shift and change. They are no longer distinct words. They are elements of a whole picture, which may be somewhat different from your original impression.

Now turn the page of writing upside down and once again step back. What happened? You completely lost your original frame of reference and were forced to see the writing as a whole object instead of single words, letters, and parts. Even if you wanted to, you could not identify individual elements of the writing. And that is our goal—to force you to look at the page as a whole.

When you analyze someone's handwriting, you can actually experience the emotions that the writer experienced as he or she drew the trail of ink across the paper. Once you are able to see the writing as a whole, you will get an instinctive feeling about it that has nothing to do with logic. It takes practice, but if you allow your intuitive sense to take over, you will learn to perceive the patterns of the writing, the rhythms, the way the writing moves on the page, the symbols—slashing knives, hearts, whirling tornadoes.

Fine Points

If you studied the stroke method of handwriting analysis and consequently can't resist picking out individual strokes, try turning the writing upside down. It's an effective way of tricking your brain into seeing the whole picture.

The "Ground" Work

We're about to dive into a concept that may at first seem strange—Gestalt psychology as it relates to handwriting analysis—but I hope that by the end of this chapter, you will understand why I've borrowed the gestalt terms, "figure" and "ground" to explain the basic principles of gestalt graphology.

Gestalt psychology is a school of psychological thought that has its roots in 1930s Germany, and grew in the United States around World War II. The most famous names associated with it are Kurt Koffka, Max Wertheimer, Wolfgang Kohler, and Fritz Perls. It is based on the concept that nothing exists in a vacuum. To properly understand what is going on in a situation, you must look at the whole picture. In other words, when something affects one part of an organism, it affects all the other parts in some way.

In Gestalt psychology there is no meaning without a context in which to put all the elements. Applying this idea to handwriting, it is possible to comprehend the essence of the personality only by viewing an adequate-sized sample of writing within the context of the whole page. Picking out a single letter or stroke, or analyzing just a scrap of writing and trying to reach a conclusion about the whole person makes little sense. The person who provides a sample of his handwriting is a whole person, and his handwriting must be examined as a whole.

According to Gestalt psychology, we tend to see things as solid objects (a figure) against a background (the ground). For example, you see your friend John as a whole person against the background of his house; he's not just an inventory of body parts. A computer is made up of CPU, cables, monitor, keyboard, mouse, and many other parts, but most people view all those parts simply as "the computer." Likewise, handwriting is made up of many different parts: strokes, letters, words, sentences, and paragraphs, but we see it as a whole object—handwriting.

In handwriting, the ground (the background) is the paper on which you prepare to write. The ink is the figure (the object). Thus, we see the trail of ink as an object against the background of the paper. And, in handwriting, the whole is greater than the sum of its parts. Singling out individual letters or strokes contributes some superficial information about the writer, but outside the context of the whole writing, they reveal very little of the whole person.

Let's take the letter "t" for example. You might examine a writing where the t's are crossed very high on the stem. In the trait-stroke handwriting analysis system, the small letter t relates to one's work and goals. The height of the crossbar indicates how high the writer sets her goals. If the t is crossed high on the stem, theoretically, the writer sets her goals at high levels.

The problem with this approach is, a lot of important information is left out. We don't know whether the writer has the energy to follow through on her goals and see them to completion. We don't know what types of goals she might have, or how firmly she is committed to her goals. Only by examining the entire handwriting can we get the answers to those questions.

Forgive me if I say it again: Pieces and parts of a handwriting sample may tell you about pieces and parts of the writer's personality, but outside the context of the whole writing, they simply cannot provide a complete picture.

To belabor the point a little further, the following illustration depicts some of the systems that make the human body work. In order for a human to live and breathe, he has to have a circulatory system, nervous system, respiratory system, skeletal system, and all the other systems working together as a whole entity. If a few parts of a system are missing or not working properly, it affects the way all the other parts work. Remember Frankenstein's monster?

Pieces of the puzzle. When is a person a person?

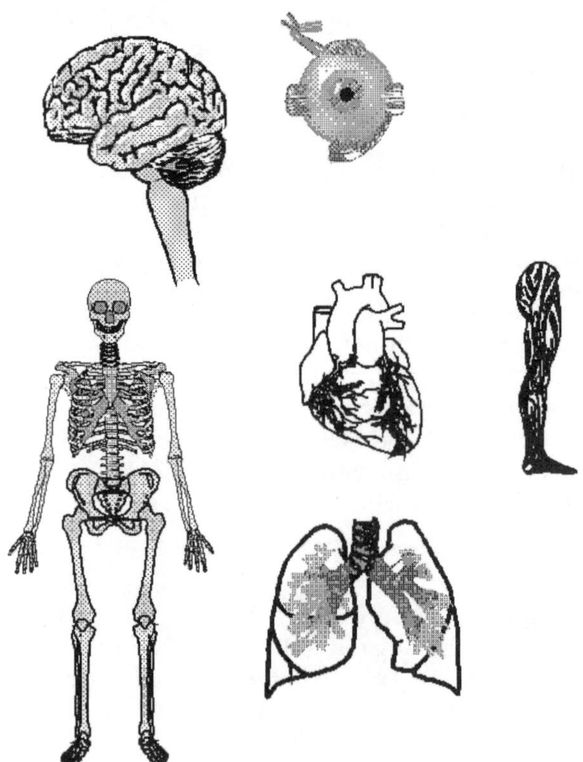

The organs in the illustration are pieces of the puzzle that make up a human being; but at what point can we say this is a whole person? When the heart is pumping blood? The lungs sucking in air? Synapses sparking in the brain? There is no such point. None of the individual organs by themselves, or even one or two together are representative of the whole, living human being. Not until all the pieces are working together can we say, "It's a person."

Handwriting is like a microcosm of the human body: The strokes that make up the letters, the letters that make up the words, and the words that make up the paragraphs are analogous to the various organs and systems that make the body work. Separately they mean little. They must be seen within the context of the page to have any real meaning, just as the various organs must function within the framework of the body to have any real meaning.

When the body is injured or disease impacts the use of some organs, some adaptations can be made. If you lose a tooth on the right side of your mouth you can still chew on your left side. If you lose the use of your right hand you can learn to use your left. Lose one kidney and you can still process toxins with the other. Loss of eyesight results in your becoming more aware of other senses, such as hearing. But even without the full use of all its normal organs, your body still functions as a whole. This is a just another way to emphasize the importance of viewing handwriting as a whole entity.

Chicken Scratch

If you have learned to look at handwriting in bits and pieces using the trait-stroke method, it may be very difficult for you to get a grasp of the whole picture. Some students find it helpful to turn the writing upside down, so they can't put their finger on any specific stroke. Things look quite different from that perspective!

A Fine Balance

Handwritings are as varied as the individuals who write them. The first glance at a writing sample speaks volumes to the handwriting analyst, even before he or she gets started on the analysis. Doubtless, you've heard it said that when meeting someone, "You never get a second chance to make a good first impression." When looking at a handwriting, you are meeting the writer for the first time. That first impression is a very important one.

Pay attention to your gut reaction. When you first pick up a handwriting sample ask yourself how well-balanced is this page? Is the figure/ground relationship (the amount of writing compared to the white space on the paper) fairly even, or does one overpower the other so much so that viewing it is disturbing?

What does a well-balanced page look like? It "feels" organized, with a pleasant harmony between the writing and the paper on which it is written. The writing is framed by even, balanced (there's that word again!) margins on all sides; the lines are clearly spaced, without loops hanging down from one line, interfering with the next.

Fine Points

When looking at a writing for the first time, ask yourself: Is it balanced? Crowded? Spacious? Airy?

Fine Points

The size of spaces around the words helps define the relationship of figure and ground.

Viewing a balanced page doesn't make you feel uncomfortable the way an unbalanced one does. When there is a lack of balance you may feel as if you need to fill in the blank spaces with something, or erase some parts because there is too much writing and too little white space. If you look at a writing and your first response is "Yuck!" there's probably a lack of balance somewhere.

This might not sound like a very scientific approach, but don't forget, some of handwriting analysis is an art that requires eye training and intuition. The intuitive part will be more difficult for those who need strict rules to follow. Still, the handwriting analyst must learn to be objective when it comes to interpreting what he sees, not allowing his own personal biases to affect the outcome. Now, if you're one of those people who need numbers and ratios to help you make judgments, don't worry, we'll get to some measurements in later chapters.

Looking for balance in handwriting involves seeing not only the writing itself, but also the negative space. Huh? The blank spaces around the writing can be just as significant as the writing itself.

Pressed in

When the page is unbalanced because of a problem with the writing (the figure), you will know it because you'll see very little of the paper. The writing overtakes the entire sheet; words and lines are *pressed in,* compacted, crowded together, leaving little breathing space. Gasp! I feel suffocated just thinking about it!

What type of person uses up all the space on the paper? Someone who feels the need to dominate the space in his or her environment. Her literal living area may be just as cluttered with furniture and other objects as the written page she produced. The writer may be a collector of fine art or a greedy hoarder. Other aspects of the writing that we will cover later will reveal which is more likely to be the case.

Spaced Out

If an imbalance is caused by too much white space, it's because the paper (ground) has overwhelmed the figure (the writing). There will be large *lakes* of space between words that draw your eye; or the appearance of a *river* is created by a pattern of wide spaces that moves down the page. Either one creates a lack of balance. Or, perhaps one of the margins is extremely wide and the other extremely narrow, making the page look lopsided.

What type of person leaves big holes of space in the writing? Someone who needs an abundance of space in her day-to-day life. The writer tends to arrange her personal space with an aesthetic eye. Her house may be sparsely furnished, or she may isolate herself and avoid contact with other people. Other signs in the writing will tell us which is true.

Exaggerations of any kind disturb the whole picture. Your eye should not be drawn to any one particular element on the page. A balanced picture is pleasant to look at with nothing jumping out at you to jar the symmetry.

Test yourself with the handwriting samples on the next page. You probably already know much more about handwriting than you think you do. Which sample is balanced? Which is too spaced out? Which is too pressed in? Check the amount of white space on the paper against the dark area of the writing to see if there is a balance.

Write Words

The spaces around words (negative space) help define the relationship of figure and ground. **Lakes** are extremely large spaces between words. **Rivers** are wide word spaces that create a pattern that looks like rivers flowing down the page. **Pressed in,** or compressed, refers to writing that is too crowded and has no breathing space.

It's Time to Start a Collection

Handwriting provides important information about the person who wrote it. Begin the process of analysis by collecting as many handwriting samples as you can and doing the exercise described earlier in this chapter, where you looked at your own handwriting from a distance. Train yourself to look at the writing as a picture and decide whether the picture is well-balanced or not. The answer will tell you how well the writer organizes his or her life.

Without exercise, muscles get weak and atrophy. Strengthen your graphology muscles by continually looking for ways to exercise your perception and eye training. Ask everyone you know to get their friends and acquaintances to volunteer handwriting samples for you to use for practice. Collect samples of as many different writing styles as you can. You may not be able to get the "ideal" sample that was described in Chapter 3, but without at least a paragraph of writing, the sample isn't adequate for a beginner's analysis.

Got an appointment at your doctor's office? Ask the office and nursing staff for samples. Ask your lawyer, your kids' schoolteachers, the local librarian, and anyone else you can think of for samples. If you know someone who knows someone in prison, ask for samples. How about celebrities? Everyone knows someone! And almost everyone

Chicken Scratch

Remember, when first starting to learn handwriting analysis, you are supposed to look at the whole page as if it were a picture. Don't try to analyze the handwriting or decide why it looks the way it does. It takes lots of practice and eye training, and that means observing many handwriting samples before you can expect to "get it."

will be delighted to cooperate, especially if you promise to return to them with some insights about their handwriting, once you've had a chance to study it properly.

Sample A

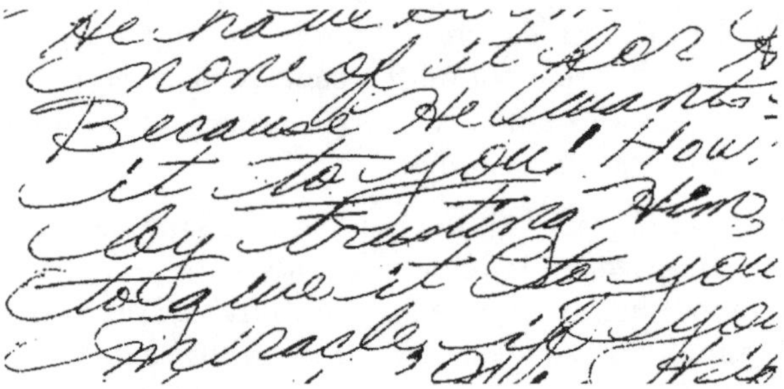

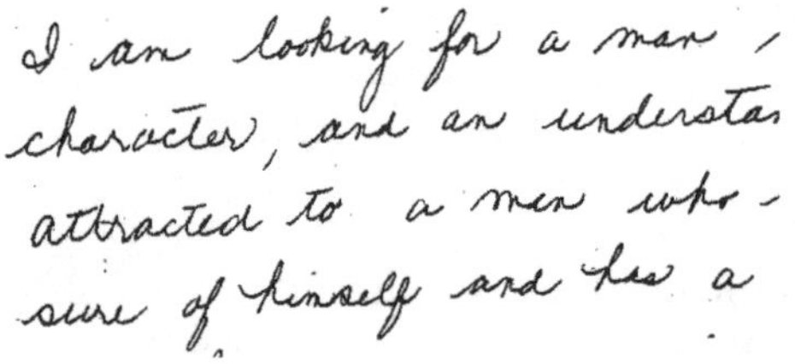

Sample B

Sample C

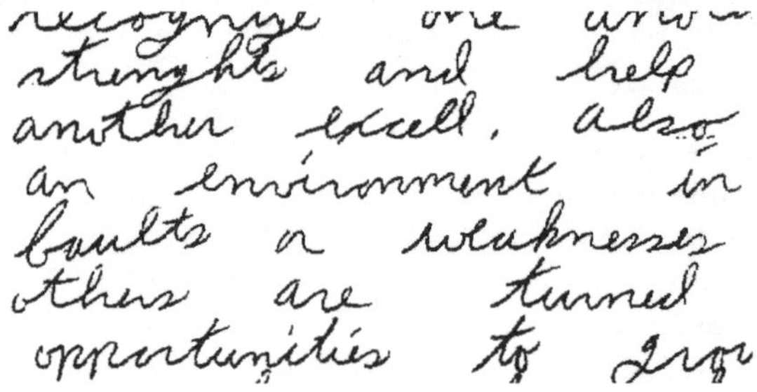

Test yourself.

It's not too difficult to recognize which are the unbalanced samples, is it? If you picked Sample B as the balanced one, you were correct. If you picked Sample A or C, you need to do some extra homework!

The following table gives you some pairs of opposites to help you decide how you to describe the writing you want to analyze.

Harmonious	Inharmonious
Orderly	Disorderly
Clear	Confused
Light	Heavy
Lively	Sluggish
Elegant	Crude
Simplified	Complicated
Regular	Irregular
Original	Commonplace

It's time to begin thinking of handwriting in terms of the words in the table. As we progress through the coming chapters, you will learn how each element of writing builds upon the others and blends into a totality that helps determine its final appearance.

When we analyze handwriting, we take on the awe-inspiring task of putting ourselves into someone else's space, that person's reality. In a very real sense, we must "become" that person by becoming one with his handwriting, and hearing the story it wants to impart. The person who examines handwriting and imposes on it what she wants to hear is likely to get the wrong message.

Let's say you and I just met for the first time and I remind you of someone you don't like. If you project what you feel about that other person onto me without letting me show you by my actions who I am, you may form a wrong impression of the real me. The analyst must put his "self" aside and ask the writing questions, then be ready to receive the right answers. Allowing the writing to speak to you lets you connect naturally with the personality behind it. Sounds confusing? Don't worry, it will become clearer with practice. For now, eye training is the key!

Tales from the Quill

Tam Deachman, a retired advertising executive and graphologist on the side, sat down with his companion at the counter of a small bistro. The daily specials were handwritten on a chalkboard in a flamboyant script. His companion issued a challenge: "Who wrote it?" The writing had been done with an obvious flourish. There were many embellishments and ornamentations. Tam looked around the restaurant at the various employees. Just then, the kitchen door flung open and into the dining room stepped a man dressed up like a French chef, complete with floppy hat and curled moustache. "There's your writer!" Tam declared. He was right.

Returning to the opening concept of this chapter, look at your handwriting and ask yourself, "How do I act within my environment?" Picture yourself in a crowded room at a party where you don't know anyone. The guests seem to be having a good time, eating hors d'oeuvres and dancing, enjoying their conversations. What do you do? Make a grand entrance, jump right in, and introduce yourself? Or do you feel awkward and sit shyly in a corner on your own, waiting for others to introduce themselves? How about when you're alone? How do you use your environment then? Or when you're at work, at school, on the road in your car, or in the supermarket?

Tales from the Quill

Handwriting is the body language of the mind. It reflects in a very real way how people act within their environment. I haven't yet seen Italian film star Roberto Bernigni's handwriting, but the way he clambered over the seats, nearly trampling Stephen Spielberg, on his way to the stage to accept his 1999 Oscar award, suggests the exuberance of a large, right-slanted, showy writing that splashes across the page with abandon. One who timidly retires to a corner all by himself is likely to have small, sober writing, crammed against the left side of the page.

How well do you organize your environment? Could a Marine drill sergeant run his white-gloved fingers over the top of your bedroom door and come away smiling? Or are there unread piles of magazines and newspapers dating back to 1982 stacked next to half-empty Chinese food containers and Doritos bags covering every inch of table space? Or, are you reasonably neat and tidy on the outside, but can't open the hall closet without risking an avalanche of old toys, games, clothes, and other collectible junk raining down on your head?

People come in all shapes, sizes, and types and their handwriting shows it. A one-dimensional handwriting analyst who understands only those who are like her makes a bad handwriting analyst. The greater the variety of personalities you can find to study, the faster you will grow into a good graphologist. You can have fun along the way, too, because you'll be helping people, and they'll think you're terrific for doing it. And they'll be right!

The Least You Need to Know

- Handwriting symbolizes how you behave in your environment.
- Looking at handwriting as a whole picture is more important than identifying individual strokes.
- Balance between the writing and the paper is the first item to check when making your analysis.
- Collecting as many different types of samples as you can will start you on the road to being a good graphologist.

Chapter 6

Space, the First Frontier

In This Chapter

- Going out and coming in
- Economy or extravagance—it's in the space
- Relationship to the environment
- Relationship with self
- Relationships with others

Space is the empty area around writing on a page, as well as the areas between words and between lines. It symbolizes the invisible boundaries we set between ourselves and others.

Space also reveals our perspective on life, how clearly we see the relationships between ourselves and others, and how we arrange our environment. Interpreting the meaning of the empty spaces is just as important as understanding the writing movement itself.

A Space Odyssey: Your Environment and How You Use It

The way we use space is the most unconscious element of handwriting. Even the most compulsive person doesn't deliberately stop to measure the distance between each letter, word, and line. Still, there is a surprising consistency that continues through the entire writing, particularly in the spaces between words.

Write Words

Perspective is the ability to judge relationships between ideas or distances.

To get a clear *perspective* of an object you have to stand away from it, but not too far back. Imagine standing two feet away from the World Trade Center building and looking up. Would you be able to tell how tall it was? No. Neither could you properly tell its height if you drove 50 miles away and tried to gauge it from there. Too close or too far, your perspective would be skewed.

Setting Boundaries

Handwriting is limited by two physical factors: the available space bounded by the edges of the paper, and by the energy you invest when writing on the paper. A small sheet of paper creates artificial boundaries that are tighter than those on a larger sheet; a small sheet forces the writer to limit himself and stay within that smaller framework, whether he likes it or not.

A small amount of writing space constricts the writing movement. That's why it is important to give the writer an ample sheet of paper to see how he handles it. If he crams a few words into the top left-hand corner of an $8^1/_2 \times 11$–inch page, it will say something quite different about him than if he takes up every bit of white space on the paper.

The writer's actions within the boundaries of paper size provide clues about how he views time, space, and money. Is he generous or stingy with his money? A profligate time waster or one who jealousy guards every minute of the day, the way Scrooge hoarded pennies?

Don't Fence Me in: Line Spacing

There are no rules about the amount of space to leave between lines of writing. Not even a school model provides guidelines on that issue. So, the choice of line spacing is a very personal one that provides the graphologist with several pieces of information about the writer:

- How she uses time
- How she uses her material resources
- How orderly her thinking processes are

Line spacing is one indicator of self-control. The amount of space left between one line and the next establishes how well the writer recognizes the need for order in her environment and how well she organizes her life.

Because writing is a form of communication, clarity should be a high priority. Someone who communicates clearly wants to make sure she is properly understood by leaving a reasonable distance between the lines of writing. Each line should be clear, with no loops hanging down to interfere with the next line. When the lines are too close together, it's like being in a crowd with someone whispering in your ear—nothing is clear.

At the end of a line of writing, you decide where to place your pen to begin the next line. If you are relaxed and know you have plenty of time, you may feel free to use up more space. The writer who feels pressured for time is more likely to start writing the new line closer to the previous one.

Fine Points

The picture of space is the most unconscious aspect of handwriting. You don't have to think about how to arrange the writing on the page. It just happens naturally.

Clear Line Spacing

Clear line spacing indicates mental clarity and a sense of order. The person who leaves moderate distances between the lines is able to plan ahead and organize his life and time effectively. He knows the importance of contingency planning; that is, leaving enough time and space in which to handle the various emergencies of daily life without leaving himself in a pinch. When a writer feels free to leave ample white space between the lines of writing it implies some self-assurance. He's not afraid to use his environment to his advantage.

Clear line spacing.

Clear line spacing demonstrates an ability to assimilate the impressions and experiences one accumulates from day to day and to express them appropriately. The writer is objective when dealing with a situation or problem, and considers a variety of potential responses and how they might affect the outcome. He reasons well and uses good old-fashioned horse sense to help him make decisions.

Narrow Line Spacing

When the spacing between the lines of writing is too narrow, the writer's perspective becomes impaired and her mental clarity is reduced. She's an impulsive person who goes with her gut reactions, rushing ahead too quickly without taking time to reason things out. A subjective viewpoint allows her to see things only in terms of how she feels about them and how they affect her, rather than keep the bigger picture in mind.

Close line spacing also tells us about the writer's spending habits. Jammed-together writing suggests compulsive caution in spending. That's a nice way of saying "cheap." Just how careful she is with her resources depends on how closely the writing is packed. When there is little or no white space to be seen, one of several options will be true:

- The writer has a "poverty consciousness," which means she expects to be poor, so fears spending.
- The writer is a stingy cheapskate.
- The writer is genuinely conscious of the need to use her resources very carefully.

Narrow line spacing.

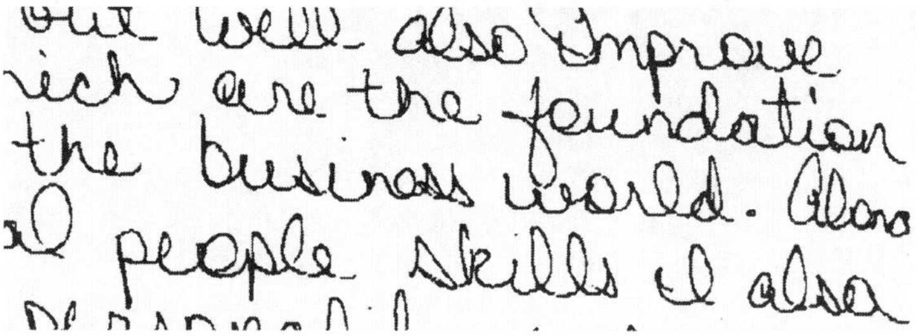

Crowded Line Spacing

The writer of extremely narrow, crowded line spacing is driven by impulse and lack of ability for abstract thinking and objectivity. He may be more imaginative than one who chooses wider line spacing. He's certainly less interested in taking time to reason things out than going with his instincts. He tends to live in the moment. Even in speech, his words are more impulsive and less discreet, and he has plenty to say! The trouble is, he doesn't think far enough ahead to measure his words. He gets so caught up in his own ideas that when the words come tumbling out, he isn't always clear and the meaning is obscured.

Crowded line spacing.

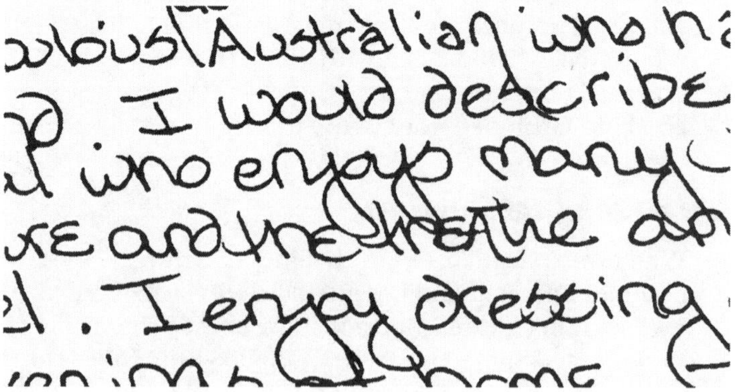

Tangled Lines

When lines are so close together that loops and/or parts of letters hang down and collide with writing on the next line (or several lines), the writer suffers from a major loss of perspective. She's too busy acting on her instincts and emotions to take the time to keep things in their proper place. Thoughts and ideas, feelings and actions are all jumbled up, ambiguous, confused. She doesn't know which end is up!

Chicken Scratch

Don't expect the tangled writer to listen if you try to offer constructive advice on how to better organize her life. She simply doesn't hear you. She may nod and say, "M'hm," but her eyes will be all over the room instead of on you.

There is always so much to do and she doesn't plan ahead, so the tangled writer's activities spill over into each other. She's at the hairdresser when she should be at a meeting, or she's playing golf when she was supposed to have lunch with mother. Without a strict schedule (which she hates), the tangled writer spins her wheels, doing what feels good at the moment. The vital but mundane routines that keep life running smoothly, like paying bills or doing laundry, are delayed or ignored entirely.

Life with this type of person can get pretty chaotic. Continually involving herself in arguments and conflicts that have nothing to do with her, she doesn't use good judgment and may allow her prejudices to overrule her common sense. She may mean well but is often inconsiderate. You can't count on her to be where she said she would be, or when she was supposed to be there. She rushes around, trying to fit in more activities than is humanly possible. Her motto might be, "Life's too short!"

Tangled lines.

Fine Points

Balance is always the key. Line spacing may be wide, but the interpretation changes when the spacing becomes too wide.

Moderately Wide Line Spacing

The writer who leaves wide spaces between the lines of writing has a logical, orderly mind and a preference for keeping things clear. He is good at analyzing situations and concepts, and always plans ahead. This is not someone who acts spontaneously or on impulse. His thinking is measured and orderly and he considers the consequences before acting.

His tastes tend to be elegant and refined, with a strong sense of aesthetics, a love of beauty. He might be more at home at the Met than the local wrestling arena.

Whether or not they actually have money, some people who leave wide spaces between their lines tend to be extravagant. They may feel less constrained to hold on to their resources, so they spend more freely.

The key to a positive interpretation for wide line spacing is that it should not be *excessively* wide. When spaces between the lines becomes so wide that you notice the white spaces between the lines more than the writing, we look at it differently.

Moderately wide line spacing.

enjoy humor, readin
in his work, what
learn from him, and
to learning from me.

Fine Points

The writer who leaves excessively large spaces between the lines may be trying to bring order to his inner world, which may seem to be falling apart. The wide spaces are an attempt to create some kind of structure and order.

Extremely Wide Line Spacing

Line spacing that is far too wide suggests someone who has lost the capacity to act spontaneously. This person isn't an active joiner. She stands back and observes rather than participates. Permanently anxious, she feels isolated, separated from her fellow human beings and the world at large.

Don't expect her to do anything on the spur of the moment, because she quickly puts the kibosh on any spontaneous feeling. She wants time to consider how any future action might affect her before making a move.

This might be the absent-minded professor who goes around with her head in the clouds, forgetting to take a lunch break because she is too busy working out a formula in her head. She tends to see things more in discrete pieces than as whole concepts or, to put it another way, she sees only individual trees rather than the whole forest. She's not particularly considerate of other people, because she's more concerned with maintaining her own space.

Extremely wide line spacing.

I believe that I

have been impressed

handwriting experts

testimony in Lya

Irregular Line Spacing

The writer who writes sometimes with wide line spacing and sometimes narrow, who sometimes lets his loops get tangled and at others keeps them separate, is inconsistent in how he uses time and money. His reactions depend on the circumstances and how he feels at the moment.

He may start out with the best of intentions (clear line spacing), but soon gets carried away with what he's talking about or the project he's involved in (his writing gets more crowded). If the line spacing is wider at the top of the page and narrow at the bottom, the more he gets swept up in his daily activities, the more difficult it is for the writer to maintain a clear perspective. He wavers between organized, abstract thinking and the need to go with his gut.

He wants to be generous, but that conflicts with a resolve to be conservative and thrifty. In any case, the writer lacks good self-discipline and is unsure of himself. He engages in a continuing struggle between the limitations of time and resources and what he wants to accomplish.

Extremely Regular Line Spacing

Extremely regular line spacing is made by the inflexible, obsessive person who feels compelled to follow a strict routine. He finds it impossible to vary from the daily rituals he has established to help him get through life. If you come across someone who writes this way, refer him to a counseling professional. You'll know this type of writing by its machine-like look.

Tales from the Quill

The handwriting of one America's best-loved poets, Emily Dickinson, is an excellent example of extremes in spatial arrangement. She isolated herself, and during her thirties saw few people but her family. Even those closest to her sometimes had to communicate with her through a closed door. The excessively wide spaces between words and lines reflect her isolation. A sample of Dickinson's handwriting appears in chapter 14.

Outer Space: Word Spacing

Inhale. Exhale. Inhale. Exhale. We speak and we pause to breathe at the end of a thought. Some people speak quickly with less breathing space between their words than others do. Some speak so fast that their words run into one another. The spaces between words have been compared to taking a breath in speech and reveal one's need for social distance.

How much space do you need to feel comfortable around other people? The amount of space a writer leaves between words is a good indication of how much personal space she demands from others and the degree of self-restraint the writer uses in social situations.

A rule of thumb as to how much space should be left between words is to measure the width of a letter "m" in the writing you are analyzing. You will find that most of the spaces between words are about that wide.

Balanced Word Spacing

The writer whose word spacing is well-balanced is comfortable asserting her need for space. She expects other people to respect her privacy and is willing to give others the space they deserve. She is comfortable around other people, but when appropriate can spend time alone. She is conventional when it comes to social interaction and likes to feel her behavior conforms to her social group.

Balanced word spacing.

Wide Word Spacing

Moderately wide spaces between words (slightly wider than the letter "m" in that writing) tell us that the writer is a clear thinker who likes to step back and pause for reflection before assimilating an event or an idea. That willingness to pause for a breath shows also that he is considerate of others, because he takes the time to see if his listener understands him.

As in wide line spacing, wide spaces between words have an effect on the writer's ability to act spontaneously. He may be charming and sophisticated, but he is also reserved and keeps his distance. This is probably not someone you should run up to and give a big sloppy kiss in public. He's not easy to get to know, because his objective outlook keeps him from becoming involved on an intimate level. He views relationships more in the abstract than the personal, and you can expect his social circle to consist of a carefully chosen few.

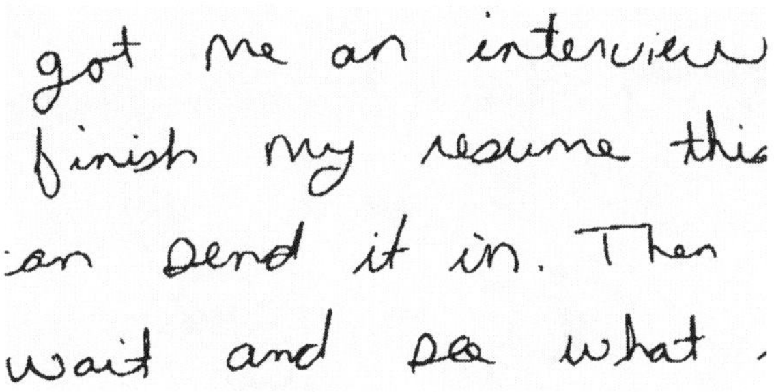

Wide word spacing.

Extremely Wide Word Spacing

Extremely large spaces between words disrupt the flow of communication. This indicates problems in the writer's ability to string ideas together in a logical progression. She is socially isolated and has difficulty getting her thoughts across. Although she may have some wonderful concepts in her head, they may not make it out of her mouth, because she gets lost in the unimportant details and forgets to keep the big picture in mind.

When words become islands in oceans of space, it implies a profound inability of the writer to connect with other people on their level. This is not a voluntary condition. The writer may have a deep desire to make contact but her fear of intimacy is stronger. The long pauses between words, rather than a moment to reflect, becomes a social

Fine Points

Teenagers who choose a wide spatial arrangement often suffer from feelings of loneliness and isolation, which they try to cover with indifference.

crevasse into which the writer falls. She feels awkward and insecure around people and, consequently, withdraws into a shell of shyness. Crowds make her very uncomfortable.

In extreme cases the writer may not even be aware of appropriate social relationships. All she knows is the need to protect and defend her ego, which to her means shunning physical and social contact.

Extremely wide word spacing.

formation you have on
rrespondence courses. I w
ppreciate some info. on
graphological analysis. I ha

Tales from the Quill

Extra large word spaces are sometimes found in the handwritings of developmentally delayed people. In this case they feel isolated and cut off from the rest of the world. The wide spaces signify an inability to communicate what they want to say and helplessness to express their inner needs.

Narrow Word Spacing

Narrow spaces between words signify an impulsive, spontaneous person who doesn't take the time to reason things out. He acts and reacts as the mood takes him. So many impressions are bombarding him all the time that it is hard for him to sort them out. Step back and take an objective look before making a decision? I don't think so! The word "rational" isn't in his vocabulary.

He is driven by a strong need for involvement and socializing, so don't expect him to keep his distance. This is an in-your-face, touchy-feely person who expresses himself through physical contact. He may pat you on the shoulder, hug you, or put his face close to yours when speaking. His conversation is "stream of consciousness"—whatever pops into his head one minute comes out of his mouth the next.

Because he's insecure, he looks outside himself to get his needs met. He can't stand to be alone for very long and will soon be looking for ways to make contact with someone, anyone. Unfortunately, he's not always very choosy about who he calls his friends.

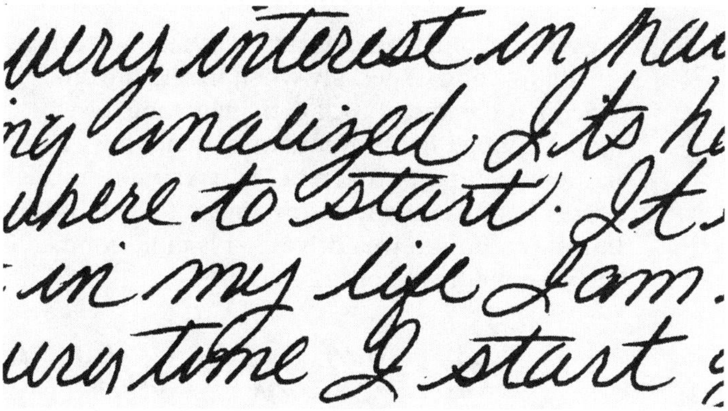

Narrow word spacing.

Extremely Narrow Word Spacing

The purpose of spaces between words is to create proper boundaries. The letters form groups that are framed by the spaces between them. When a writer disregards the proper boundaries he is behaving like the guy on the subway who stands so close that you can hear him breathing in your ear, even though the train isn't all that crowded. You want to elbow him out of your way!

Words so close together that they almost (or do) touch, suggest the writer with an extreme need to surround himself with other people. He leaves no space for self-exploration and, since he requires no space for himself, he also has no regard for the space of others. That is, his social boundaries—his sense of what is socially appropriate—are very blurred.

Common sense has little meaning for this person. He acts purely on instinct. Like a puppy, always on the heels of whoever walks into the room, he needs constant attention and approval to feel good about himself. Without continual reassurance from others he gets anxious, and the moment he's not getting attention, his self-esteem plunges. The problem is, when it comes to the need for approval, the writer of very close word spacing is a bottomless pit.

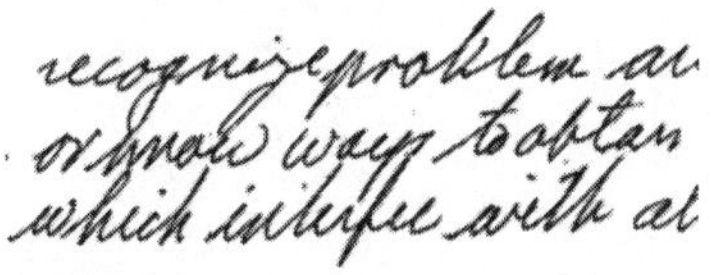

Extremely narrow word spacing.

Chicken Scratch

Extremely narrow word spacing, especially when combined with narrow letters, can be one sign of obsessive thinking. Stalkers may adopt this type of spacing (though not everyone with extremely narrow word spacing is a stalker!).

Irregular Word Spacing

Irregular spaces between words suggests emotional instability, that is, someone whose behavior changes unpredictably from moment to moment. You can't count on her to act consistently. Filled with inner conflicts, she's unsure of how to behave, either in the company of others or when alone.

This is someone who is always on the move. She can't sit still for long (especially when irregular word spacing is combined with extremely long lower loops), though her movements may not have any particular purpose. When her letters spill over their proper boundaries she doesn't mean to be impulsive, but the confusion that drives her is more compelling than her ability to control herself.

an excellent additi
already spectacular seri
wait to get my hand
of this book.

Irregular word spacing.

Inner Space: Letter Spacing

Spaces between the letters give us clues about the degree of freedom the writer allows herself internally and her receptiveness to others. They show her gut reactions to emotional situations and her ability to act on them appropriately.

The ideal amount of space between the letters (intraletter spacing) should be about the width of the letter "n". In "ideal" writing, this amount of space would indicate adaptability, a capacity for give-and-take relationships. The writer is spontaneous and friendly, with the appropriate amount of warmth in relationships. She has the capacity to learn new ideas and is open to changing her mind when she finds a better way of doing things.

Average letter spacing.

Wide Letter Spacing

If the letters themselves are also wide, the writer is talkative, spontaneous, and outgoing. He is open to everything and does whatever comes naturally without a lot of restraint. He doesn't take the time to analyze a situation using logic, but "lets it all hang out," responding according to what's happening from moment to moment.

Wide letter spacing.

Narrow Letter Spacing

Letters crammed together reveal an impetuous person who rushes to judgment and overreacts to everything. He is impulsive and often confused about what he feels and what others feel. His need to fit in with a social group can push him to behaving inappropriately. He desperately wants acceptance, so he'll do anything he thinks will help him fit in. This is the type of person who will give in to either internal emotional pressures or external peer pressure.

Chicken Scratch

Large, inconsistent gaps that appear between words may be accidental or caused by some interruption. Therefore, it is important to have an adequate amount of writing to analyze, so you'll know which is which.

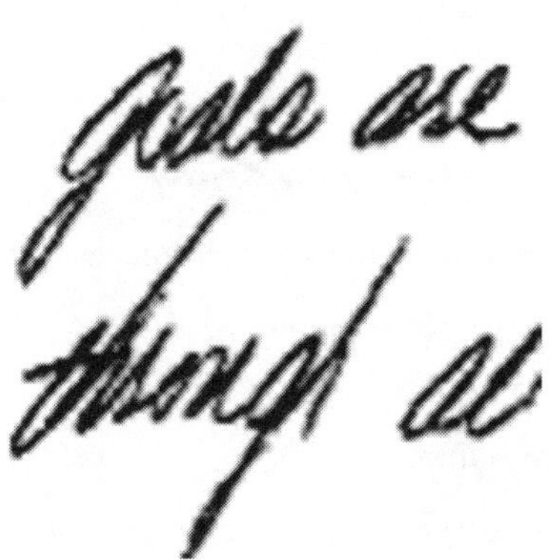

Narrow letter spacing.

Tales from the Quill

When the letters bump up against each other, the writer may be stingy with her affections and emotions, especially when the letters themselves are narrow. The letters in the handwriting of "Killer Mom" Susan Smith knock up against each other (Smith's handwriting appears on page 20). Some graphologists see this as one of the indicators for suicidal thoughts. Of course, there have to be several other signs before that kind of extreme conclusion can be made.

Inconsistent Letter Spacing

Inconsistency in any area of writing symbolizes ambivalence. In letter spacing, the ambivalence is about whether the writer should move forward or stay back in the shadows. She's uncertain and worried about what to do. An internal tug of war keeps her unsettled most of the time.

Inconsistent letter spacing.

Secondary Expansion

A special situation called secondary expansion is where the letters themselves are narrow but the spaces between them are wide. On the surface the writer seems to be outgoing, but inside he shrinks away from social contact. Yet, despite his insecurity and shyness, he pushes himself to interact, at least in groups where he knows the people.

The Least You Need to Know

- Spatial arrangement is the most unconscious aspect of handwriting.
- Someone who writes with a clear spatial arrangement can get along in the world, even though he doesn't have a good self-image.
- Clear line spacing suggests clear thinking.
- Word spacing shows how close you want to be to other people.
- Letter spacing shows how much space you give yourself.

Chapter 7

Margins, Back to the Future

In This Chapter

- It's about time—past, present, future
- More about balance
- Have you left the past behind?
- How you approach the future
- What margins have to do with respect for authority

In the margins that frame handwriting, we find out about the writer's emotions and mental outlook as they relate to time and space. We'll discover how he feels about the past and his outlook on the future, as well as his social manners.

When you think back over your childhood, what comes to mind? Are the memories mostly happy, with a few experiences you'd rather forget? Or is it difficult to look back and re-experience what should have been a carefree time but was instead filled with sadness and pain? The margins on the page reveal whether you have moved on from the past or whether it holds you back from emotional growth.

Somewhere in Time

Are you punishing yourself for the past? Raring to race into the future? Ambivalent about what lies ahead? *Margins* reveal how you perceive time. Whether the past is a hospitable place to visit in your memory, or a scary nightmare that you'd rather run away from, your left margins will tell the truth. The right margins shows how we view the future, whether it is something to look forward to with a hopeful, optimistic view or perhaps with anxiety and dread, something to delay facing as long as possible.

Write Words

Margin is the perimeter area bordering a page of handwriting.

Writing in English and other Western-style languages starts on the left side of the page and progresses to the right side. Margins are created first by the position where the writer initially places his pen—the beginning of the writing effort—and the spot where the line ends before returning to the left side of the page to start the next line. These positions form a pattern as the writing progresses down the page.

The writer starts out by consciously making a decision about where to place the pen. At the end of the line on the right side of the page, a new decision is called for—where to start the next line; will it begin exactly under the beginning of the previous line, or somewhere slightly different?

Handwriting is filled with symbolism. Since the writing starts out on the left, the left side of the paper symbolizes the past. After moving across the page towards a goal, the writing ends up on the right side, which represents the future. What goes on in the middle, therefore, represents the present.

The left margin also represents the self ("me") and the right margin, other people ("you"). As the writer moves from "me" to "you" he reveals whether he faces the future and other people with hopeful optimism or fear and trepidation.

Suitable for Framing

The average margin consists of about one inch of blank space all around the page. Yet, as a handwriting analyst you will be confronted by many handwritings with virtually or literally *no* margins at all, or others with margins so all-embracing that the writing takes up barely any room on the page. At times, a left margin will start out narrow, at the very edge of the paper, then pull towards the right side of the paper so strongly that it ends up quite wide.

The opposite is likewise true. The left margin might begin at one inch or more, but by the time the writing reaches the end of the page, it has pulled back to the left, creating a wide-to-narrow pattern. Then, of course, there are also right margins that start out wide and end up very narrow, not to mention right margins that start narrow and end up wide.

We haven't even begun to comment on left and right margins that bow out or bow in, or margins that waver with the wind so you're not quite sure where they are going. Then there are the ever-fascinating top and bottom margins! Did you ever think that blank space could be so varied and stimulating? Well, maybe that's carrying it a bit far.

But you'll be surprised by some of the knowledge waiting to be uncovered from around the edges of the page.

Fine Points

For a seemingly simple element of handwriting, the margin comes in a surprisingly wide variety of patterns. In fact, margins are blank spaces, not writing at all. So this is a reminder that blank spaces on a page can be just as revealing as the writing between them.

Well-Balanced Margins

A handwriting that is well-framed by nicely balanced margins (they shouldn't be absolutely perfect) on all sides looks like a picture in a frame. Balanced margins reveal a careful planner with a good sense of timing. The writer creates structure and order in her environment and doesn't appreciate it when disruptions threaten to mess things up. She prefers to carry out her activities according to a plan. She isn't stingy, but neither is she likely to spend lavishly. She uses common sense to budget her resources (time, energy, and money).

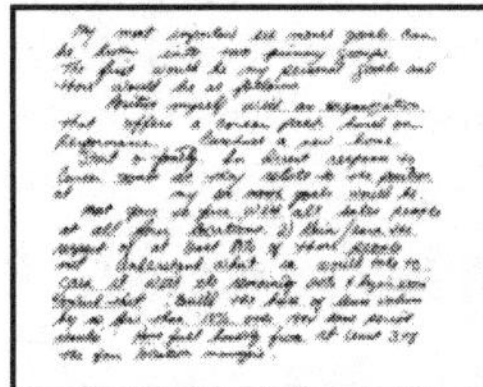

Well-balanced margins.

Her social manners are slightly formal and reserved. She's polite and courteous, and probably won't go beyond the boundaries of convention. She feels most comfortable when she stays within familiar limits.

When the margins are too exact, too careful, appearances mean more to the writer than substance. His home is likely to be just as orderly as his handwriting. In fact, his motto might be, "A place for everything and everything in its place." When things get out of place or unexpected events happen, the writer's anxiety skyrockets. He can't stand for anyone to see him at less than his absolute best.

Extremely Wide Margins All Around the Page

The person who places a small amount of handwriting in the middle of a vast desert of space is terrified of getting involved with life. She feels inadequate, and so keeps herself apart from others in an effort to hide what she thinks are her deficiencies. Her limits are self-imposed, but that doesn't make it any easier for her to reach out and make connections.

Extremely wide margins all around.

Chicken Scratch

If the writing with extremely wide margins is undeveloped or immature, the writer may simply be showing off and attempting to pass himself off as sophisticated and cultured when in reality he is not at all.

Physical contact is especially difficult for this type of person. The only way she will allow touching is if she initiates it, which is unlikely. If you reach out for a hug or to pat her on the back, she'll shrink away from your touch. She might even take a step backward to put more distance between herself and the other person—a greater *margin* of distance, that is.

Narrow Margins All Around the Page

Looking for someone to take on that tedious project? Ask the person with no margins. Running a few bucks short for the rent? No problem, ask the guy with no margins (unless his letters are narrow). He may not have the time or money, but he gets involved in anything and everything, whether he can afford to or not.

Fine Points

If writing with no margins is also large, money burns a hole in the writer's pocket. No matter what resources he has at his disposal, he feels obliged to use them up.

He doesn't know when to say no, which means he's often overextended. This habit can become problematic when his time and energy is wasted on trivia that doesn't get him anywhere. Not only does he waste his own time, he'll make demands on yours, as well. He is the juggler of innumerable activities who tries to keep so many balls in the air at the same time that it would be a miracle if he could complete half of what he takes on.

The writer with no margins usually crowds other parts of writing, too, such as lines and words. If that's the case, he feels compelled to control "all space," which includes other people's space. He gets involved in others' lives to the point of intrusiveness.

Narrow margins all around.

Ghosts of Christmas Past: Left Margin

Let's begin at the beginning. *All* the way back, as far as you can go. Life experiences begin with birth, and the initial placement of the pen symbolizes that magic moment. The left margin represents how the writer feels about the past.

Narrow Left Margin with Wide Right Margin

A narrow left margin combined with a wide right margin suggests that the writer finds the past a more comfortable place than the present or the future. Safety and security are very important to her, and she is afraid to spend her resources. The need to economize nags at the back of her mind.

Going into unfamiliar places and situations or trying new things is stressful for her, so she keeps the stress at bay by limiting herself to who and what she already knows. She looks to old friends and family for support. The downside is, she may miss out on opportunities for growth when they threaten to take her out of her depth.

Narrow left margin with wide right margin.

Wide Left Margin

Moderately wide left margin shows a strong desire to move forward and leave the past behind. The writer is willing to get involved with life. He welcomes opportunities to meet other people and quickly takes hold of new ideas and projects. That he doesn't cover all the space he reasonably could indicates some degree of extravagance. He is not overly concerned about utilizing all his resources, but will spend the time and money it takes to get where he wants to go.

Chicken Scratch

The writer of small or narrow writing with no margins hoards everything she has. This is the one about whom it is said, "She still has the first nickel she ever made."

Courage is evident in the way the writer forges ahead into new territory and charts new goals. Especially when the right margin is narrow, the writer is more interested in what is coming up in the future rather than worrying about the past. He doesn't concern himself about conforming to convention or doing things the way they were always done before. An extremely wide left margin suggests running away from something in the past.

Wide left margin.

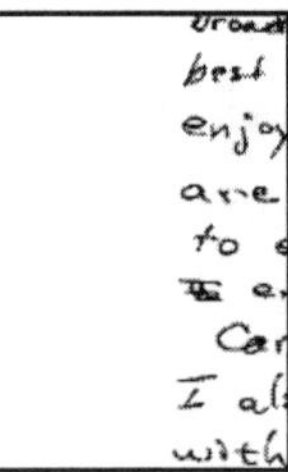

Fine Points

The top third of the paper represents the past, the middle third represents the present, and the bottom third represents the future. You can see where in the project—beginning, middle, or later—the writer begins to lose confidence. Just look for the point where the line starts to move back towards the left margin.

Shrinking Left Margin

When the left margin starts out wide but moves towards the left edge of the paper as it progresses down the page, the writer starts out with plenty of enthusiasm, but doubts begin creeping in. She starts backing off, wondering whether she is doing the right thing, or whether that new project was a good idea.

She begins to look for ways to return to the safety of the past, which could mean going home, or calling old buddies, or following some ritual that makes her feel secure. Her misgivings will have to be put to rest before she'll go back to her original plans.

Shrinking left margin.

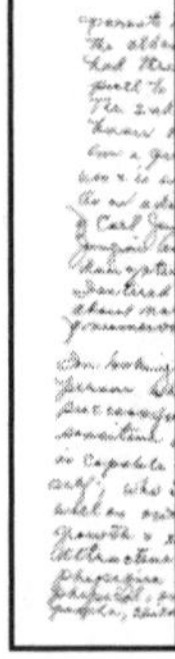

Growing Left Margin

As you might guess, a left margin that gets wider as it moves down the page represents the opposite of the shrinking left margin. The writer is a slow starter with many fears and trepidation about taking on anything new; but his enthusiasm grows by leaps and bounds as he gets more involved.

If the writing is also large, there is a tendency towards extravagance. The writer may not show the appropriate restraint when it comes to spending his time, energy, and money.

Growing left margin.

Concave or Convex Left Margin

You're in a department store with your girlfriend, and she's about to splurge on a $75 black lace teddy but changes her mind at the last minute because it's too extravagant. Check her left margin for the concave pattern.

When the left margin starts at one point, gets wider, then somewhere down the page begins to get narrower again, we call it a *concave* left margin. This phenomenon is usually found in writing where the basically thrifty person has to fight a desire for extravagance but pulls himself back before he gets completely carried away.

Convex is the opposite of concave. Something convex pushes outward, like a lens. The left margin starts at one point and moves further to the left for a while, then starts back towards the right again.

Write Words

A **concave** margin dips inward towards the middle. A **Convex** margin bows outward and away from the middle.

You've probably already figured it out—the writer continually puts the brakes on her behavior, which tends to be a bit more openhanded than she can afford. She recognizes her tendency to be extravagant and tries to control it. Yet, because the end result is movement towards the right, we know that she can't always resist the temptation for a more freewheeling lifestyle.

Right concave margin.

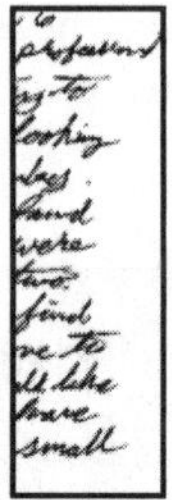

Left concave margin.

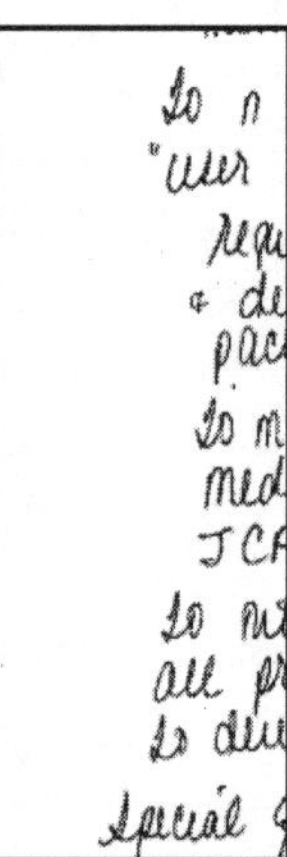

Right convex margin.

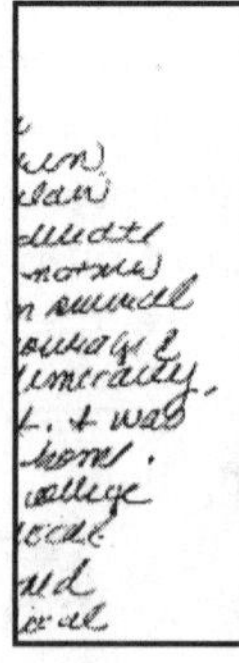

Rigid Left Margin

The left margin is consciously chosen, whereas there is less control over the right margin. The left margin represents the ideal self, or who the writer would really like to be. The right margin is more symbolic of his real self—who he actually is.

Strong self-discipline and will power are needed to begin every new line in exactly the same place under the previous one. It also takes longer to maintain a strict left margin, suggesting someone who doesn't make decisions without first considering the potential outcome.

A rigidly straight left margin is usually formed by someone who is highly conscious of appearances and who doesn't allow himself or others any slack. Just as his margin is inflexible, so are his attitudes and behaviors. Someone who is this rigid is not an easy person to live or work with because his expectations are so high.

Chicken Scratch

If the left margin is too wide, the writer may be running away from some past event that she would rather not face.

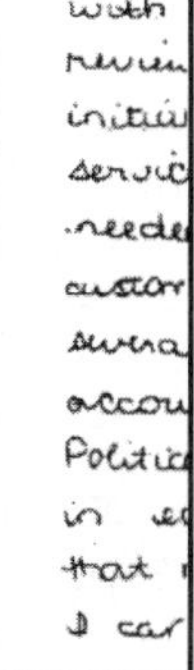

Rigid left margin.

Irregular Left Margin

A left margin that has a new starting point with practically each new line signifies conflict about what to do next. The writer doesn't care about sticking with society's convention and standards, but prefers to make things up as she goes along. She is a poor manager of her resources and probably runs out of money long before payday.

If the writing is done on lined paper with a printed left margin but the writer begins to the left of the

Fine Points

Juvenile offenders are among the writers who ignore the left margin and create their own. They refuse to follow the standards and rules set for them by society. Yet, at the same time, they may be easily influenced by their peers.

rule, it suggests someone who makes his own rules, literally. Moody and easily influenced by his peers, he is not interested in doing what anyone else expects of him.

Irregular left margin.

Future Perfect: Right Margin

Courtesy of the left margin, our virtual time machine has taken us on a voyage through the past. Now we are about to move forward in time and explore the writer's attitudes about the future. The right margin tells us how eager she is to face what's ahead and more about how well she handles her time, energy, and money. It also shows how cautious she is when it comes to making contact with other people.

Wide Right Margin

Leaving a wide right margin is like stopping your car about 15 feet behind the stop sign. It's just a little too soon. But the person who stops so far back is telling us that she is being cautious, very cautious. She wants time to see what's coming before deciding how to proceed.

Chicken Scratch

When the right margin is overly narrow, almost to the edge of the page, it can be a sign of an eager beaver without enough self-discipline. His impulses take over and he doesn't consider the consequences before acting.

Past experience has taught her to dread the future, to view it as an unfriendly place where she can get hurt if she's not careful. She feels overwhelmed by life and fears she won't be able to cope with any additional stress. Staying away from the right margin allows her to avoid reality for a while. She creates a safe framework for herself and rarely extends her reach beyond those self-imposed limits. Maybe she thinks that if she doesn't risk, she can't fail.

A wide right margin may be temporary and related to a particular situation, such as job loss. An out-of-work single mom, worried about how she's going to feed her kids next week, may show her concern by pulling back from the right margin (the future). When she's bringing home a regular paycheck again, the right margin will return to a more normal width.

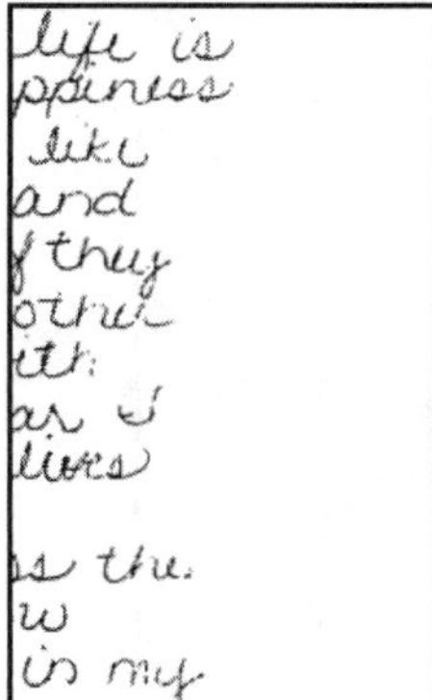

Wide right margin.

Narrow Right Margin

The spontaneous, action-oriented person makes a narrow right margin. Eager to set new goals and work on them, he cares about progress and he's constantly looking ahead to see what he should do next. He is outgoing and at ease meeting new people and trying out new things.

If a wide left margin is balanced with a narrow right margin, the writer is poised, ready to jump at the chance to move forward on his goals. He believes in the maxim, "Success is what happens when preparation meets opportunity."

Narrow right margin.

Expanding Right Margin

As the writing proceeds down the page the margin begins to pull back, so it is wider at the end of the writing than at the top. Although she may jump in with enthusiasm, the writer needs encouragement to keep on going. She reverts to behavior that has proved safe and effective in the past rather than travel into uncharted waters. Completing new projects may be a bigger challenge than she can comfortably handle, unless she receives a lot of encouragement from the people she loves or respects.

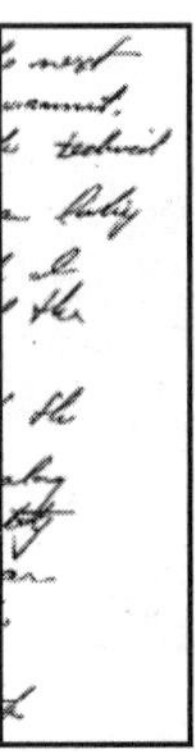

Expanding right margin.

Shrinking Right Margin

When the right margin moves ever closer to the right edge of the paper, the writer is unafraid of taking on new challenges. In fact, he welcomes them. The more he gets swept up in his interests, the more his excitement grows. His is progressive and goal-directed, and, without a second thought, involves himself in things he's never done before.

He may be shy on a first introduction, but once he gets more familiar with new acquaintances his reticence falls away. In a group he probably watches everyone until he understands the power structure, then he'll put in his own two cents.

Fine Points

When the writer uses a long, horizontal ending stroke to fill in the ends of lines, he's carrying out a superstitious routine, done for his own protection, like "touching wood."

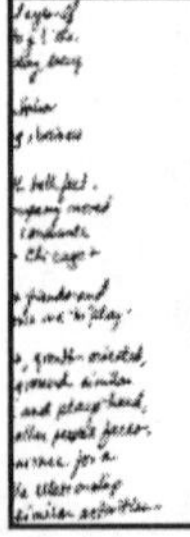

Shrinking right margin.

Extremely Straight Right Margin

Making a straight right margin is a much harder task than making a straight left margin. The writer has to hyphenate words and take great care to line up last words of lines. Someone who goes to this much trouble has lots of self-control. She also needs a tremendous amount of structure to function at her best.

Whatever this person does, it's going to be something she's done before and strictly by the book. Don't expect her to act independently or quickly. She's self-protective and has trouble adapting, so she needs time to adjust to new situations and people. She can't trust others because she doesn't trust herself. In an effort to safeguard her ego she creates the most predictable environment possible.

Chicken Scratch

When words careen off the edge of the page, the writer is rushing headlong into the future. At the extreme end of the future, death awaits. Therefore, the writer whose words fall downward and crash into the right margin may be having thoughts of suicide. Or, he may be suffering from temporary financial embarrassment because he has spent beyond his means.

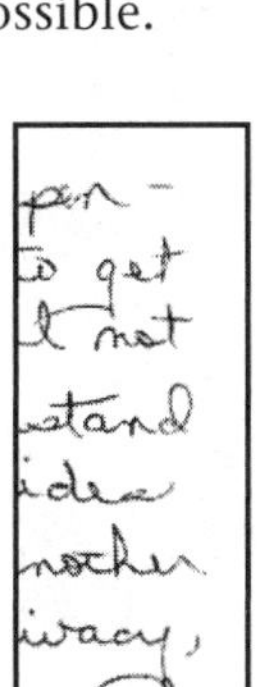

Extremely straight right margin.

Extremely Irregular Right Margin

Some variability is expected on the right margin, because it's not always possible to predict how the line will end. However, when the irregularity is extreme, the writer is guaranteed to be unstable.

A poor planner, he's unsure of how he feels about other people or the future. An adventurer who is quite content with the turbulent life he creates, he'll take whatever comes next, the more exciting the better. Pressured by a strong need for variety (especially when combined with very long lower loops), he vacillates from one position to another. He seems unable to stick with a steady point of view about anything or anyone.

Extremely irregular right margin. JonBenet Ramsey ransom letter.

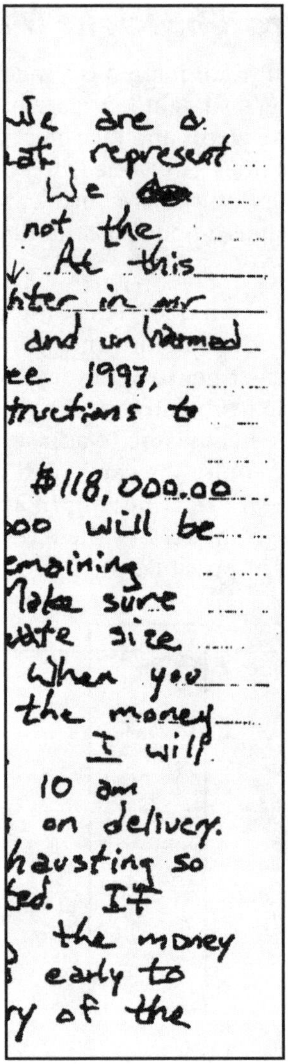

Greetings, Your Majesty: Upper and Lower Margins

In bygone days it was customary to leave a very wide upper margin when addressing a letter to an important personage, such as royalty. It was as if the writer were putting a respectful distance between himself and the recipient of the message. Although that rule doesn't seem to apply so strictly in modern times, it is still appropriate to leave a respectful space at the top of the page.

Tales from the Quill

The ransom letter in the murder of child beauty queen, JonBenet Ramsey, is a good example of an extremely variable right margin. As you can see in the illustration on the previous page, the writer was feeling under a lot of internal pressure at the time of writing. The right margin weaves back and forth, in and out, as the writer tries to decide which direction to take. The writer hesitates, goes forward, then pulls back. There is no real pattern to the forward movement.

As a gauge of personal space, a narrow upper margin is analogous to starting the conversation in the middle—the writer doesn't care whether the other person understands what's going on or not. This inconsiderate kind of behavior may show a lack of discretion and appropriateness, especially if there are other supporting factors, such as narrow word and line spacing.

The lower margin is less significant, because there is no standard by which to judge. All the same, a narrow margin at the bottom of the page does seem to indicate enthusiasm and spontaneity. The person is so wrapped up in the message that she doesn't want to take the time to stop and turn over the paper or start a new sheet.

A lower margin that is too wide for the message, on the other hand, may indicate that the writer is more concerned about appearances than what she has to say. She doesn't reveal much about herself, and may not tell the whole story.

The Least You Need to Know

- Margins reveal where you are in time and space.
- The left margin reveals how you feel about the past.
- The right margin shows how eager you are to meet the future.
- Upper margins indicate your respect for the reader.
- Lower margins reveal enthusiasm.

Chapter 8

From Here to Eternity: Baseline

In This Chapter

- The ground rules, or standing on the baseline
- To rule or not to rule—writing on the line
- How to measure a baseline
- Going for the goal—the right margin
- The ups and downs of baselines
- Your health plays a part

The *baseline* of handwriting represents the ground we stand on. The question is, how steady is the ground as you move from one place to another? Is it solid concrete, asphalt, loamy soil, or quicksand?

Solid ground, not trembling and shaking ground, offers a measure of security. If you've ever been caught in an earthquake or tornado, you know that when terra isn't so firma, you feel insecure and anxious. Keeping your balance, finding something substantial to hold on to, or hiding under for protection is all you can think of. When the earth stops moving, you breathe a sigh of relief.

The graphologist examines the baseline of writing to see how firm it is, or how much it fluctuates as it winds its way across the page. The direction the line runs is also important: Does it move uphill, downhill, or straight across? We'll consider these and other aspects of the baseline in detail in this chapter.

Write Words

The baseline is the invisible line on which handwriting rests. It is created by the bottoms of the individual letters and their connections.

The Invisible Line

When kids begin learning to write, the teacher supplies paper with ruled lines printed on it. This gives the kids a road map of where to go and how to get there. Without that printed line, and left to their own devices, there's no telling where the little writers would travel. After all, the empty page offers an unlimited playground where anything goes!

Later, after the child understands the rules (literally and figuratively), he is able to form a mental picture of the baseline to follow. Whether or not he actually follows it is a question for the graphologist to ponder.

When Is No Line a Line?

Although the baseline of writing may be an actual ruled line on the paper, it also may be invisible. How can a line be invisible and still be a line? Examining the points at which the lowest parts of letters join together solves this apparent riddle. The bottoms of letters and the connections between them (called *ligatures*) form an imaginary line that moves from one side of the page to the other.

Several elements can affect the direction and shape of the invisible line we call the baseline. Probably the most obvious factor is the position of the paper on the writing surface (desk, table, or other), with the writer's body position coming in a close second.

Some people like to turn the paper at an angle to the writing surface, which tends to push the writing uphill and also produces a rightward slant. It may also force the body to turn to the left, which will affect the tension/release pattern of the writing (we'll cover the concept of tension and release in handwriting in great detail in Chapter 12). This position allows the right-hander more freedom of motion, which in turn means a greater release of tension. The same is true of the left-hander, but from the opposite direction.

Write Words

Ligatures are the connections that join one letter to the next. We'll tell you more about them in Chapter 14.

Others prefer to place the paper square to the edge of the desk and sit very straight. The writing they produce is more likely to be upright or left slanted. Here's an experiment you can try:

Sit straight, facing the table or desk on which you are preparing to write. Put both feet flat on the floor and the writing paper square in front of you. If you're right-handed, you'll find that your writing arm is pulled leftward, while your hand is slightly torqued to the right, producing tension in the writing movement.

The Underground Is Not Just the Subway

Whether invisible or on ruled paper, the baseline separates the handwriting into two parts: above the baseline and below the baseline. In handwriting symbolism, the baseline represents the actual ground, so it follows that the area below the baseline represents *under the ground.*

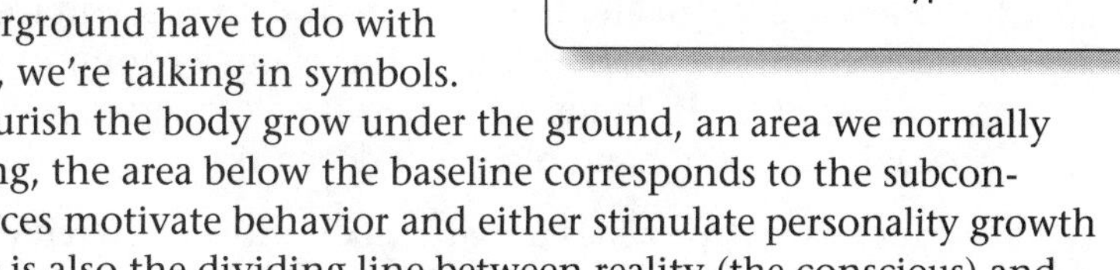

> **Fine Points**
>
> Experimenting with various writing styles and positions helps to better understand different types of writers.

But what does the underground have to do with personality? Remember, we're talking in symbols. Plants that feed and nourish the body grow under the ground, an area we normally don't see. In handwriting, the area below the baseline corresponds to the subconscious, where *unseen* forces motivate behavior and either stimulate personality growth or stunt it. The baseline is also the dividing line between reality (the conscious) and fantasy (the unconscious).

Logically then, it follows that the area above the baseline represents *above the ground,* where the fruits of the underground growth are visible. In terms of the writer's personality, this area represents the conscious aspects or expressed behavior (but more on all that in Chapters 9 and 10).

How Far Is Far?

Remember our discussion of line spacing in Chapter 6? We learned that there is no absolute law about how close a baseline should be to the next one below it. However, a good rule of thumb is that the lower loops on any given line should not interfere with the upper loops on the next line. Extra long lower loops or extra large writing require that baselines be spaced further apart, while shorter loops or overall smaller writing allow for closer line spacing.

> **Fine Points**
>
> The baseline is the dividing line between conscious reality and the unconscious self. The closer the writer stays to the baseline, the more realistic and less imaginative she is.

Let's say you've just written a line. When you begin the next line you already know where the lower loops from the first line are placed. If you write over the top of them, allowing the loops from the new line to tangle with the old ones, it's because you make the choice to do so. It's just as easy to choose not to allow the loops to interfere (In Chapter 9 we'll discuss what long lower loops mean).

Following the Rules

Even as adults, some writers prefer to use a printed ruled line. It makes them feel safe. The response to a request for a handwriting sample on unlined paper is often unmitigated horror—"You want me to do *what?*" Anyone would think you'd asked for the writer's firstborn child. The person who feels that she cannot write without a ruled line to guide her has a strong need for direction, for specific rules, structure, and a pattern to follow. Without the security of a strong framework of rules she is insecure and ill at ease.

More compulsive still are those who choose to write on ruled paper, and place a ruler on the ruled line to boot. Although this is not a common occurrence, it's not so rare that you won't see it. In my 30-something-year career as a graphologist I've probably witnessed this phenomenon about a dozen times.

The "ruler writer" provides us with an example of extreme insecurity. Think of how it feels to enter an unfamiliar room in the dark. You cautiously feel your way around the perimeter, afraid to step out into what might be empty space or a space filled with unfamiliar objects that might trip you. That's how the ruler writer experiences life. He doesn't know what might be waiting for him in that empty room, and that is intolerable to him. Thus, he sticks like glue to what is familiar—the baseline.

Tales from the Quill

The ruler writer often has unresolved difficult sexual issues and uses the ruler to separate the upper and lower zone. In some cases, he puts entire lower zone letters into the middle zone. In others, he will make lower zone letters in two segments. A dramatic demonstration of sexual conflict was seen in the handwriting of a man who was an incest victim of his mother. He cut the lower loops in half at the baseline.

Jittery and high-strung, he lives with the continual threat that his internal chaos will overwhelm him. His fear is that if he lets go, even for an instant, his life will spin out of control. Returning to the baseline—something familiar and safe—is like a ritual that gives him a point of reference he can count on. Knowing what to expect allays his anxiety to some degree.

How About a Hug?

Among other things, the baseline tells the graphologist how much stability and security the writer needs. The degree to which the writing clings to the baseline tells us how firmly she needs her feet planted on the ground.

When the letters in a handwriting sample look very even and always return to the bottom of the line, they are said to *hug the baseline*. This happens when writing shows generally strong regularity with little variation.

The writer believes only what she sees. She's not particularly imaginative, but has a pragmatic outlook, and because she takes things so literally often misses the irony in subtle humor. She is motivated by a need for security.

The baseline hugger makes sure the basic essentials are handled before attending to anything else. Her focus is on putting plenty of food in the fridge, getting insurance coverage, and depositing money in the bank. It's too bad that no matter how much she stockpiles the material goods and money it never seems to be quite enough to make her feel really secure.

Fine Points

In general, the person who hugs the baseline has very regular, controlled handwriting. It is usually made by the insecure writer who chooses familiar forms.

Pretending to Follow the Rules

Then there are those who choose paper with ruled lines but fail to follow the line. They write above or below it. This says that the writer wants us to believe he is going to follow the rules, but when it comes right down to it, he really prefers to be independent. Whether the writing floats above or hangs down below the ruled line gives additional information.

Writing that hovers above the ruled line suggests enthusiasm and a spirit of adventure. Pragmatic reality and security are not as important to this writer as they are to someone whose feet are stuck to the ground as if held there by a magnet.

Imaginative with a spiritual bent, this type usually doesn't expend a lot of energy pursuing creature comforts—the cool stuff that makes life more comfortable. What the future might hold intrigues him. He focuses more on the possibilities and what might be, rather than what already exists. He doesn't need to see something to believe in it.

The person whose writing falls below the ruled line focuses entirely on the tangible, material realities of life. There is little or no energy left over for spiritual matters, as he exhausts himself pursuing his most basic needs. Depression or illness may be a factor in this case, as psychic heaviness drags him down.

Tales from the Quill

Sally, who used lined paper but wrote well above the line, seemed like a pretty conventional lady. She dressed conservatively, held a respectable job as a secretary, and her manner was quiet and reserved. It was in her "other life" that her individuality flowered. Sally's night job was acting! On stage, she was flamboyant, ebullient, and totally outrageous. Like her handwriting, she outwardly followed the rules, but only to a point.

Charting Your Goals

The baseline is a major indicator of how goal-oriented the writer is. The beginning of a writing line symbolizes the beginning of an effort, starting out towards a goal. The end of the line stands for the end of the effort, or completion of the goal. What happens in the middle tells us how the writer goes about attaining her objectives.

Ask yourself, "Do I have a set of life goals?" How about a five-year plan for your business? How clear in your mind is your plan for the future? Perhaps you are the type of person whose motto is, "Let's just wait and see what happens." Or, maybe you prefer to plan ahead and be pro-active, taking responsibility for making things happen. The way you approach the baseline helps us find the answer.

The steadier the baseline of writing, the more focused the writer is on her goals. At the same time, don't forget that balance is important—a compulsively straight baseline (i.e., ruler writing) is too much of a good thing.

As an example, when you're going to take a road trip, how much planning do you do? Do you decide on a destination, call your auto club for a map, check the weather channel to make sure you have the appropriate dress, pack a cooler with snacks and drinks, fill up the car with gasoline, plan each stop carefully to make sure you have the proper amount of fuel, and let those who are expecting you know exactly what time you'll arrive?

If so, your baseline is probably very straight. You are highly goal oriented. You focus on what you want, making certain that you won't run out of resources before reaching your goal. But at the same time, unplanned events are very difficult for you to deal with. If you run into a roadblock and have to make a detour, or traffic is unexpectedly heavy and delays your arrival time, you may over-react with anger and frustration because your plans are impacted.

Tales from the Quill

Rick decided on the spur of the moment to visit his girlfriend who lived 50 miles away. He jumped in his car and sped off down the road. About halfway there he remembered that he wanted to do some paperwork. He got off the highway, turned around and headed home. A few miles later he decided it would be more fun to see his girlfriend and turned around once more. Rick has a variable baseline.

On the other hand, are you the type who suddenly decides you want to go somewhere, though you're not at all sure where; you just grab a jacket, jump in the car, and head out on the road? You don't bother to check the gas gauge, and might end up sleeping in the car because you have no hotel reservation.

As a result, you might find your unknown destination is somewhere exciting and wonderful, or you might discover the less attractive side of society in a yucky part of town. But it doesn't matter because for you, the action is more important than the goal. Your baseline probably wavers.

How to Measure a Baseline

There are two ways to measure baselines. Each one gives you different kinds of information. The first is to find which direction the line is going, and the second is to determine how well the writer adheres to the baseline. (See the following illustrations.)

Measuring Line Direction

Place a ruler or any straightedge on a page of writing. Slide the ruler until its left edge rests on the bottom of the first letter on the line. Measure across to the last letter on the line and draw a line between the two points. (Don't do this on the original—make a photocopy.) This technique tells you the direction of the baseline, whether it is straight across, rising, or falling.

Measuring Across the Baseline

Now place the ruler on the page of writing so that the end of the ruler touches both the left and right edges of the paper. Place the ruler at the bottom of the first letter of a line and then lay it straight across the page. Draw a line to see if the words stay on the baseline, rise above it, or fall below it.

Measuring the baseline.

Rigidly Straight Baseline

The rigidly straight baseline, especially one written without a printed line to write on, indicates a person whose emotions are kept under strict control at all times, and her behavior is restrained to the point of rigidity. Once she decides on a goal, nothing will stop her from reaching it. Like a horse wearing blinders, she pushes on, seeing nothing but the goal.

Chicken Scratch

The rigid-baseline writer doesn't know how to balance his need for control with the appropriate emotional release. When he lets go, he really lets go, explosively. You might be surprised when the person who is normally very quiet and polite suddenly begins yelling and cursing.

Rigidly straight baseline.

Moderately Straight Baseline

A moderately straight baseline varies to some degree. Overall though, it proceeds directly from one side of the page to the other. It goes where it is supposed to go (from left to right), but is reasonably flexible about how it gets there. The writer has good willpower and can be relied upon to pursue his goals persistently, using common sense. There is no doubt he will follow through on what he starts out to do.

He handles unexpected events without getting too distracted, finding ways around obstacles, and getting back on track. The writer is generally calm and emotionally steady, well-balanced, and reasonable. He knows how to express his emotions when it's appropriate and hold them back when it's not.

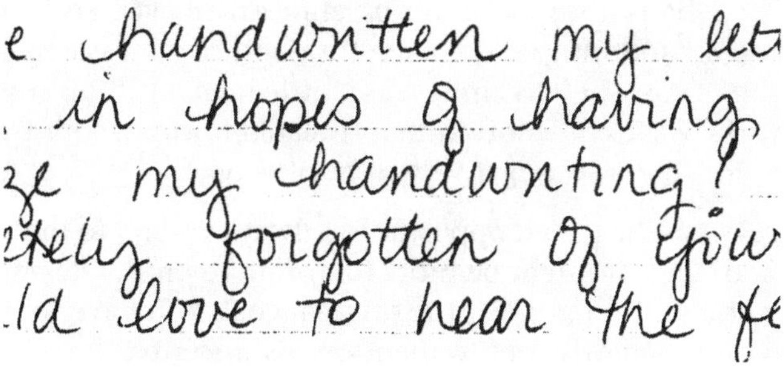

Moderately straight baseline.

Slightly Wavy Baseline

As the baseline gets wavier, more emotion creeps in. The writer whose baseline meanders casually across the page is easily distracted by outside influences. Her sense of direction is not so firm that she can't be persuaded to change her goals. She doesn't have a problem stopping what she's doing to handle something else. In fact, she probably welcomes the interruption. Will she return to finish the original project? Maybe. Maybe not.

Sensitive to what is going on around her, the writer adapts to different kinds of people and circumstances without difficulty. She is emotionally responsive and her feelings are suddenly aroused and quickly expressed. You can expect her to laugh and cry easily, because she experiences more emotional ups and downs than the writer of a straighter line.

Fine Points

Researchers have found that blood sugar levels have an effect on the baseline. When blood sugar is low, as in hypoglycemia, the person's mood plunges and her baseline becomes erratic. Blood pressure and muscle tension can likewise have an effect on the straightness of the line.

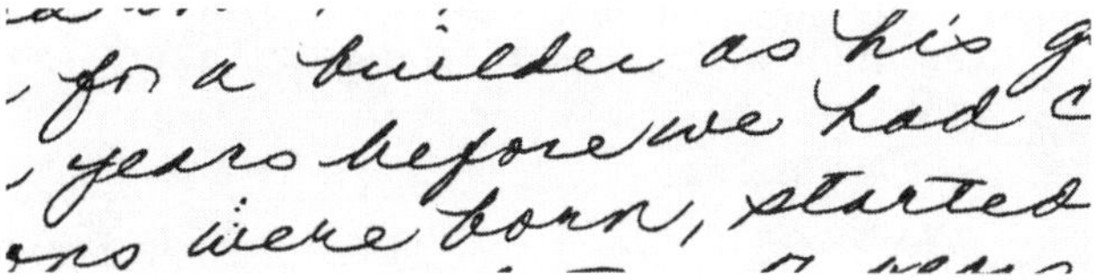

Slightly wavy baseline.

Extremely Wavy Baseline

Someone who can't make up his mind on even the smallest detail leaves a baseline that moves across the page snakelike. He doesn't know whether to go east or west; to the movies or play video games; wear green or pink, wool socks or cotton. And it doesn't matter what he chooses anyway because the moment he decides, he'll change his mind. Something better might come along as soon as he makes a choice, and then what would he do!

It's as hard for him to think straight as it is to keep his baseline on an even keel. Don't expect him to take a firm stand on anything, even when his point of view is challenged, as he avoids conflict at all cost. He's as aimless as a little boat adrift on stormy seas, tossed here and there by the waves of emotion that threaten to capsize him. Even the smallest event affects him in a big way, negatively or positively.

The writer of an extremely wavy baseline is an opportunist, always willing to quit what he's doing if something else looks like it might be more fun or more profitable, and it doesn't matter who was counting on him to meet the original goal. You have to wonder about his ability to plan coherently, not to mention his sincerity.

Extremely wavy baseline.

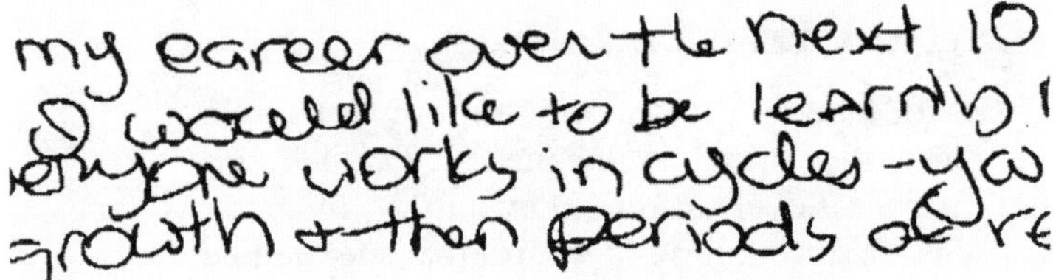

Chicken Scratch

The excessively wavy baseline is one of the signs sometimes seen in the writings of criminals (but never judge criminal behavior or any other type based on only one sign!). One thing is certain, the writer is unreliable and not to be trusted with important decisions.

Ready, Set, Goal!

The direction of the baseline (does the baseline as a whole move up, down, stay even across the page?) has something to do with enthusiasm and optimism, but other factors also affect it. The direction of the baseline is one of the elements of handwriting strongly affected by mood or emotional state. A sudden welling up of emotion may cause a change.

If you see something unusual in the direction of a baseline, ask for other samples of writing done over a period of time. Then you can better determine whether something related to a specific issue is causing the effect or if it's the writer's normal state of mind.

Uphill Baseline

Most graphology books claim that an uphill baseline means the writer is optimistic. Now, get ready for a controversial statement: *This is not necessarily true.* A lot depends on the degree of the uphill slope. A baseline with an exaggerated uphill slope is more likely to be made by someone fighting depression rather than an optimist.

Remember the story of Sisyphus in the Greek myth? As a punishment for offending the gods, Sisyphus was doomed to push a massive boulder uphill. Once he reached the top of the hill, the boulder would roll back down to the bottom and he had to begin all over again, eternally.

That's how the person who creates an exaggeratedly uphill slope feels: as if she were fighting an unending uphill battle. However, she works hard at keeping a positive mental outlook. Her attitude is "If I just keep on pushing, things are bound to get better tomorrow."

autograph & business card on
it in my appointment book
the photo of us together.

Uphill baseline.

When the uphill slope is moderate, we interpret it as eagerness, ambition, and hopefulness. To interpret optimism there must also be self-confidence and self-assurance. The writer is influenced to some degree by her emotional state, but not unduly.

The extreme uphill baseline rises at about 45° from the edge of the paper, which suggests impulsiveness. The writer is highly excitable and wholly driven by her urges and emotions. It takes a certain amount of forcefulness and aggressiveness to produce this type of baseline, so it's a good guess that she pushes to get her own way.

Chicken Scratch

Be careful of how you interpret the falling baseline. Before deciding that the writer is a pessimist or has a generally negative outlook, ask whether she has been ill recently, or has experienced a major life event, such as becoming unemployed, which might have a temporary effect on the direction of her baseline.

Falling Baseline

Generally, a falling baseline is a sign of fatigue or illness, or it could indicate a generally pessimistic outlook on life. Again, only by examining a series of handwriting samples done over a period of time will you know which is true.

The bottom line, however, is that the writer is suffering from weakness for some reason, and he lacks the energy and enthusiasm needed to pursue his goals effectively. Assuming the writer is reasonably healthy, you can infer that he's probably easily discouraged and feels worn down by external events.

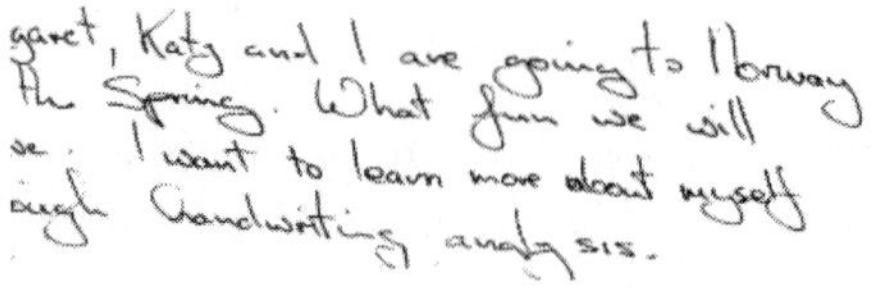

Falling baseline.

Convex Baseline

In Chapter 7 we discussed convex margins. That's the one that bows outward. There are also convex baselines. This baseline rises in the middle, then falls back down by the end. It signals a writer who starts out consumed with passion about what's coming up, but his interest and enthusiasm quickly dies out. In other words, he's a better starter than a finisher.

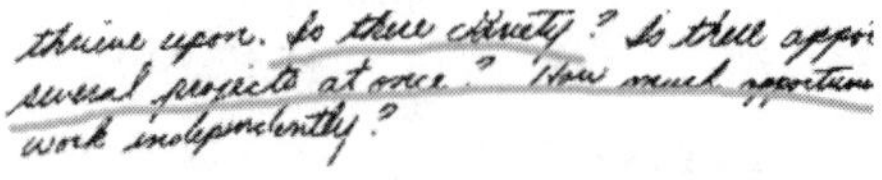

Convex baseline.

Concave Baseline

We have also discussed concave margins—the kind that cave in. The concave baseline writer is a slow starter who bellyaches about how much she has to do, and how put-upon she is, but who nevertheless finishes what she starts. Bit by bit, as her enthusiasm and confidence grow, she pulls herself up out of her negative attitude and does all she can to meet her goal. Even when she's afraid she won't be able to pull it off, a strong sense of responsibility pushes her to make a strong finish.

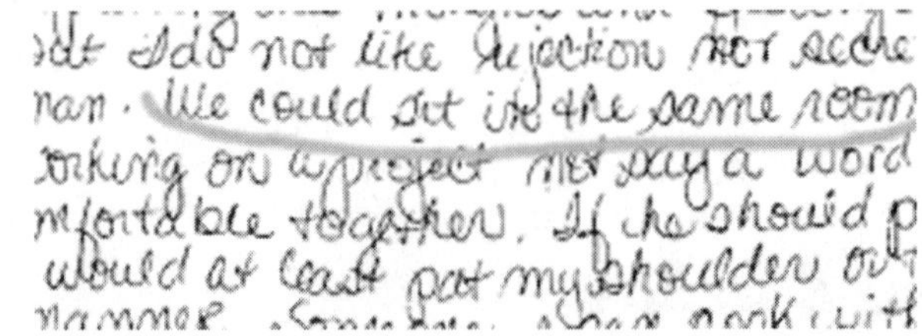

Concave baseline.

The Step-Up and Step-Down Baselines

Neither the step-up or step-down baselines will usually appear over an entire page of writing—they'll show up more or less sporadically. Think of them as the baseline of individual words. Note which words slant up or down, because they may be emotionally charged words that will help you understand the writer's emotional state at the time of writing.

The so-called step-up baseline is created when the baseline of each word rises, producing a tiled effect. In this case, the writer struggles to keep his emotions and enthusiasm under control.

The step-down baseline is made by someone who experiences life as a constant struggle. He expects things to go badly and must pull himself out of depression on a daily basis. No matter how much he fights the tendency towards discouragement, and no matter how many times he picks himself up, he just seems to fall back down into a dark pit of despair.

Fine Points

When a word falls below the baseline or jumps up above it, note what the word is. It may have a strong emotional association for the writer and provide an important clue to his personality.

Step-up (above) and step-down (below) baselines.

Sometimes a baseline will be reasonably straight, but plunges downwards at the end of the line. This indicates a lack of planning on the writer's part—he didn't see the end of the page coming. He's often unrealistic and extravagant and gets into financial hot water. He spends beyond his limits and has to pinch pennies to make ends meet. By using up most of his resources at the beginning of a project, he runs out of budget too soon and is forced to skimp later on the more important parts.

The Least You Need to Know

- The baseline of writing is the invisible line that you write on.
- A super-straight baseline isn't a good thing, but neither is a super-wavy one, either. Balance is the key.
- Some slight variations in the baseline mean flexibility.
- An uphill baseline doesn't necessarily mean optimism, but a downhill baseline could point to pessimism, if only temporary.

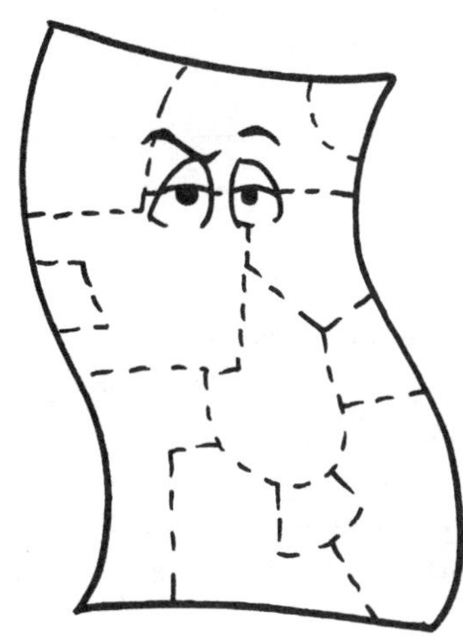

Chapter 9

Calling Dr. Freud: The Zones

In This Chapter

- Three isn't always a crowd when it comes to zones
- The middle zone—it's your daily life
- The upper zone: Imagine that! The intellect
- The lower zone—a trip into the subconscious
- Sex and the single loop

Many cultures around the world have a habit of dividing things into threes. A multitude of religions, both Western and Eastern, have triune gods. There are the concepts of heaven, earth, and hell; mind, body, and spirit, and so on. Max Pulver (Remember him from Chapter 1?) is credited with being the first to classify handwriting into three individual zones: upper, middle, and lower.

The zones show how the parts of personality interact with each other. Although each zone serves its own function, none acts independently of the others. When one or two zones is either overdeveloped or underdeveloped, the effects span the entire handwriting and the entire personality.

In the Zone

As hard as it is to choose a "most important" zone, the middle zone wins the prize. Everything passes through it to get to where it's going, and the middle zone is where

Tales from the Quill

Although Pulver is best known for creating the three zones in handwriting, the English translation of his best-known book, *The Symbolism of Handwriting* (reprinted by Scriptor Books, 1994), refers to "i = height," and the upper and lower "extensions," rather than zones. In fact, there is no chapter on zones. The closest he comes is a chapter called, "Dimensions of Handwriting." As the title of his book implies, he was more concerned with the overall graphic symbolism than any of the individual parts of which handwriting is made up.

letters connect. In Chapter 8, we talked about the baseline as the dividing line between reality and the unconscious. The middle zone sits right on this dividing line. But what is this "reality"? The reality defined by the middle zone includes:

- The self
- Day-to-day life
- Interactions with other people
- Communication
- Expression or control of emotions
- Acting out moral principles
- Ego needs and ability to satisfy them
- Ability to adapt

Middle-zone letters include the vowels, a, e, i, o, u, and other small letters that have no upper or lower extensions. They are c, m, n, r, s, v, w, x. Some letters have upper and lower extensions, but parts of the letters fall into the middle zone. They are the circle parts of b, d, g and the hump on h and y. Really, any stroke passing through the middle zone counts.

Like the middle zone, the upper zone is part of the conscious area of personality. The movement the hand makes going into the upper zone is up and away from middle zone, away from the body, then back down to the baseline. When we go into the upper zone, the upward movement of the pen, it symbolizes reaching up into the mental sphere, where our minds are free to wander, unfettered by the material world. The mental sphere of the upper zone includes:

- Mental processes
- Spirituality
- Standards, principles, conscience
- Abstract reasoning
- Ambition
- Intellectual pursuits
- Imagination
- View of authority figures, including the Father

Fine Points

Although handwriting is split into three zones, which represent different areas of personality, there is always an overlap. What affects one zone will have a corresponding effect in the other zones.

Upper zone letters have extensions rising out of the middle zone: b, d, f, h, k, l, t. Letters or parts of letters from other zones that wander into the upper zone where they don't belong are given special attention.

The lower zone is especially intriguing. We're taught to write lower-zone letters by making a downstroke from the baseline into the lower zone. At the bottom of the downstroke a smooth turn to the left is called for (to form a loop), then an upstroke to the right for a return to the line of reality (the baseline). The unconscious, hidden, instinctual aspects of personality, as well as our attitudes toward work and productivity, are stored in the lower zone. The lower zone includes:

- Biological imperatives: food, sex, money, physical activity
- The past, including experiences and memories that influence our behavior in the present
- View of the Mother and nurturing
- Dreams and fantasy
- Release or repression of anger
- Susceptibility to stimulation
- The energy of the personality
- Productivity

Lower-zone letters have extensions that drop below the baseline: f, g, j, p, q, y, z. Letters or parts of letters that don't belong in the lower zone but sneak a peak down there anyway are a sign of problems.

Back to School with Freud

Okay, now we know which letters are found in which zones and what the zones represent. Let's take a trip back to Psych 101.

Good graphologists understand personality development. You don't have to have a psychology degree, but without a basic foundation in psychology, the best you'll be able to do is make a list of unconnected personality traits, and that won't help you or your client. Knowing how those traits work together as a dynamic system will help you create meaningful, helpful analyses.

Around the time Pulver published his zonal theory, Freud's *Psychoanalytic Model* was attracting attention. Pulver discovered that Freud's concepts of personality fit in very nicely with his concept of zones. Freud's ideas may have been hotly contested over the years, but it's generally accepted that most systems of personality development have their roots, at least partially, in Freud's time-tested concepts of id, ego, and superego.

Write Words

Freud's **Psychoanalytic Model** of personality development includes the id, ego, and superego.

The Id Did It

Every living organism uses *"psychic energy"* or life force to meet its needs in the physical, emotional, and spiritual areas of life. Energy, according to Einstein, cannot be destroyed; however, it can be transformed for different uses and distributed where needed.

Picture a lake filled with water. When part of the lake is dammed, some of the water gets redirected into another area. The same amount of water is still there, but it isn't all available at the same time for the same purpose. We can relate this image to the available energy in the human organism. We have a certain amount of energy to use for all our different activities. We might expend some mentally at work, then maybe go to the gym and use some for physical exertion, then use more energy in socializing when we go out for dinner with friends. Our energy is transformed for use in different parts of the personality at different times.

Sigmund Freud gave human energy a name. He called it the id and identified it as the earliest part of personality to appear after birth.

Freud said the id serves one purpose and one purpose only: to reduce tension and increase pleasure. The id knows only that it must provide relief from discomfort and it doesn't matter what form the relief takes. If the source of discomfort is hunger, cold, sadness, or sexual tension, it makes no difference. Its sole function is to provide relief, to make you feel good. That's why the id is called the Pleasure Principle.

Let's say you're walking past a bakery around lunchtime. The yeasty aroma of freshly baked bread wafts out to the sidewalk and curls around your olfactory sense. You immediately feel compelled to duck inside and order a sandwich. Blame it on the id. In fact, you can blame your urge to buy that new dress, tell your boss what you think of him, and your sexual impulses on the id.

The id knows only that it wants what it wants, and that it wants it NOW! "Wait" is not a word the id understands. Like an infant who can't delay the urge to eat, the need to have its diaper changed, or the desire to be cuddled, the id demands instant gratification. Hungry, wet, or frightened, a baby will scream to get relief, and that's appropriate for a baby. But the same behavior is not at all attractive in an adult.

Write Words

Psychic energy is the basic life force available for all the activities carried out by the personality.

We've all seen adults who, when they don't get their own way, have a tantrum. They'll yell and pound the desk and jump up and down, making unreasonable demands. We say to ourselves, "Oh, how infantile!" Such people act like babies because their emotional development never progressed past the infant stage. Their id impulses drive them, rather than the more mature adult quality of self-control.

The distribution of energy in the personality is seen in the zones of handwriting. In a mature personality, the energy is distributed throughout the writing. Some parts may have a little more emphasis than others, but overall there is symmetry and balance.

Where the personality is stuck in the infantile id stage the writing runs wild. There is unevenness and variability in practically every area: size, style, baseline, slant. Loops may balloon grotesquely, as the energy bursts out into places where it doesn't belong. "Id" writing explodes into impulsive action, as demonstrated in the next handwriting sample. Having fun and doing what comes naturally without restraint is what life is all about for one driven entirely by id impulses.

Off at the
nursery. I was
angry & grabbed
my mother's

Uncontrolled id writing.

For the id energy to be used effectively, it must be properly channeled. That is the job of the ego, which, in Freud's view, is the next area of personality to develop.

Chicken Scratch

Unusual forms in the lower zone (the unconscious), which might include hooks, knots, twists, and angles, indicate an unhappy id. The writer's drives are not being satisfied in the usual, standard ways.

Ergo, the Ego

The ego is the "traffic cop" of the personality. It directs energy where needed and helps the individual make appropriate choices based on common sense and reasoning. The ego is called the Reality Principle.

A healthy ego uses self-discipline and self-control to ensure the appropriate amount of energy is available as and where needed. If you're playing racquetball, you need more energy for the physical than for the intellectual area. In the handwriting analysis class you are attending, you need more intellectual energy than emotional energy. When you and a couple of classmates go out for a latté after class, the ego channels the energy into the social area.

Returning to our bakery example: you smell the warm bread and your stomach grumbles longingly. Your conscious mind starts a debate with your biological urge to eat: "You're on a diet and need to cut down on carbs," the mind says. "But it smells so good," argues the id. Hmmm, what to do? A well-developed ego gains the upper hand and says "Not now, wait until you've lost five more pounds. Eat a salad instead."

A handwriting with good overall balance says the writer has developed common sense and self-discipline. He is even-tempered and has learned to delay what he wants until the time is right. He's probably nice, and can be counted on to act maturely in most circumstances. Of course, he may not be the most interesting person in town, but nobody's perfect!

Although its effects are imprinted on the entire handwriting, the ego is specifically found in the middle zone. That's where the day-to-day routines and social interactions are revealed, and where the traffic cop directs the energy where it needs to go.

If a handwriting looks fairly neat and well-organized, and nothing pops out to hit you in the eye, chances are the writer has a healthy ego and the ability to get his needs met in socially acceptable ways. The next handwriting sample shows the smooth flow of reasonable control and balance.

Healthy ego writing.

and a sense of
be desirable th
for the natura
They should be

Note, though, that *excessively* organized writing, like any other excess, is out of balance and is not a good sign. In fact, excessive organization indicates an overly active super-ego, the last part of personality to develop.

Tales from the Quill

Many teenage girls write only in the middle zone. (Their upper and lower extensions are so short they're practically nonexistent.) They are interested solely in what is happening from moment to moment, and they live for today. A large middle zone does not signify a strong ego, but a weak one (See Chapter 10). Middle zone emphasis in the writing of an adult is generally a sign of immaturity.

Superego to the Rescue!

As the child learns to live by the rules of society and his conscience evolves, the superego is acquired. Its function in the personality emphasis is to reward and punish. It acts like a parent who peers over your shoulder every time you want to do something and says, "Don't do that!" or "You should do this, not that!" If you hear a little voice in your head constantly whispering "shoulds" and "shouldn'ts" it's a sure sign of a strong superego. This is called the Morality Principle.

A super-strong superego is like a strict dean of discipline mixed with Santa Claus. It punishes you with guilt feelings when you don't do what you're supposed to—you give in to the id's temptations and overspend your credit limit. Or, if you are good and fend off the naughty urge, the superego might reward you with pride and self-satisfaction. Maybe if you're really good, it will give you a vacation in Hawaii!

Handwriting of the person with a too strict superego, such as the one in the next sample, looks rigid and overcontrolled. It is brittle and stiff, with very tall upper loops. The writer's internal parent is a stern taskmaster that never relaxes and won't allow the writer to experience anything that looks enjoyable. The first response of her superego is, "No! You can't have it!" The "superego" writer is usually very serious. She doesn't know how to have fun, as opposed to the id writer who wants *only* to have fun.

Too strong superego writing.

Welcome to My World: The Middle Zone

The middle zone, where the ego resides, tells us how the writer acts around other people, how well-adjusted she is, and whether all the parts of her personality are working together harmoniously.

In the middle zone we pursue the goals that were conceived in the lower zone (unconscious) and planned out in the upper zone (conscious). When one zone is much larger or smaller than the others—for example, a tiny middle zone with an extremely tall upper zone; or a large middle zone and stunted lower zone—the writer's goals conflict with her ability to meet them.

The uniformity of the middle zone size tells how sensitive the writer is to the needs of others. The middle zone represents where we interact socially, so a little variability in size shows sensitivity for dealing with different types of people. But while some fluctuation is normal and expected, when letter size varies too much, the writer lacks confidence; his ego is in a constant state of flux.

Chicken Scratch

Handwritings with middle zone letters that suddenly flare up over other letters paint a picture of sudden outbursts. This phenomenon is known as jump-up or pop-up letters. The writer may normally be mild-mannered and low-key, but without warning, comes on strong.

How much variation is too much? When the middle zone looks very uneven, with letters randomly jumping up and squishing down, it's too much. Is the word "balance" becoming your mantra yet? If not, it should be.

Middle zone letters of more or less the same height indicate a degree of self-confidence. But too much regularity is no better than too much variation. The writer is so fixed in his own ego needs that he can't understand or isn't interested in what others need. If the handwriting looks machine-like this means overcontrol resulting in robotic-type behavior.

aeioucmnrsvwx

The middle zone.

Soul Survivor: The Upper Zone

The upper zone represents the place where the writer can expand his knowledge, let his imagination run wild, explore various philosophies and satisfy his intellectual curiosity. To effectively use the ideas and philosophies he contemplates in the upper zone, the writer must bring them back into the middle zone in a reasonable length of time. Otherwise, he is just wool-gathering or building castles in the air. That means the upper zone shouldn't be too tall in relation to the middle zone (You'll find some guidelines in Chapter 10).

When too much emphasis is placed on the upper zone, either by making loops too tall, too wide, or too elaborate the writer is compensating for problems in the ego (the middle zone). He has difficulty functioning in the real world in some area. Maybe he feels inferior socially, so he escapes into the intellectual world of the upper zone. There, he can create his own reality, which feels safer.

An **extra-tall upper zone** is like someone standing proud, as if he has just achieved some wonderful goal. Whether or not the pride is deserved and based in reality depends on how well-developed the other zones are. If the upper zone height is too tall in relation to the other zones, the writer may be an intellectual dilettante who lacks the ability to manifest his ideas in middle-zone reality.

A **very narrow upper zone** allows little room for the writer to expand his ideas. In a very real sense, he is narrow-minded and may be afraid to explore philosophies that threaten to draw him outside the realm of his experience. He'd rather stick with what he knows.

A **tall, narrow upper zone** suggests that the writer may have been raised in a strict or authoritarian household. One's attitude toward *authority figures* is found in the upper zone, and the writer of tall, narrow loops views authority figures as extremely powerful, towering over him. Feeling inferior to those in authority, the writer tries to compensate by dominating others over whom he feels superior.

Those who expend too much time and energy thinking about things rather than doing them often make **overly wide upper loops.** The imagination is given free rein. The writer is hypersensitive and believes others are talking about him in a critical way. The wider the loops, the more unrealistic the outlook.

Write Words

An authority figure can be an individual such as father, boss, teacher; or a group such as the government, police, or the army.

Without the balance of practicality in a well-formed middle and lower zone, an overemphasized upper zone shows someone who is unable to properly meet the demands of everyday life. Everything is filtered through the intellect, so his reality testing may be poor.

A **short upper zone** indicates a writer who generally doesn't have strong religious or spiritual beliefs, and who isn't interested in questioning his values. More materialistic than intellectual, he is interested in people and things that he can see and touch, not abstract ideas and philosophies.

The upper zone.

What Dreams May Come: The Lower Zone

Keeper of secrets, gateway to the unconscious, the lower zone holds the mysteries of the psyche. The lower zone begins under the baseline and descends into the darkness of the past.

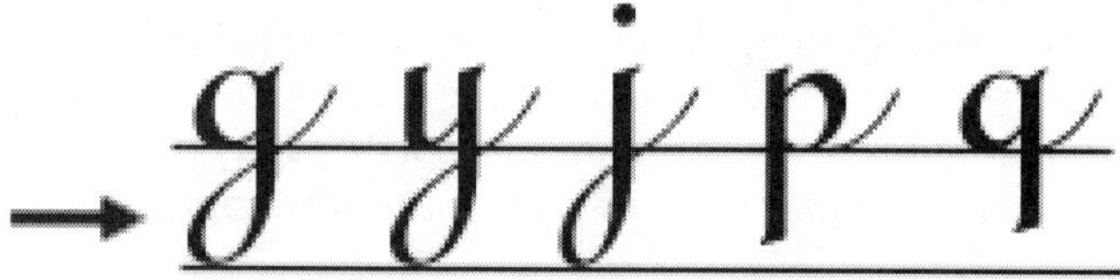

The lower zone.

Chicken Scratch

The writer of an elaborate upper zone with many unnecessary flourishes and curlicues draws attention to himself. This is a sign that the writer is overcompensating for feelings of inferiority. His tendency to be unrealistic may signal delusional thinking. He fabricates the facts to suit himself.

How the writer expresses her sexual and material desires and how well she suppresses them, are found in the lower zone. Whether she is moderate and reasonable or extremely inhibited; whether she feels inferior or powerful when it comes to sex, the lower zone tells at least part of the story.

It also reveals whether the writer is apt to be a sensitive, considerate lover, or one who prefers to use brute force to subdue his partner. However, it is important to keep in mind that sex is more than just a physical expression, so different aspects of sexuality will be seen throughout the handwriting, not just in the lower zone.

Moderately full lower loops balanced with the other zones signify the writer's ability to satisfy her sexual and other biological urges adequately. She has the ability to plan (upper zone), call on past experience and draw on the necessary energy (lower zone), and effectively act on her plans (middle zone).

Good pressure on the downstroke shows vitality. Check to see whether the loop is just weakly falling into the lower zone or if the thrust below the baseline is strong and purposeful. Is the writer easily led, or does she do the leading?

The downstroke that moves purposefully from the baseline into the lower zone is akin to going underground, into the basement, where we have a chance to look around at all the stuff stored there in the subconscious. There's a lot of old junk down there, but some bona fide treasures, too. What we bring "back upstairs" in the upstroke, to use in the reality of daily life is our own choice.

What if your particular basement is a dank and dirty dungeon, and there's nothing there you want to use? What if, in fact, you have a strong aversion to going there at all. You might decide to fly back upstairs as fast as you can, pretending you never visited. This is the writer who, in the middle of a word, makes a straight downstroke but no return loop.

The writer of **extremely long lower** loops has a basement deep under the ground. She likes to delve into the past and is very interested in learning about her heritage, her roots, and even the skeletons in her closet.

Very short loops suggest someone who's uncomfortable in her basement and quickly returns to the middle zone. Consequently, she is unlikely to learn from past mistakes. Her mind is on what she's going to have for dinner, or whether the mail has arrived yet. There is little interest in remembering last year, last month, or even yesterday—it's all in the past. And she certainly doesn't want to bother with what might or might not happen tomorrow. All that counts is the present.

Chicken Scratch

Here is an important caveat concerning the straight downstroke with no loop. When it occurs only at the ends of words it is a form of simplification and does not have the same meaning as when it appears consistently in the middle of words.

The **standard lower loop** upstroke returns directly to the baseline without deviating from its path. When the loop veers off in a direction other than straight, chances are, the writer's sexuality has suffered some insult, probably in childhood. As a result, the emotions attached to sex are not expressed in the usual, standard ways. What should have been a natural expression of the basic drives becomes self-conscious, perhaps shameful and humiliating.

Off the Beaten Path

More often than not, when unusual loops appear in handwriting, a miserable childhood, clouded by sexual and physical abuse or neglect, is an underlying factor. The uncommon formations of the loops suggest that the writer has been unable to resolve the past events, whatever they were.

Extremely wide lower loops that look like an inflated balloon tend to be made by those who have an amazing fantasy life. They put a tremendous amount of energy into talking about their sexual interest and prowess, but when it comes down to action, their intended partner finds they're full of hot air. The writer feels sexually unsure and inadequate and the extra width helps him compensate—like a rooster, puffing himself up.

Lower loops ending in a **short, sharp hook** are made by one who is generally quick to nit-pick. He's irritable, cranky, and short-tempered. When found in combination with other negative signs, such as very heavy pressure, he may also be a bully.

For some interesting and unique lower zone forms, see the next illustration. Some general explanations follow.

Tales from the Quill

Hook-shaped lower loops symbolize feelings of guilt. Such writers may unconsciously set themselves up for punishment because they think they deserve it. One person who made hooked lower loops had a habit of gossiping about a particular friend to others. The way she did it ensured that the talk inevitably got back to the friend, who would angrily confront her about it and make her feel guilty.

Unusual lower zones.

Sometimes the lower zone pulls strongly to the left (more often seen in men's writing.) This signifies a strong attachment to mother or a need for mothering that was not satisfied in childhood. On the other hand, lower loops that pull to the right (more often seen in women's writing,) are usually made by those who rebel against male authority. Variable slants in the lower zone are sometimes made by writers who question their sexual identity.

Mom Always Gets the Blame!

A **triangular-shaped** lower zone has sharp corners pointing to the left (mother, past), indicating unresolved issues with mother that spill over onto other women in the writer's life. There is hidden aggression or hostility in this formation; hidden, because it is in the lower zone, below the baseline, the line of reality, and in the unconscious. The aggression may take the form of nagging and constant criticism. When the angles have soft edges, it mitigates the implication somewhat.

Big, rounded lower extensions that look like **cradles** don't return to the baseline but hang in the lower zone. The stroke ends in a leftward movement, towards the past and mother. The writer may have missed the nurturing, loving care that she would like to have had, and continues to seek it out in adult relationships. Her behavior in intimate relationships may be childlike and quite different from what she shows to the world.

Loops that **curl inward** like a snail's shell show strong self-involvement. They are made by an egocentric, insincere person who cannot be trusted to tell the truth. In relationships, this writer only has room for himself.

When the upstroke crosses the downstroke too soon (before the baseline), it may indicate a lack of the proper emotional release in sex, resulting in frustration.

Tales from the Quill

Handwriting can't determine someone's guilt or innocence in matters of sexual misconduct, but it may demonstrate the writer's attitude about the opposite sex. President Bill Clinton's two terms in office were marked by accusations of misconduct, including sexual harassment in the workplace. What does his handwriting show? The soft triangles in the lower zone do seem to indicate some unresolved issues with women. (See a sample in Appendix E). The rounded edges of the angles soften the interpretation.

A well-developed lower zone, balanced with the other zones shows good coordination, self-confidence, and an ability to relate effectively with other people. As in every other aspect of handwriting, no zone should be interpreted separately from the others.

The Least You Need to Know

- Handwriting is divided into three zones, upper, middle, and lower, which correspond to areas of personality.
- The middle zone is the most important because all parts of handwriting pass through it.
- The upper zone represents conscious thought (how you think).
- The middle zone represents where you live (how you feel).
- The lower zone represents the unconscious (how you act).
- Although each zone has its own significance, all work together and affect each other.

Chapter 10

Size Does Matter: Writing Size

In This Chapter

- What height and width mean in handwriting
- What does "size" really mean?
- How tall is tall, how wide is wide?
- From me to you—width and social skills
- Aspiring to visions of greatness—tall writing
- The material girl and boy—middle-zone emphasis

In Chapter 9 we discussed the general areas symbolized by each zone. So, let's review: the upper zone is where you think, the middle zone is where you feel, and the lower zone is where you act.

Now, we'll discover how size affects the activities that take place in those areas of life. But first, we need to define what "size" means, because there are two ways to look at size in handwriting. Absolute size encompasses the entire scope of writing from the tops of the upper loops to the bottoms of the lower loops. The most important size, however, is "relative size." which is the ratio between the heights of middle zone letters to the height of upper-zone and length of lower-zone letters. In this book we are concerned with relative size.

The middle-zone measurement is the most important one because several other measurements are based on it. Don't worry about making your measurements exact though, because a ballpark figure is good enough. Besides, once you have some experience under your belt, you'll be able to eyeball a writing and decide on the size.

We're going to talk about measurements in terms of height and width of the letters in each zone, beginning with the middle zone (MZ). The middle zone provides us with a frame of reference for measuring the other zones.

Fine Points

It's very unlikely that all letters will measure exactly the same, and that's good. Mechanical regularity in any area of writing is a negative because it shows rigid, regimented behavior.

Leggo My Ego

The middle zone is where you live. It's the zone of the ego and it answers the question, "How tall does the writer feel?" Someone who isn't very tall in a literal sense but has a healthy ego can seem like a giant. What counts is how tall you feel *inside*. The middle-zone height (MZH) is an indicator for how tall the writer is inside and how much recognition makes her feel good about herself. We'll call this measurement her *ego needs*.

Middle-zone width (MZW) involves expansive movement from left to right (from me to you), and tells us how free the writer feels to move out into the world to satisfy her ego needs. The person who is not afraid to ask for what she needs has a wider middle zone than the one who is shy and shrinks back. We'll call that measurement her *ego strength*.

Small, Medium, Large— As Opposed to What?

Write Words

Ego needs are what it takes to make an individual feel good about himself. **Ego strength** is the ability to get one's needs satisfied appropriately.

The American Palmer school copybook (CB) is the standard we'll use to decide whether the middle zone height is small, medium, or large (see Chapter 4 for a copy of the Palmer model). According to Palmer, the middle zone should be 3 mm high.

To measure the middle-zone height (MZH), take a writing sample and pick several letters in the middle zone (a or o are easy to use). Using a metric ruler, measure the letter heights from top to bottom. If you aren't sure where to measure, check the following illustration.

If most of the middle zone letters measure 3 mm, we'll call the middle-zone height medium. If the letters are taller than 3 mm, we'll refer to the middle zone as large or tall. If they're smaller than 3 mm, we'll say the middle zone is small or short. If there is a wide variety of measurements, the middle-zone height is variable.

Next, measure the middle zone width (MZW). Again, use the letters o and a. Copybook dictates that MZW should be about the same as MZH or just slightly less. That makes the ratio 1:1. If the letters measure less than 3 mm wide, the middle zone is narrow. If they measure more, the middle zone is wide. If there a wide variety of measurements, the middle-zone width is variable.

Measuring the middle zone.

Following is a list of abbreviations for commonly used graphological terms.

Abbreviation	Meaning
CB	Copybook
LZ	Lower zone
LZL	Lower-zone elaboration
LZW	Lower-zone width
MZ	Middle zone
MZH	Middle-zone height
MZW	Middle-zone width
UZ	Upper zone
UZH	Upper-zone height
UZE	Upper-zone elaboration
UZW	Upper-zone width

How About Those Loops?

In (CB), the upper-zone height (UZH) is one and one-half times as tall as the MZH, which means they measure $4^{1}/_{2}$ mm from the baseline to the top of the loops. Use the letters l, b, or h, measure the tallest upper loops. Here's the catch: To be considered medium, the *width* of the upper loops (UZW) should be only about one-half as wide as the middle zone height. Since 1.5 mm is the copybook measurement, the ratio of MZH to UZH is 1:1.5. Measure upper loops at their widest point. The MZW ratio is 1:.5.

Fine Points

Someone who wants to seem taller than she really is may put on high-heeled shoes or pouf up her hair. In handwriting, she writes a tall middle zone. But if the writer doesn't also have sufficient self-confidence, the middle zone will be narrow.

What about the lower zone? Using the longest loops on g or y, measure from the baseline to the bottom of the lower-zone loops (LZL). The LZL should be twice as long as the middle zone is high, and the lower-zone width (LZW) should be half as wide as the middle zone height. That means loops measuring 6 mm long and 1.5 mm wide are medium. The ratio of MZH to LZL is 1:.5. The ratio of MZH to LZW is 1:5. Measure lower loops at their widest point.

Measuring upper and lower loops.

Handwriting is a tool which can be
valuable in many ways. I hope to assist

Bigger Than Small, Smaller Than Big

A middle zone that is medium in height and width suggests a writer who is well-adjusted, realistic, and generally conventional. He is able to focus on what he wants to do and get it done with adequate self-confidence. Socially, he knows his place and does what is expected of him within his chosen social group. Someone who follows instructions well it bothers him when others break the rules or step too far out of line.

Chicken Scratch

Describing the middle-of-the road, average writer is one of the biggest challenges for the graphologist. It's like giving a description of a man in his mid twenties, with a medium build, brown hair, brown eyes. There are no distinguishing characteristics!

A moderate degree of fluctuation in the middle zone is expected and indicates some social sensitivity. The writer is responsive and reacts to emotional events in his environment. His self-confidence may waver to some degree, but he is ready to open himself up to whatever may come.

When the middle zone is fairly uniform in height and width it indicates that the writer is emotionally calm and even. It implies a degree of inner security, so that wherever she is, the environment doesn't seem to affect her too much. There is give and take in her relationships with others, and she feels comfortable in her own skin. If there is little or no fluctuation, check the writer for a pulse.

Medium middle zone.

secure, financially and
intelligent, interested
him and has a sen
myself as generous a

Too Wide

The wider the middle zone, the more important it is to the writer to be accepted by others. An MZ wider than it is tall is made by someone who tends to be indiscriminate in relationships. Quantity becomes more important than quality. Such an exaggerated need for acknowledgment and approval sets the writer up for disappointment. He is hurt over and over again on discovering that once more he has chosen the wrong friends.

It's the Little Things That Count

The writer of a small MZH with medium width doesn't much care what others think of her. She is more intellectual than social and content to spend long periods on her own, concentrating on the things that interest her. She works well under pressure, especially when small details are important.

She seems modest, but her unassertive behavior stems, at least partially, from lowered self-confidence. She recognizes her limits in social situations and her manner is restrained around other people. This writer is comfortable being an introvert, so don't try to talk her into being more sociable.

Small middle zone.

Small and Narrow

There is insecurity in narrowness and the narrower the MZ letters are, the greater the insecurity. When the writer refrains from moving outward, the letters become ovals instead of circles and "from me to you" becomes "from me to me." A lack of confidence restricts her, so the writer feels tense and apprehensive in an unfamiliar environment with people she doesn't know.

That short MZH says her self-concept may already not be so hot (she feels she doesn't deserve to

Fine Points

When you measure the loops, it's unlikely they will all measure exactly the same, and that's good. Mechanical regularity in any area of writing is a negative.

command much space in the world). Add to that narrowness, and her world becomes limited to what and who she knows. She may have few great passions or strong emotions. In fact, others may see her as impassive or apathetic.

Small, narrow middle zone.

Very Small

A tiny middle zone is the sign of a shrinking violet. Rarely will anything get him to venture out of his confined space. He prefers his own company to that of others. He's afraid that others will see him for what he believes he is—nothing. When forced into the company of others, he'll be picking nits and generally being petty toward them. This is the porcupine defense—I'll attack you before you get a chance to attack me. As soon as he possibly can, he'll retreat to the security of his safe little shell.

Tiny middle zone.

An extremely small middle zone may be a sign of mental illness if the letters are so simplified that they become skeletal.

Big Is Beautiful

The large middle zone writer is less realistic than the smaller writer. The tallness of her strokes take her away from the baseline (the line of reality) so she sees things less pragmatically. She thinks BIG, and, because she doesn't believe she can fail, she happily takes on jobs that others might feel are beyond them. If there is also adequate width, she has the confidence to carry through her plans.

The large middle zone with proportional width reveals the extrovert who wants to act upon the world, rather than have the world act upon her. She is determined to stand out in a crowd and behaves in ways that will put her at center stage with the spotlight directly on her. Her large ego, as reflected in her large MZ reveals a need for approval and admiration from all. Refusing to recognize any limitations, the writer is ready to try anything at least once if she thinks it will bring her the recognition she believes she deserves. Satisfying her own needs is her top priority. It's not that she doesn't care about other people, it simply doesn't occur to her that they might have needs too.

A man who
loving, honest,
and available.
extremely Suc

Large middle zone.

Tales from the Quill

The person who prints in all block capitals shares many personality traits with the all MZ writer. Both have a large ego and take up a lot of space. One all-caps printer became frustrated when she attended a social function where she wasn't the center of attention. She sulked and pouted for awhile, but when no one showed any interest, she quickly sought a more positive way to grab the limelight: She began to tell jokes and got everyone laughing.

Large but Narrow

This ebullient personality is more show than go. The tallness in the middle zone is a compensation for the feelings of anxiety demonstrated by the narrowness. The writer may brag about all the things he is going to do, but when it comes to performing, he is afraid to try, unless he knows with certainty that he will succeed. Consequently, he doesn't offer much of himself to others, tends to be miserly with his true feelings and also, perhaps, with his time and money. His viewpoint is subjective. Rather than looking at the big picture, his judgments are based on how the outcome will affect him. When he is unable to produce what he desires he feels unbearably frustrated.

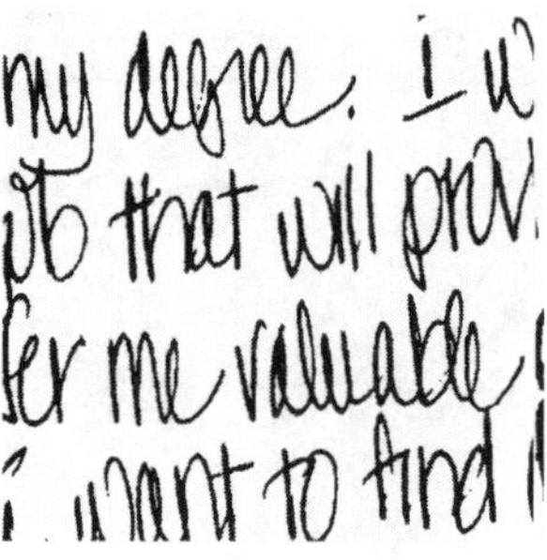

Tall, narrow middle zone.

Too Much of a Good Thing

An extremely large middle zone doesn't mean an extremely healthy ego. Quite the opposite is true, in fact. The writer believes the world revolves around her and that she's better than others. She's a know-it-all who behaves as if anything that doesn't serve her ego didn't exist.

Don't expect her to listen to reason. She believes she can do anything she wants. Even though inside, a vague nagging sense reminds her that her bragging isn't based on truth, it doesn't stop her. The excessive MZ writer is grandiose and makes mountains out of molehills. Nothing is too small for her to turn into a major issue. When she fails, don't expect her to accept responsibility. It's always someone else's fault.

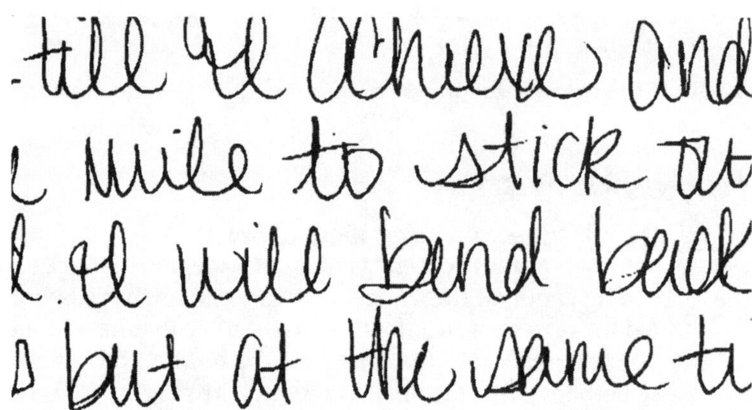

Extremely large middle zone.

Decision, Decisions—I Can't Make Up My Mind

A variable middle-zone height shows emotions on a continuum from sensitivity or touchiness. Whether the writer is emotionally lively or simply unstable depends on the degree of variability. *Some* variability shows the capacity for adapting to the needs of the moment, but when the variability becomes extreme, the writer is a victim of his own moods.

When the MZH fluctuates too much, you'll know that the writer's confidence level is inconstant. He feels sure of himself now, but in five minutes he may be berating himself for being so inadequate. If he's feeling good, he might get involved in a project, then suddenly fear he won't be able to handle it and want to back out. Life is certainly never dull around this type.

The writer of changeable middle zone *width* is likewise unpredictable. You never know what he's going to do next because *he* doesn't know. He might act friendly and welcoming one moment, then withdrawn and aloof the next. It all depends on how he's feeling, and that can change in the blink of an eye.

Write Words

A typical **variable middle-zone height** may range from 2 mm to 4.5 mm or anywhere in between.

Variable middle zone.

Up, Up, and Away

If you want to know about someone's values, check the state of her upper zone (UZ). The upper loops show the writer's degree of interest in the realm of ideas, philosophy, and spirituality. The higher the loops climb, the more the writer wants to reach into the theoretical domain. For the mental activity to be productive the height should be in balance with the lower zone and the middle zone.

The upper zone goes away from the self and out towards other people before returning to the baseline with what it has learned. If the writer is successful in incorporating the new information into her life she will make a strong downstroke. A weak downstroke shows an avoidance of reality: the writer has trouble integrating what is real (MZ) with what is theoretical (UZ).

An upper zone that is proportionate to the middle and lower zones is made by a more or less conventional and practical person.

Moderate upper zone

Fine Points

Some graphologists call extra-wide lower loops "money bags," because they symbolize an emphasis on money and enjoyment of the good things in life.

Tall Upper Loops

A moderately tall upper zone suggests the writer is searching for greatness. The motion of going into the upper zone is like reaching for the stars. If the upper zone is taller than twice the MZH the writer is more concerned with the theoretical than the practical. Driven to understand the universe, if he thinks there's more to know about a subject he finds interesting, it makes him crazy until he has ferreted out every last bit of information there is to find.

He tends to be more idealistic than realistic. By focusing on distant goals so absolutely, some of the important realities waiting in the middle zone are overlooked.

Tall upper zone.

Too Tall

When the loops reach too far into the upper zone, the writer is dissatisfied with who she is. The movement is away from the self, towards something else, something "out there," so she is looking outside herself to get her needs met. The loops seem to be reaching into the heavens (this is not necessarily a sign of spirituality), aspiring to please an authority figure, someone she sees as a higher power. Usually the authority figure is the writer's father, whether she is aware of it or not. especially when the loops are also narrow, an extra-tall upper zone often signifies someone who had an ultrareligious upbringing with an abundance of rules and regulations to follow.

The writer wants everyone to know how clever he is, the type who complicates even the most trivial matters and uses jargon at every opportunity. Because it takes longer to make taller loops than more normal ones, the person who makes them may waste time expounding on theories that have little basis in reality. And, the longer he spends on thinking, the less time there is to act.

Narrow or Retraced Loops

When the loops are narrow or *retraced* (the downstroke covers the upstroke), there is no room for intellectual growth. The writer is narrow-minded and prejudiced against any new ideas. He isn't interested in broadening his horizons, but continually recycles the ideas and concepts he learned while growing up.

If the loops are tall, he probably reads a lot and spends a great deal of energy contemplating a very narrow range of thought. He can't deal with the unconventional, so don't expect him to come up with innovative or revolutionary ideas. Having to deal with anything really new and different is threatening to him, so give him plenty of time to assimilate major changes.

Write Words

Retracing refers to laying the final stroke on top of (retracing) the original stroke, and may be found in any zone.

Tall, narrow upper zone.

Tall and Wide

Tall, moderately wide loops are a sign of imagination. The writer leaves room to create new thoughts and listen to new ideas. She is able to learn from experience and keep a reasonable perspective on what others have to say. She's not afraid to hear anyone else express an opinion, and finds it easy to visualize unfamiliar concepts.

When the loops are too wide (more than twice the MZH) the writer lacks discrimination in what she takes into her mind. An overdeveloped upper zone is a way of compensating for dissatisfaction in one or both of the other zones. The writer prefers to escape into her daydreams or intellectual woolgathering, rather than return to the reality of the middle zone. Her ideas are many, but tend to be impractical and unrealistic. They'll probably never get off the drawing board. Extremely wide upper loops suggest imagination gone wild, perhaps to the point of delusion.

Tall, moderately wide upper zone.

Look Ma, No Loops!

Some writers simplify their writing by making straight, unlooped downstrokes. We'll cover this more in Chapter 17, but in the meantime, all you need to know is that the writer thinks in a direct, practical manner. He may be very creative, but he doesn't spend a lot time fantasizing. He'd rather just get down to business.

Unlooped upper zone.

Short Upper Loops

Chicken Scratch

If the middle zone is much larger than the upper and lower zone it is a sign that the writer is avoiding the intellectual and material areas of life in favor of social relationships and emotional concerns.

The person who hasn't the energy or interest to rise above the middle zone is rooted in the real world. She finds intellectual discussions boring and will quickly seek an excuse to leave when the conversation turns to abstract ideas. People and things are her idea of more interesting topics in her view.

The writer of short upper zones is quite self-involved. She doesn't spend time planning, which is an upper zone activity, but prefers to "just do it." Whatever you do, don't give the short upper zone writer a book for her birthday. It probably will never be opened. She isn't interested in expanding her knowledge base because she cares only that things happen, not *why* they do.

Short upper zone.

Variable Upper Loops

As you might guess, the person whose upper loops are short or wide in one word or letter, and tall or narrow the next, is inconsistent in his thinking. This writer doesn't have a consistent opinion or point of view to offer on any subject. The same topic might be viewed from totally opposite directions, depending on how he looks at it from one moment to the next.

Down in the Boondocks

The lower zone is the area of activity, sexual and otherwise. It contains our attitudes towards the material and biological areas of life. Pen pressure, which will be discussed in Chapter 12, is an important element in interpreting the lower zone.

When the pen dips below the baseline into the lower zone, its purpose is to recapture past experiences and put them to use in daily life above the baseline. An emphasis on the lower zone shows a strong interest in money, sex, and the material life. Loops that are too short show either a lack of interest in biological urges or little energy to invest in satisfying them.

Short Lower Loops

It doesn't take much determination or persistence to make short strokes into the lower zone. The writer probably shouldn't take on projects that can't be quickly completed, because she may lose interest or become discouraged over a period of time. If there is strong pressure, she may work hard but has limited endurance and stamina and just doesn't have it in her to keep on going. Then again, if the pressure isn't firm she might very well be lazy. She has minimal interest in sex. Because she stays close to the middle zone, she focuses her energy on the necessities of daily life.

Short lower zone.

Medium Lower Loops

The writer of a moderate lower zone is active and productive, but he also likes to relax and recharge his batteries. If there is also moderate width, endurance and persistence increase as the lower-zone loops increase in length.

Tales from the Quill

Max Pulver, one of the most quoted early graphologists said: "The dangers of intellectualism are lack of persistence, of perseverance with projects, and of attention to material, physical and sexual matters. Those who write in the opposite way remain to some extent imprisoned in the foundations." If you find Pulver's meaning a little obscure, here's my interpretation: People who live in their heads (too tall upper zone) are often impractical, but those who spend too much time in the lower zone (the foundation) tend to get stuck in material concerns.

Slightly wide lower loops, as in CB writing, reveal a conventional lover who may not spend much energy developing his sex life. He does what is expected of him and no more. This is not the type you would expect to find searching the Internet for Web pages featuring kinky sex.

Long Lower Loops

The longer the loops, the greater the interest in satisfying physical and material desires. The writer of long lower loops prefers to jump right into activities without a lot of planning (especially when she has short upper loops). She reacts on a physical level and enjoys sexual activity. She is motivated by opportunities to acquire money. She doesn't easily let go once she gets fixed on an idea and has a tendency to be dogmatic and opinionated about her beliefs.

Chicken Scratch

Retracing in the lower zone may be a sign of sexual dysfunction. At the very least, the writer may be inhibited to the point of being unable to function satisfactorily.

When the lower loops are more than twice as long as MZH, the writer can't sit still. She is constantly moving, drumming her fingers on the table, tapping her toes, or pacing around the room. She can't relax and hates routine in anything. She uses sex as a tranquilizer, and may have a long list of partners to call on when she's feeling frisky. Sex relieves her anxiety, but only temporarily.

Narrow Lower Loops

Just as in the upper and middle zones, narrowness in the lower zone signifies inhibition. If the lower zone is long (showing an interest in sex and other lower zone activities) but narrow or retraced, it will take some doing to get

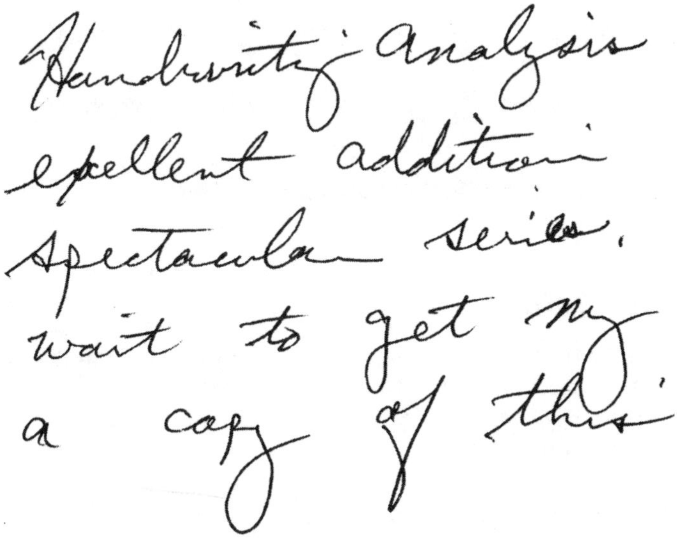

Long lower zone.

the writer to act on her desires. Because she is afraid that she won't be able to perform adequately, she creates a self-fulfilling prophecy.

Risking failure is out of the question, so she's unlikely to experiment with anything new or outside the bounds of convention. If she does allow herself to be persuaded to try something new and it doesn't go well, she'll never try it again.

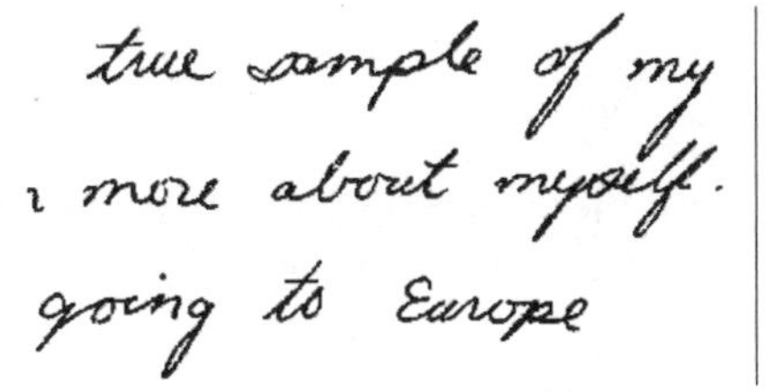

Long, narrow lower zone.

Moderately Wide Lower Loops

Moderately wide loops balanced with moderate length are a sign of a self-confident person who is not afraid to act spontaneously in intimate relationships. He has a strong sex drive and is resourceful and willing enough to branch out and go where he hasn't gone before. Long after the honeymoon is over, the writer of wide lower loops (as long as they aren't *too* wide) will be finding new adventures to try with his lover. He is imaginative, fun-loving, and ready for anything.

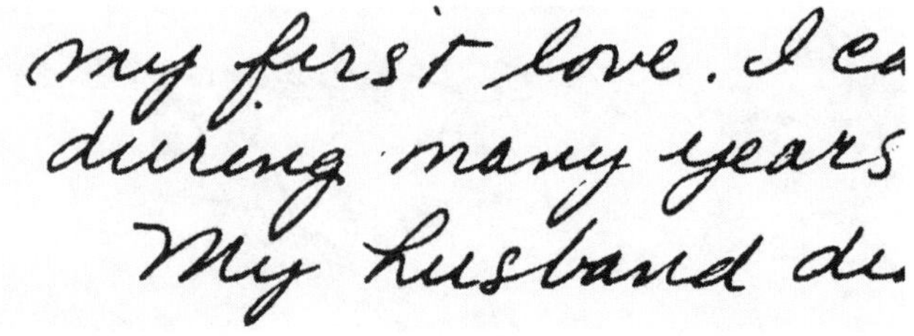

Moderately wide lower zone.

Extremely Wide Lower Loops

As the lower loops swell to more than twice as wide as the MZH there is a danger of fantasy overtaking reality. This writer overreacts to everything, exaggerating and distorting the facts until they are unrecognizable as the truth. He may brag about his sexual prowess, yet be unable to perform.

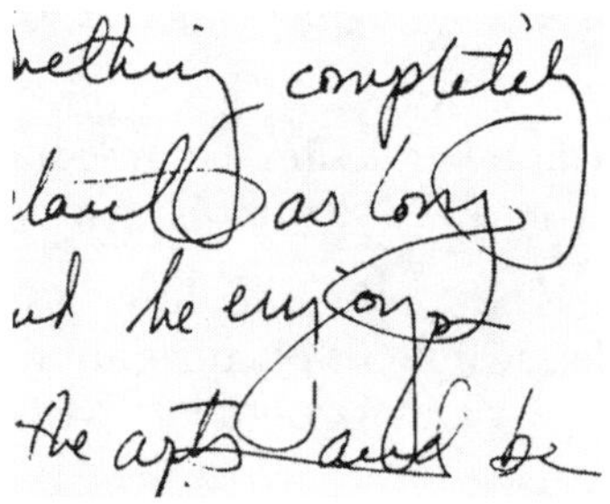

Extremely wide lower zone.

Some Last Remarks

As in all other aspects of handwriting, extremes upset the balance and often are a sign of immaturity. Excessive size or lack of harmony in any zone is a negative indicator and intensifies the possibility of instability.

Never make an analysis based on one sign or one zone, because it is impossible to know a person based on just one aspect of her personality. There are always confirming, verifying factors, and contradictory ones that must be considered in developing an accurate picture of personality.

This really is a sneaky way to lead into the Chapter 11 where I discuss rhythm, as rhythm is all about balance.

The Least You Need to Know

- Writing size tells how much space you feel you deserve.
- Middle-zone height reveals how much your ego needs; width shows how willing you are to get your ego needs met.
- Upper-zone height symbolizes aspirations, principles, and standards; width shows how open-minded you are.
- Lower-zone length and width tells how active and productive you are.

Part 3

Let's Dance: Movement

Here's where we'll move even deeper into handwriting. The basic rhythm, speed, pressure, and other vital aspects are explored in detail. These are some very complex concepts, but once you grasp them you'll be able to analyze any writing in any language.

You'll find it's worth the effort to study this section over and over again, until you feel comfortable with the theories presented here. It may be tempting, but don't just skim through it. You'll miss out on a vital part of your graphological education.

Chapter 11

I've Got Rhythm: Writing Rhythm

In This Chapter

- Going out and coming in—the ebb and flow of rhythm
- Rhythm versus regimentation
- Will you or won't you? Rhythm and will power
- A rhythm all their own

In this chapter we'll explore *rhythm* in handwriting. You'll learn how to recognize the individual rhythms of space, form, and movement; separate the parts; then put them back together into a picture of the writer's movement patterns, her own unique rhythm. This is one of the more complex concepts in graphology, but if you learn to unravel the enigma of rhythm, you will be well along the road to becoming a good handwriting analyst.

So, let's begin at the beginning. I warn you, it may seem heavy going at first. You'll need to read this chapter again and again—or come back to it when you've finished the rest—until you are confident you've mastered it. It's an indispensable part of your graphological education.

Handwriting is movement, as surely as you put one foot in front of the other to walk from here to there. The pen touches down on a sheet of paper and it begins *moving* from the starting point to your goal, the end of the line. Without movement, all that would result is a dot on the paper.

Write Words

Rhythm is movement or variation characterized by regularly recurring elements or activities.

But more than just the hand is involved in writing movement. Writing is controlled by the central nervous system and every part of the brain is bound up in the act. Both physiological and psychological factors affect the movement you produce on paper.

Different Strokes for Different Folks

Movement expresses the writer's basic life force, her own unique temperament. There's a world of difference between a mechanical, dull temperament that functions like a robot, and an intense, vivacious one that treats life as a party. Calm or excitable, stilted or natural, the writer's emotional life is encapsulated in the rhythm of writing.

The inherent rhythm in writing movement reveals, perhaps more than any other factor, how the writer adapts to and functions in the world. Many different types of rhythm exist along a wide spectrum, from extremely irregular, to weak at one end, to disturbed in the middle, to strong at the other end. But before diving into our discussion of rhythm, let's examine the smallest element of writing movement, the stroke.

Handwriting is comprised of two types of stroke: curved and linear. Curved strokes are smooth and continuous. They move in two directions—centrifugal, which moves counterclockwise, (outward and away from the center) and centripetal, which moves clockwise (inward and toward the center). Linear strokes, on the other hand, are straight and sharp. They go in one direction at a time. To change the direction of a straight line, you have to make an abrupt stop and an acute turn. Try drawing a series of curves and straight lines like the ones in the next illustration, and you'll see what I mean. Both curved and straight lines are needed to produce good rhythm. It's the proportion and balance between them that makes the difference, as we'll soon discover.

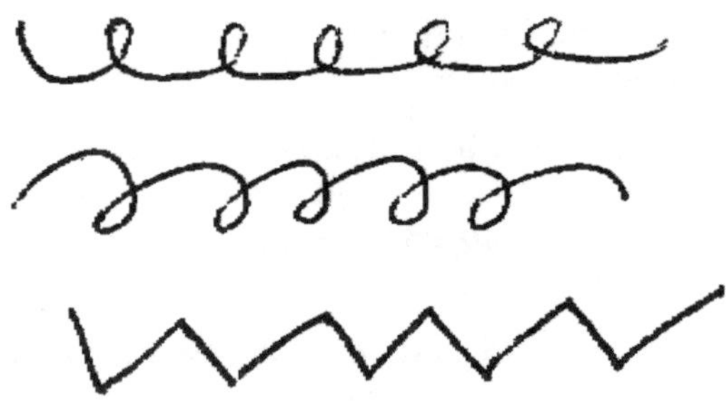

Curves (above and middle) and lines (below).

As they thrust or slink or dance their way onto the paper, the various combinations of strokes fall into a pattern, a portrait of how the writer experiences the world and how she expresses her experiences. A predominance of straight strokes draws one type of picture; a predominance of curved strokes draws another. The writer bends or straightens these shapes to suit her own temperament.

Fine Points

Rhythm is one of the most important and one of the most difficult aspects of handwriting to learn. Think of it as the ebb and flow of energy.

Energy Balancing: Contraction and Expansion

All living organisms have their own natural rhythms. The ebb and flow of energy that comprises rhythm involves two types of movement: one contracts, the other expands. In breathing, for instance, you inhale in a contracting movement; you exhale in an expanding movement. Ebb and flow, in and out, give and take, anticipation and realization, centripetal and centrifugal. You get the picture.

For an example of expansive movement, think of winning the lottery. How would you react? Doesn't it make you want to leap out of your chair just to think of it! You even start breathing a little faster! When you're excited and happy (or excited and angry), you act expansively. Now, to experience regressive energy, think back to a time when you felt really sad about something. Your body contracts, you seem almost to fold up and go inside yourself. It's as if you actually take up less space.

So, energy expands and contracts. It forms a pattern of activity called rhythm or "periodicity." That's a fancy word for "doing the same thing periodically, but not exactly the same way every time." Each breath you take is similar to the others, but not identical. Some breaths are shorter, some are longer; some are ragged, some are smooth, but always, there is an in-and-out motion you can count on.

A handwriting with good rhythm suggests a harmonious personality. The various elements, the physical, emotional, and spiritual, are all working together to produce balance. Writing that is not rhythmic reveals a lack of unity within the personality. Something is out of whack. There is no symmetry and the person's day-to-day functioning is impaired in some way. It's important to remember, however, that good rhythm doesn't necessarily equate to a "good" person or disturbed rhythm to a "bad" one.

Chicken Scratch

Beware of mistaking poor rhythm for a "bad" person. Rhythm simply tells you how well integrated are the various parts of the writer's life. Poor rhythm says that something is out of whack.

Will Power or Won't Power?

Rhythm is affected by one's strength of will. "Will," as defined for our purposes, is the quality of mind that sets activity in motion and also controls it; will provides the impetus to get things done and to call a halt when necessary. It is sometimes called "motive power" or "self-control."

> **Fine Points**
>
> School writing models are mechanical. Well, after all, they were written by a machine! Handwriting that you examine should not look like this, though it sometimes does. As Max Pulver said, "Copybook should never be viewed as an ideal."

A handwriting that shows good will power is rhythmic. Rhythmic writing allows impressions from the outside world to impact the writer. He then assimilates them and expresses them outwardly in a reasonable manner. There is a "periodicity" in his behavior and his writing, a sameness within a particular range, but not so much the same that it looks mechanical or machine-like.

One of the purposes of the will is to regulate natural impulses. Its job is to inhibit some of the basic urges that might be harmful to the organism (As we learned in Chapters 9 and 10, this is the function of the ego and superego when they work together properly).

Good will power (above) and weak will power (below).

The Regularity Continuum

Socrates wrote, "In all of us, even in good men, there is a lawless wild-beast nature, which peers out in sleep." The person who controls every impulse is inhibited, afraid to allow her emotions free reign, ever. She believes, deep in her psyche, that if she fails to keep every urge in check with the strictest controls at all times, she will become completely wild. This is unacceptable to her, so she invests enormous amounts of energy denying the very existence of the beast.

We could talk about the origins in childhood of such rigidly disciplined behavior, and of how strict the writer's parents were. But for this discussion, let's just say that the more regular the handwriting, the greater force the will exerts on the personality. The rigid writer's behavior is stiff and formal, emotionally withholding. The energy returns to the self in a centrifugal, contracting movement, which is reflected in her handwriting.

The movement patterns of a person who maintains extremely strong self-control tend to be highly regular, such as a clock, or a metronome, or your heartbeat. A high degree of regularity in handwritings is not considered good rhythm. Writing that looks as regular as a clock ticking indicates severe psychological problems. The rigid, mechanical sameness represents absolute inflexibility and inability to adapt to the ups and downs of everyday life. Such rigidity is an extreme example of the contracting movement.

On the other hand, there are those whose handwriting is altogether irregular, like a hurricane. The rhythms are wild and uncontrolled, which is just as much a problem as the over-controlled personality. The irregular writer is so impressionable that every input is immediately expressed in action. Such irregularity is an extreme example of the releasing movement.

Chicken Scratch

Will power keeps us from doing things that are harmful, such as using drugs or alcohol excessively or engaging in promiscuous sex. A person with weak will power tends to be self-indulgent and doesn't seem to know when to quit. Too little will is the sign of a person who lets the world act upon her instead of her acting upon the world.

The degree of balance between expansion and contraction is what creates our own particular rhythm. It reveals how receptive we are to outside stimuli, how we assimilate it, and, finally, how we express it outwardly.

Remember, movement comes in and it goes out. Someone who only takes in and doesn't give out has no emotional growth. Someone who only gives out, but doesn't renew and refresh the spirit by taking in from the outside, depletes his energy and has nothing left to give.

Irregularity Breeds Contempt

Now we'll tackle the other end of the regularity spectrum: irregularity. Irregular writing is a sign of powerful emotionalism. If you've ever seen a seismograph (an instrument that measures earthquakes) you'll have an idea of what the irregular writer's emotional life is like. There are magnificently soaring highs and profoundly plunging lows, with little uniformity or order. Some like to call this type of personality "high-strung."

Tales from the Quill

During the O.J. Simpson murder trial, prosecutor Christopher Darden was often criticized for his angry, emotional displays. Even his fellow district attorneys seemed not to know what was going to come out of his mouth from one moment to the next. Darden was portrayed in the press as a loose cannon (remember the "glove" episode, where he insisted Simpson try on the bloody glove, only to find that it apparently didn't fit). Not surprisingly, his handwriting has a highly irregular rhythm, the hallmark of a rash, unpredictable temperament.

The writer is never sure of how she feels, what she wants, even who she is. She is deeply impacted by every external event. Every urge, every need, every desire is seen on her face, heard in her tone of voice, acted out in her body language. There is little or no restraint of emotion.

Such impulsiveness can wreak havoc on the person who experiences it, as well as everyone witnessing the outbreak. Being tossed about so violently by the impressions the world makes on the writer leaves little time or energy for her to develop any depth of feeling. Others experience her as superficial or shallow. A woman of this type is often referred to as an "airhead."

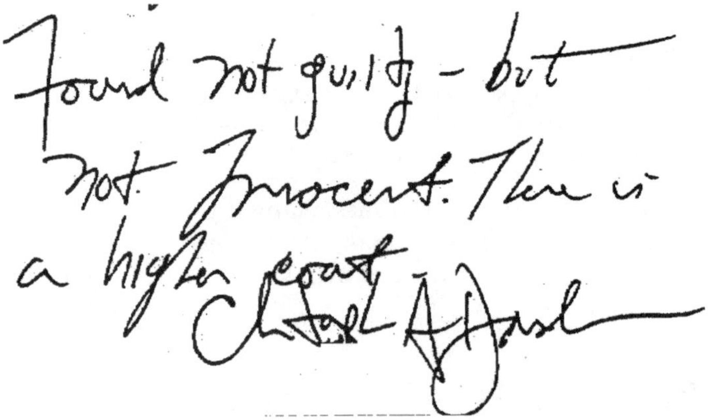

Christopher Darden, a prosecutor in the O.J. Simpson trial. An example of arrhythmic writing.

Irregularity in handwriting is seen in variable size, a wavering baseline, and changing slant. Strong rhythm is lacking, which negatively impacts the writing's aesthetic quality and indicates a temperamental, capricious disposition.

Past, Present, or Future? Left and Right Trend

Carl Jung suggested that we can properly meet the demands of the *outside* world only if we have first developed inner harmony. Writing rhythm reveals how well harmony has been achieved.

Jung spoke at length about the importance to personal growth of progression *and regression*; that is, the flow of psychic energy moves both backward and forward. When energy is regressive it reduces the impact of what is experienced when it is progressive. Here's an example: Someone hits a tennis ball toward you at 70 miles an hour. If you stand still, the ball will hit you with tremendous force. Moving backward allows some of the force to dissipate, so when the ball strikes, some of its impact will be lost. Psychically, too, we have to go backward to go forward. Like backing off the tennis ball, stepping back to look at what went before lessens the impact of going full-bore into new experiences unprepared. It allows us to learn from our successes and our mistakes. In handwriting this back and forth movement is seen as contraction and release.

Fine Points

Early graphologists disagreed with Ludwig Klages (the father of German graphology) on the importance of rhythm as a central organizing principle. He viewed rhythm as the most important of all the features of graphic expression, while Pulver rejected the "exclusive meaning of rhythm as a key sign of interpretation of handwriting."

Trendy in the Right Direction

Any movement to the left (the past) in handwriting is called *"left trend."* Movement to the right (the future) is *"right trend."* It's very simple: Any part of the writing movement—strokes, letters, words, margins, space—that travel in a leftward direction is left trend. Any part of writing movement that travels in a rightward direction is right trend. Both are fundamental to writing. You can't have one without the other, unless all you want is a straight line in the middle of the page.

When the left-tending elements are stronger than the right-tending ones, the writer is seeking refuge in the past. For some reason, he fears the future and does everything he can to avoid going there. It's like a tug of war, with the left side winning. Left-tending elements are:

- Left slant
- Leftward-pulling lower loops
- Narrow spaces between words
- Margins pulling to the left side of the page

- Loops that balloon leftward
- t's crossed to the left; i's dotted to the left
- Long beginning strokes
- Small size
- Linear forms

Write Words

Left trend is movement toward the left side of the page. **Right trend** is movement toward the right side of the page.

Writers with excessive right trend appear to be in a hurry to get to the right side of the paper. In that case, they may be running away from something in the past, or enthusiastically pursuing a future goal. We'd have to look at the whole picture to know which is which. Right trend includes elements similar to left trend, but they move in the opposite direction. Right-tending elements are:

- Right slant
- Wide spaces between words
- Margins pulling to the right side of the page
- Loops pulling to the right
- t's crossed to the right; i's dotted to the right
- Long t bars
- Large size
- Curved forms
- Long ending strokes

Write Words

A **counterstroke** is any stroke that moves counter to proper direction.

Strokes that travel opposite to the direction they properly should, are called *counterstrokes* because they contradict the original intention. In Western writing, we move from left to right. Elements of the writing that migrate to the left when they should have gone right suggest either a rebellious personality or, perhaps, one that seeks comfort in the familiarity of the past. If some elements move to the left when they should be going right or straight; or if they are moving right when they should be going left, as in the following illustration, it infers someone who is either rebelling against authority (the right) or running away from the mother influence of the left.

Counterstrokes.

Rhythm and Blues

Rhythm in handwriting is an indicator of how well the writer controls her impulses. Good rhythm is a sign of healthy impulses and reasonable impulse control. Disruptions in the rhythmic flow of energy suggest some sort of inner physical or mental imbalance that manifests in the writer's inner and outer life.

Although we judge the overall rhythm of writing, the chief aspects, space (the way the handwriting is arranged on the page); form (the chosen style); and movement (the way the writing progresses across the page) have their own rhythms and their own functions. But, to create a harmonious balance, all three must work together.

Movement consists of several elements. These include: the basic stroke, pressure, left-right movement, slant, zonal proportions, beginning and

Fine Points

To recap, when something goes wrong in the elements of Space, Form, and Movement, here's what it signifies: Disturbance in the rhythm of Space = problems with intellect; Disturbance in the rhythm of Form = problems with ego; Disturbance in the rhythm of Movement = problems with the basic energy of the personality.

ending strokes, and degree of connections between letters. If these elements stand out more than any others, the writing has a dominance of movement. Dominance of movement reveals an impulsive, person whose emotions and instincts rule. She goes with her gut reactions, is spontaneous, unconventional, and may not have adequate impulse control.

The elements of space include the overall arrangement of the page, margins, alignment, space between letters, words, and lines.

A dominance of space indicates someone who has over-developed her intellect at the expense of her social life. She relates to the world through her mind and carefully filters every experience through her intellect before acting on it.

Form is the most conscious part of handwriting, which we will consider in Chapter 17. It consists of the writing style, which may be school type, simplified, elaborate, or printed. Writing that has a strong dominance of form reveals someone who is more concerned about appearances than substance. Social standing is usually a very high priority for this type of writer.

In the following tables, we'll use categories of "strong," "weak," and "disturbed" to examine the rhythms of movement, space, and form in graphic expression. If one part of someone's personality is weak or disturbed, generally, another aspect takes over or compensates for it. Someone who suffers a physical loss, such as loss of eyesight, develops her hearing or another sense to make up for the loss. The same thing happens psychologically.

Chicken Scratch

In many cases, a handwriting that looks lazy and sluggish infers those personality traits in the writer. Unless there's a medical reason for the lack of energy in the script, the writer simply hasn't any "oomph." His get-up-and-go got up and went.

For instance, the person with poor social skills may compensate by exercising his intellect to make up for what he's missing socially. The compensation will be reflected in his handwriting through a disturbed rhythm of Form (which relates to the ego). The compensated intellect will have a better developed rhythm of Space (which relates to the intellect). If the compensation took place through physical activity rather than intellect, it would be evident in a stronger rhythm of Movement (which relates to the physical).

By zeroing in on the elements that are weak or disturbed, we can determine which parts of personality are affected. When there are problems in all three elements a serious underlying disturbance that affects the entire personality is at fault.

The following series of tables will help you identify where disturbances appear: in the rhythm of Space, Form, and/or Movement.

Tales from the Quill

Surprising results came from a survey on self-image. The survey included a self-assessment and a handwriting sample. In most cases, respondents whose handwriting was rhythmic and well-balanced stated that they had a poor self-image, while those whose handwritings were less rhythmic felt they had a good self-image. Just goes to show—no one aspect of handwriting should be judged by itself. As important as rhythm is, it must be evaluated as part of the whole picture.

Rhythm of Movement Table

Strong	Weak	Disturbed
Rhythmic	Slack	Curved letters changed to angles
Sharp turning points	Sluggish	Straight strokes
Swinging	Listless	Angular
Curved	Dragging	Jerky
Elastic	Hesitant	Brittle
Fluid	Awkward	Stiff
Firm	Lacks pressure	Uncontrolled
Natural	Passive	Lacks harmony
Dynamic	Lethargic	Choppy strokes
Complex movements	Simple movements	Hesitations
Centrifugal movement	Centripetal movement toward center	Uneven tension
Moderate regularity	Emphasis on inner direction	Irregularity
Without constant fluctuations		Fluctuations in size, slant, pressure, form, connectedness
Right trend		

Rhythm of Space Table

Strong	Weak	Disturbed
Good proportions	Conventional	Awkwardly spaced
Well-arranged margins	Extra wide spaces	Irregular gaps Irregular margins, word spacing
Balanced margins, lines	Poor distribution of space	Overall size too large: writing stands out too much
Words clear and evenly spaced	Drifting margins	Overlapping lines
Good balance of zones	Upper zone emphasis; lower zone emphasis; letters too wide	Zones not balanced
Initial strokes missing	Letters too narrow; emphasis on end strokes	
End strokes missing or Emphasis on initial strokes	Overall size too small; emphasis on white space rather than the writing	Letter spacing too wide or too small

Rhythm of Form Table

Strong	Weak	Disturbed
Lively	School model	Exaggerations
Spontaneous	Conventional	Unnatural forms
Departs from school model	Monotonous	Distortions
Legible shortcuts	Narrow or retraced loops and ovals	Over-embellished
Original	Awkward	Inharmonious
Harmonious	Undeveloped	Highly angular
Some embellishments		Ungraceful
Creative forms		Poorly developed

Do You Wanna Dance?

Various types of rhythms make dance and music fun. The graceful 1-2-3 waltz rhythm is unlike the steady 1-2-3-4 of a military march. The brisk 1-2-1-2-3 of a cha-cha bears little resemblance to the laid-back beat of Reggae, or the mercurial sound of acid rock. Let's have fun with some examples of different types of rhythm in handwriting.

Waltz rhythm.

devotion and secu
older man can offe
I have had rel
with men of my
and it has never

Acid-rock rhythm.

e open to my interests and idea
and who will be as proud and sa
I will be proud and satisfied t
like the outdoors, especially skiing

March rhythm.

Thank you so much for making
time in your schedule to talk
to the Hospital Auxiliary. Everyone
enjoyed your presentation.

Reggae rhythm.

Sense of humor, genero
sion. Passion and "conne
feelings is also importa
ture and Spontaneity as

Extreme, Dude!

Some handwritings have extremes that seem to jump off the page and hit you in the eye. These include:

- Lower loops so long and wide they look like big, sad teardrops on the page
- Upper loops slanting so far to the right that the writing looks like it could fall over in a breeze
- Pressure so heavy it tears through the paper
- Ornaments that wouldn't even look good on a Christmas tree

Tales from the Quill

A young man whose lower zone looked like giant teardrops felt frustrated and angry because his lover had been diagnosed with a serious illness. He didn't want to express his negative feelings and make his partner feel worse, so he stuffed them deep down inside. Reflecting his subconscious, his emotions manifested in his handwriting as a profound, but temporary condition. If the analyst failed to explore what was happening under the extreme lower zone, she would draw a wrong conclusion.

Extremes hint at some form of compensation for a lack in one area or another. The writer prefers to deny what is really going on inside, so tries to cover it up by distracting you with the exaggerations. Until you get the underlying picture in mind, pretend the exaggerations aren't there. It may not be easy, but try to ignore them, because they may draw you away from the truth. The handwriting sample in the next illustration has extremes in several areas: beginning strokes (which we'll cover in Chapter 19), lower-zone width, and punctuation (also in Chapter 19).

Extremes in writing.

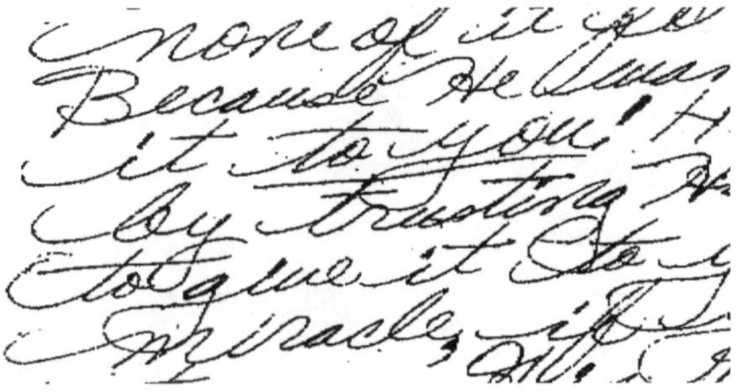

Rhythmic writing, which shows "good enough" balance, has periodicity—a similar, but not identical pattern of movement. Over-control of the will produces highly regular, almost machine-like writing, which is not considered rhythmic. Highly regular writing tends too much toward sameness, which indicates fear of reaching out and experimenting with new experiences, resulting in stunted emotional growth.

"Perfect" balance never can be achieved because people experience continual input that requires adjustments and growth. "Good enough" balance, however, is absolutely attainable.

In Chapter 12 we'll discuss pressure, which is an integral part of movement and rhythm.

The Least You Need to Know

- Writing is movement.
- Movement expands and contracts. As always, look for the degree of balance in how much the writing expands and contracts.
- Movement to the right is natural. Strong movement to the left is contrived.
- There are many different types of rhythms, which symbolize different types of temperaments.
- Extremes or exaggerations are never given a positive interpretation because they impede rhythm.

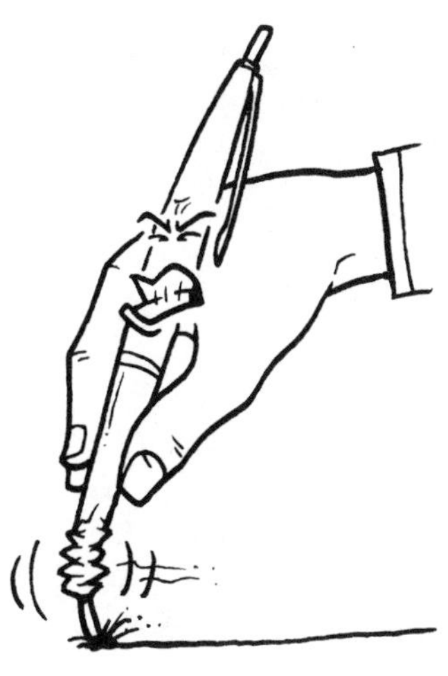

Chapter 12

Contents Under Pressure: Pressure

In This Chapter

- Energy gets things done
- Choose your writing instrument with care
- How intense are you?
- Keeping up with the flow

In this chapter we'll explore writing pressure as the characteristic that most closely expresses the energy of the personality. Like blood pressure, which strongly influences physical energy, writing pressure regulates the flow of ink as it is expelled from the pen. We'll cover which factors affect the stability and quality of the ink flow, and a few other important items.

Whether a task is physical or mental, doing it takes energy. The energy needed for physical tasks comes from the food we eat. Psychic energy, which is used to accomplish the work of the *personality*, comes from emotional experiences. Since the human body is a closed system, what happens on a physical level affects thoughts and feelings, and what happens on an emotional level affects the body. When the flow of energy is smooth and the human system is working harmoniously, things get accomplished. When the flow is disrupted, it impacts the entire organism.

Ready for Action—Tensing and Flexing

Energy produces movement and, for any part of the body to move, it requires muscular tension. Without tension, we'd be as limp as the characters on a boneless chicken ranch (drawn by cartoonist Gary Larson). It keeps the body in a constant state of readiness to act. As we discovered in Chapter 11, the degree of tension and release creates a pattern of activity.

Tales from the Quill

Very sensitive people find it irritating when forced to use a pen that is uncomfortable for them. Using writing instruments they dislike may cause their writing to be unrecognizable. It's not unusual for a handwriting examiner to be called upon to identify a signature that the alleged writer claims was not his. Sometimes the writer fails to recognize his own signature due to an unfamiliar pen.

Too much tension means the body is always on the alert, which eventually results in physical and mental fatigue. Too much release results in flabbiness and inability to react quickly when a response is called for. You know what I'm going to say next. Say it along with me: *A reasonable balance between the two extremes gets the most positive interpretation.*

The physical movement of the hand when writing involves two sets of muscles that allow the hand to tense and flex. Downstrokes use the tensing muscles and upstrokes use the flexing ones. The motion of the downstroke—the tensing, contracting movement—brings the pen back to the self. At that moment the emphasis is on conserving energy and self-preservation. Therefore, if a handwriting demonstrates extra heavy emphasis on downstrokes, the writer is excessively concerned with the most basic of instincts of personal survival, more than other aspects of life.

The motion of the upstroke is the flexing, stretching movement, which takes the pen away from the self, toward others. During that movement the energy is expended on moving outward toward the ideals, and in releasing stress. If the writing emphasis is more on the flexing movement, the writer's focus is on outer concerns, such as altruistic or idealistic efforts, or on developing her spiritual side, more than her basic instinctual needs.

To summarize, tension is created by a need. Release comes from satisfying the need. Bottom line: the strength of the writer's needs and desires, whatever they are, are expressed in her output of energy. They will affect her writing pressure and the tension/release pattern.

External Influences

Several factors influence writing pressure. They include the type of writing instrument, pen hold, choice of paper, and writing surface.

Writing Instrument

Choice of writing instrument can make a tremendous difference to the writing trail it produces, yet some handwriting analysts insist on analyzing only samples written with ballpoint pen—I'm not sure why. If forced to use an instrument he doesn't like, the writer with a strong preference for a particular type of pen may not produce his normal style, which may skew the analysis. Let the client use the pen he likes best.

Pen Hold

The way you hold the pen influences the width of the stroke it creates. Here's an experiment for you to try: Hold your pen near the tip (called a *short hold*). You'll find the pen wants to stand almost upright, and the ink line it produces is thin and sharp, with a very precise stroke. Now, grasp the pen further back on the barrel (a *long hold*), about $1^1/_2$ inches from the tip. When you write, the ink flows more readily and spreads out in a thicker line. We'll talk about what these two types of line, or *ductus,* signify a little further on. By the way, ductus means "writing stroke" and refers to the quality of the line of ink that flows from of your pen.

Rock, Scissors, Paper

If the writing paper is thick and porous, the ink soaks into it like blotting paper and the ductus looks fuzzy or blurred under magnification. Very smooth or glossy paper leaves the ink sitting on its surface and may not give a true impression of pressure. The commonly used 20-pound bond seems to be the best type of paper for accurately estimating pen pressure.

Write Words

Holding the pen near its tip is called a **short hold.** When the pen is held further back on the barrel, it's called a **long hold. Ductus** refers to the quality of the pen stroke produced by the flow of ink.

Writing Surface

Where you choose to write is another factor that affects handwriting. Here's another experiment: Place your paper on a hard wooden surface, write something, then check the pressure. Next, put a soft pad underneath the paper and see what a difference it makes to the pressure. A hard writing surface doesn't allow as much play on the paper, so the pressure doesn't make as much of an impression. A softer surface allows too much play and makes the pressure appear much heavier than it really is.

Chicken Scratch

A handwriting sample that looks very shaky may have been written on a rough surface. When you see something that looks out of the ordinary, don't analyze it until you get further information.

A Gripping Tale

There are three types of pressure in handwriting. The first is grip pressure and refers to how tightly you hold the pen. That's part of our earlier discussion about tension and release. Do you cling to your pen like a limpet, leaving a nasty dent in your finger? If you often get writer's cramp, your grip pressure is probably too strong.

The second type is called primary pressure. This expresses how heavy-handed you are as you press the pen into the paper. Primary pressure shows how much you assert yourself in the world.

The third type is secondary pressure, which shows the rhythm of tension and release. Remember: upstrokes should be lighter than downstrokes because the upstrokes release the tension. Sometimes it's easier to detect the secondary pressure pattern on a photocopy. The next figure illustrates the different types of pressure.

Types of pressure.

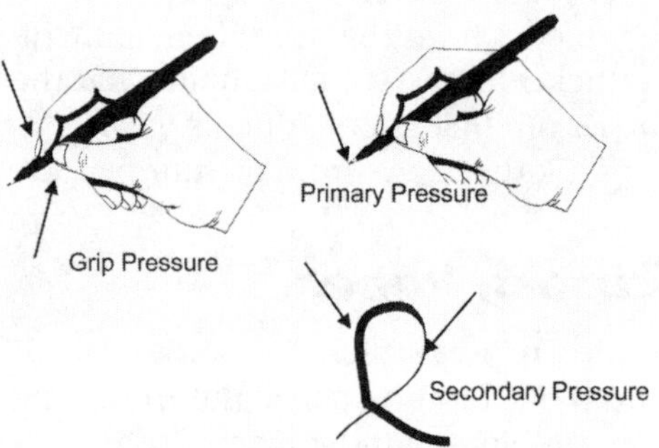

Internal Influences

In addition to all the external influences on pressure, health, and mood can have an effect. When you're feeling ill the pressure may get lighter because you just don't have the energy to invest in the writing movement. The same is true of someone who is depressed. She just doesn't feel like making the effort. On the other hand, the angry person tends to write heavier, digging into the paper.

Pussycat or Storm Trooper?

Graphologists view pressure as the third dimension of handwriting. The writing zones carry movement across, as well as up and down on the paper. That's the first and second dimension. Pressure moves *into* the paper and has been labeled the depth component. It reflects, in a very literal way, the impression the writer makes on the world.

The timid, shy person tiptoes onto the paper in his house slippers without making even a dent. The medium-pressure writer has healthy self-confidence and isn't afraid to make her presence known. The angry, frustrated guy or gal who rages at life storms onto the page in combat boots, leaving deep gouges in her wake, perhaps even ripping holes through the paper.

Fine Points

The dimensions of handwriting include: 1) movement across the paper from left to right; 2) movement up and down as the writing goes across the page; 3) movement above the paper; and 4) movement into the paper.

What Does It Weigh?

Pressure in handwriting is not an indication of physical strength. A 98-pound grandma may have much stronger writing pressure than a 300-pound fullback. The degree that the writer presses into the paper depends on the amount of psychic energy expended.

Klara Roman invented the Graphodyne, a machine for measuring pressure. It seems to have disappeared from use after her death and, apparently no one has replaced it. As a substitute for the Graphodyne, some graphologists found it helpful to use six sheets of paper with carbon paper in between. If the message reached the bottom layer, the pressure was considered very heavy. These days carbon paper isn't used as frequently, but it's a method you might want to try.

Don't worry about measuring pressure exactly. Light, medium, or heavy is close enough. How can you tell how heavy the pressure is? Easy! Turn the paper over and feel the back. Can you feel the words pressing into the paper? Or, is the back totally smooth, the pen having made no impression at all? If you can't feel anything, the pressure is light. If you can barely feel it through the paper, the pressure is medium. If the paper is heavily scored, and you can feel the writing almost as if it were braille, the pressure is heavy.

A Word About Copies

A photocopy or facsimile doesn't let you detect pressure, which is a very important component of handwriting analysis. This doesn't mean you can't analyze faxed or copied handwritings, but you'll need some experience under your belt before knowing how to gauge the writing depth of a photocopy or facsimile of a handwriting.

The truth is, sometimes a photocopy offers a better idea of the *pressure pattern* (though not the depth) than the original. Set the copier on a "lighter" mode and often, the light/dark pattern of secondary pressure will stand out.

Chicken Scratch

In Europe, analyzing a faxed or photocopied handwriting sample is a violation of the graphologists' code of ethics. Organizations in the United States, however, take a more relaxed view.

Breaking the Surface: Medium Pressure

"Medium" is the most common pressure, so we'll start there. Medium-pressured writing will be moderately dark, and you may feel a slight indentation on the reverse of the paper. In terms of need for physical contact, the writer is moderate and conventional.

Because pressure is an expression of one's vitality, a good pressure pattern suggests someone with adequate will power, stamina, and a moderate sex drive. If other characteristics support it, the writer is reliable and dependable, with sufficient backbone to help him get through difficulties.

Running on Empty: Light Pressure

The pen dragging on the paper produces friction, which the moderately light-pressure writer prefers to avoid. It may be that she's had to face a lot of conflict in the past, and can't stand the thought of dealing with any more. Consequently, she avoids obstacles whenever possible and takes the path of least resistance every chance she gets. She would rather switch than fight.

More spiritual than physical, the light-pressure writer's sexual energies are sublimated into the mental realm. He probably doesn't expend a lot of energy on sex or other activities requiring a lot of vitality and stamina. It's not that he doesn't work hard. In fact, he may work very hard, but in bursts of energy that leave him absolutely exhausted by the end of the day.

The light pressure writer is usually very sensitive, sometimes (if the writing is also irregular) to the point of being temperamental. He can't afford to let things touch him too deeply, so his emotions tend to stay on the surface. An emotional event may flatten him momentarily, but then he'll let it go and move on.

Fine Points

Strong pressure doesn't necessarily mean heavy pressure. It means a rhythmic pattern of light/dark strokes, indicating balanced tension and release.

Blowing in the Wind: Extremely Light Pressure

Extremely light pressure has an almost ghostly quality. The writing lacks substance and barely glides over the page, leaving almost no mark. Depression is often a factor, because the writer feels overwhelmed by the stress of life. For her, friction of any kind is like rubbing a towel over sunburn—unbearable! It may help to find out why her will to make an impact is so weak. Remember, sometimes we have to ask for additional information. Handwriting is not like a crystal ball that "tells all."

The extremely light writer is highly suggestible and doesn't have the inner strength to stand against someone with stronger will power. Because she has little interest or drive for experiencing life in all its fullness, she compensates by living in her mind. Anything that suggests power and vitality disturbs her sense of equilibrium, so she may choose a quiet environment with light colors and unseasoned foods.

Pressure Fades Away

Downstrokes that start out strong but fade away before the releasing upstroke suggest someone whose energy peters out before the effort is complete. If the pressure returns just before the end of the upstroke, a short rest may be all he needs to revitalize and complete what he started.

Mount St. Helens: Slightly Heavy and Extremely Heavy Pressure

Moderately heavy pressure can be easily felt on the reverse side of the paper. It signifies someone who sees the writing surface as a force to be overcome, and she believes she has the will to overcome anything. The heavy-pressure writer with a good contraction/release pattern is a hard worker who gets things done. When other people get tired and quit, she keeps on going. Her stamina takes her through a long day and she's still got the energy to party at night. She's usually a sensual, hearty lover with a strong sex drive. Activities that call for bodily contact and physical strength attract her. She enjoys pitting herself against difficulty and, especially with strong downstrokes, is determined to beat the odds. She's not afraid to demand what she wants.

Tales from the Quill

Jennifer, a 26-year-old "California girl," works nine hours a day in a busy county office as a secretary and goes to medical school three nights a week. On weekends and free evenings, she's out night-clubbing with her friends or spending time with her boyfriend. Her two cats have almost forgotten what she looks like! Jennifer's stamina is evident in the moderately heavy pressure of her handwriting.

This is a practical, down to earth person whose primary objective is to ensure that she'll get her basic needs satisfied. The moderately heavy pressure writer is the type who enjoys spicy foods, fine wine, bright colors, and rough textures.

Extremely heavy pressure is a primary sign of frustration and anger. The increased tension on the pen results in deep scoring of the paper. If pressure symbolizes the degree to which the writer wants either to embrace or to pummel the world at large, extremely heavy pressure suggests hostility and aggression. He's stubborn and inflexible, and you can expect to see a very nasty temper, especially when the heavy pressure combines with a strong right slant, slashing i-dots and heavy t-crosses.

This writer has a ferocious drive for sensual gratification, but has no finesse and may be brutish in satisfying his needs. For him, everything is brought down to its basest level. The image of a "bull in a china shop" comes to mind. When he's happy, he shouts. When he wants something, he shouts. If you disagree with him, he shouts. If he is unhappy, he shouts.

If there is a positive side to the extremely heavy pressure, it is that he isn't afraid of doing the dirty work. When something unpleasant needs handling, this person will do it.

Sudden Bursts of Pressure

When you see a sudden burst of pressure, check the word. It may be emotionally charged. Otherwise, the sudden pressure signifies a flare-up of suppressed emotion that has been smoldering for some time. If the pressure subsides right away, it simply symbolizes a burst of irritation that quickly passes.

When the sudden burst is on the horizontal axis (left-right), especially on an end-stroke, the writer is forcing his will on the world. He must have the last word. If the extra pressure is in the lower zone, he probably is not even aware of this tendency to be domineering. Certainly, he won't admit to it! This is a difficult element to illustrate without showing you an original sample, but the next figure gives you an idea of what bursts of pressure look like.

Bursts of pressure.

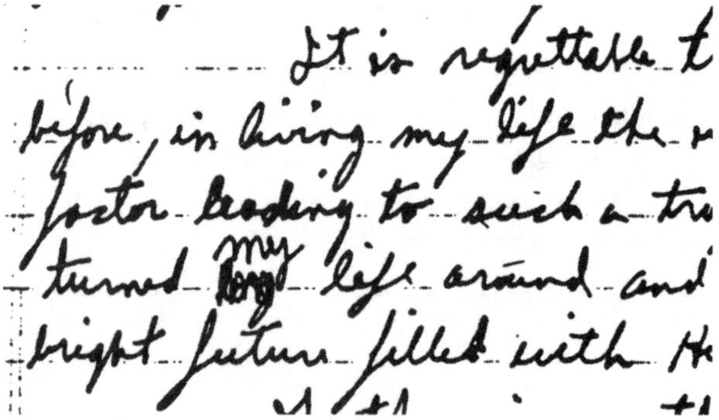

Life's Hard Enough—Displaced Pressure

To stay balanced, it's just as important to take time out to play as it is to work. Without regular times to relax and let go of the tension that builds up from day-to-day events, the body eventually rebels. Tension without release can lead to stroke, heart attack, and other unpleasant health problems.

Some people find it extremely difficult to relax and do nothing. They keep on pushing and don't know when to quit. Sometimes the tension is displaced, or channeled into an area where it doesn't belong. In handwriting, this results in a phenomenon called *displaced pressure.*

Pressure Displaced on the Horizontal

Pressure that is displaced onto the horizontal axis (as in t crosses), rather than in the vertical (up/down) axis of handwriting, is a sign of domination and force of will. Instead of directing the energy where it properly belongs, into the unconscious instincts of the lower zone, it gets hijacked. Extra strong, long t crosses are symbolic of aggressive will power. The person whose pressure goes horizontal rules others with an iron fist. Oh, it may be camouflaged in a pretty velvet glove, but there is no doubt about who has the say-so.

Write Words

Instead of the upstrokes being lighter than the downstrokes, in **displaced pressure** the pattern is either reversed or emphasized on the left-right movement instead.

When the horizontal pressure appears in underlining, it is a matter of emphasis. The writer is trying to exert her authority like an instructor who thinks you don't understand her. If the horizontal stroke is a long final stroke at the baseline and not for the purpose of underlining, it suggests holding off and distrusting others.

Pressure Displaced onto Upstrokes

Very little has been written about displaced pressure. It usually is not discussed in a positive light, yet, it can be a sign of successful adaptation. Klara Roman often found it in the handwritings of successful women who, for whatever reason, had sublimated much of their sex drive into their work.

The reversal of pressure means that when the writer should be releasing energy (light upstrokes) she is actually contracting (pressure on the upstrokes). She is, in effect, swimming against the tide of libidinal energy, making things much harder than need be. By forcing her will against the environment, she doesn't allow things to flow naturally.

On the surface, she may appear quite calm, but the lack of inner balance causes frustration. The pressure moves away from the middle zone (ego activities) where it belongs, and into the upper zone, displacing energy into an area where it doesn't belong. In other words, the writer is thinking when she should be feeling and feeling when she should be thinking.

When pressure is displaced in the lower zone (light downstrokes, heavy upstrokes, as seen in the next illustration), sexual energy is displaced into the middle zone area of daily life. This doesn't mean writer isn't interested in sex. Quite the opposite might be true in fact, but there is no appropriate outlet for the sexual energy. The expenditure of energy into the middle zone is a compensation for it. According to Roman, "if the displacement is carried out without loss of force or rhythm, the compensation is successful."

Chicken Scratch

When the pressure is displaced onto the horizontal, as in very heavy t-bars, look for other signs of con-trolling behavior, such as extra-heavy pressure and a crowded spatial arrangement.

Manipulative behavior is a natural by-product of reversed pressure. The writer is determined to get done what she wants, by hook or by crook. If she can't get it by being nice, she'll force the issue. Insecurity generally is at the root. The writer's instinctual needs aren't being directly satisfied, so she exerts her will in some other area to make up for it.

Displaced pressure.

Fine Points

Directional pressure can come from any direction. If the "caving in" is on the tops of strokes, there is pressure from authority figures; on the left, there is pressure from the past; on the bottoms of strokes, pressure comes from the instincts; and on the right, the pressure comes from the future.

A Word About Directional Pressure

When graphologist Felix Klein was imprisoned in the concentration camps at Buchenwald and Dachau during World War II, he discovered an interesting phenomenon in the handwritings of some prisoners. Those who survived had something in common: The strokes on the right sides of letters that were supposed to be straight were bent, or caved in. This seemed to indicate stress coming from the direction of the future. Makes sense—they didn't know if they would be alive from one moment to the next. Those whose handwritings were more rigid were killed more often, because they didn't have the capacity to adapt or bend to life in the camps. (Directional pressure doesn't refer to the depth component, but it is a sort of pressure nonetheless.)

Directional pressure. Bent strokes that should have been straight.

Your Erogenous Zones

There is a difference, I'm told, between sensuousness and sensuality. Sensuousness has to do with gratifying the five physical senses: sight, sound, touch, taste, smell. Sensuality, on the other hand, is what results when indulgence in sensuous pleasures goes to its extreme. At least, that's the definition we'll use here. Sensuousness is seen in a phenomenon known as pastosity.

Pastosity and Clam Sauce

Pastosity. What kind of word is that? A made-up one, actually, and its creation is credited to that prodigious early modern graphologist, Klara Roman. Dr. Roman used the word pastosity to describe the broad flow of ink that today we see produced by felt-tip pens. It comes from the word "pasta," and intends to represent a soft, doughy quality.

As you can see in the next illustration, the stroke is wide, both on upstrokes and downstrokes, but there is no real pressure. The stroke looks as if it were painted on with a brush. The lack of release that comes from heavy pressure on both up- and downstrokes is not present in this case because the pastose stroke is a released movement in itself. Lots of ink is discharged onto the paper.

Pastose writing is produced by people who are physically oriented and very much in tune with their senses. What they can touch, taste, smell, see, and hear are the things that turn them on. The scent of a rose or the sound of the birds singing early in the morning might drive a pastose writer wild. Warm and earthy, he enjoys sex for its tactile sensations.

Write Words

Pastosity derives from the word "pasta" (which is doughy or soft) and refers to the quality of certain handwritings. Some graphologists call it "pastiosity."

For the pastose writer, it is important that the sensuous experience be natural. Don't try to palm some knock-off perfume or fast food on this type of writer. He wants the real thing.

Because the pastose stroke is produced without heavy pressure (it's made by a long hold on the pen), it suggests that the writer wants to enjoy his creature comforts but not expend a lot of energy to get them. If the "good things" come to him easily, fine. If not, that's okay, too. But he'd much rather sit in the lap of luxury than on the cold dirt floor.

Unlike sharp writers, who we'll consider later, pastose writers are not judgmental. There are many shades of gray between black and white, and the pastose writer usually is somewhere in between. On the negative side, this individual lives mostly by his senses, expending far less energy developing his philosophical or spiritual side of life.

Pastose writing. (thick strokes)

Mud Wrestling

Muddy handwriting, related to blocked pressure, is at the extreme end of pastosity. Writing is muddy when it looks smeared and smudged, the oval letters are flooded with ink, pressure suddenly billows, and/or there are numerous heavy cross-outs. Compare the muddy writing in the next illustration to the pastose writing in the previous one. You can probably see the difference in the quality of the stroke. The muddy stroke is heavy and flooded with ink.

Muddiness comes from eroticism gone wild. That's different from a healthy sexual appetite. Muddiness is found in handwritings of some people whose sexuality may be linked to all sorts of unconventional practices frowned on by society. It suggests unbridled excesses and unbalanced discharge of energy. The flood of ink depicts a flood of impulses that the writer makes little or no effort to curb. Guilt and anxiety are often a big part of the picture.

Muddy writing.

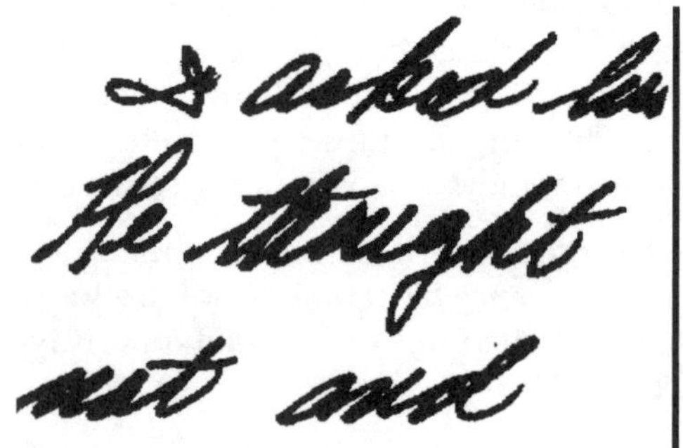

Blocked Pressure

When the pressure is unrelieved, both the upstrokes and downstrokes are heavy. This is not the same quality as pastosity, which is created *without* noticeable pressure. Blocked pressure looks unhealthy. In fact, it may be time for the writer to go for a physical checkup. Circulatory problems, alcoholism, menopause, or heart disease may be possible contributing factors.

If the cause is not strictly physical, we can deduce that the writer feels stuck in a rut. What happens if you drive your car into a sandbank? You can't go forward and you can't go backward. You just sit there, spinning your wheels. And that's what life feels like for the writer of blocked pressure.

Signs of blocked pressure are muddiness, combined with:

- Slow speed
- Lack of dynamic movement
- Inhibition seen in narrowness and left trend

Chicken Scratch

Klara Roman describes areas on the writing that have been colored in, as a "black spot" in the life of the writer. She said the writer is preoccupied with a secret that is choking the inner person. The patch of ink serves to cover up something the writer doesn't want the world to know.

Oh, What a Relief It Is: Shading

Shaded writing looks like the sculpted bas-relief of an ancient temple. It is also called "writing in relief" or "shading" If you are unsure of what I mean, look in a book on ancient Greece or Rome, or Medieval Europe. The stone carvings on the temples and castles seem to stand out from the walls ("in relief"). Certain pens produce this effect, such as a fountain pen or calligraphy-type pen, sometimes with a chisel tip. They produce an artistic, though not a particularly spontaneous script. The shaded writing in the next illustration provides a perfect example.

Aesthetics—the way things look—are of paramount importance to the writer of shaded writing. She is cultured and refined, socially polished; someone who demands excellence in her presentation.

As of today, this is Jenny's new home!

Shaded writing.

Sharp As a Tack

Sharpness in handwriting can best be identified under magnification. A sharp stroke is thin with clean, clear edges. The illustration of "Dr. Laura's" handwriting shows a razor-sharp edge.

The aesthetic person enjoys the crispness of this type of stroke, and usually has a critical nature. The sharp writer enjoys an argument but don't expect him to bend even a millimeter. His aggressive, dogmatic way of dealing with people may push others away. A very sharp stroke, combined with a tall upper zone, is sometimes seen in the type of person with a "do as I say, not as I do" attitude.

For the sharp writer everything is either black or white with no gray area in between. When combined with angles, there is a certain coldness of personality and absolute refusal to adapt. He likes others to see him as moral and righteous. However, the kindness and compassion that go with morality and righteousness appear to be lacking.

Tales From The Quill

Radio talk show host, Laura Schlessinger, well-known for her acidic tongue, writes with a very sharply-honed stroke. Emphatic and intolerant of those who disagree, she exhorts callers to stay in unhappy marriages, to always tell the truth, and never bend their principles. She recently published a book about the Ten Commandments. Yet, her own past behavior came under fire in Vanity Fair magazine in 1998.

The pen is WONDERFUL –
I am crazy about it – and am
touched by your thoughtfulness.
Warmly,
Laura Schlessinger

Dr. Laura Schlessinger, talk-show host, a sharp-stroke writer.

The Least You Need to Know

- Handwriting is movement in the fourth dimension.
- Pressure reflects "psychic energy," not physical strength.
- Pressure in handwriting symbolizes the energy available for the work of the personality.
- Extremely heavy pressure is a sign of frustration.
- Extremely light pressure is a sign of depression.
- Moderate pressure suggests physical health.

Chapter 13

Faster Than a Speeding Bullet: Speed

In This Chapter

- What the heck is graphic maturity?
- Putting on the brakes
- Signs of speed and slowness
- Speed and personality
- Speed and legibility

It's easy to gauge speed when driving your car. The flashing red lights behind you on the highway tell you it was more than 65 mph. Drive too slowly and the honking horns will let you know. Measuring speed on paper is more of a challenge, especially when you weren't present to watch the writer's pen progress across the page.

Speed is a very important, though oft-neglected, factor to consider when analyzing handwriting. It relates to intelligence, spontaneity of thought, and dynamic action. Movement goes in two directions: forward and backward, but it should end on a forward thrust. In the forward movement we see how the writer approaches the world: enthusiastically, spontaneously; or hastily rushing forward, never quite having enough time to get everything done. When forward movement is inhibited, or there is too much movement to the left (backward), it signifies either caution and forethought or lack of ability and know-how.

The Age of Innocence

Many factors influence writing speed, both internally and externally. The most powerful of those is graphic maturity, an internal factor. *Graphic maturity* is a term that was coined by Robert Saudek in the early 1920s. He helped lay the scientific foundation for handwriting analysis.

Write Words

Graphic maturity is the ability to write fluidly without having to consciously think about the act of writing.

Saudek published several books on handwriting, including *Experiments with Handwriting* (George Allen & Unwin, 1922, reprinted by Books for Professionals, 1978). *Experiments* details his research on speed and is still considered the most important work on the subject. If you aren't up on the vernacular of the 1920s, it's a tough book to get through, so unless you have a very strong interest in the physiological aspects of handwriting or are a masochist and want to wade through it yourself, I'll summarize some of the basic tenets for you.

Before learning how to write a word, you first must learn how to form single letters. Graphic maturity is the point at which you can write fluently without having to stop and think how to form the letters and the words. There are several checkpoints that must be reached before we can say that a writer has reached graphic maturity. The steps to graphic maturity are:

- The writer has learned how to control the writing instrument and feels comfortable with it.
- There is no physical impairment that would affect the writer's ability to write.
- The writer has become familiar enough with how to form an individual letter that when she hears the name of the letter, a mental picture of it appears in her head.

Fine Points

When an adult writing looks awkward and undeveloped, ask the writer whether a physiological problem, such as a wrist or shoulder injury, or even writer's cramp, is at fault.

Once these first three checkpoints have been reached, another condition is added that contributes to the writer's ability to write whole words smoothly: She knows how to spell the words she wants to write, and when the words are said, she is able to form a mental picture of them.

Before an entire sentence can be written automatically (that is, without thinking about each word before writing it), one more condition must be met: The writer focuses on what she wants to write about to the degree that she isn't paying attention to the details related to the act of writing itself. She ignores or overlooks problems that may be directly related to the writing such as:

- Poor legibility (sometimes caused by a faulty writing instrument)
- Concern about how attractive the writing looks
- Uncertainty about the spacing or other part of the writing pattern that makes the writer pay closer attention to the act of writing than the content. (Hesitancy of any kind impacts the flow of writing.)

The next checkpoint in the development of graphic maturity is familiarity with the language. The writer is considered familiar with the language if:

- The writer is comfortable with the language.
- There is a change of language mid-text and it doesn't disrupt the continuity.
- The writer is just as comfortable with the written word as with the spoken word.

Parlez Vous Handwriting?

Even after reaching graphic maturity, some circumstances impact the ability to write without hesitating. Something in the text itself—a word or a thought that arouses painful memories—can cause the writer to falter or pause momentarily. Or, he may reach a word he is unsure of and is forced to stop and sound it out in his mind.

People write differently depending on the purpose of the writing. Content makes a difference, too. If you're writing a check to the IRS you might go slower because you don't want to do it. Or, if you're writing an enthusiastic account of your vacation in Hawaii in a letter to your friend, the writing may be faster than your normal pace. Mood also has an effect on speed. Angry or excited writing is faster than sad or tired writing.

A smooth, fluid writing movement shows that the writer is comfortable with the act of writing, that it comes naturally. What contributes to fluidity, and what detracts from it? That's where we'll head next.

Chicken Scratch

If a handwriting shows many stops and starts, ask the writer questions about the writing instrument. Your analysis may be dead wrong if you assume personality characteristics that are actually the result of a sticky pen or some other external factor.

Speed Bumps

Speed in handwriting depends on many details and circumstances. Let's consider them one at a time.

- *Direction of movement.* Fast writing moves to the right. How far would you get if you applied the brakes every few feet? Any interruption to the writing movement is like stepping on the brakes.

- *Shapes of letters.* Rounded movement is faster than angular movement (we'll cover this in more detail in Chapter 15). Angles require abrupt stops—that's like *slamming* on the brakes.
- *Size of letters.* Larger and smaller writing takes longer to make than medium sized writing. Any exaggerations take longer and slow down the writing.
- *Extra strokes.* Strokes that are unnecessarily retained or added take longer to make and slow down the writing.
- *Pressure.* Heavy pressure takes longer than medium or light pressure. Using our car analogy, when you step on the brakes it produces friction between the tires and the road, and that's what slows the car to a stop. As we discussed in Chapter 12, heavy pressure on the paper creates slowing friction.
- *Quality of pen and paper.* A pen that has ink clogging the tip impacts speed. Being forced to constantly stop and shake the pen to get the ink flowing slows down the writing. Writing on ragged or poor-quality paper also slows things down by creating pen drag.
- *Physical disability.* A disability may influence writing speed. Someone suffering from Parkinson's disease or another illness that affects muscle control may write slowly out of necessity. Such a person may also produce a writing so distorted that undertaking an analysis becomes risky. Slow speed due to physical illness is illustrated in the next example.

Fine Points

Someone who is angry or upset may write at a faster pace than when he is feeling calm and composed. Avoid analyzing handwriting that has been done under less than optimal conditions, unless there is a specific reason for doing so, such as when making a determination that the writing was done under stress. Of course, this is something only an advanced graphologist might do.

- *Mental illness.* A problem such as chronic depression may slow down the writing. Other types of mental illness, such as the manic phase of bipolar disorder speed it up.
- *Drugs.* Drugs, including prescribed, over-the-counter, or "recreational" and medications, may alter writing speed for obvious reasons.
- *Unfamiliarity with the language.* If the person is trying to write in an unfamiliar language, her speed will be affected.
- *Self-consciousness about the appearance of writing.* Fear that the writing isn't as beautiful as the writer would like may cause a person to write slower. The writer pays more attention to *how* rather than *what* she writes.
- *Dislike of writing.* The handwriting of someone who hates to write may not be well-developed, which will slow it down. Or, he may be in a hurry to get the act of writing over with, which will speed it up.

- *Hurried writing.* A hasty note dashed off to someone as you're going out the door isn't fair for analysis.

Slow speed due to illness.

Setting the Pace

The *pace* or speed at which we write is affected by how we respond emotionally. The well-balanced person who expresses her emotions appropriately writes at a steady tempo. Someone who is tense and anxious makes many starts and stops.

Each individual has his or her own natural tempo. Some people are slow in everything they do, from getting up in the morning to getting around to making breakfast. The day moves at a tortoise pace. They're even slow about going to bed. Others have energy to burn and never sit still. The day flies by in a whirlwind of activity without a second to spare between tasks.

Environmental factors, such as the telephone ringing or someone walking into the room while the writer is in the act of putting her thoughts on paper, temporarily effect speed. If you have to stop to answer the phone or speak to the person who pokes his head around the door, the disruption will appear as a hesitation in the writing speed. Physical illness or emotional crises may precipitate permanent changes in writing speed.

Write Words

Pace refers to the rate the pen travels across the page—a very personal detail of handwriting, which develops with graphic maturity.

Speed and Speech

Speed in handwriting mimics the writer's personal pace in her day-to-day activities, and even reflects the way she speaks. Those who speak fast tend to write fast as well. When you're in conversation with someone who zooms along so fast you can hardly understand her, ask for some handwriting. Chances are you won't be able to read it because she thinks faster than she speaks or writes, which results in poor legibility.

The slower speaker is more deliberate in her writing as she is in her speech. Someone who is unsure of herself and feels nervous communicating tends to speak and write hesitantly, starting and stopping numerous times before being able to express what is on her mind. There are those who speak in short, rapid staccato bursts. They write that way, too, like machine-gun fire.

Reading the Handwriting Speedometer

Saudek's experiments reduced writing to milliseconds in order to measure the time it took to write. We won't go into that kind of minute detail. In the following table is a summary of many indicators representing speed and slowness in handwriting.

Indicators for Fast and Slow Writing

Speed	Slowness
t crossed to right of the stem	t crossed to left of the stem
Long t bars	Short t bars
Loops balloon slightly to the right	Loops pull to the left
Increased right slant	Left-slanted loops
Left margin gets wider	Upright loops
Right margins gets narrower	Left margin gets narrower
No sudden stops or changes of direction	Right margin gets wider
Moderately connected	Very even margins
Light-medium pressure	Frequent change of direction
Clear ovals	Many breaks within words
Sharp strokes	Heavy pressure
Few covering strokes	Ink-filled ovals
Accents and i dots look like dashes	Retouching or soldering
Fluent, smooth writing	Many covering strokes
Medium size	Accents and i dots round, careful
Garlands, thread, mixed forms	Strong consistency
Illegibility	Large or small size
Words taper off	Angular forms
Simplifications	Slow arcade forms
Neglect of detail	Supported forms
Expansion	School-type writing
Short or missing initial strokes	Elaboration
End strokes to the right	Attention to detail
Slightly rising baseline	Narrowness
Loops moderate in width and length	Long end strokes

Speed	Slowness
Final strokes decrease in size	Blunt end strokes
	Rolled-in strokes
	End strokes turned leftward
	Final strokes increase in size

To determine the speed of the handwriting you are analyzing, add the number of indicators in each column. In most cases there will be some items from each side. Whether the writing is slow or fast depends on which side is more heavily weighted.

Rarely will a writing sample be comprised of either all fast or all slow elements. Some signs of slowness almost always appear in a fast script and some signs of speed almost always appear in a slower script. It is helpful to check the areas where the speed was arrested to find out what caused the slowness and vice versa.

Saudek's rule was that a writing sample with at least two more indicators for speed than slowness is a writing that is primarily fast but has been slowed down. Conversely, if a sample has at least two more indicators for slowness than speed, it is primarily slow but has been speeded up. The question is, what caused the variation from the writer's normal tempo? We may not always know the answer. Some internal or external condition may have influenced the speed. Maybe the writer had a cold and stopped to blow his nose; or he saw something on the news that got him excited. Sometimes it has to be enough just to take note of the difference.

Slow As Molasses

Just how slow *is* molasses, anyway? Can you picture a stream of sticky syrup meandering down the side of the jar, taking its time and enjoying the scenery along the way? That's the way the slow writer approaches life.

Assuming no mental or physical causes, slowness in writing indicates a reduction of emotional spontaneity. The moderately slow writer generally uses school-model forms, which are more conventional and less natural than a rapid, spontaneous script.

Chicken Scratch

A slow writer may be quiet and profound, or lazy and timid; it takes a complete analysis to discover which. Remember: Not speed, nor any other element of writing can provide a full picture of the writer's personality on its own. Everything must be considered within the context of the entire handwriting sample.

Moderately Slow Writing

Moderately slow writing is a sign of inhibition and self-control, as well as circumspection. The writer doesn't have the comfort level of someone who has no trouble going into new things unprepared and unrehearsed. She is most comfortable when she has the time to thoroughly prepare ahead of time and follow a familiar routine that lets her know what's coming up next.

The slow writer is passive and thoughtful, so don't try to hurry her along or get her to make quick changes. She'll only go slower to prove that you don't control her. In fact, she can become quite piqued and her stress level rises when she's under significant time pressure. On the other hand, when you need help with a project that requires patience or involves a lot of mundane details, the slow writer is the one to call on.

Fine Points

An interesting paradox of slow writing is that, although the writer takes extra time to ensure correctness, he is more likely to scratch out words or make corrections to the writing than the fast writer who cares less about making mistakes.

In social settings, you can expect her manner to be pleasant yet somewhat formal and reserved. Deliberate and cautious, she puts on the brakes before acting and takes the time to ponder over what she's going to do and say before doing and saying it. Usually, she is not willing to just go with her gut reactions.

The moderately slow writer carefully weighs and evaluates each new thought before expressing it. She wants to assess how it might affect her and anyone else involved. She digs deep for the facts and questions the whys and wherefores before accepting new information and making it her own. It may take her a bit longer initially to learn new tricks than it does her faster cousin, but once she's added something to her mental database it sticks with her over the long haul.

Moderately slow writing.

The Tortoise: Very Slow Writing Speed

There is a difference between the careful deliberation of the moderately slow writer and the sluggish, plodding movement of one who is mentally impaired. In the case of very slow writing, lack of graphic maturity or mental impairment is generally the cause.

How do you separate slow from very slow? The extreme slowness of the unskilled hand will be obvious, as distinguished from the writing of someone who has reached graphic maturity but has a careful, contemplative nature. Analyzing extremely slow, unskilled writing goes beyond the scope of this book. If you are handed a sample that looks extremely slow, as in the following illustration, the smart thing to do is refer the client to an experienced graphologist.

Very slow writing.

Tales from the Quill

In a study of children who were performing lower than their grade level, it was found that their writing speeds were significantly slower than those of their higher-performing peers. This was not necessarily an indicator of lower intelligence. Stress may have been a factor, such as problems at home.

Deliberate Slowness

Sometimes a writer will intentionally slow down the writing pace. You may not recognize what she is doing unless there is a full page of writing, which would be enough to allow for comparison. The writing starts off at a steady clip, then at some point you notice a change. The writing may get larger, spaces get wider, or the letters more carefully formed. In that case, look for other signs of deliberate calculation. The writer is probably trying to hide something that could be detrimental to her. Fear of betraying what she wants to keep hidden makes her very careful about how and what she writes. Underlying the deliberate slowing down of the writing act may be pathological anxiety or, possibly, criminal acts. We'll cover the latter in more detail in Chapter 22. It takes extra time to create the deliberately slow writing illustrated in the next figure.

Deliberate slow-speed writing.

Steady As She Goes: Medium Writing Speed

Medium speed signifies a conventional approach and reasonable impulse control. The writer's personal tempo is moderate and restrained. He can handle delays without getting too upset (if other factors in the writing bear this out), and doesn't mind waiting for someone slower to catch up with him. He likes to process new ideas and thoughts, but isn't fanatical about making sure he has all the latest facts and data to support them. For him, good enough is good enough.

Medium-speed writing.

The Hare: Moderately Fast Writing Speed

Fast writing is done by someone with a reasonably good measure of self-assurance. Because she is not self-conscious about the way she writes, the focus is more on the message than the style.

This writer reacts quickly and wants to see things happen quickly. Like the guy at a one-hour photo store, she doesn't like waiting for things to develop. The fast writer is efficient. She dislikes waste and wants to use her time and resources wisely. Translating thought into action is easy for her, and she takes the initiative when something needs to be done.

Her ability to quickly comprehend the essence of a matter says she's a fast learner. She can put new knowledge to use almost as soon as she assimilates it, and it really ticks her off when she has to wait for a slower thinker to catch up with her. It drives her crazy, having to wait for someone to choose exactly what he wants to say. She'd like to put the words in his mouths for him!

Write Words

Fast writing speed is made by a rapid writer who is unimpaired physically, intellectually, and mechanically; or by a slower writer who is in a hurry.

Expressive and articulate, she knows how to put down what she wants on paper without hesitating. The moderately fast writer is composed and smooth in her interactions with others. Her ability to respond rapidly indicates someone who is good at thinking on her feet. She'll come up with a ready retort and is never short of a quick answer.

Let's Play Jeopardy!

Legibility is an important factor to consider when judging fast writing. Since writing is done for the purpose of communicating, it obviously should be legible enough for the reader to understand what the sender wanted to get across. When writing is so fast that the words become illegible, the words lose their meaning and the basic purpose of writing—communication—fails.

Busy doctors are often accused of writing illegibly, due to the speed at which they write. When prescriptions are misread by those whose job it is to administer care, their patients lives can actually be put in jeopardy. This is one case where deliberate slowing of the writing can be beneficial—especially when the message is one that affects other people's well-being.

Fine Points

Is it true that all doctors' handwritings are illegible? No. Many doctors make an effort to write legibly. Like any other human being's, a doctor's writing reflects his personal style and temperament.

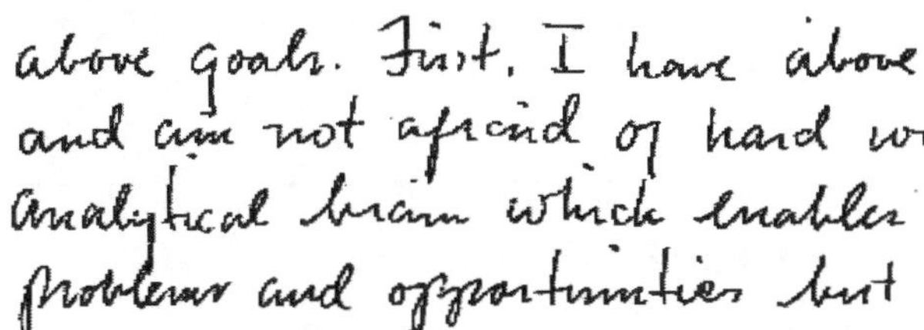

Moderately fast writing.

Moving at the Speed of Light

There's fast, and then there's fast. One has the ability to get things done quickly and efficiently. The other is rash and impetuous, always in a hurry, regardless of the time available.

The difference between the fast writer and the hurried writer is a sense of agitation found in the latter. Borne along by the winds of necessity, he turns his attention to whatever is most urgent at the moment. He feels the hot breath of Father Time on his neck and fears he won't be able to accomplish all that he wants to do. But it really doesn't matter how much time is available, as the pressure to hurry up is internal and unrelenting.

Impatient and impulsive, the extremely fast writer's thoughts travel almost faster than his synapses can fire. Even when his body is at rest, his mind is never still. Moving at such a rapid pace significantly impacts his ability to be thorough and careful. He also tends to be somewhat superficial because digging deep takes up more valuable time; so, the knowledge he picks up is usually directly related to what he needs to know right now.

The hurried (or is that "harried"?) writer has a nervous temperament and lacks the sense of control of the moderately fast writer. He races to get the words out, both oral and written. When he pauses briefly to take a break, mind chatter intrudes.

In his haste, he often leaves out letters, diacritics, and punctuation, which contributes to illegibility. When he remembers to dot the i's and cross the t's, the dots and cross-bars usually are made in a sharp jabbing motion, symbolizing his irritability and a tendency to overreact.

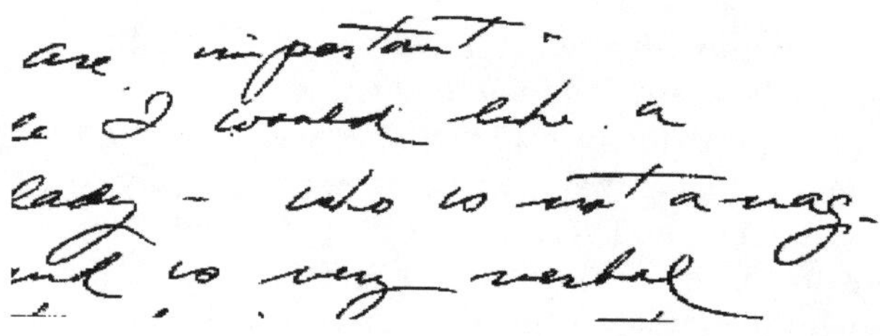

Extremely fast writing.

If you want to start World War III, put a very fast and a very slow writer in a small room and lock the door. How long do you think it would take them to drive each other to distraction? All bets are off!

The Least You Need to Know

- Speed of writing depends on the graphic maturity and skill of the writer.
- Speed and spontaneity are closely related.
- Speed depends on the direction of the movement, shape of the letters, size, and pressure.
- Fast thinkers write fast. Deliberate thinkers write more slowly.
- Extremely slow writing is generally a sign of mental or physical impairment.
- Slow writing is an important contributing factor for premeditated dishonesty.

Chapter 14

Reach Out and Touch Someone: Connections

In This Chapter

- The writing impulse pattern
- Writing in the air
- Connecting the dots
- Breaking the bridges
- You can analyze printing

Can you imagine a conversation where there were no pauses between the words?

Itwouldbereallyfrustratingtryingtofigureoutwhatthemessageis.

See what I mean? Pauses in conversation give both the speaker and the listener a chance to catch their breath and contemplate for a moment what was just said. Without pauses, information floods in, obscuring the meaning of the message. On the other hand, pauses that are too long impair continuity. Ideas become discrete bits of information without any means of linking them together:

h o w   c a n   y o u   r e m e m b e r   t h e   l a   s t   t h o u g h t   w h e n s o   m u c h   t i m e   h a s l a p s e d ?

Impulse Patterns

Handwriting consists of a series of impulses echoed on paper. The spaces between them are like pauses in conversation. Some pauses are short, some are long; some are smooth, some are choppy. The smallest writing impulse is found in a single stroke, which proceeds to the next impulse, the letter, then the word, and finally, the sentence impulse.

Tales from the Quill

Early in the 20th century, Klara Roman discovered that poor writing impulses had a relationship to problems in speech. She found that those who spoke fluently and articulately wrote with smooth, continuous writing impulses. The handwritings of those who stuttered or stammered, or who had other difficulties in communicating coherently, also matched the way they spoke. Using handwriting movement as therapy, Dr. Roman was able to help many speech-impaired people improve their ability to speak. As a result of her research, clinics in Europe began using handwriting analysis to help diagnose and treat speech-impaired patients.

Writing impulses mimic the writer's speech. Some people speak rapidly, rushing to get their thoughts out, while others are more deliberate and careful in delivering their message. Someone who speaks with many starts and stops creates a considerably different impulse pattern on paper than another person who speaks smoothly and expresses himself well.

A writing impulse begins when the pen starts moving on the paper and ends when it is lifted. Depending on the number and quality of the impulses that are linked together, a graphic pattern is formed. The next figure depicts one type of writing impulses. As you can see, a word written in one continuous movement creates a writing impulse that is longer than a word that has been chopped up into several graphic sequences.

Writing impulse patterns.

Unquestionably, different impulse patterns reflect behavioral styles unique to each individual. Our challenge is to discover what these patterns tell us about the writer's ability to function in the world, intellectually, socially, and emotionally.

Fine Points

Collect handwriting samples from people whose speaking styles differ radically. Chart the impulse patterns of slow, smooth speakers and compare them to samples from rapid, uneven speakers.

The degree and type of linkage from one letter to the next is symbolic of how well the writer:

- Connects her thoughts
- Functions in social relationships
- Coordinates her activities

Before we begin examining the linkages, or connections, on paper, there is one other aspect that needs to be defined: airstrokes.

Some People Say I'm Psychic: Airstrokes

Handwriting exists in several dimensions. One of those dimensions is "above" the paper.

Writing actually starts in the air. Like an airplane on final approach to the runway, the hand hovers briefly above the paper as the writer decides where to bring the pen in for a landing. In between writing impulses, too, the pen rises off the paper momentarily before moving into the next writing impulse.

Ideally, while the pen is raised, the hand proceeds in the same direction through the air as it was moving on the writing surface. When the pen touches down again, the flow of ink resumes as if there had been no interruption. Movements above the paper are called *airstrokes*.

Remember the connect-the-dots pictures you enjoyed as a kid? Drawing a line from one numbered dot to the next made a picture. Airstrokes connect writing impulses in the same way, but, invisibly, above the paper. Think of it as drawing in the air.

Smooth airstrokes are created when the writing continues moving in the same direction. Blunt airstrokes are created when the writing movement stops abruptly or makes infinitesimal changes of direction.

The hesitant writer who is unsure of his next move stops suddenly to reconsider or adjust his path. The confident writer creates a continuous, smooth airstroke that advances along the *graphic path* in the same direction. Use a stylus (or work on a photocopy) to trace the movement along the graphic path from the end of one writing impulse to the next. If you can't trace the movement in a smooth line from one stroke to the next, the airstrokes are abrupt.

Write Words

The **graphic path** is the trail of ink made by the writing movement as it proceeds from left to right. An **airstroke** is the movement of the hand in the air, which continues in the same direction as the writing on the paper.

You'll need to whip out your trusty magnifying glass and examine the starting and ending strokes, to find out whether an airstroke is smooth or not. Under magnification, the point at which the movement tapers off as the pen was raised will show a lightening in the trail of ink. Stopping to change direction creates an abrupt airstroke where the ink does not taper off.

Disruption of the writing movement impacts the rhythm. In handwriting, frequent stopping and starting is like walking along a dark street at night, breaking stride every few yards to look back and see if anyone is following. It suggests a lack of self-assuredness, unlike someone who has a strong command presence and moves forward with a sense of purpose and self-confidence.

Smooth (above) and abrupt (below) airstrokes.

Smooth Breaks

Aburpt Breaks

A handwriting with smooth airstrokes is produced by a mind that makes leaps of logic faster than a speeding bullet and grasps whole concepts at a single bound. The writer spends a lot of time "in the air," which, in graphology, symbolizes the mind. She seeks efficient solutions to problems, avoiding the friction caused by contact with the paper.

Ties That Bind

Now we're ready to explore the world of connectedness. Connectedness refers to the degree to which a group of writing impulses join together to form words. The correct term for the connecting strokes is *ligature*. (Yes, that's the same word referred to in crime stories where the victim was tied up or strangled.) It means something that ties or binds. The more friendly meaning in handwriting is, "to unite two or more letters into a single unit."

Write Words

Ligature is a line connecting two or more letters together.

A handwriting is considered connected if shorter words, about six or eight letters long, are joined together. If there are breaks, they should be after syllables or in other expected places, such as breaks to dot the i's or cross the t's. When the connections are broken in unexpected places, or the connections in a short word are mostly or all broken, the writing is considered disconnected.

As in all other elements of handwriting, connectedness leaves clues about the writer's personality and how she functions intellectually and emotionally. Connectedness is one of the indicators that shows how well the writer strings her thoughts together (uses her intellect), and how comfortable she is dealing with the outside world and adapting to her present circumstances (handles her emotions).

The Ups and Downs of Connectedness

Connections between letters are made by joining upstrokes and downstrokes. Downstrokes are like the spine or backbone of writing. Without them there is nothing to support the body. See the next illustration. Legibility may be impaired somewhat, but you can still decipher the message. When the downstrokes are removed (example a), it is impossible to read what the writer is trying to get across.

Writing without downstrokes (above) and writing without upstrokes (below).

Our discussion from this point centers on the degree to which writing connects. We'll go from one end of the spectrum to the other, from highly connected to totally disconnected, keeping in mind that balance and moderation are given the most positive interpretations. Overkill in any handwriting or personality trait or characteristic is interpreted negatively. Whatever the "normal" interpretation is of any characteristic, the opposite will be true when the same characteristic goes to its extreme.

Unrelenting connectedness is one extreme. Total disconnectedness is the other. Let's find out how the degree of connectedness affects the way the writer thinks, feels, and acts.

Do Let's Stay in Touch: Connected Writing

"Connected" doesn't mean that every single element in every single word is linked together. Pausing after syllables or for *diacritics* (i dots and t crosses), doesn't count as breaking the impulse. *Where* breaks occur is important. If they come at the beginnings of words it signifies something different than if they are made at the ends. If they occur in the middle zone, it affects a different area of behavior than in the upper or lower zone.

Write Words

Diacritics, also called diacritical marks, are t crosses and *i* dots and other marks added to words to help with pronunciation, such as accents.

Moderately Connected Writing

Moderately connected writing, which is connected, except for letters after syllables and diacritics, is made by the moderately adaptable person. Provided the airstrokes are smooth, she is able to use either logic or intuition, whichever is appropriate to the situation. Her thoughts flow smoothly, and she is able to string together a series of ideas into a whole concept. She needs to be able to relate the small details to the bigger picture for it to make sense to her.

The ability to reason things out and associate ideas is known as deductive thinking, which is the moderately connected writer's preferred mode. Her thoughts flow easily from one to another. She thinks logically and solves problems by integrating new information with what she already knows.

Socially, the moderately connected writer wants to relate to others in some way. She is attracted to group activities and (with supporting evidence, such as a well-developed lower zone) welcomes other people into her life. Feeling connected to a circle of friends she can count on makes her feel emotionally supported and comfortable.

Moderately (above), highly (below) connected writing.

to make it wo
he wasn't helping
years ago. I w
These events d

to teach in California.
I met in our apartmen
ix years we had our f

Highly Connected

The highly connected writer links most of his letters. He may pause occasionally after capitals but, for the most part, he connects everything else.

He has a good memory for facts, although he may not be as quick to associate them with the events they represent. For instance, he might remember that November 9 is an important day for some reason, but not that it's my birthday (well, it's important to me!).

The highly connected writer enjoys handling details, putting things where they belong, and dealing with the practical necessities of life. Once he has started a project, don't bother to interrupt him because he needs to keep going until he's finished it, the same way he finishes writing a word before taking a break.

Fine Points

Although there is no absolute measurement for connectedness, the rule of thumb is that a strong degree of connectedness exists when relatively long words are written in one impulse; a moderate degree consists of four or five letters being linked; and a low degree is less than four letters joined together.

Tales from the Quill

An example of the highly connected writer is the person who needs a detailed, step-by-step explanation when she doesn't understand a new concept. She has a difficult time picturing something that isn't spelled out, or it isn't right in her line of vision. This can be a very positive trait, used in a job where being detail-minded counts. Or it can seem nit-picky and annoying when it's your mom and she wants to know where you were last night!

Linking letters is a progression from left to right to, from Me to You. The highly connected writer feels a strong need for involvement with others. His behavior and attitudes are consistent from one day to the next, and he can be counted on to respond similarly in like situations.

Overconnected

The overconnected writer makes no breaks at all, even after capital letters. If the writing is also narrow or crowded, what was consistency in the moderate to highly connected writer has burgeoned into obsession. The unrelieved effort reflected in overconnected handwriting is the hallmark of a refusal or inability to let up, even for a moment. The persistent connections at the baseline are made by someone who needs to feel her feet firmly in contact with the ground. She expends much of her energy taking care of the practical, material aspects of her life. She doesn't trust her intuition, but needs to gather as much logical data and as many facts as she can before making a decision.

The overconnected writer can be overwhelming. Her need for contact, if combined with close word spacing, suggests someone who doesn't have good social boundaries. She discharges an avalanche of thoughts and ideas without giving you a chance to assimilate them. Just as she can't seem to relinquish the writing impulse, she goes on and on, whether you want to hear her or not. She may give lip service to allowing others to have their say, but doesn't really hear them. She's too focused on her own thoughts.

Chicken Scratch

In discussing the overconnected writer, Klara Roman said, "Overconnected configurations are produced by rhetoricians, verbose persons, time wasters, individuals who make much ado about nothing."

Have you ever met someone who insisted on enlightening you on a topic of absolutely no interest to you? A religious fanatic, perhaps? You would rather walk away, but she doesn't give you any space in which to politely take your leave. If she thinks her listener isn't "getting it," she'll go to great lengths to explain herself further. Don't try winning a debate with someone like this. She will out-argue you until either you get tired and walk away or you capitulate. Yet, what others may interpret as a habit of argumentativeness is, to the overconnected writer, simply a desire to make others hear her.

In extreme cases, the emotional excitation implied in overconnected writing is sometimes a sign of a psychological disturbance. The writer's refusal to give anyone else any space suggests some sort of paranoia. She doesn't trust anyone else, so she feels compelled to control as much of her environment as possible.

I Need My Space: Moderately Disconnected Writing

Writing that has many smooth breaks, when simplified and original (that is, it's made simpler than Copybook), is the sign of a quick, facile mind (the concepts "simplified" and "original" will be discussed in detail in Chapter 17). The writer is able to leap nimbly from one thought to the next without waiting to have all the data before him. Especially if there are smooth connections and airstrokes in the upper zone, it shows an ability to proliferate a series of ideas and combine them into a workable system.

With his propensity for sailing off the page with many airstrokes, the moderately disconnected writer tends to be more mentally than socially oriented. He is generally more comfortable in the theoretical world than in the company of others. Although he may have plenty of friendships, it isn't quite as easy for him to connect with others as it is for the connected writer.

If the airstrokes are choppy, the writer's emotions are less controlled and a bit more erratic. His behavior is not so consistent, and he may surprise you by suddenly changing his attitude. You may think you're having a very pleasant conversation, when all of a sudden he abruptly gets up and walks off. He abruptly disconnects his written words in the same manner.

Those who make many breaks between writing impulses don't seem to view the world in quite the same way as highly connected writers. They are generally less conventional and more flexible, willing to bend their standards to some degree.

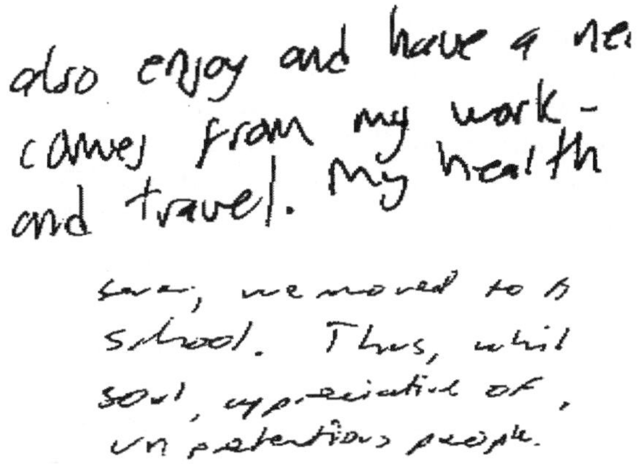

Highly (above), moderately (middle), and low(bottom) disconnected writing.

Looking for Breaks in All the Wrong Places

Extreme disconnectedness is different from printed writing. Here, we're talking about cursive writing that has been chopped up into very small writing impulses. It's unusual to find many smooth airstrokes in totally disconnected writing. Constant, restless, movement in many directions and nervous activity are the order of the day for the extremely disconnected writer.

The highly disconnected writer is often highly creative. The question is, is he able to put his creativity to work productively? The ideas gush out, spattering in all directions like paint from an aerosol can. Some of them may be pure genius, but others are just flights of fancy not worth spending the time and energy to develop. He isn't always able to clearly define which is which. He is often quite moody and inconsistent. You never know how he is going to react from one minute to the next. Establishing close relationships is much more difficult for this individual. The breaks between letters suggest a breaking of the bonds between himself and the outside world. He finds it easier to stand alone than have to bother cooperating with others.

Fine Points

When the disconnected final letter is g, the writer is often someone who has trouble making emotional commitments in intimate relationships. Such a writer may live with a lover for years, and even get married, but it's as if he feels compelled to withhold that last little bit of himself.

Tales from the Quill

Rick and his girlfriend Marcia were spending a romantic evening alone by the fireside. Marcia thought it would be the perfect time to talk about making plans for a ski trip to Big Bear Mountain, but when she raised the subject she immediately felt Rick withdraw. Soon, he went upstairs to bed. Alone. Marcia didn't know that he wanted to surprise her with a trip, and now the surprise was spoiled. Like many disconnected writers, Rick's moods can change without warning.

Some handwritings are generally connected, but the writing impulse breaks consistently in one particular spot, perhaps always after the first letter, or always after the last letter. The next sections cover the significance of breaking after the initial letter of a word or before the final letter of a word.

Making a Break for It

You start to write a word, but after the first letter you pause and reconsider. Is that what I really wanted to say? Yes. It is. And, having broken the connection, you go on to finish the word. Art is imitating life. When the writer pauses after the first letter of a word, it mirrors a tendency to reconsider after having made a decision. The writer feels she needs to step back and take a deep breath, or to wind herself up before carrying on. Pulver suggests that the person who leaves a pause after the first letter doesn't have a natural ability to adapt to circumstances, but had to learn how, later in life.

Let's Break It Off

Do you know someone who has trouble making and keeping commitments? Check her connections. Chances are, the last letter of some words will be separated from the rest. This often happens when the writer rushes headlong into a new relationship or makes a major decision. As the time draws closer for her to put her money where her mouth is, she gets cold feet and pulls back. After reconsidering, she may move forward and fulfill the commitment. But first she's likely to do this push-pull cha-cha several times before fulfilling her commitment.

According to Pulver's research, breaking off the last letter of a word suggests someone whose natural capacity to adapt to circumstances has been disrupted at some point. Continuing to break off the last letter stems from unwillingness or inability to take the necessary steps to accommodate disruptive events.

Disconnected final (above) and initial letters (below).

Bring Me My Soldering Iron

Sometimes a writer will realize that breaks have crept in where she didn't intend, or doesn't want them. So, she goes back and tries to connect them after the fact. Strokes that are made in an attempt to fix a break are called mending, retouching (going back over the strokes), or soldering.

A soldering iron, such as you'd find in a machine shop, is used to melt and apply solder to two pieces of metal in order to join them together. In effect, that's what happens when the writer wants to connect a "hole" in his writing, only the soldering material in this case is ink.

The significance of mending and soldering is that often the writer is anxious to make things look better than they really are. She doesn't want to be seen as wrong, so she makes an effort to correct and improve herself. Some writers use this method to hide something they don't want seen, so it may be a form of dishonesty. As usual, it all depends on the whole configuration of the writing. Often, the retouching (in the form of mending or soldering) just makes matters worse, as the following example illustrates.

Retouching.

Viva Variety! Printscript

Some people combine printing and writing. Graphologists call this writing style printscript. Depending on whether the overall graphic picture is harmonious or not, the writer may be wonderfully creative, or merely impulsive and erratic.

Tales from the Quill

John, who divorced after a traumatic two-year marriage, went through a series of relationships, some of which were serious. When he and Rosemary became engaged after a two-year courtship, it seemed as if he had finally overcome his fear of commitment. Not quite. Every time he and Rosemary got especially close, John would pick fights with her, until they almost broke up. When Rosemary consulted a graphologist, she found out the problem was—his disconnected final letters! (Well, okay, the finals were a *symptom* of the problem, which was commitment phobia.)

Creative Printscript.

The Complete Idiots Guide to Handwriting Analysis will make an excellent addition to an already spectacular series. I cant wait to get my hands on a copy of this book.

Reading the Fine Print: Printed Writing

Using the principles of gestalt graphology it's almost as easy to analyze printing as cursive writing. As graphic movement, printing utilizes space, form, and movement just like any other style of writing.

There are several types of printed writing, with block printing and manuscript printing being the most common. Block printing is done in all capital letters, while manuscript printing uses upper and lower case letters. Manuscript printing is taught as a lead-in to learning cursive writing.

Printing is a relatively new phenomenon. Klara Roman's *Encyclopedia of the Written Word* (Frederick Ungar Publishing Company, 1968) tells us that "The reform of using basic letter forms related to Roman capitals in teaching the young to write was initiated by Edward Johnston of the Royal College of Art, London. In an address on penmanship, in 1913, Johnston suggested 'that in the early stages of teaching children to write, the Roman alphabet might with advantage be used as a model.'"

Some people (most notably police officers, architects, and engineers), print because it's a requirement of their type of work. If they print only at work, but write cursive at home, we would analyze the cursive. However, if they print in social settings too, such as writing personal letters, the printing will reflect the true personality.

One aspect of printing that always puzzled me as a new graphologist was how to interpret the breaks between letters. Did this mean that, like disconnected writers, printers repudiated logic? That they were flighty and unpredictable? That certainly didn't fit with the printers I knew, especially when their cursive writing was highly connected, which it usually was. What I discovered was, you have to look at the whole picture (as if I haven't been saying that for 13 chapters already).

Interestingly, many printers, while breaking the connections between their letters, place the letters close enough to touch. This suggests that while their conscious desire is to keep their distance, their inner need is for closeness.

Some types of printing, like cursive, allow the writer to go into all three zones (upper, middle, lower), but block printing isn't one of them. Block printing is viewed in the same manner as writing with an emphasis on the middle zone. The writer's energies are concentrated in the day-to-day area of routine and social interaction. Like other middle-zone writers, the block printer's ego is central to all aspects of her life. She doesn't mind sharing her opinions, and expects you to agree with her. But if you don't, it won't change her mind.

Fine Points

Most printers say they print because they want to be perfectly clear in what they are saying. Those who write in all block capitals, especially, tend to be logical thinkers who are grounded in reality (providing there are other supporting indicators).

The Complete Idiot's Guide to Handwriting Analysis will make an excellent addition to an already spectacular series.

Printed writing.

The Bare Bones: Skeletal and Disintegrated Writing

Skeletal or fragmented, or disintegrated writing is writing that is stripped down to its absolute bare minimum, but still retains legibility. That is, the downstrokes are still present, but not the upstrokes. The writer is ascetic and stingy in his attitude and manner. There is no flesh on the bones of his writing—no loops or flourishes to enrich it. His emotional detachment hints at little or no connection between himself and the world. If he is not just plain eccentric, mental illness (impending or present) is a possibility.

Children learn to write by first forming singular strokes, then proceeding to learn letters, letter combinations, words, and finally whole sentences. In cases of severe mental illness or distress where the mind begins to break down, it is manifested on paper. As the mind deteriorates, the writing regresses through the various stages, all the way back to the basic stroke impulse. At that point, regression to an infantile stage is complete. The writing of a Down syndrome adult is a stunning example of her ability to organize the page, while being entirely unable to go beyond the basic stroke in communicating with others.

Writing of an adult with Down syndrome.

Tales from the Quill

The handwriting of American poet Emily Dickinson, in her later years, disintegrated almost to the point of illegibility. As she became more reclusive, the letter forms became more difficult to read. You can see from the next sample that the letters bear absolutely no resemblance to any copybook. Emily created her own original forms, but the positive interpretation that normally comes from originality is lost due to their eccentric, even hieroglyphic appearance.

Emily Dickinson's disintegrated writing.

I Don't Know How I Know It, but I Do

Everyone has it, but not everyone uses it. Some people develop it to an astounding degree, while others prefer to shun it altogether. What is it? Intuition. What can handwriting uncover about this special means of perceiving?

Many graphology books claim that breaks between letters are a sign of intuition. That's not always true, as confirmed by the early modern graphologists, such as Pulver, Saudek, and Roman. Let's consider what intuition is. My favorite definition is pretty basic: Intuition is knowing what you know, without knowing how you know it.

For our purposes, intuition is an instinctive, unconscious process that begins in the lower zone, the area of the unconscious. It is quite unlike the deliberate theorizing, measuring, and computing a series of ideas that you would do in conscious thought. But neither is it stuff just popping into your head out of the blue.

Intuition seems to have some relationship to previous knowledge. When the unconscious (lower zone) recognizes a truth about something within the realm of your experience, the perception quietly germinates, unfettered by logical thought processes. When insight is ready to manifest, it erupts into the conscious mind above the baseline and blossoms in that "Aha!" sensation. If the perception happens to come mid word, a smooth break or an airstroke, results.

But what if the airstrokes are not smooth; isn't that also intuition? Well, sort of.... Abrupt breaks do signify a torrent of ideas popping into consciousness, but they seem to be more on the order of sudden hunches, not connected to anything in particular.

Tales from the Quill

Although you might think that psychics' handwritings would have the type of disconnections that point to intuition, their writings don't necessarily show disconnectedness. As in every other field, there is more than one type of psychic and some of their handwritings are, in fact, highly connected. They say that their information doesn't come from intuition, which is based on past experiences, but from a source completely outside themselves. Other psychics have very spread-out writing with thready forms (We'll be covering connective forms, including thread, in the next chapter).

It is extremely difficult to force a change in the degree of connectedness in an individual's handwriting. Try to print for an extended period if you normally write cursive; or try writing cursive if you only print. It feels yucky (that's the technical term). Once a writer has reached graphic maturity (he knows how to write), his tendency to connect or disconnect comes naturally.

To discover how easily someone connects with the world, mentally, emotionally, and practically, examine the way she links her letters. If they are excessively flourished, unnatural linkages, she is trying hard to make an impression. However, simplified, original connections, particularly in the upper zone, signify intelligence and creativity. What is most important is that the connections are fluid and enhance the writing movement, not detract from it.

It is the *type* of connection that tells us how the writer relates to others, and we will consider those connections in Chapter 15.

The Least You Need to Know

- The disconnections (airstrokes) between letters are just as important as the connections.
- Connected writing shows an ability to connect thoughts.
- Overconnected writing is a sign of argumentativeness.
- Disconnected writing shows a break in the flow of thought.
- Printed writing is not the same as disconnected cursive writing.

Chapter 15

From Me to You: Connective Forms

In This Chapter

- Adapting, inside and out
- Rounded, angular or ???
- The secondary connective forms
- How a shark's tooth can bite in handwriting

How well do you adapt to different environments? Are you flexible and quick to adjust to new situations and people? Or do you stubbornly stick with what you know and insist that everyone else defer to your habits? The answer is found in your basic temperament.

Basic temperament is most clearly seen in the shapes of letters and the connections between them. In Chapter 14 we discovered that the degree to which words connect reveals how much we desire contact with other people. The types of connections we make and the shapes of the letters themselves provide the next piece of the puzzle: *how* we relate to others. The connections are called *connective forms*.

There are four major connective forms: two rounded (arcade and garland), one angular, and one thready (or indefinite), which combines the two rounded ones. Although arcade and garland are both rounded forms, the arcade is open at the bottom and the garland is open at the top. Angular form are closed at both the top and bottom.

The easiest way to find the connective form is to check the tops of the lowercase letters m and n, and the connections from one letter to another at the baseline.

Write Words

Connective forms are the shapes of the linkages between letters.

Fine Points

An easy way to determine the primary connective form is to look at the tops of the letters m and n. If they are rounded on top, the primary form is arcade. If the m and n looks more like a w or u, it is garland. A wavy top is thready (or indefinite), and a pointed top is angular.

The school model teaches a combination of the garland, arcade, and angle forms, and most adults adopt one of these three types as a primary way of forming and joining letters together. Generally, the other forms will also be used to some degree. We add the "thread" type, which is a combination of the garland and arcade, but flattened out.

A good mix of all the connective forms suggests someone who has an innate ability to relate to many different types of people on their own level, rather than stick with those who are just like him. Someone who uses one type of connective form exclusively tends to be a one-dimensional personality. His behavior is regimented and premeditated; he lacks the capacity to act spontaneously.

The connective form illustrates the writer's social attitudes and is an expression of his true nature. Pulver described the connective form as defining the way the writer adapts, both to his inner and his outer world. For instance, the choice of rounded forms is made by the more passive individual (the more rounded the form, the more passive the person), angular forms are chosen by resistant people (the more angular, the more resistance), and thready forms are adopted by those who refuse to be forced into making any choice at all.

Changing your natural form is extremely difficult. Try it sometime! In fact, let's do it right now. The following figure shows the four major connective forms. Pick one that is unlike your own writing and copy it for several lines. How did that feel? Probably pretty uncomfortable, since you were imitating a form that doesn't reflect the way you naturally function.

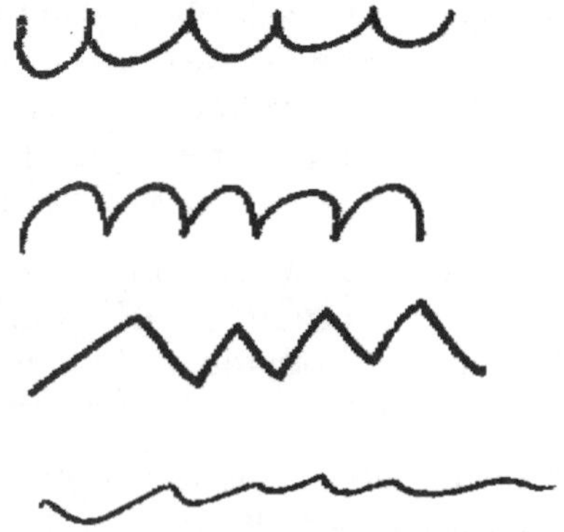

The four major connective forms. Garland (top), arcade (second), angle (third), thread (bottom).

In the following pages we'll be exploring each of the four major connectives, and some sub- or minor forms, in detail. I can already see those of you with rounded forms nodding cooperatively, the angular writers getting their arguments ready, and the thready people shrugging, "whatever." So, let's begin.

Why Can't We All Just Get Along? Garlands

The first of the major connective forms is called the garland. There are several variations of the garland and we'll cover the basic form first. It has firm pressure and a natural, free flow of left-right movement.

Although both sexes use all the connective forms, the garland is viewed as a more feminine type. Rounded on the bottom and open at the top, the garland is like a bowl, ready to receive whatever you are prepared to give.

Remembering that the writing movement is from Me to You, you'll recognize the garland as a spontaneous movement outward, opening itself up, extending itself toward others. Sociability is implied in this movement, and a willingness to please.

Because the bowl is open from the top, it is influenced by outside forces. The garland writer is trusting and open, the type of person who reaches out to others with a smile and expects you to smile back (think, "California Girl"). The rounded form symbolizes emotions, so you can expect warm, emotional responses from this writer. The writer has an informal manner and doesn't mind displaying how he feels.

Good-natured and easygoing, the garland writer wants everyone to get along and be friends. He usually opts for the path of least resistance because he doesn't want to do anything that might upset anyone or make them unhappy.

Tales from the Quill

Princess Diana's handwriting uses the garland form. Her love for children and work with AIDS patients and other people in need is well-known. She also admitted to her struggle with an eating disorder. Her behavior was typical of a garland writer (see the sample of her handwriting in Appendix E). Many, if not most, writers with eating disorders have very rounded handwritings.

The garland writer is usually quite hospitable and willing to share what he has. When unexpected guests stop by, chances are they'll be greeted with a warm hug and a sincere invitation to stay for dinner. Male or female, this is the mothering, nurturing type who enjoys listening to what happened to you today, sticking on a band-aid when you scrape your knee, and being as supportive and encouraging as you could possibly need.

Kind and compassionate, a little on the sentimental side, the writer's basic needs frequently are tied to home and hearth. Very rounded writing is often done by those who are more comfortable with kids and animals than with other adults. This writer won't argue or fight about anything else, but when it comes to defending his home and family he can be a tiger.

Wilting Garlands

When the garland is made without firm pressure and a good sense of direction, much of the positive interpretation is lost. Instead of being merely receptive, *flat, shallow,* or *weak garlands* indicate extreme susceptibility and dependency. Certainly, the shallow or weak garland implies weakness of character. In some cases, it might be construed as just plain laziness.

Write Words

In the **flat garland,** the connecting strokes hug the baseline. In the **shallow garland,** the connecting strokes droop. Strokes of the **weak garland** are made without pressure.

Made by those who talk much but say little, the writer is easily influenced and may go overboard in indulging herself. She lacks the energy to resist outside pressure and allows others to push her in directions she might not be eager to go. Gullible and naive, the writer is ready to believe anything she hears, so if she happens to fall in with the wrong crowd, she's likely to find herself in hot water, right along with them.

The shallow garland is sometimes a sign of depression. The writer simply doesn't have the heart to withstand the onslaught of a stronger-willed aggressor. She goes with the flow to avoid having to fight for what she wants.

Faking It—Sham Garlands

The sham garland (sometimes called "clothesline garland") is another less-than-stellar form of the friendly connective. With this form there is no free flow of movement, as in the genuine garland. Although the letter connections are rounded on the bottom, the movement is slow and careful. Upstrokes are partially concealed by downstrokes, which implies a need to hide something. Since connecting strokes generally occur at or near the baseline, the concealing is taking place in the middle zone, the zone of relationships, emotions, and day-to-day life.

The sham garland writer wants to appear affable and adaptable, but something in her environment has her worried or afraid to act naturally. Consequently, she covers her fear with a veneer of congeniality. The friendliness of the normal garland has become a mask.

Tales from the Quill

The word "garland" was probably much more commonly used when Abbe Michon was developing his graphological system. When I asked my husband what he thought of when he heard the word, he said "Christmas trees." The blank look on my face prompted him to explain that he meant the popcorn or tinsel that is sometimes strung around the tree for decoration. A garland could also be a necklace of flowers, like a Hawaiian lei.

In some instances, you'll find looped garlands. Since the loop is made by a slight turn to the left, it is a regressive or counterstroke. In other words, it's going the wrong direction. Roman says the looped garland is a case of balancing tension and release by momentarily going inward. Some other writers call it the "worry stroke," and say it is made by those who carry the woes of the world on their shoulders.

Garland

Shallow Garland

Sham Garland

Garland forms.

Cover Me, I'm Going in: Arcades

The second type of rounded major connective form is the arcade, named for its arch-like shape. While the garland connective form is bowl-shaped on the bottom, the arcade turns the bowl upside down, making it rounded on the top. The garland writer is open to influences from the outside, but the arcade closes off at the baseline, making it inaccessible from any direction except within. If you put an apple on the kitchen counter and placed a bowl over it, how accessible would the apple be? It wouldn't be. And that's the effect of the arcade form in handwriting. There's a sense of impenetrability.

Because the arcade form is rounded, the arcade writer, like the garland writer, is basically an emotional person. The difference is, she doesn't like to show it, preferring to hide her emotional responses under the arch. Think, for a moment what an arch represents besides McDonald's Golden Arches, that is. Look at the Marble Arch in London, or the Arc d' Triomphe in Paris. That's some very impressive architecture that has stood for aeons and weathered all sorts of assaults, including WWI and WWII.

Chicken Scratch

In graphological literature, the arcade has traditionally been given a bad rap. It usually is listed as a major sign of dishonesty, as well as other nasty stuff. While that may be true in some cases, it isn't always. Just as in many other aspects of handwriting, speed is the modifying factor.

The arch is a super-strong structure that may be used as a bridge to travel over; an aqueduct to carry life-sustaining water under; or a means of protection under which to hide from a variety of hazardous conditions. It becomes an impenetrable bulwark against the outside world.

The need for the arcade writer to conceal her emotions sometimes gives others the impression that she is cold or unfeeling. Nothing could be further from the truth. However, she would rather let them believe that than have to explain herself.

An arcade in fast writing is interpreted quite differently from an arcade in slow writing—they even *look* different. We'll examine the fast arcade first.

Fast Arcades

The fast arcade begins with a releasing movement toward the upper zone, which shows the writer's interest in achieving great things. Driven toward success and accomplishment, she pushes herself to ever greater heights. The arcade ends with a downstroke, coming back toward the self and the lower zone, and indicates strong determination. The writer keeps her eyes on the goal, not allowing obstacles to deter her. Because the arcade is closed at the top, the writer is able to shut away outside distractions and single-mindedly pursue her objectives.

The negative side of the fast arcade writer's one-track mind is that others may see her as pushy and overbearing. Especially when the pressure is displaced onto the upstroke (see Chapter 12), the energy is sublimated from other areas and permits the writer to keep on driving herself until she has achieved her goal.

Many times, fast arcades are seen in the handwritings of highly creative people. (If I weren't so modest, I'd point out my own golden arches.) Those who work in the arts, as well as architects ("arch"-i-tects—get it?!) tend to use the arcade form because the structural appearance appeals to them.

Fine Points

When the arch is tall and comes at the beginning of a word, you can bet the writer wants to make an impact. He wants be seen as impressive and imposing, without having to say a word.

Similarly, structure and form are important to the fast arcade writer. In fact, she may be quite attracted to architecture on one level or another. Her concern with appearances indicates a more formal approach than her garland-writing sister. That formality puts the brakes on spontaneity, and in social situations, makes her reserved, maybe even a bit shy.

The fast arcade writer tends to be very interested in the past. Remember, the arcade is open at the bottom, toward the past and the subconscious. She wants to know where she came from, what her roots and genealogy are (especially when combined with a long lower zone). A traditionalist, she would like to maintain life the way it was, and it takes some time and effort on her part to accept progress. Some fast arcade writers can be quite snobbish and class conscious.

Slow Arcades

The slow arcade writer shares some characteristics of the fast arcade writer because the form is similar. However, the interpretation of slow arcades is less flattering. The statuesque arch is now more like a baseball cap, pulled down low over the forehead to conceal the wearer's identity. Or, like a turtle who has retreated inside his shell.

The maker of the slow arcade is self-oriented and defensive. He doesn't wait to be attacked, but barricades himself behind the walls of the arch, just in case. The slow arcade is a controlled form, unlike the free and easy movement of the garland.

Tales from the Quill

When the last stroke of a word returns to the left in an arcade, it usually has a negative connotation. It is a sign of deliberate secretiveness and withholding of information. Pulver, who was very big into symbolism, likened the final arcade to the writer biting his lip to keep from saying something that he doesn't want you to know. The return to self also suggests selfishly keeping things to himself for his own ends.

Especially when the arcade is narrow, it is signifies secretiveness and inhibition. Some graphologists see it as the sign of a hypocrite, or a wolf in sheep's clothing.

An arcade at the end of a word is a deliberate, inhibiting movement. The writer withdraws the outgoing gesture and returns it to himself. This may indicate defensiveness, embarrassment, or insincerity.

Arcade forms.

Fast Arcades

Slow Arcades

No More Mr. Nice Guy: Angles

Okay, I've got my boxing gloves on. Now we can move on to discuss the angular writer. Why the gloves? Because the angular writer is always looking for a fight or argument. Friction is part of his daily diet, as much as the garland writer seeks peace and harmony. When things are going too smoothly he gets unsettled and feels compelled to make waves.

In order to form an angle, the hand is required to make an abrupt stop and change of direction. There is little room for flexibility in the writing movement or in the angle writer's nature. He refuses to adapt to the needs or desires of others, but expects, even insists, that others should accommodate him. For him, every situation is a new opportunity to exert his will.

The angle writer doesn't sit around waiting for something to happen. He is driven to make decisions and act, especially when acting gives him a chance to provoke a power struggle. With heavy pressure added to a primarily angular writing, the writer may treat people with a ruthless heavy hand. The handwriting of Heinrich Himmler, head of the dreaded Nazi SS in World War II, is a case in point, as you can see in Appendix E.

One of the angular writer's positive characteristics is that, when he uses his power for good, he can be extremely effective. When he needs to stand firm, there is no shaking him. He doesn't give up, no matter how high the odds are stacked against him. Some call it stubbornness, but he sees it as persistence.

There is no doubt about his opinions or his wants, because he expresses them directly and candidly. He's a strict disciplinarian of himself and those who report to him, be it his children or his employees.

Fine Points

If the writing is also sharp, rather than pasty, the angular writer is moralistic. Doubly so if he also has a tall upper zone. If the stroke is muddy as well as angular, brutality is a given.

Your Guardian Angle Is Watching

When the angle is slightly rounded rather than making a completely sharp point, it's called a soft angle. The softness mitigates some of the more difficult aspects of the angular form and gives the angular writer more moderation. Her obstinacy becomes a gentler persistence, and inflexibility becomes just plain firmness.

All in all, the soft-angle writer is much easier to get along with. She has developed some tolerance and adaptability. She may still have strong opinions, but they will not be expressed so directly and severely. The better nature of the angle is allowed to shine through.

Biting with the Shark's Tooth

So named because it looks like one, the *shark's tooth* form is an angle with a bend in it, which you can see in the following figure. The bend is a type of directional pressure (see Chapter 12). The stroke bends inward, as if something from the right side were pushing it. That makes it a counterstroke (going in the opposite direction to the way it should go).

Write Words

The **shark's tooth** is an angle made with a curve and signifies a cunning, shrewd personality.

The meaning of the shark's tooth isn't very pleasant. It is a smooth-looking stroke that hides cunning, crafty behavior under a courteous exterior. The writer smiles at you while calmly stabbing you in the back. If this form is seen only once or twice in an otherwise positive script, the inference is that the writer can be pretty nasty when pushed, but that the trait pops out only under duress. There's an illustration of shark's tooth in Chapter 22.

Angular forms.

applying my education
studying various subje
management. Now that

to think of myself as
specialty and am now
xpert in my offbeat

Handwriting Analysis will make c
addition to an already specta
series. I can't wait to get my

Write Words

A **thread** is an indefinite form that combines elements of the garland and the arcade.

Chicken Scratch

The thready writer is generally unassertive, avoiding, and evasive. She dodges conflict even more than the garland writer does. The thready writer is like an eel, twisting away from unpleasantness.

Don't Pin Me Down: Thread

The *thread* form isn't taught in any schools. It combines the arcade and garland, but breaks them down so it isn't easy to identify which is which. The result is a rather flat and wavy form, ambiguous, indefinite, and equivocal.

Thread, like the arcade, is often treated negatively in graphology texts. It is assumed that all thread forms should be treated equal, which is not so. There are two distinct types of thready formations—primary and secondary. Remember how, in the case of garlands, a positive interpretation depended on firm pressure? It's the same with thready forms.

It is impossible to make either primary or secondary thread slowly. Thus, the mind that makes it thinks fast. In primary thread, legibility remains unimpaired and the form helps the writing movement progress to the right because it accelerates the speed. Secondary thread produces illegibility because the writing thins out, in many instances, merely to a wavy line.

Primary Thread

Primary thread is made with moderate pressure and is seen mostly at the ends of words. The last letter breaks down and, to some extent, thins out. Or, some letters (most notably the m's and n's) lose their definition and become slightly wavy-looking. Overall though, letters retain their basic shape.

> **Write Words**
>
> **Primary thread** is a sign of fast thinking. Usually seen on the ends of words, where the final stroke thins out to a point, it is made with pressure and does not impair legibility.

The primary thread writer thinks and acts fast. She's not interested in going into information in depth, but tends to skim the surface. Although at her best when handling complex matters, she tends to get impatient when someone tries to feed her too many details.

If connective forms symbolize the writer's ability to adapt, then thready writing is created by the King of Adaptability. Adaptability is the very essence of the thready writer's being. He takes on the shape of his environment. We could call him the "chameleon," because wherever he is, he fits in.

The thready writer lives by his instincts and goes with his gut reactions. He quickly jumps to conclusions—often too quickly—without the benefit of logic. So, while his basic assumption may be correct, the final judgment is sometimes flawed due to lack of supporting information.

The writer suffers from a general angst about being exposed. He equivocates, hoping not to have to take a stand and promote a particular viewpoint. He won't expend the energy to fight and avoids friction or conflict at all cost. Interestingly though, when forced into a corner with no other way out, he'll come out swinging.

Once again, connective forms are found in the middle zone, which has to do with day-to-day functioning, ego needs, and social activities. When word endings thin out in a thready form, it suggests diplomacy and tact. Why? Because the thready form is able to penetrate the defenses of others and get under their facade.

Socially, the thready writer has great charm. In conversation she doesn't wait to hear an entire thought before getting the gist. In fact, she has a disconcerting way of knowing what others are thinking, almost as if some invisible antenna were implanted in her head, allowing her to pick up the thoughts of the people around her. She is already thinking of how she is going to respond before the other person has finished speaking. Her ability to relate to others on their level makes them quickly feel comfortable talking to her. Hopefully, her talent is used for good; otherwise she can become manipulative and exploitative, as is often the case with secondary thread.

Secondary Thread

Secondary thread is made either without pressure or with very light pressure, resulting in a formless scrawl in the middle of words. It is a sign of inner hysteria. The writer feels crushed by life's burdens and feels as if he can handle no more. The secondary thread writer is like a piece of elastic that has been stretched so many times it has lost its resilience. His motivation is self-preservation, which for this writer means hiding out. The only strength he has left is for flight. He always leaves a back door open so he can wriggle out in case of trouble.

When the writing is illegible, there is a complete lack of concern for others. If he doesn't care whether they can read his message, what does that say about his level of compassion and fellow-feeling? His only concern is to stay afloat.

Fine Points

The writer of secondary thread can be a genius, an executive, or an opportunistic criminal. As with all other factors, the secondary thread form must be evaluated within the total graphic picture.

Secondary thread is often the connective form of choice of the con artist, the person who refuses to make a commitment of any kind, and one who feels unable to take a stand. Actually, it's no use for these people to make a choice, because once they make one, they're just as likely to abandon it for something more attractive. Whatever will advance their objectives is the course they will choose, regardless of the consequences.

The Double Bow

The double bow, like the thread form, combines the arcade and the garland, but retains more of their form. It suggests someone who wants to appear conventional and sincere, but doesn't want to make a choice. She is always working at maintaining equilibrium, hopping from one foot to the other, changing sides. She has no opinion of her own and won't give you her point of view because it depends on who she is with at the moment.

This type of writer could be called an opportunist who does what she believes is expected in order to avoid conflict. If she finds herself in a position where she could be taken to task for her actions, she simply slides over to the other side. Her main objective is to avoid the complications and responsibility that comes with having an opinion.

Primary Thread

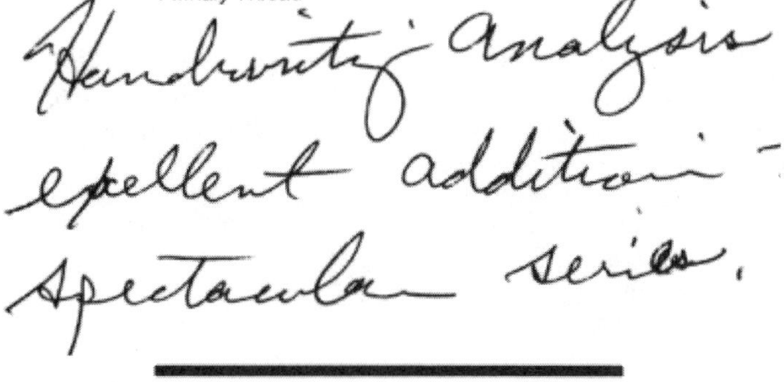

Secondary Thread

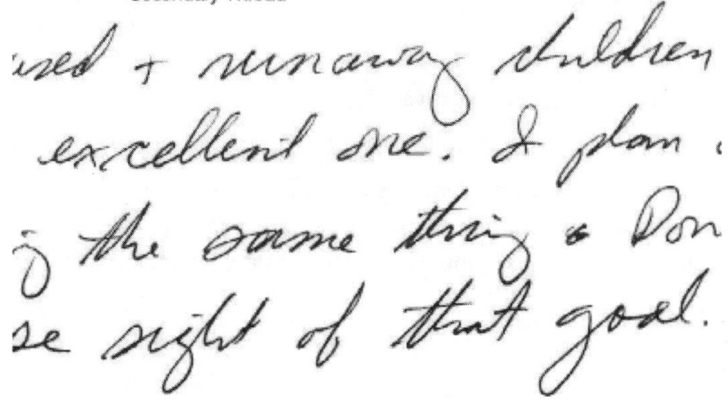

Thready forms.

Sacre Bleu! It's Sacre Coeur: Supported Forms

The Sacre Coeur (Sacred Heart) type of connective form was taught in French convent schools and in some British schools. It is a form of calligraphy that allows for no individuality or spontaneous expression of the writer's true personality.

It is called a supported form because, in order to make it, tops and bottoms of letters are actually covered by the stroke that comes before. The writer's personality is immersed in the convention of the system, and someone who chooses this form is more concerned with being socially correct than morally sound. Thus, supported forms generally signify hypocrisy.

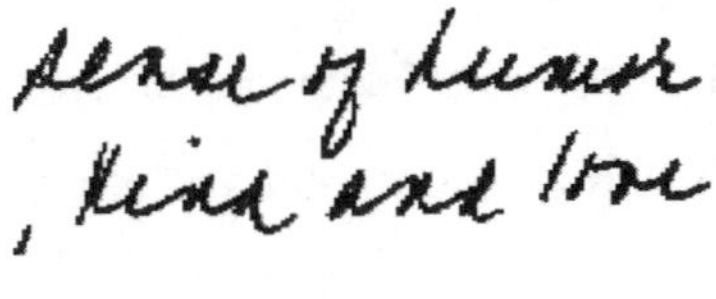

Supported forms.

Combining Forms

Some combinations of forms are particularly desirable, such as the garland/angle combination. The softness of the garland derives strength and support from the angle, so the writer is not a complete pushover, driven by her emotions. The angle is made softer by the garland, showing a greater willingness to adapt.

Some garlands in arcade writing temper the arcade writer's reserve and allow for greater spontaneity. Likewise, some fast arcades in a generally garland writing brings a little more reserve and caution to the gullible garland writer.

Tales From the Quill

President Richard Nixon's handwriting, some of which appears in Appendix E, is comprised largely of thready forms with some angles thrown in. You can't see it in the sample excerpt, but both his margins moved inward, making the whole page of writing look like the funnel shape of a tornado. Overall, Mr. Nixon's writing, like his personality, is filled with conflicting characteristics.

The angle/thread combination is a dominant sign of the exploiter who capitalizes on the weaknesses of others. He is sneaky and undependable. The worst of both connective forms is found in this duo. Don't trust him with your kitchen trash!

The Least You Need to Know

- The shape of connections between letters and within letters reveal the writer's style of relating to other people.
- Rounded forms are made by passive, accepting types.
- Angular forms are made by active, self-assertive types.
- Thready forms are made by avoidant types.
- A combination of forms are used by the healthiest personality types.
- The least desirable combination of forms is the thread and angle.

Chapter 16

In the Mood: Slant

In This Chapter

- Handwriting is like body language
- How to measure a loop
- Right, left, or indifferent, which way do you slant?
- All over the place—variable slant
- What about lefties?

Writing slant tracks the moment-to-moment flow of feelings and responses. It demonstrates surface reactions but not the deeper emotional expression found in some other areas of handwriting, such as pressure. Because it is the easiest characteristic to change deliberately, slant is considered one of the superficial signs in handwriting analysis.

Handwriting is a lot like body language. When you are interested in what someone is saying, the tendency is to bend forward to hear better and pay closer attention. If you don't like the message, you may lean backwards as a show of resistance. With a so-so attitude your posture might be upright—you don't care, either way.

As we've discovered, handwriting symbolism has it that the left represents the self (the personal "I"), and the right represents other people (the global "You"). The degree to which handwriting slants to the right or left reveals how much the writer wants to be involved with "you."

Fine Points

If the slants could speak, they might say: "I think, therefore, I am." (vertical slant); "I'd do anything for you." (right slant); "Nothing exists except Me." (left slant); and "Oh dear, what should I do?" (variable slant)

The person who uses a right slant is the type who leans forward to listen to the speaker in a conversation, and openly shows his interest. The one whose writing reclines to the left can be expected to show a more skeptical expression; and the person with vertical writing assumes a neutral posture until he decides whether or not he approves of the subject matter.

Slant also shows how spontaneous one's emotional reactions are, and how receptive the writer is, both to internal and external events. It also reveals how well he controls his responses after filtering them through his rational mind. In other words, slant depends on how fast the writer responds and reacts. The steadiness of the slant reveals the writer's emotional equilibrium.

Culturally Speaking

Nationality has some influence on slant. In the United Kingdom for instance, the school model teaches an upright writing position and a large proportion of British people stick with the school model. They have the reputation for being more cool-headed, which is one characteristic of the neutral slant.

Fine Points

Some graphologists prefer the designation "slope" instead of slant. They refer to an inclined slope, which is right slanted, or a reclined slope, which is left slanted.

In the United States, the learned slant is moderately rightward; but there is a much wider range of variability in the writings of Americans, which, in itself, is an indicator of cultural independence, a well-known American trait.

At some periods in history, writing was far more right-slanted than it is now; at other times, it is more upright. In his book, *The Psychology of Handwriting* (George Allen & Unwin, 1926; reprinted, Books for Professionals, 1978), Robert Saudek describes some of the changes in handwriting slant in various European countries over time. That's another reason why it's important to check the school model if you are analyzing writing done by someone from another country. Deviating from school model is as significant as if school-model style is retained.

Gauging Slant

The most profound effect on slant is produced by the angle at which the paper is placed on the writing surface. Pen hold and the position the arm is held in relation to the writer's body also affect the slant.

Tales from the Quill

Klara Roman studied the handwritings of 283 pairs of identical twins. In most pairs she found that one twin wrote with a right slant, but the other twin used a left slant. In most cases one twin was right-handed and the other left-handed. Handedness does have some effect on slant. Graphologists are continuing to study the effects on handedness of being a twin, but so far none have contradicted Roman's findings.

Two types of slants exist in handwriting, and both are found in all three zones. They are upslants, which are made by strokes going upward, away from the self; and downslants, which are made by strokes going downward, back toward the self.

In the upper zone, slant is measured by drawing a line from where the upstrokes and the downstrokes of an upper loop cross at the baseline, to the top of the loop. (See the next illustration) The angle is now determined between the line we've drawn and the baseline. This clues us in on how responsive the writer is intellectually to outside influences. The letters l, b, and h are the easiest to use in measuring upslant.

The downstrokes of middle-zone letters are also measured, using the last stroke of the letters m, n, and h. Because the middle zone is where we live from day-to-day, we can learn how quickly the writer reacts outwardly on his inner responses, his gut reactions.

There are all sorts of possibilities for slant. A 90° angle is the midpoint, which we'll call vertical, or upright. Slants between 90°–45° in either direction are considered moderate. Any slant leaning further than 45° to the baseline is extreme.

Some writers can't seem to make up their minds and adopt a variable slant. As you might guess, variable slant has a meaning all its own.

So, how do you measure the upstrokes and downstrokes? An inexpensive plastic protractor will do for measuring slant. The flat side of the protractor should line up with the baseline of the writing you want to measure. Slide the gauge along the upper loops until one of the slanted lines passes directly through the middle of the loop (or close to it), from the apex (top) to where the downstroke crosses the upstroke at the baseline. This allows

Fine Points

If you don't have a protractor, you can photocopy the slant gauge shown in this chapter and have it printed out on a transparent sheet. You can lay it over the handwriting to get a good idea of where the slant falls.

you to find the angle between the upslant and the baseline.

To measure the downstrokes in the middle zone simply find the slanted line that most closely approximates the final downstroke on the m's, n's, and h's. This allows you to find the angle between the downstroke and the baseline.

Some graphology schools require their students to measure 100 slants on a page. I would never graduate from that school! I don't think I could make it past 20. In my experience though, it isn't the number of exact measurements that counts. The most important thing is to get a good feel for the direction the letters slant. Of course, if you feel compelled to measure 100 letters, go for it. You have my blessing. Now, let's see what slant reveals about personality.

Measuring upslant (above) and downslant (below) angles.

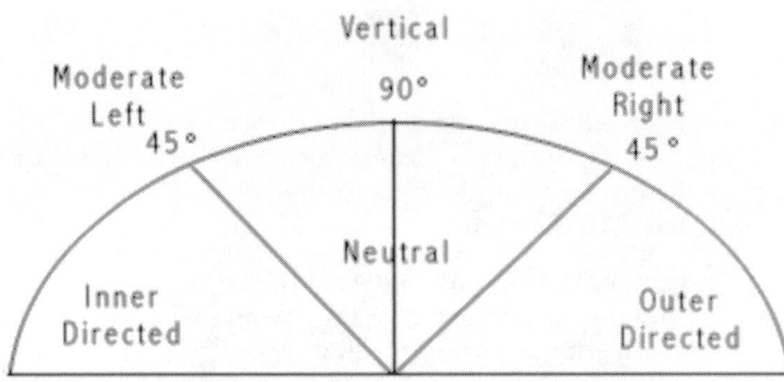

Slant gauge.

Feeling It in the Heart: The Right Slants

The amount of right slant tells how much the writer is willing to spontaneously show her feelings. If your spouse brought home a new friend to meet you and you wanted that person to feel welcome, how would you act? You might reach out, maybe even with both hands, to grasp his hands in a warm clasp and tell him how glad you are to meet him. The act of reaching forward and extending yourself is reflected in right-slanted handwriting.

Moderate Right Slant

The writer with a *moderate right slant* is sociable and affectionate. A strong right slant, however, suggests someone who might impulsively throw herself on you and give you a big hug and kiss. She is expressive and enthusiastic, a bit sentimental, and easily able to love others.

Right slant suggests some degree of subjectivity. The writer doesn't care so much about logic and reason, she just knows how she feels. However, she uses some restraint and doesn't get totally carried away with her feelings. She may share her opinions and viewpoints with others, but is not afraid to allow someone else to influence her when the situation calls for it. Emotions are involved though, so the writer's decisions may be a tiny bit colored by her feelings about the subject matter.

Write Words

A **moderate right slant** is where the upslant in the upper zone measures between 120°–130°, and in the middle zone, between 110°–130°. These numbers are approximate, not absolute.

The warmth and sincerity found in a moderate right slant are desirable characteristics. But, as in every other area, balance and moderation are important factors. As the slant moves further to the right, the controls begin to weaken.

The Complete Idiot's Guide to Handwriting Analysis will make an excellent addition to an already spectacular series. I can't wait to get my hands on a copy of this book

Moderate right slant.

Strong-Extreme Right Slant

The stronger the right slant, the more subjective the writer. When the slant becomes extreme, the writer is responding on a purely gut level, seeing things only from his own point of view. His attitude says "How will this affect me?". He is too impatient to put the brakes on and examine the facts before acting, so it doesn't take long for him to make a decision. He just acts, regardless of the consequences.

The very strong right-slanted writer is quick to jump to conclusions and overreact. He makes assumptions and proceeds accordingly. He rushes ahead, with little restraint. There are times when his rash, reckless responses might put others at risk, but it never occurs to him that he might be at fault when things go wrong. Taking time to check things out before hurtling into them headlong would probably save everyone a lot of grief.

Chicken Scratch

Adolf Hitler's handwriting careened to a manic right slant, word by word. His maniacal impulses are seen in the way his signature falls over (see a never-before-published sample of his handwriting in Appendix E).

With supporting evidence, such as narrow word and line spacing, the extreme right-slant reveals a writer who responds hysterically at the drop of a hat. Especially when letters and words become progressively more slanted to the right, real emotional problems are a strong possibility. Whatever he experiences is expressed in an instant. Expect him to broadcast his feelings openly and extravagantly. When he is angry, he is explosively angry. When he is loving, he is passionately loving.

Although he may have later regrets, he impulsively throws himself into new adventures without evaluating the consequences. In the meantime, if it feels good, he'll do it and not look back. His actions are overly informal, often irresponsible, and tactless. He'll blurt out whatever comes to mind without censoring himself. His attraction for behaving with such reckless abandon could easily alienate the people around him.

Strong right slant.

Upright, Uptight?

A vertical or upright slant is midway between left and right slant. Self-control and self-discipline are needed to maintain such a neutral posture. Try standing up straight for an hour and see what a strain it can be! If handwriting is like body language, the vertical writer is standing very straight and projecting a rather austere manner.

His unsentimental, levelheaded demeanor may make him look as cool and detached as James Bond. The apparent lack of emotion is not because he isn't emotional, but because he would rather deny that he is. Being very concerned with controlling his behavior, he weighs his words before speaking and thinks before acting. The closer to upright the writing, the more the writer curbs his initial impulses.

This is not the type who blindly goes where fools rush in; he listens to his inner voice, which speaks the language of logic, not emotion. Being fair is very important to the vertical writer, so he takes great pains to stay impartial and carefully weigh the facts before making a decision. He thoughtfully considers the various sides of a matter, balancing all the pros and cons to reach a conclusion.

Impassioned appeals do little to sway him, even when he cares deeply about the people involved. He is able to put his compassion to sleep and consider the facts rationally without getting carried away by personal feelings that might affect his judgment.

He denies being dependent on anyone, preferring to stand on his own. An observer from the wings of life, he is more of a perceptive watcher than one who participates fully. In a crisis he can be a rock, the one guy who doesn't lose his head when everyone else is panicking.

The complete Idiot's Guide to Handwriting Analysis will make an excellent addition to an already spectacular series. I can't wait to get my hands on a copy of this Book.

Upright handwriting.

Tales from the Quill

San Francisco Graphologist Marcel Matley says of girls who choose a left slant, "She says in her heart, if not out loud, to the father figure who threatens her, 'I'll show you, you bastard, I will become a better man than you are.' So she tends to become the kind of 'male' he is, out-drinks him if he drinks, out-sexes him if he is a sex addict, outperforms him in business if he is a businessman, etc."

You'll Never Know How Much I Really Love You: The Left Slants

When you have a real aversion to someone and unexpectedly run into her on the street, what do you do? You might turn away, give her the cold shoulder. In effect, that's what left-slanted handwriting does. The left slant is a formal rejection of the world at large; a literal turning away; a slap in the face to anyone who wants to approach the writer with social overtures.

Even a moderate slant to the left shows an oppositional attitude toward the world in general. When she needs encouragement and emotional feeding, who does she turn to? Herself. The writer is leaning away from "you," to go inside. She doesn't feel comfortable asking anyone else for anything important. It would be too much of a risk.

Risk of what? Rejection of some kind, perhaps. She's felt it before and prefers not to repeat the experience. It doesn't have to be childhood experiences that prompt the left slant. In one case an individual said she switched her slant after her parents divorced; another, when his wife left him for another man. And another after he discovered his lover had an abortion without discussing it with him.

The left-slanted writer is just as impressionable and emotional as the right-slanter, but she keeps her responses to herself. The greater the degree of left slant, the more emotional and the more self-contained she is likely to be. In fact, if you mentally flip the angle of left slant to the same angle of right slant, the emotions indicated are doubly strong, yet doubly inhibited.

Such a writer may be very friendly and outgoing, yet, even after a long period of acquaintance, reveals little of herself beyond what you see on the surface. So you'll have to guess at what left-slanters are thinking and feeling.

Left-slanted writers are almost always pleasant to work with and they make an effort to do a good job. When things start going wrong, however, they may take refuge in an "everyone for themselves" attitude. They'll watch their own backs before covering for someone else.

Fine Points

Graphology pioneer Alfred Mendel taught that slant indicates the writer's position between the mother (left) and father (right); or, according to Klara Roman, between male and female leadership. The more left-slanted, the more inclined the writer is toward females. The greater the right slant, the more the writer is influenced by males.

Teenagers who are feeling rebellious about knuckling under to their parents' and teachers' influence often use left-slanted writing. Since the right symbolizes authority, one who deliberately turns to the left is defying authority and convention. Think of it as "thumbing their nose" at the rest of the world, saying, "I'll do what I want, regardless of how you feel about it."

Left slant is never taught in school models, so when someone adopts one, she's made a conscious choice to reject the norm. It takes sustained effort to preserve a left slant over a long period of time. Thus, while a moderate right slant is considered spontaneous, a left one is always viewed as unnatural.

Moderate Left Slant

Chances are, the person with a *moderate left slant* was the victim of some really nasty experiences. As a result, he feels compelled to protect himself at all costs. In men, the left slant often stems from an unhappy childhood, which meant conflicts with the father, stepfather, an older brother, or some other influential male. He may never have been acknowledged by his male role model, or worse, he may have been abused.

A boy child's response to the disappointing relationship may be to repudiate any behavior or attitude that approximates anything close to that person. Sometimes he'll compensate by growing into an especially sensitive or refined young man. More aggressive boys may even accuse him of being a "mama's boy."

To the moderate left-slanted writer, being in control is all-important. Consequently, he takes the time to screen his emotional reactions through the fine mesh of logic. He believes he can think his way through life as a substitute for experiencing his feelings.

Moderate left slant.

Extreme Left Slant

Alfred Mendel conducted a study of famous authors who wrote with a strong left slant. It turns out that they shared a common background: a very unhappy childhood and parents who were out of harmony with each other. Mendel concluded that left slant is an indicator of unresolved difficulties very early in life, resulting in a generally negative attitude in the writer as an adult. This type of writer opposes people, ideas, and everything else, just for the heck of it.

Write Words

A **moderate left slant** is where the upslant in the upper zone measures between 80°–90°, and the downslant in the middle zone measures between 80°–90°. These numbers are approximate, not absolute.

Even if he wanted to respond emotionally, the extreme left-slanter feels paralyzed by his inability to trust. Surely, he thinks, if someone is "acting nice" to him, she must have an ulterior motive. He desperately wants to avoid being susceptible to any more emotional damage than he already has experienced. His self-protective attitude is like a turtle refusing to come out of his shell, even for a hug from the right-slanter.

The past is where mothering and nurturing are supposed to have been. The extreme left-slanter is preoccupied with the past and all the awful things (real or imagined) that happened to him there. He is looking for something to hang on to, some stability. Someone who didn't get what he needed in the past returns there again and again, hoping to find some way to make up for what was lacking—in this case, by slanting his letters to the left.

Staying aloof takes a lot of energy, leaving little for the more important activities of life. The extreme left-slanted writer is exhausted by the conscious need to repress his reactions and his lack of energy may lead others to conclude that he is passive and lazy,

Tales from the Quill

One graphologist told me about a moderate left-slanter who, at first, came off as Ms. Wonderful. Everyone thought she was the most giving, fun-loving person in town. Sadly enough, my friend came to know her too well. His comment was, "She gave new meaning to the word bitch." Of course, the same could be said of some right-slanters, too! It's very important to avoid generalizations when characterizing left-slanters or any other type of writer. Look at the *whole* picture before interpreting the handwriting!

which might well be wrong. If he is able to find some way to successfully compensate for the disappointments he experienced in the past, there will be signs of strength in the handwriting, such as good pressure and vitality, and a well-formed middle zone.

Extreme left slant.

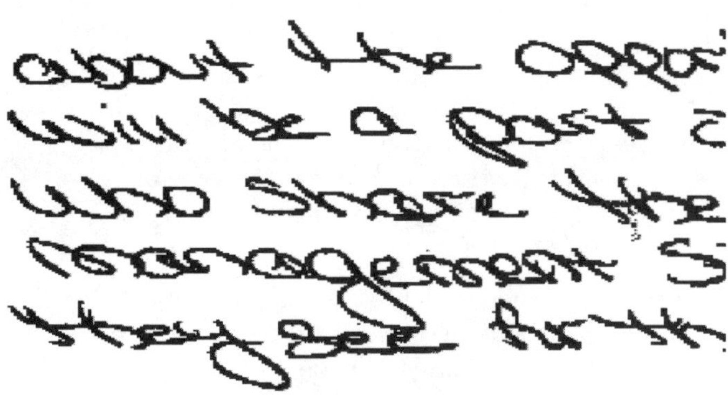

Every Which Way But Loops: Variable Slant

If slant were an electrical current, it would be important for the current to flow smoothly. What happens to a computer when it isn't protected by a line conditioner or a surge protector and there are spikes of electrical current? The motherboard is fried. No more computer. When electricity doesn't flow smoothly it leaves a lot of damage in its wake. The person whose loops slant in every direction is like someone who is being zapped with electrical current every five seconds or so. Yeow!

Decisions, decisions. The variable slant writer turns indecisiveness into an art form. She is consumed with ambivalence. Making up her mind about anything and sticking with it is close to impossible. She can't even decide which way to write, for heaven's sake! Oh, she tries to control her responses, but the constant excitement and restlessness subject her to the capricious waves of emotional input which fling her in every direction.

Torn on every front, her internal agitation communicates itself through her nervous demeanor. She can't decide which way to go, what to do, whom to believe. An inner battle rages, and, what's worse, it's not a war she might have a chance of winning because the enemy is within.

Just when she makes up her mind about something, someone comes along with a better argument and she switches over to the other side. Of course, she may just as quickly switch back again and for those who were counting on a firm decision; this can be extremely frustrating.

From a positive angle, if you want her on your side, you're in luck. She willingly explores all sides and is on all sides.

Chicken Scratch

Convicted Oklahoma City bomber, Timothy McVeigh's handwriting reveals a strong left slant in combination with a tiny middle zone—lack of reality; wide letter and word spacing and printing—isolation; heavy pressure—frustration. It looks like a slingshot, pulled taut, ready for launching.

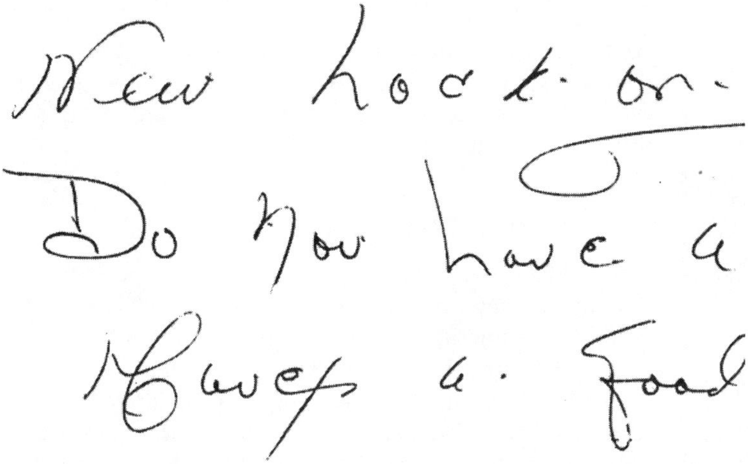

Variable slant.

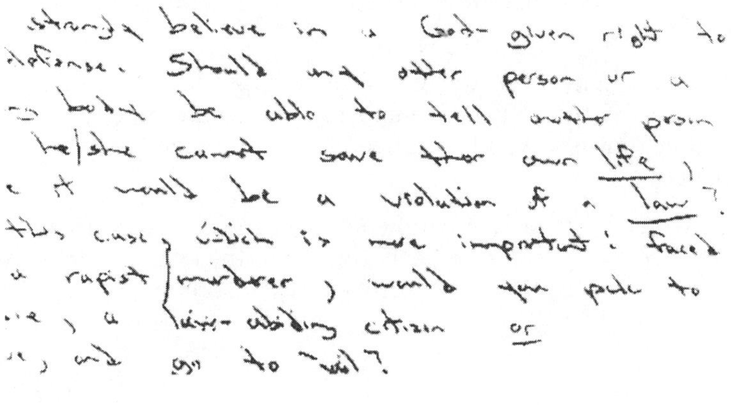

Timothy McVeigh, Oklahoma City bomber.

Lefties Are in Their Write Minds

The left-handed person has many more challenges in the graphic field than the right-hander. As the mother of a left-handed son and daughter, I remember how much harder it was for them to learn to write than it was for my right-handed son. According to Klara Roman and other graphological trailblazers, the natural mode of the left-hander is to write upside down or backwards (mirror writing), which goes against the grain in the right-handed world we live in (supposedly, only about 15 percent of people are left-handed).

We've already established that left-*slanters* are rebellious, but Roman further claims that when a left-handed person adopts a left slant, he is protesting the pattern that is imposed on him by the outside world. For a lefty to be able to write with a right slant, he is forced to turn his paper in a counter-clockwise direction. When the paper is absolutely straight to the edge of the writing surface it is nearly impossible for him to write correctly because he would be dragging his hand across what he had just written. Try it. You won't like it.

Fine Points

Fellow graphologist Pauline Clapp and I undertook a study to find out how often a left slant would be adopted in a large group of writers. The sample of 120 writers consisted of 60 left-handed and 60 right-handed writers. In each group, 30 of the writers were men and 30 were women. Of the entire sample, only two people wrote with a left slant. Both were right-handed.

The lefty who manages to successfully compensate for writing in a right-handed world should get extra credit. So, when a left-hander adopts a right slant, pat him on the back for having made the adaptation. The same goes for when he makes rounded forms, which are more difficult for him to make than angular ones.

Slant and the Sexes

Women who use a left slant seem to find it especially difficult to relate to men and even more so, male authority figures. Sometimes they are highly competitive with men, either directly or indirectly challenging their leadership. The pull to the left suggests that any close relationships they develop are likely to be with mother substitutes. Especially when the writing is also rounded, these women tend to be more possessive than some other types and have trouble letting go of a relationship, once it's over.

Women whose lower zone slants right, while the rest of the writing slants left, are also rebelling against male authority. With a left-slanted upper zone in addition to the right-tending lower zone, they probably won't rebel openly, but find more passive ways to express their defiance.

Additionally, the right-slanted lower zone in either men or women pulls away from the left, the mother influence. Therefore, there is probably conflict in the relationship with the mother or some other close female role model, such as a sister, aunt, or other mother-substitute.

Tales from the Quill

Werner Wolff, in his classic, *Diagrams of the Unconscious* (Grune & Stratton, 1948), described an experiment with slant. One student wrote, "I can write faster with a right slant but feel as if I was running ahead of my thoughts; I like to write this way, not much thought is involved." Others said it felt strained, unnatural, tense, reactionary, self involved. Right slant was experienced by some as pleasing, artistic; by others as an expression of haste, sluggish and weak." Wolff's experiments found that choice of slant is a very individual matter.

A left-slanted upper zone in men's writing is fairly uncommon. It suggests a strong attachment to ideas about women, particularly the mother. The writer prefers to steer clear of situations where other men can dominate him. Such men are often eager to please and work hard to make relationships succeed. However, when the left slant is in the lower zone, it infers disappointment in his intimate relationships and he may have doubts about his ability to satisfy a lover.

Other Stuff About Slant That Doesn't Fit Anywhere Else

An unvarying slant, like any other mechanical-looking handwriting, is a sign of overcontrol. The writer is predictable and consistent, but also emotionally inhibited and passive. She is afraid to let go and respond to her feelings.

Sometimes one letter in a word will unexpectedly tip over toward the baseline. Some handwriting analysts call these "maniac" letters because they're a mini volcano of emotion. This is not a particularly uncommon characteristic, and certainly not always the sign of a maniac (I even make them myself, once in a while) if they occur only occasionally. The Zodiac Killer's writing, however, is one example where "maniac" is an appropriate term for the sudden extreme right slant. You can see his handwriting in Appendix E.

A capital letter that tilts more to the right than the rest of the word suggests someone who is quick to control her initial strong impulses. When the slant becomes stronger the further the writer goes into a word, it implies that her enthusiasm is growing and her self-control is slipping. She starts to get carried away with what she wants to say and just can't hold back. If there is a sudden pulling back to a more vertical slant, you'll know she managed to put the brakes on before crashing into a wall.

The opposite is, of course, also true. With a strong slant in the beginning that pulls back mid word, or toward the end of the word, it's a sure sign that the writer recognizes his tendency to let it all hang out and makes a conscious effort to control himself. He wants to look cool, but also he doesn't trust you. By making his strokes more vertical than they naturally are he puts up a deliberate barrier that says that he fears making himself vulnerable.

The personal pronoun "I" (which we'll be covering in detail in Chapter 18) that slants to the left in a normally right-slanted writing suggests feelings of guilt. The writer is pulling away from others, and since the single letter I represents the self, he wants to hide something from the world.

When the upper zone slants in a different direction from the lower zone, this indicates conflict between the way the writer thinks and acts. If the upper zone slant conflicts with the middle zone slant, the disagreement is between thoughts and feelings.

The Least You Need to Know

- Slant is a gauge of emotional responsiveness.
- Upstroke slant shows your gut reactions.
- Downstroke slant shows how quickly you respond to your gut reactions.
- Left-slanted writing is never natural.
- Slant is one of the easiest elements of handwriting to deliberately change.

Part 4

Just My Style: Form

Flamboyant Fanny? Ostentatious Oliver? Simple Susan? Elegant Elfred? Plain Jane and no nonsense? You'll find out what the style of writing says about the way a writer presents himself or herself to the world.

You'll also discover what part form plays in the big picture.

Chapter 17

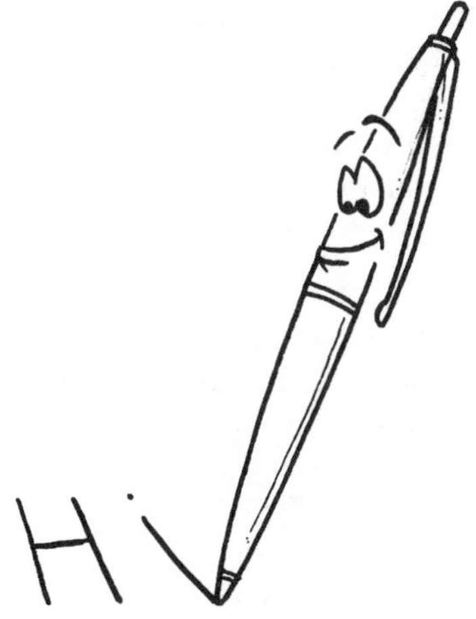

Keep It Simple, Sweetheart

In This Chapter

- Copying the copybook
- Simplifying matters by cutting away the extras
- Going to extremes—embellishments galore
- Adding something beautiful with stylized writing

Handwriting is not like walking or breathing, which comes naturally. It's a learned behavior, more like speech. The penmanship teacher spends many hours instructing her students in how to create the strokes and forms that make up the letters of the alphabet.

Each country has its own unique school model. Chapter 4 shows examples of copybooks of several different nations. More than one copybook is taught in the United States, and geographical location generally determines which one is used in any particular school system. But, whether the copybook is Zaner-Bloser, D'Nealian, or another, one thing is true of all students: They start out learning to write alike.

In Chapter 13 we discussed graphic maturity, which is the point at which a young writer no longer needs to consciously think about the letter forms as she writes them. Letters and words begin to flow naturally. Then, depending on the child, at some point something else happens.

Perhaps the margin begins to move away from the left side of the page. Or, the writing size may begin to shrink or grow beyond copybook size. The slant, baseline, and letter forms may look entirely different from what the school model dictates. What's going on here?

Chicken Scratch

Some people believe that it's good to write just like they learned in school. The truth is, many convicted felons write exactly the way they first learned! It's a matter of conforming, and some people conform to the wrong crowd.

The letter forms and their placement on the page have begun to deviate from what she learned in school. A more personalized writing style is taking shape, which mirrors the youngster's personality development. As she grows and matures, cultivating her own style and tastes along the way, her handwriting will gradually reflect the internal changes she experiences.

Let's say she loves sports and has energy to burn; her lower zone will probably expand and the pressure will increase. If she is shy about meeting new friends and venturing forth into the world, her right margin may grow and the writing size contract. If she is running for class president and has a flamboyant style, she may enlarge and decorate the capital letters. She didn't learn to make those flourishes and ornaments from her penmanship teacher—they just appeared naturally. The aspect of handwriting that exhibits personal style is called "form."

To Conform or Not to Conform, That Is the Question!

Form is the most conscious aspect of handwriting and represents a deliberate choice of writing style. It is how the writer wants others to see him. He may choose copybook, simplified, printed, or embellished styles to project his self-image.

Those who stick closely to the school model and write copybook style tend to be followers more often than leaders. They are most comfortable when the rules are clearly stated and they have a good idea of their parameters. Rather than being mavericks who develop their own individual styles, adult copybook writers prefer to follow instructions and guidelines given to them by someone else. They like to do things the way they have always done them, and feel threatened by major changes. Their motto is, "If it ain't broke, don't fix it."

Fine Points

Handwriting that shows a strong degree of regularity is often close to the school model. The writer feels safer when he sticks with what he knows—from the way he learned to write in grade school, to choosing the same cereal for breakfast every morning.

Lest you jump to the conclusion that writing copybook style is a "bad" thing, consider this: Many who adhere to copybook style perform some extremely important functions in our society. Nurses, grade-school teachers, secretaries, and administrators often choose copybook style (see some examples in the next figure), and where would we be without them! But, while our grade-school teachers might be happy if their students all maintained copybook writing style, the healthiest relationships, groups, and organizations embrace a variety of styles of being.

and able to be in a
loving relationship.
uld be successful in his
life as well as career.

a man who is a lot like
would like to meet a ma
happy and secure in his
but who is ready and w

for honesty, integrity,
fection. I am looking
minds, for that

Nurses, teachers, secretaries.

Straying from the Straight and Narrow

Almost everything we do says something about our individual style. We project who we are in our body language, facial expressions, tone of voice, and handwriting. Some people feel more comfortable blending in as part of a crowd. They act like the others because they don't want to be thought of as nonconformists.

Others have more original, individualistic styles and prefer to stand out from the crowd. They do things their own way and don't care what people think of them. And, within the group of "original" people, there is a wide range of possibilities.

The form the writing takes on—the way it looks—demonstrates the writer's personal style. Using copybook as a starting point, the degree to which the writing departs from the school model is the degree to which the writer feels compelled to express his own original style.

In what ways could one depart from the school model? As a graphologist, you'll examine handwriting to see how closely it adheres to the school model or how much it diverges from it. Are the shapes of the letters the same as the shapes in the copybook? What about the size, slant, beginning and ending strokes, and margins? Or, has the writer stripped away some of the nonessential strokes, changed the basic form, or added ornamentation?

Originality in handwriting can be expressed either by simplifying the school model or elaborating on it. A tremendous scope of possibilities falls between one end of the spectrum and the other. Copybook, or school model, sits in the middle. Let's start with copybook and work our way backward toward simplification.

Tales from the Quill

Teachers have a strong influence on the young mind. One woman reports remembering when her third-grade teacher very seriously informed the class, "You need to join up all your letters and write cursive—not printed—capitals, or else when you grow up, they won't let you vote, they won't let you have a job, they won't let you drive a car...." Children tend to believe what adults tell them. A seemingly innocent remark such as this may have a long-range effect on an impressionable young mind.

The following figure demonstrates just six ways the letter "S" can be made along the spectrum from highly simplified to extremely elaborate. Apply this illustration to all of handwriting to get the idea of what it means to simplify or elaborate.

The simplification to elaboration spectrum.

Just the Facts, Ma'am

Write Words

The **beginning stroke** leads into a letter but is not an essential part of the letter. The **ending stroke** follows the end of a letter or word but is not an essential part of the letter.

Writing is done for the purpose of communicating, so it needs to be clear and easily readable. It doesn't have to be fancy or ornate. To qualify as "simplified," a handwriting has less ornamentation and less superfluous elements than copybook. To some degree, the unnecessary parts are stripped away.

For example, *beginning strokes* are dispensable. You don't need them to make a word understandable. The same is true of *ending strokes*. (Beginning and ending strokes will be covered in detail in Chapter 19.) Upper loops are also optional. It is quite possible to make a downstroke that steers directly into the next letter without first moving into an upstroke. The following handwriting sample is simplified down to the bare bones.

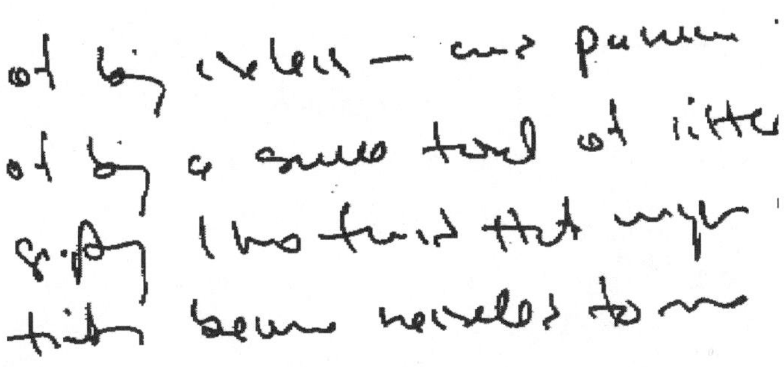

The bare bones.

Letters which, in copybook, have pointed tops, such the small s or r, can be simplified by rounding them (as in the next figure). Basically, simplifying handwriting is a way to take shortcuts and get the message across quicker. Writing that is simplified overall (see the moderately simplified writing example) is made by the person who wants to be efficient and expeditious. She gets impatient if you bombard her with a lot of extraneous details and just wants to get down to basics. Don't waste her time with long explanations—she isn't listening anyway.

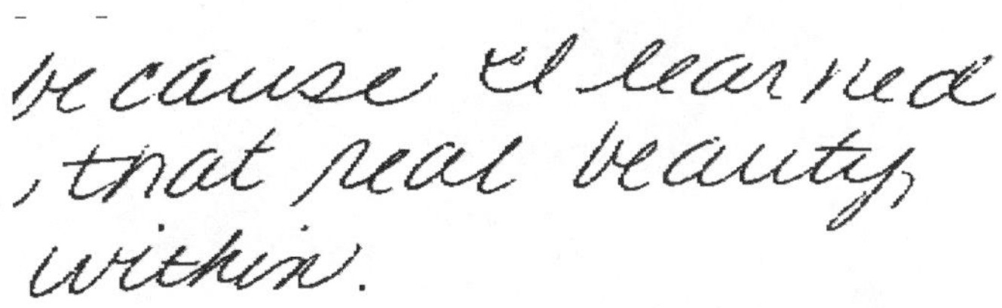

Simplifying by rounding.

The simplified writer's home echoes his writing style. Ornamentation may be sparse, with a few high-quality knickknacks gracing the bookshelves. In combination with an overall wide spatial arrangement (which is common in simplified writing), the writer feels uncomfortable in a crowd. Whenever possible she elects to spend her free time with a few carefully chosen friends.

Simplified writing that is low on loops signifies a direct personality that "tells it like it is." The writer can't stand verboseness and doesn't indulge in the kind of flowery speech that is liberally sprinkled with flattery. What you'll get is the bare facts with little embellishment.

Socially, the simplified writer takes her time getting to know you before she will allow any type of intimacy. The emphasis is on the intellect more than the emotions, and the writer is generally objective and realistic. It takes a fast thinker to cut through all the irrelevant matter and get to the bottom line.

Moderately simplified writing.

The Complete Idiot's Guide to Handwriting Analysis will make an excellent addition to an already spectacular series. I can't wait to get my hands on a copy of this book.

Ingenious Solutions

Because one of the aims of simplified writing is efficiency, writers who like to cut out the details often create very interesting shortcuts. The next figure illustrates some nifty ways to get from one letter to the next, which the writer certainly never learned in penmanship class!

Ingenious shortcuts.

Idiot's Guide to
lysis will make an
tion to an already
ies. I can't wait to
on a copy of this

Tales from the Quill

Sometimes simplifying takes time. Writing a concise letter, for example, isn't always as easy as it sounds. Benjamin Franklin once wrote to an acquaintance, "I would have written you a shorter letter but I didn't have the time." It's easy to write at great length about a subject, but making the writing clear and concise takes much more effort.

The ability to find efficient means to get from one place in writing to the next suggests that the writer is proficient at constructing solutions to problems without relying on the standard, tried-and-true methods. She is resourceful and innovative, finding fresh, sometimes even revolutionary ways of doing the same old thing.

There is, however, the danger of (as my grandmother used to say) "throwing the baby out with the bath water." In her need for efficiency and innovation, the simplified writer may repudiate what has worked well in the past simply because it isn't new. She may jettison some systems that are doing just fine as they are, in favor of something untried.

I Go to Pieces

Simplifying handwriting is possible to achieve without damaging the basic structures of the letters. Writing that is simplified by removing the upstrokes can retain its legibility. However, when the downstrokes—the backbone of the writing—are eliminated it becomes impossible to read the message. Remember in Chapter 14 the illustration of downstrokes without upstrokes, and upstrokes without downstrokes? For a positive interpretation, the handwriting must be spontaneous, natural, and easy to read. The next figure is a handwriting made up mostly of downstrokes.

Chicken Scratch

The extremely simplified writer often is not considerate of other people. He lives at a high level of stress and is too impatient to put a little meat on the bones of his writing. His behavior in the world is just as impatient and irritable as his writing.

THE COMPLETE IDIOT'S GUIDE TO
HANDWRITING ANALYSIS WILL MAKE
AN EXCELLENT ADDITION TO AN
ALREADY SPECTACULAR SERIES.
I CAN'T WAIT TO GET MY HANDS
ON A COPY OF THIS BOOK.

Keeping the essentials.

When too many details are eliminated the writing may look emaciated, like someone who has been fasting too long. There is little meat on the bones. We say the form is neglected, as in the next illustration. Yet, if the downstrokes are present, the bare essentials are still there and the writer generally manages to function in the world.

The overly simplified writer is ascetic. He has little interest in form. Creature comforts and the extraneous trappings of life mean nothing to him. He views the world through objective eyes, sustained by purely intellectual interests. He doesn't consider other people's needs; in fact, he is probably barely aware of their existence. Reason and intellect are developed at the expense of his emotional life.

Overly simplified writing.

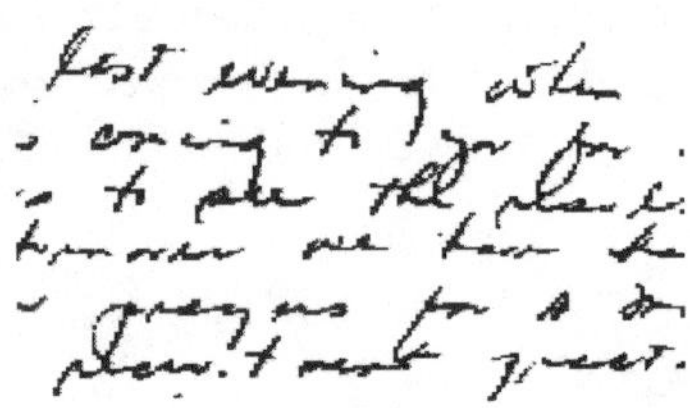

Skeletons in the Closet

Fine Points

In determining whether simplification in a particular handwriting should be interpreted positively or not, we need to ask ourselves a couple of questions: Does the writing retain legibility? Is the simplified style natural and spontaneous or does it look as if it were carefully drawn?

As in many other aspects of handwriting, "simplification" is a matter of degree. When the handwriting is so oversimplified that it has deteriorated to the most basic strokes and legibility is totally abandoned, it is called fragmented or skeletal writing. Whereas the writer of simplified writing wants to be clear and efficient, the skeletal writer achieves the opposite result—the writing becomes hard to read because it lacks some of the essential structure, the "backbone."

Extreme simplification is a sign of emotional self-denial and an impoverished spirit. The writer may feel so profoundly stressed and unable to deal with the pressures of his daily existence that he is forced to divest himself of every emotion or experience that might add to the fullness of life.

Neglect of form in handwriting can also be a sign of narcissism or egocentric behavior. The person who is so consumed by his problems tends to become wrapped up in himself—to the point that he ignores the people and events around him. Emotional reactions are withheld and responses kept to the barest minimum effort. His emotional life is decaying, falling apart, and so is his handwriting. Communicating with the outside world is impaired at best, nonexistent at worst.

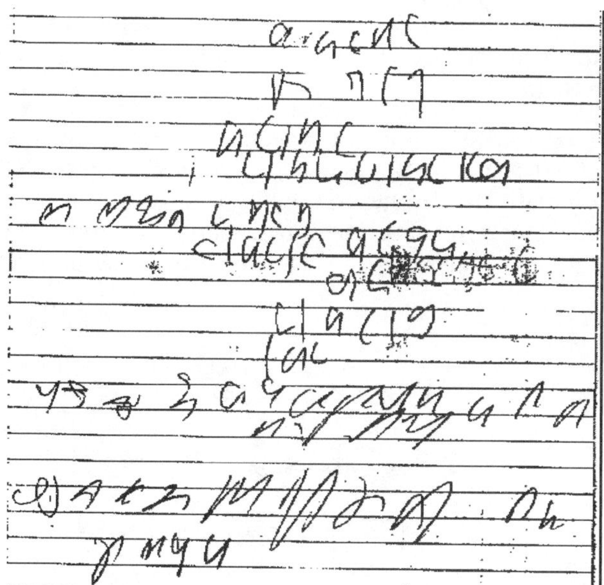

Skeletal writing due to mental illness.

Dressing Up Is Fun

Now it's time to go to the other end of the spectrum and visit the enrichment/elaboration continuum. While simplification is spontaneous and unconscious, any type of ornamentation added to handwriting is done consciously. Again, we have to ask ourselves: Is the writing legible and is it spontaneous and natural? If answers to both questions are yes, then the interpretation can be positive. If, on the other hand, the elaboration detracts from the message or legibility in any way, a negative meaning results.

Chicken Scratch

Skeletal writing may be a sign of mental impairment in the form of retardation or mental illness, such as schizophrenia. This is not a job for the beginning graphologist. Call in an expert!

Think of handwriting as a sponge cake. Simplified writing is the plain, ungarnished cake. Add frosting and you've got copybook writing. From there, your imagination can run wild. Do you like birthday cake with frosting flowers? That might be "embellished" writing. How about wedding cake with flowers, sugar bells, and silver sprinkles? Now, that's elaborate!

Elaborated writing can run the gamut, from richly enhanced to gaudy and overly dramatic. Someone who decorates her writing with many extra strokes, wide loops, and other embellishments, such as we see in the next writing sample, is a visual person for whom form is often more significant than content. This is not a value judgment. It's a fact: the writer spends more time making the writing beautiful (at least, beautiful in her eyes), than on what she writes.

The elaborate writer is likely to have a home filled with objets d'art—pictures and sculptures—with an emphasis on design. She is attracted to flamboyant, eye-catching, showy things. Her manner is dramatic, sometimes to the point of theatrical. You can bet she'll make an entrance when she arrives at a meeting or party. When she describes an event, it's not a dry recitation of the facts, it's a full-blown story. In her life, everything is BIG and EXCITING.

Ornamented handwriting.

to California in
6 continued educ
rior to marriage
as fashion design

Artistic Additions

To be considered artistic, the ornamentation must add to the form picture, not detract from it. In other words, if the form stands out too much, it may reduce the positive meaning. Usually, positive ornamentation includes some type of flourish and original or unique letter forms. Ornaments that are superfluous and overly complex become mere gaudy junk that serves no useful purpose. Always keep in mind that legibility is the first consideration. Artistic writing with some simplified forms appears in following sample.

Artistic handwriting.

courses were taken as
only married to a high

Distinctive Details

Writing that is full and round without being overly elaborated suggests fullness of emotion and imagination. In a harmonious writing where the forms are balanced in a well-organized space, the interpretation could be an exuberant spirit with a zest for life.

Elaboration in disorganized, inharmonious writing, on the other hand, could signify one who overexaggerates or overestimates himself. Both types of writers have an abundance of ideas, but express them differently. Think of it as the difference between having a gift wrapped by a professional or by someone who is all thumbs. The gift is still wrapped, but which would you rather give?

The Complete Idiot's Guide to
Handwriting Analysis will make
an excellent addition

Elaborate writing.

There's a big difference between enriching writing and overembellishing it. The difference is an aesthetic one. When the adornments are in good taste and not overdone, the analysis will be more positive than one where the handwriting is bedecked with a myriad of curlicues, inflated loops, and extra strokes, as the writing of the next sample is.

Both types of writers are attempting to beautify their scripts, but for different reasons. The enriched writer wants to enhance his writing and improve it. The embellished writer wants to impress others for his own self-aggrandizement.

Chicken Scratch

Writers of highly embellished handwriting tend to spin their wheels. They may devote many hours attending to details that will make their environment look impressive without leaving time to handle the mundane obligations that pay the bills.

Much Ado About Nothing

Exaggerated embellishments are a waste of time—the writer's and the reader's. The writer spends an exorbitant amount of time fussing over the most unimportant details. There is so much "stuff" in her subconscious that it overflows onto the paper and displays itself in excessive ornamentation on her handwriting.

The overly embellished writer is likely to be vain and ostentatious in her presentation, loudly drawing attention to herself. Her need to be in the limelight is an overcompensation for a poor self-image. She feels that the only way she can get the recognition she so desperately craves is to demand it. Unfortunately, her over-ornamentation trivializes her efforts, and the attention she gets is likely to be of the negative variety.

The more extravagant the flourishes and ornaments, the more inflated the capital letters, the less the writer is in touch with reality. She may be conceited and narcissistic, boasting of her supposed accomplishments, which probably exist only in her mind. Such people are often social climbers who are impressed with other people's money.

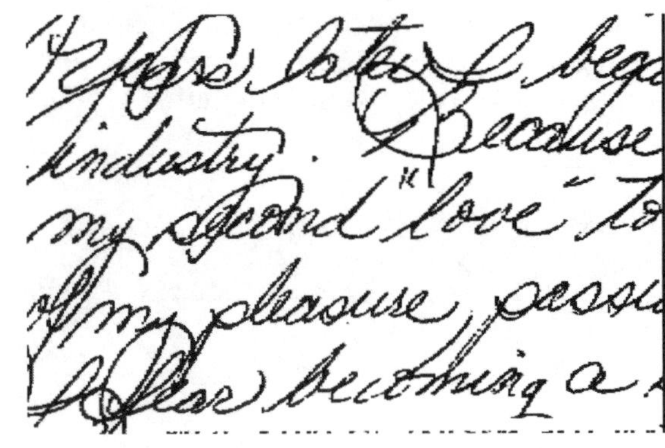

Over-elaborated writing.

The Icing on the Cake

Everyone has different faces or masks that they use in different situations. Carl Jung called them our *persona*. We wear our masks to cover up the less desirable parts of ourselves (Jung's shadow side), so others won't see them.

The masks we wear change according to circumstances. We don't wear the same face when dealing with the boss as the one we wear in bed with our lover (at least, one would hope not!). The mask we wear when a policeman pulls us over in traffic is probably not the one we wear at a party, and so on.

Write Words

Persona is the outer self that masks the shadow side of personality. An overly strong persona is seen in carefully constructed handwriting called persona writing.

Some people are more concerned than others about controlling their shadow side, and consequently develop a stronger persona to keep it under wraps. Those who are most afraid of their shadow peeking out and giving them away develop a strong persona, which means lots of self-control.

Strong self-control requires a lot of maintenance and energy, and is developed at the expense of spontaneity. It shows up as a pictorial-style handwriting, like Elizabeth Dole's handwriting is shown in the next figure. The writing looks as if it were drawn, rather than written naturally and spontaneously. It may be quite beautiful to look at, and is more of a work of art than communication.

The writing is elaborate and ornamented, but with little spontaneity. Mrs. Dole has a reputation for having extremely strong self-control that rarely, if ever, slips. Her mask is kept firmly in place, and the public sees only what she wants us to see. Her handwriting is shown in the next figure.

Persona writers are often successful in the world of culture or design. They may be performers, artists, or orators who keep their private selves completely separate from the ones they show to others. The persona writer is polite and formal, sophisticated and charming, but onlookers may get the sense that the smile is painted on and unchangeable, regardless of what is happening inside.

Elizabeth Dole's elaborate writing.

The important question is: What is the purpose of the mask? Is it an attempt to deliberately disguise and hide something, or is it adopted out of a need to appear more beautiful, more sophisticated, more charming than the writer feels?

Persona handwriting is somewhat more difficult to analyze than natural handwriting, but the careful graphologist will be able to peek behind the mask and see what's back there. Certainly, the person who maintains her individuality, who is courageous, independent, and strong-willed in her drive to break away from the norm, stands out from the rest. Those who insist on "doing it their way" feel less need to adapt to the world than the copybook writer does.

Fine Points

Well-balanced form is natural and spontaneous, with good simplification and originality. It indicates maturity, ability to achieve goals, creativity, and receptivity to new ideas. Persona form is stilted or overornamented, which would indicate an unbalanced self-image.

The Least You Need to Know

- Copybook style is the point of departure in analyzing handwriting.
- Communication's the thing—whatever the style, handwriting needs to be legible and clear.
- Simplification means cutting away unnecessary elements, such as extra loops or beginning and ending strokes.
- Too much simplification breaks down the ability to communicate clearly.
- Elaboration on copybook writing is done by someone who has a more social, dramatic style, who deeply cares about appearances.
- Over-elaboration may be a sign of perfectionism or showiness and is called persona writing.

Chapter 18

A Rose by Any Other Name

In This Chapter

- Who are you?
- Signing on the dotted line
- Ideal self versus real self
- Who am I?

We've just completed a discussion of the most conscious aspect of handwriting, its overall form. Now, we'll delve into some very specific conscious form choices—capital letters, the signature, and that extra-special letter, the personal pronoun I.

When someone discovers that I'm a handwriting analyst, very often, she'll thrust her signature at me, expecting an instant opinion. It's doubtful that the same person would go to the doctor's office and expect to get a clean bill of health based on a quick peek down her throat; yet she thinks a handwriting analyst should be able to draw a full personality portrait from just a signature—the equivalent of a cursory glance at her tonsils.

Clearly, the signature is a very meaningful part of the whole handwriting picture. It explains some things about the way the writer functions that the body of text might not. But while some graphologists are willing to make an analysis based on the signature alone, the Old Masters always caution against it. The signature represents the personality on its best behavior, but it doesn't tell what goes on behind closed doors.

Tales from the Quill

A woman who suffered through a long, difficult marriage finally got her freedom through divorce. She detested her husband so thoroughly that, although she kept his name, she completely changed the way she wrote it. Soon afterward, the woman got a call from her bank, wanting to know if she had written a particular check, since the signature was so different from the one they had on file for her. Her public image had changed.

How Do I Look?

In the days before handwriting, people used pictographic drawings to transmit information. These symbols represented the message that they wanted to get across. When you sign your name to a document, whether it's a legal contract or a personal letter, you are leaving a symbolic representation of who you are, not so unlike those early pictographs.

One's signature is carefully crafted to project what we want others to know about who we are. It identifies us as us. Once we've chosen a signature we like, it usually remains constant for most of our lives. Only after undergoing major life changes does our signature alter in any significant way, if at all. The signatures of several world leaders suffered dramatic changes as their owners' power declined. Napoleon Bonaparte, Adolph Hitler, and Richard Nixon are compelling examples, as you can see at the top of the next page.

A signature can sometimes symbolize one's profession. A hairdresser might unconsciously draw scissors in her name. Liberace deliberately drew a little piano with his. In the following illustration, see if you can find the symbol of the ship in the captain's signature. It's not too hard to see boxer George Foreman's definite KO, and Mario Andretti's race car is clearly seen in his dynamic autograph. Some graphologists claim to see a building in architect Frank Lloyd Wright's moniker, and Walt Disney, who used to wear an engineer's hat on his Sunday evening TV show, makes his signature into a train. Once, Klara Roman noted that sometimes the signature may be symbolic of a wish, rather than the reality.

Developing one's signature is a highly individual and personal matter. It's rather like choosing a suit of clothes to cover the body underneath. One who believes his body is covered with horrible blemishes might select a heavy overcoat to completely cover himself; or, perhaps he feels the need of a suit of armor to hide away from a world that seems threatening. On the other hand, maybe the writer is a nudist who doesn't mind if others see his...er, well, you know.

Changes in signatures of world leaders.

The signature is one's public image; how someone wants to be seen. To discover whether what he's displaying is the genuine article or not, we'd have to examine his regular handwriting, too. Text that looks entirely different from the signature suggests duality. The personality has two very distinct sides. Either the writer has something to hide, or else is hiding from something. It's the body of writing that will uncover the true story.

A signature similar to the text is a primary sign of a genuine, up-front person who has nothing to hide. His personality is consistent and dependable. He faces the world with equanimity.

Symbols in signatures.

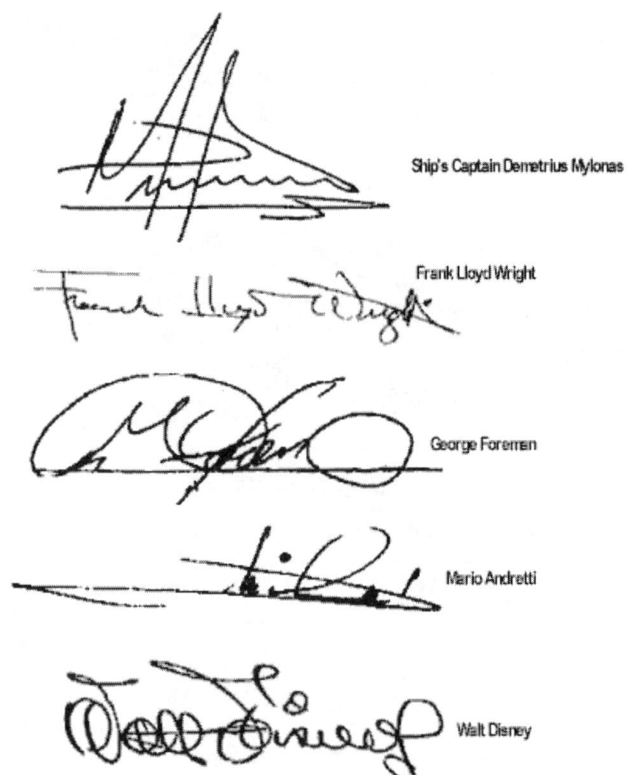

Chicken Scratch

Unscrupulous people have been known to deliberately disguise their signatures so they could later deny having authored certain documents. Changing the capital letters is a common method of attempting to disguise one's own signature.

Some people, especially those in public life, have two entirely different signatures. The public one is more like the gift-wrap on a package. What's inside may not look exactly like the wrapping implies. The one they choose for private correspondence is more revealing of the real person.

Do You Read Me?

The readability of one's signature speaks volumes about the writer's willingness to be known. Following are some of the ways people commonly present themselves in their choice of signature:

- *Clear and legible.* The person whose signature is absolutely readable has nothing to hide. She feels good about who she is and doesn't care whether you like it or not. What you see is what you get, warts and all.

- *Illegible signature.* Makeup, dentures, hair dye, high-heeled shoes; the methods we use to change our outer appearance are many and varied. There's nothing wrong with wanting to improve on the basic model, unless it's for the purpose of deliberate deception.

  An illegible signature may result from someone who is in a hurry and has had to sign many documents. Or, it may be that the writer doesn't want others to know the truth about her. She creates an illegible signature to conceal the person behind the mask. It's possible that by writing her signature so it can't be read, she is looking to absolve herself from responsibility for what she signs. Desire for privacy, or something more ominous? Examining the body of writing will tell.

  The signatures in the next samples are an example of someone with a public signature and a personal one. Grammy winner Paula Cole has a very private side that is revealed in her illegible signature.

- *Middle name or initial included.* Including the middle name or initial is a sign of pride. It's a very formal, official way of presenting oneself. Like Hillary Rodham Clinton, or Lance A. Ito, for example.

Legible and illegible signatures of singer Paula Cole.

All in the Family

The family name represents one's ability to interact on a social level. The given name symbolizes one's personal ego. If the person behind the signature is balanced and harmonious in both roles, the first and last names will be compatible and congruent. Sometimes they're not, as we'll see next:

Fine Points

The height that the capitals reach indicates to what degree the writer is driven to achieve. Extra large initials are frequently employed as compensation for low self-esteem.

- *Surname larger.* Pulver spoke of one's surname as being his history or trademark. In the case of a man, it tells the story of his regard for his family (or, for a woman who takes her husband's name, her husband's family). If the initial letter of the surname or the whole name is made larger than the given name, it denotes great respect for tradition and pride in the family name. In some cases it could possibly represent fear. Nicole Brown Simpson's signature is a case in point, as you can see in the next figure. The one after that is Oprah Winfrey's. Notice the difference in size between her given name and her surname.

Signature of Nicole Brown Simpson.

- *Given name larger.* Someone who makes his given name larger than the family name may not be too enamored of his family. The writer may have suffered some disappointment at the hands of his father or other family member and devalues their name by making it smaller. A woman who hates her husband may symbolize her animosity by shriveling up his name. Alternatively, a larger first name suggests that the writer would rather be known as "Bill" (see President Bill Clinton's signature in Appendix E), rather than "Mr. Clinton" for example.

  If the given name and the surname slant in different directions, it's a good bet that there is an inner conflict being waged between the writer's ego and his social life. Check the body of writing to discover the cause of the conflict.

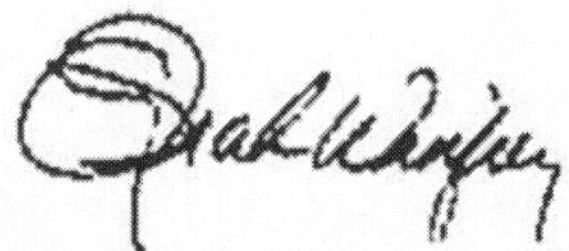

Oprah Winfrey. Which name is larger?

- *Surname illegible.* If the given name is written clearly but the family name is illegible, you can be sure that the writer has issues (that's a nice way of saying "problems") with his father. On the other hand, an illegible given name with a clear surname points to an insecure ego.

Tales from the Quill

There is a popular misconception that by using an elaborate signature one will be protected from having his name forged. Quite the opposite is true. A simple, straightforward signature is much more difficult to forge than one with lots of swirls and curls or one that is completely illegible. The easiest type of signature to copy is the squiggly line.

All the Trimmings

When my kids were little I used to spend a lot of time shopping in the fabric store. They hated it, because they naturally would rather be playing outside. But one thing they did enjoy was helping me choose which trimmings I would sew onto the clothes I was planning to make for them.

Some people enjoy ornamenting their signatures, much like sewing fancy buttons and beads onto a garment. It makes them feel important, or it's just fun to dress things up. The question for the graphologist is, is the writer choosing to do it for fun or because she feels compelled to do it.

Write Words

A **paraph** is a flourish appended to the signature. It may take the shape of an underscore, wavy line, scroll, or other decorative form. In "olden days," it was used as a means of preventing forgery.

The answer will be in how natural and genuine the embellishments are. A free and easy movement, one that adds attractive swirls, will produce a very different interpretation than carefully drawn ornamentation. The former represents a playful free spirit, while the latter has a premeditated quality that shows forced, unnatural behavior.

The Wrapping on the Package

Anything that goes beyond the plain and simple writing of one's name is considered an embellishment. From ornate capitals to flourishes and swirls, there are any number of ways to elaborate the signature. When placed underneath the signature, these decorations are called *paraphs.* Although the paraph used to be commonly used, it's fairly rare in the United States. It is still used in some Middle Eastern and South American countries.

What is the significance of underlining and other additions to the signature? That's our next area of discussion.

- *Signature embellished.* Embellishments represent a need to draw attention to oneself in some way. The writer feels his accomplishments deserve recognition. Exercise maven, Richard Simmons, makes elaborate capital letters in his signature (see the next figure). Anyone who's seen Richard on television knows it's impossible to overlook him!

Richard Simmons.

- *Signature underlined.* Underlining the signature is a way to emphasize it. The writer is proud of the poise and confidence she projects. It may be either a bold statement or a defiant, compensatory gesture.
- *Signature encircled.* The person who puts a circle around her signature feels in need of protection. In effect, she is the turtle withdrawing into a shell that she believes nothing can penetrate. In some cases, the circle is used to hide information about the writer from prying eyes. Reverend Jimmy Swaggart, before he was (allegedly) found with a prostitute, wrote an illegible signature and put a circle around it. Note in the next illustration that later, his signature opened up, apparently with relief, and became clear and legible.

Jimmy Swaggart.

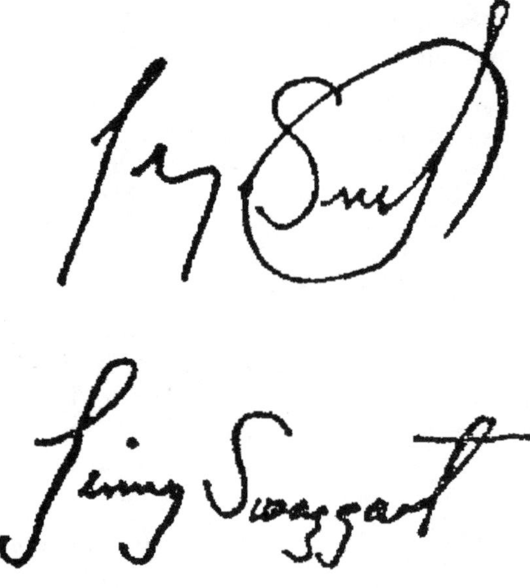

Chicken Scratch

Have you received a letter where your name was written smaller than the "Dear"? Maybe the writer doesn't really like you! Or, if words like "Dear," "Darling," "Honey," are written with a small initial, the sentiment may be insincere.

- *Signature crossed through.* When the final stroke of the signature goes back to the left and lines through it (or an intended underline slashes through it), it represents a gesture of canceling oneself out. A wife who detests her husband might unconsciously cross right through her married name, or a man who hates his father might cross through his own name.
- *Signature with a covering stroke.* As the term implies, this extra stroke is used to cover over or protect the ego. When the stroke goes under the signature and moves to the left it is a sign of caution and intent to cover up some aspect of the writer's life.

- *Signature with period or dot at the end.* Someone who makes a period at the end of his signature is putting a full stop to the action. It is a sign of caution, of backing off, inhibition, and mistrust. Possibly, the writer may have a "black spot" in his past that leaves him feeling like a guilty sinner. He knows in his heart what he's done, even though he hasn't yet been found out.

Ups and Downs

The position of the signature and its size are also significant.

- *Signature smaller than text.* Either the writer underestimates himself or she wishes to appear more modest than she really is. The text will tell the truth.
- *Signature larger than text.* This is a show of bravado. The writer wants to appear supremely poised and self-confident, even though she really feels quite small inside. She needs to impress others with her competence and stature.
- *Ascending signature.* The writer whose signature soars is ambitious, hopeful, and goal-oriented, especially if he also makes tall capitals. If the signature rises at too extreme an angle, he may be defending against a fear that things will not turn out as well as he hopes.
- *Descending signature.* Extreme discouragement, fatigue, or illness are all possibilities for why the writer's signature slopes downhill. The writer may have lost all hope and is simply giving in to depression.

Memories of Bygone Days

Leftward tending strokes—a long beginning stroke that swoops in from the left, or strokes that return to the left, suggest a mental return to past memories. When the leftward stroke is in the upper zone, the emphasis is on cultural or philosophical recollections. In the middle zone, the memories have to do with the emotions; and in the lower zone, with sexual and material remembrances. If the pressure on the leftward stroke is strong, this indicates that great passion is tied up in the memories the writer seeks to recapture.

Fine Points

Next time someone sends you a letter signed "love," so-and-so, check to see whether there is a comma after the word "love." If there is no comma, the request becomes a command—"love so-and-so," which is an altogether different closing.

In the next illustration, we see left- and right-tending strokes in the signatures of two politicians. Representative Jack Kemp makes a long, strongly right-tending stroke, while former governor Pete DuPont starts his signature to the far left.

Leftward- and rightward-tending strokes in Jack Kemp (above) and Pete DuPont (below).

A final stroke that gets larger in a rightward direction is an emphasis on the self and outer life. The writer is pleased with himself and wants others to know it.

Which Way Did He Go?

The placement of the signature on the page has its own story to tell. Normally, we expect to see the signature toward the right-hand side. The writer who exceeds that expectation and goes all the way to the right drives himself mercilessly. He is always on the go. He never lets up.

The nearer the signature is to the center of the page, the stronger the inhibiting movement. Since the right side represents the future, the more the signature hangs back, the greater the writer's fear of the future.

Chicken Scratch

A signature written at the far left side of the page is a danger sign! Especially when the writing is also small and narrow, the writer may be contemplating suicide.

The Man Behind the Curtain

Remember in the *Wizard of Oz,* when Dorothy and her companions finally made it to Emerald City? They stood quaking in their boots in front of this frightful image with a booming voice. That is, until Toto the dog revealed the feeble little man behind the curtain. Capital letters are the big scary voice the writer projects, and the small letters are the reality behind the curtain: the ideal self and the real self.

School models call for the capital letters to be about two to three times the height of the middle zone. Some writers take it even further and exaggerate their capital letters to great extremes. Others shrink them to barely copybook height. Capitals may also be more elaborate or more simple than copybook. The next list covers what various styles mean:

- *Capitals copybook.* When the capital letters are written the way the school model prescribes, the writer is conventional and conservative. He has little interest in breaking away from what he was taught and going out on a limb. Sticking within the confines of his chosen social group is much more comfortable for him.

- *Capitals plain and simple.* The writer has no illusions about who she is. Her manner is direct and up-front.
- *Capitals ornate.* The writer may be impressed with himself, and thinks others should be, too. He is likely to be attracted by status, wealth, and social prominence. Some degree of narcissism is evident in this showy display.
- *Capitals very small.* Modesty and constraint are suggested by small capitals. The writer desires to shrink into the woodwork, rather than be swept into the limelight. She may be submissive and pliable, or just plain spineless. As always, the whole picture of writing will differentiate the two.
- *Capitals very large.* The person whose capitals are large but not extreme, has self-confidence, pride, and ambition. She believes in her ability to accomplish what she sets out to do.
- *Capitals extremely large.* This is the self-aggrandizing person who comes on strong. He makes himself the center of attention and exaggerates his accomplishments to anyone who will listen. Whether what he says is based on reality or is mostly in his mind is another story.
- *Capitals well–formed.* The writer presents himself well. His obvious sense of pride and dignity indicate someone who understands where things fit.
- *Capitals poorly formed.* The self-concept is not well-developed. If this is the writer's "ideal self," he may need some help in improving his image.

Tales from the Quill

A graphologist was shown the handwriting of a young radio announcer who wrote with extremely tall capital letters. "You're looking for bigger and better things," she told announcer. The announcer laughed and shared that she had just accepted a more prestigious job at a much larger station.

Let's Get Personal

English is the only language in which a single letter represents the personal pronoun. In French it is *Je,* in German *Ich,* but in English I stands on its own as the personal symbol. That makes it a highly significant letter.

Fine Points

The school model of the personal pronoun I (PPI) has been compared to a little sailboat. The top part is the sail and the bottom is the boat. Some writers simplify the school model to one simple stroke, while others elaborate, using various twists and turns.

Entire books have been written on the subject of the personal pronoun I, which will be referred to as "PPI" from here on. Jane Nugent Green's, *You & Your Private I* (Llewelyn, 1975) goes into great detail to describe the various aspects of the self in relation to the PPI. My personal favorite on this subject, *The Freudian I* (Reprinted, Graphex, 1998), by Terry Henley, uses Freudian concepts to explain the complexities of this single letter.

Our discussion here intends to present only an overview of the more common styles of PPI. The number of possible types is practically boundless. It should go without saying by now that the following interpretations will be confirmed or modified by the body of writing and are only generalizations.

The school model calls for a PPI of about twice the height of the middle zone. Anything higher than that is considered tall; anything shorter is short. Besides the height, the width, or scope of the letter is important. So is the pressure, placement, and most telling of all, the shape of the I.

According to Henley, the downstroke or the backbone of the PPI represents the Self. The straighter the downstroke the more independent the writer. Conversely, the more curvature there is in the backbone, the more the writer depends on others for emotional support.

Fine Points

One of my favorite books, *Handwriting Analysis, the Complete Basic Book* (Newcastle Publishing, 1980), by Amend & Ruiz, is the only place you'll find the mother/father interpretation of the PPI reversed. The authors later amended their position to say that the top loop represents the nurturing parent and the bottom loop the disciplinarian parent.

As in all parts of handwriting, the initial writing impulse represents mother, and the final stroke represents father. According to copybook, the first stroke starts at the baseline and moves into an upstroke, which turns at the apex, returns to the baseline, moves left into a curve, and finally ends to the right. Thus, when made this way, the upper loop (the sail) represents mother and other females, and the bottom loop (the boat) represents father and other males. You'll find my attempt at imitating the copybook PPI in the next illustration.

The following list describes some of the more common types of PPI. I've included a wide variety of PPIs in the illustration for your amusement or amazement, but of course they must be analyzed and interpreted in the context of the whole handwriting. See if you can match the descriptions to the various examples.

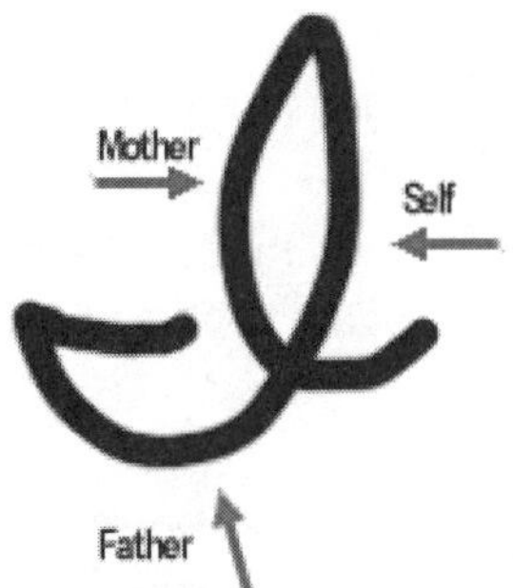

Copybook PPI.

- *Copybook PPI.* The writer has conventional attitudes. He probably had a "normal" family life in a two-parent home. Whatever issues he had with his parents as he grew up did not do any long-term damage to his ego.

  In some schools, children are taught to write the PPI in the reverse of what was described earlier. Also, some writers who were not taught to reverse it, do. What do we mean by "in reverse"? The bottom part of the I is made first, then the top. It's not always possible to tell which way the I was made, unless you check the pressure pattern under a magnifying glass. The heavier pressure will be on the downstroke.

Fine Points

One way to tell if a PPI is written in reverse is to find another word in the text that begins with a capital I, such as Indiana. If the capital connects to the word, you'll be able to trace the writing movement and see whether the writer began at the top or the bottom of the PPI.

- *Reversed PPI.* Henley says the reversed PPI (when not taught) is a sign of rebellion. Others define it as the writer seeing himself differently from how others see him.
- *Printed PPI.* The PPI made in one single stroke (called a *stick figure I*) or with a crossbar at the top and bottom (called a *Roman I*) is a sign of independence. The writer has either rejected the influence of her parents, or just wants to stand on her own two feet. This form looks like a number one, so we could extrapolate that to mean that the writer makes her own opinions and principles Number One in her life.
- *PPI with an upper loop only.* The writer was strongly influenced by her mother (or other female figure). The father may have been missing, either physically or emotionally or both.

Write Words

A **stick figure I** is a PPI made in one single downstroke. A **Roman I** is a PPI with a crossbar at the top and bottom added to the downstroke, like a Roman numeral I.

- *PPI with a lower loop only.* The writer's mother-image is missing from her life. She may not have been present for her, either physically or emotionally. The male image was a stronger influence.
- *Very small PPI.* The writer is modest and unassuming. She doesn't like to draw attention to herself. She may have been devalued at home, and hasn't developed a strong self-image.

Various forms of PPI.

- *Lowercase PPI.* This may be an affectation, as in the writing of e.e. cummings, who wrote almost everything in lower case. Or, if other signs in the writing bear it out, the writer's self-concept may be poor. He feels he doesn't deserve to give himself the reward of a capital I.
- *Large and wide PPI.* The writer takes up a lot of personal space. When the upper loop is wide it suggests that the writer has an expansive, open view of women in his or her life. The same would be true in reverse if the lower loop were wide—men are given a lot of latitude.
- *Lower loop turns left.* When the final stroke of the PPI ends toward the left, it is a gesture of rejection. The writer's father has disappointed or hurt her and she can't deal with it.
- *Angular PPI.* Angles are not prescribed by the school model PPI; therefore, there are significant ramifications when they are added. The angle is a sign of rigid inflexibility, and in the upper loop of the PPI it signifies anger and resentment toward the mother/females. Angles in the lower loop show aggression directed toward the father.

- *Retraced PPI.* Sometimes you'll find a retraced upper loop in the PPI, which suggests that the writer squeezes her feelings about her mother into tight little packages that she doesn't want to look at. In some cases, the writer who blames her mother for a separation from her father retraces the PPI's upper loop.
- *Very round PPI.* The soft, bloated PPI looks almost like a fetus, and the person who write it may be a bit babyish in her behavior. She needs a lot of mothering and may have come from a home where she was pampered and overindulged. As a result, she has a hard time standing up for herself. This type of PPI is more often found in women and some gay men.

Chicken Scratch

If you interpret an odd formation in a PPI to be a problem with the writer's mother and find out you were wrong, it may be that the problem was with some other significant family member. An aunt, sister, or stepmother could be the one.

- *PPI with a figure eight.* A figure eight lying on the baseline indicates unresolved issues or conflicts with the father/males. The bottom loop becomes a counterstroke, with the energy being convoluted into an unusual shape.
- *PPI looks like a number 2.* When the PPI looks like a number 2, you can be sure that the writer sees himself as a second-class citizen in his own life. He puts everyone else first, himself second, third, or last.
- *Top and bottom loops are separated.* The upper and lower loops are made separately. Frequently, if you question the writer, you'll find that her parents were separated, either physically or philosophically. Maybe both.

Tales from the Quill

Richard Speck, who stabbed to death eight Philippine student nurses in the 1960s, made a PPI with sharp triangles at both the top and bottom, with a very rigid downstroke in between. The triangle is never taught in the copybook, and signifies extreme hostility and tension. Note: This doesn't mean that everyone with an angular PPI is a potential murderer! It does mean, however, that there is tension and aggression present in the way they view their parents.

- *PPI is isolated.* When the PPI stands away from the other words, with an island of space around it, you can guess what it tells you about the writer: She feels alone, or she needs to be alone. Check the rest of the writing to determine which it is.
- *PPI leans left.* A PPI leaning to the left in handwriting which otherwise is right-slanted is an indicator of guilt feelings. As is so often the case, the guilt usually has something to do with sex or religion.
- *PPI lays on the baseline.* If you see a PPI that looks like it's fallen over on it's side, chances are, the writer is disappointed in his father but has decided to accept him for who and what he is. Nicole Brown Simpson made her PPI this way.

These are just a few of the myriad of possibilities. I encourage you to do your own research, questioning as many people as you can about their history and try to see how it fits in with the PPI they choose to represent them.

The Least You Need to Know

- Your signature is your public image. It's what you want the world to know about you.
- Capital letters represent your ideal self, while lower case letters represent your real self.
- The personal pronoun I tells about your self-concept and your attitudes toward your parents.

Part 5
Sweating the Small Stuff

Now that you've got all the hard stuff out of the way, it's time to coast for awhile. Learning about the character traits that have been assigned to various letters is something like learning how to play chords in music after you've learned the theory. It fills out the melody.

This is where we'll also cover important information about some of the more unpleasant aspects of handwriting—the danger signs.

Chapter 19

The Finer Details

In This Chapter

- How it all begins...and ends
- Tying things up
- Digging in with hooks
- Too much punctuation is *negative*!!!
- When color counts

Finally, after 18 chapters, we've come to a discussion of beginning and ending strokes. If it seems odd to wait so long, it's a case of going from the general to the specific. You had to learn about the vagaries of space, form, and movement before we could get to the fine points. But now, here we are.

As in all the other areas of handwriting, depending on where they start and finish, beginning and ending strokes can be interpreted on several levels: the physical (lower zone), social/emotional (middle zone), and intellectual (upper zone). And, always, the movement from left to right symbolizes going from me to you.

Beginning strokes show how the writer advances from within himself out into the world. On a physical level, the type of beginning stroke provides clues about how eager he is to get going on a new project or activity; on a social/emotional level, his sense of independence; on an intellectual level, how much preparation he needs before starting out, and how well he understands the basics.

Write Words

In copybook writing, all letters have a **beginning stroke** that leads into the letter. It's also sometimes called an "initial" or "lead-in stroke." All letters also have an **ending stroke** that leads into the next letter. It is sometimes called a "final stroke."

Ending strokes tell us how the writer relates to the outside world. On a physical level they indicate his eagerness to move forward; on a social/emotional level, his attitude toward his fellow man; on an intellectual level, his ability to think progressively.

The variety of beginning and ending strokes is astonishing and diverse. They come in all shapes and sizes, and, as small an element as they are in the overall writing sample, they can fill in some very important details about the writer's personality.

In the Beginning

Remember when you got your first bicycle? Your dad attached training wheels so you wouldn't fall over and hurt yourself. You needed that extra support to help keep your balance until you learned how to stay on the seat and ride in a straight line by yourself. Before long though, you wanted Dad to get rid of the training wheels because you felt all grown up and could now ride without help.

Initial strokes are the training wheels of handwriting. In the beginning, when you're first learning to form the letters, initial strokes are necessary and important. They provide the beginner with the support she needs to steady her hand as she proceeds into each word. Once graphic maturity is reached however, most initial strokes become superfluous and could be discarded without losing legibility.

There is a second aspect to retaining or rejecting those lead-in strokes. As part of the original handwriting training, keeping them might signify one's willingness or desire to follow the rules. Once one understands the reasons behind rules she can choose her own path and follow them, or not. No one will be harmed should the writer choose to discard this particular rule, and she can prove her spirit of independence by omitting the expendable initial stroke.

When the initial strokes are jettisoned, it reveals a self-confident, independent writer who relies on herself. She has the capacity to act quickly, without spending a lot of time on preliminaries. She no longer wants or needs training wheels to guide her along her chosen path. She understands what is important and what is not.

Can't Let Go

The writer who retains the initial stroke is either unable or unwilling to remove the training wheels. He believes he needs a crutch, and has difficulty letting go and "riding" on his own. He has difficulty getting started, either with a new project or activity, or making a social connection. The shape of the initial stroke will tell us whether the inability of the writer to let go of the past and move from me to you is because the past was a comfortable place where he'd like to stay, or because he's afraid to leave it and go forward.

Any type of long initial stroke indicates that the writer feels compelled to think about it for a while before starting anything new. He isn't comfortable going into unfamiliar territory unprepared.

The very long, straight initial stroke that starts well below the baseline is known as the "springboard stroke," and hints at difficulty in the past. However, the stroke is made with great energy going into the middle zone, and that suggests a strong desire to use past difficulties and turn them into achievement. The longer the stroke, the greater the obstacles the writer has had to overcome in order to feel successful.

Fine Points

Few men make long, curved initial strokes. The adult women who do are usually very attached to home and family. They may have been babied long past babyhood, which has impacted their ability to act independently. The longer and the more curved the stroke, the more the writer has been sheltered from the Big Bad World.

The shorter, straight stroke has been called, by the trait-stroke school, the "resentment stroke" (see the following figure) Whether the writer is actually resentful or not, what the theory tells us is that this type of stroke forms an angle with the following stroke, and that is a sign of tension and aggression. The aggressive acts take place in the middle zone, and the writer's behavior is quarrelsome and contentious. He is on the defensive, always on guard against criticism, seeing himself as a victim, rather than as someone who is powerful in his own right. He feels threatened by change, and, if someone tries to force a new course of action on him, he'll do his best to thwart them.

Long, straight initial strokes.

As you'll see in the next figure, a long, curved initial stroke has a friendlier implication, but is still a sign of immaturity. Chances are, the writer was babied at home, which can be a very seductive memory when things aren't going well. So, she returns to old friends and/or family for support and encouragement, rather than standing on her own and trying to sort things out for herself.

Curved initial strokes that start out high, in the upper zone, look like a smiley, and the writer has the demeanor to match. You'll find that people who begin with a curved or wavy initial stroke smile a lot and are generally cheery folk. They have a good sense of humor and prefer to look on the bright side.

Tales from the Quill

That graphological icon Felix Klein used to say that the person who retained the long initial stroke needed a second cup of coffee before he could get himself going in the morning. He would have to wind himself up before he could face the day. The long extra stroke symbolizes the need of the writer to put a little distance between himself and the new activity. He has to think about it for a while before getting going.

Curved initial strokes.

I know that this is a true sample of my handwriting. I am having a great time at the party

The small, cramped loop on an initial stroke has been called the "jealousy loop." I'm not sure of the reason for that one, but the definition offered by the trait-stroke schools is, "jealousy focused on one person." Try it out and let me know what you find.

The End

The last stroke of a word signals the end of an effort. The project is done and it's time to rest. What does the writer do? Does she want to reach out and socialize? Or does she put up a wall between herself and others?

Where there is no final stroke, and the last letter is abruptly cut off, the writer is likewise abrupt or even rude in her social transactions. She is very impatient and hates "wasting time" on the polite amenities. You may be speaking with her, when suddenly she turns on her heel and walks off without a word.

The long, garlanded final stroke is like a hand reaching out generously, in friendship. The writer wants to move forward and she wants to take others along with her.

Fine Points

A special case is the large initial letter. When the first letter of a word (not a capital letter) is larger than the rest, it shows a need for recognition and superiority. The writer comes on strong at first, to make his presence known. After the initial burst of energy he backs off.

She is kindly and empathetic, willing to share her resources and time. In the same gesture, she is holding her hands out to be filled, showing readiness to receive, as well as to give.

When the long final stroke is not garlanded, but straight, the meaning is entirely different. It is a holding-off gesture, as if the writer were putting out a stiff arm to keep others away. He doesn't trust people and doesn't want them getting close enough to hurt him, as seen in the next sample.

In some writing, the long final stroke is made only at the end of lines, filling up the space between the last word and the edge of the paper. In this case, it signifies a superstitious sort of "touching the wall" for safety, as we did as children.

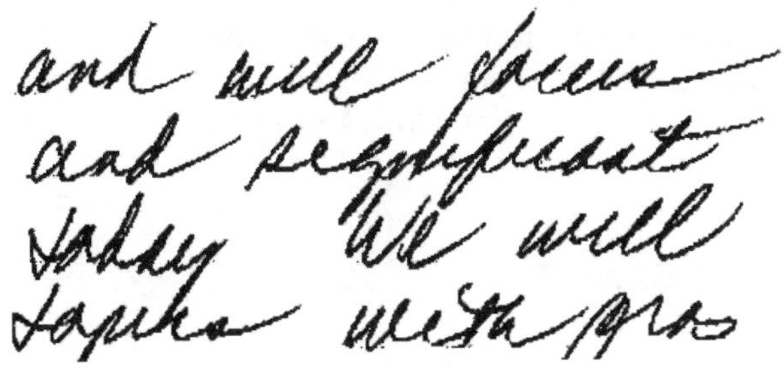

Long straight final strokes.

A final stroke that returns to the left, arching back over the word like an umbrella, like the one in the example, is a self-protective gesture. Think of someone crossing her arms over her head to ward off a blow. This type of ending stroke also effectively builds a wall between the writer and others who might like to become friends with her. If it happens only occasionally in a handwriting, it's likely that the writer uses the final return to the left as a defense only when she's feeling particularly vulnerable.

When the final stroke returns to the left *under* the word, below the baseline, it is a way for the writer to emphasize herself. She wants to draw attention to her achievements and have others applaud her for her contributions.

Chicken Scratch

A final stroke left suspended in mid air is called "trait suspendu." It is like ending a conversation in the middle of a sentence. There is more to be said, but the person has thought better of saying it. He would rather keep the information to himself.

Covering return strokes.

Final strokes that rise into the upper zone are said to denote someone with a tendency to worship. It is also a seeking for higher truths. The writer who goes into the upper zone when she doesn't need to is interested in philosophy and exercises her intellect every chance she gets. She may also be ambitious and optimistic, especially if the baseline also rises.

A final stroke that ends abruptly with pressure on the downstroke is self-assertive and the writer can be dogmatic in defending her point of view. Add to that an increase in the pressure and you get belligerence.

Final strokes that tend to turn down (see the next example) show a pragmatic, matter-of-fact way of dealing with the world. There is a certain ponderousness in this seeking the baseline or below. If other signs support it, pessimism is possible.

Heavy-pressured final strokes show signs that the writer experiences unbearable surges of emotion. If the final stroke is in the middle zone the writer will have unexpected outbursts of temper and aggressiveness. If it is in the lower zone, she may turn the aggression inward in depression and self-sabotage.

Final strokes turn down.

Fine Points

A final letter that grows suddenly larger than the rest of the word is a sign of someone who blurts out whatever is on his mind. He has a childish, immature way of demanding what he wants, using no finesse or tact.

Most handwriting samples will have more than one type of initial and final strokes, with one standing out more than another. Look for a preponderance.

I Love You, Period: Punctuation

Not much is said in the classical texts about punctuation, and I'm not going to say much about here. However, there are a few things to be aware of when considering those seemingly insignificant exclamation points and question marks!?

Some writers use excessive punctuation, adding heavy underlining, quotation marks, and exclamation points. Some add little asterisks or smiley faces here, there, and everywhere. The effect on the page is often confusing and disturbing. The person who turns punctuation into ornamentation doesn't really understand where things belong. He overdoes everything. He is theatrical and melodramatic, and simply doesn't know when to quit.

Overdone punctuation is done by someone who feels obliged to draw attention to himself in some way. He craves excitement and adventure. He can't sit still, but is always on the move and looking for action.

When making a period or a comma, the writer goes over and over the same spot, grinding the pen into the paper. Dot grinding is a form of compulsion, often seen in the handwritings of both abusers and victims of abuse. We'll discuss dot grinding briefly in Chapter 22.

Round, careful commas and periods suggest a careful, meticulous mind. The writer is a methodical thinker who wants to take the time to do things properly. More often than not, this type of punctuation is found in copybook writing and is a sign of the conventional personality.

Periods that look like commas, with the final stroke fading into a tail thanks to a fast pen, denote impatience. The writer may have a quick temper and an irritable nature. He can't stand to wait, and wants to "get on with it." His rather careless attitude implies that it's okay with him if some of the details fall through the cracks. He has more important things to do than hang around, trying to get it right. Thready connective forms usually will also be found in the sample.

Tales from the Quill

People suffering from some types of mental illness often use excessive punctuation. Particularly those diagnosed with paranoid disorders write with extremely heavy punctuation of all types: periods, commas, quotation marks, exclamation points, and question marks. They also tend to underline more than normal, and, in some cases write all around the edges of the page. They feel obliged to control all space on the paper.

Yoo-Hoo! Here I Am!

Inappropriate or lavish underlining is done for emphasis and signals someone who wants to feel important. He draws attention to his own words, as if to say, "Here I am! Listen to me!" Very heavy underscores that almost (or actually) tear through the paper are a sign of a strong emotion, usually anger. If the writer makes a habit of using this form of punctuation, he may have an explosive temper. Someone who underlines too much feels frustrated because he isn't getting the recognition he feels he deserves. Accordingly, he wants and demands that everyone appreciate even the most trivial things about him.

Heavy crossing out demonstrates a need to be right. The writer doesn't want you to see that he's made a mistake, so he completely blacks it out. He simply can't be told he's wrong or take criticism from anyone. The writer demands his own way, no matter what. As long as things go according to his wishes, everything is fine. But push him or expose his weaknesses, and you can expect an unpleasant eruption of anger and hostility. This type of crossing out is seen in numerous places in the so-called suicide note written by O.J. Simpson after his wife's murder.

Don't Let Go!

You may use a plastic or metal hook to hang your robe on the back of the bathroom door. You use hooks if you go fishing. Grappling hooks are used by those who like to climb mountains. Hooks are made for many different situations, but they all have the same basic purpose: holding onto something.

In handwriting, too, hooks symbolize holding on. Some hooks are large and round, such as the garlanded initial or final strokes we discussed earlier. Others are tiny, seen only under magnification. Each type has its own significance. Where they appear, their shape and size, add yet another piece to the personality puzzle.

In this section, we'll talk about hooks and ties (another form of holding on). Hooks are found in angular writings more often then they're found in garland writings, but depending on the type of hook, they may be present in fast or slow writing. Ties are often seen in rounded handwritings, and may serve the purpose of lending some strength to the normally flexible writer.

Chicken Scratch

Beware of the sneaky little hook at the ends of words. The writer may appear generous in extending himself on your behalf. At the last minute though, he throws out a hook to keep hold of what he had offered and selfishly pulls it back to himself.

Hooked on Handwriting

Hooks have two basic meanings: tenacity and acquisitiveness. They can be made on initial or final strokes, or both. In the upper zone a hook means grabbing onto an idea and holding it. In the middle zone it could represent a refusal to let go of a social attachment. In the lower zone, it usually has to do with sexual attitudes.

Hooks at the beginning of a letter or word suggest holding on to what is past, while hooks at the ends of letters or words imply reaching out and actively attempting to acquire something new. Because hooks are superfluous appendages, they are not usually considered a positive sign.

Small initial hooks are made with speed and express impatience and irritability. Large initial hooks represent holding on to past experiences. Large final hooks may be a sign of greed and a desire to acquire as many possessions as possible.

Writing with many hooks is done by someone who can't let go—of the past, of relationships, of anything. It's even hard for her to take the trash out on pickup day. If the writing is also narrow and cramped, you can bet she's a packrat whose home is filled with all sorts of miscellaneous stuff.

The easiest place to spot a hook is on t bars, as well as initial and final letters. Use your magnifying glass.

Hooks.

The Old School Tie

Like a hook, a knot or tie, is used to hold something together. In handwriting, knots are a sign of persistence. It's not enough that this writer forms the stroke or letter, she has to tie it up with a neat bow, too.

Fine Points

Hooks can appear in any part of handwriting. They may be large, such as the kind of hook that you hang your bicycle on; or they may be tiny tics that are barely seen.

The knot is made by someone who, once she gets hold of an idea, will not let it go. She stubbornly persists in her beliefs. There is a tendency for her to get caught up in the small details, so she may miss the importance of the big picture. By wasting energy on trivia, she has less time for more important considerations.

Another, slightly more sinister interpretation for knots and ties, is secretiveness. When the tie is in the form of a double looped oval in the middle zone, the writer is locking her lips and hiding the key. We know she's got something to hide, but we don't know what it is. The tie in the next example looks like the bow you make when you tie your shoes.

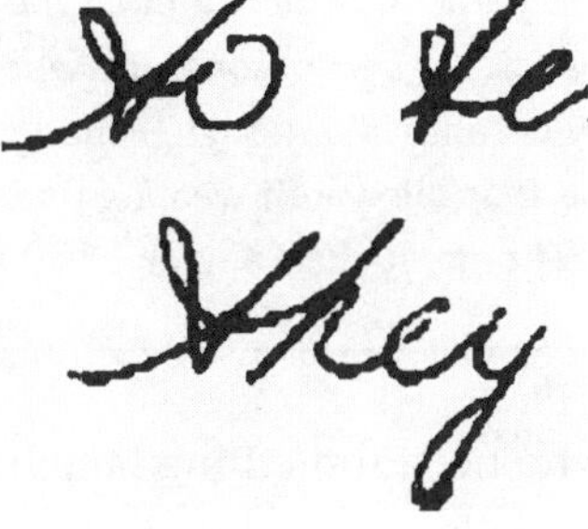

Ties.

Purple Haze: Choice of Ink Color

Little is written about ink color and its relationship to handwriting and personality. My comments are based on personal observations, not scientific research.

The angriest man I've ever met chose to write with red ink. His writing pressure practically tore through the paper, and the sharp angles he favored looked like knives. He was a surgeon. This man would stand outside a patient's room and shout at the top of his lungs, slamming his fist into his open palm, barking orders at his nurse, not caring that the patient could hear.

The choice of red ink for communications that are written for other people to read is quite telling. The color of blood, its bold, powerful look demonstrates a desire to take charge and be the leader, rather than be on the receiving end of an order. Aggression and tension are also evident. The positive side of red is energy, vitality, and strength.

Black ink is also selected as a power color. Business people, engineers, and other conservative types who aren't driven to stand out from the crowd generally use it. They need to be precise and clear in their communications, and black stands out against the white background of the paper.

Blue is a friendlier, soothing color, often selected for personal communications. Sensitive, emotional, or spiritual types who understand others are likely to choose it.

Green ink is frequently used by those who are seeking harmony. They are willing to adapt to circumstances when necessary.

Purple is sometimes picked by those who want to stand out as different, dramatic, and one of a kind. Yet, their need for recognition may have immaturity at its root.

Tales from the Quill

There are those who insist on using only one particular color of ink. One such woman invariably chose to write with purple ink, which is a sign of someone who wants to stand out and be different. That was not her only eccentricity, though. Among many other oddities, this woman enjoyed telling people that she wasn't wearing underwear. After her suicide, police found some odd items in her home, such as a stack of 300 butter wrappers.

The next chapter is especially for those who need something tangible to hold on to. We'll be diving even deeper into the particulars, to find the meanings that have been assigned to some of the individual letters.

The Least You Need to Know

- Initial strokes reveal how comfortable the writer is in leaving the past behind, as well as how she deals with essentials.
- Final strokes tell about social attitudes and whether the writer is interested in extending himself on behalf of others.
- Punctuation plays an important part in handwriting analysis.
- Some hooks may be seen only under a magnifying glass, but their significance should not be underplayed.
- Ink color can be telling.

Chapter 20

Making It in the Minors

In This Chapter

- t time
- Looking them in the *i*
- x marks the spot
- p, r, and a bunch of other small letters
- It's all Greek to me
- The oral o's and a's

For those of you who have been a teensy bit frustrated by the seemingly nonspecific aspects of the gestalt method, this chapter is for you.

Here, you'll find some of the "this-means-that" indicators that seems to make the left-brained graphologist so happy. Of course, everything you see in handwriting should always be analyzed in context, but there are some specific letter forms that we can pick out, just for fun. It's sort of like learning how to play chords on the piano rather than studying the theory behind the music. You might not be able to play the really complicated pieces, but you can make it sound pretty darn good.

The interpretations that follow are my take on some items taught by the atomistic or *trait-stroke school* of handwriting analysis. These are the bits you can use to "amuse your friends and amaze your neighbors." They are not meant for the serious analyst, unless used as secondary information to fill out the analysis. I can't always give you the theory behind them, because no one seems to know it! But the interpretations do seem to "work."

The discussion that follows applies to lower case letters, which may be printed or cursive. We discussed capital letters separately in Chapter 18 and printing in Chapter 14.

Don't t's Me

According to the book, *Tattletale t's,* by Geri Stuparich (American Handwriting Analysis Foundation), there are more than 400 ways to make the letter t. We're not going to cover them all here, but we'll consider some of the more common forms.

Write Words

The **trait-stroke school** of handwriting analysis assigns personality-trait names to individual writing forms. This method builds a picture of personality as if using bricks, laying one atop the other, and seeing what results at the end.

The letter t has two parts, a stem and a crossbar. The cross bar requires a dynamic left-right action and traditionally, represents one's ability to set goals and meet them.

The Stem

The height of the t stem is a clue to how strong the writer's self-image is in regard to his work life. If the stem is moderately tall, about twice the height of the middle zone, he feels good about himself and is independent enough to assert himself when the situation calls for it.

A very tall t stem (more than 2.5 times higher than the middle-zone height) is a sign of pride that has grown to the extreme of vanity. We often find that the writer of a very tall t stem had a strict, demanding father who was never satisfied with the writer's accomplishments. As a result, the writer continually tries to impress his father, whether he realizes it or not. Yet, he feels he never quite measures up. To compensate for his feelings of inadequacy, he flaunts his accomplishments through his swaggering manner and by bragging about them (ornate capital letters often appear along with the tall t's).

A short t stem is made by the independent person who follows his own drummer. His own self-approval is more important to him than what anyone else thinks. He doesn't need the approbation of others to feel good about his successes.

The copybook height t stem is made by someone who is more comfortable following than leading. Don't expect him to branch out on his own, because he is conservative, conventional, and happy to go along with the crowd.

Looped t stems supposedly mean the writer is sensitive to criticism about his work. Of course, any wide loop is a sign of emotionalism and sensitivity.

Height on the Stem

The height at which the t is crossed tells us how high the writer sets her goals. Copybook height is around two-thirds up the stem. It's important for most of the t bars to actually cross the stem because that keeps the writer in touch with reality—the baseline, where the t sits.

Chicken Scratch

When the t bar is too high—right at the top of the stem—the writer may be unrealistic in his goals. Chances are he is a daydreamer who builds castles in the air, rather than take the steps to make his dreams a reality. Look for some t's crossed lower, to balance out the idealism.

The person whose t's cross at copybook height sets her goals at practical levels that she knows she can accomplish. She doesn't reach out for attainment greater than she feels she can reasonably meet.

There are two possibilities for a t crossed very low on the stem. On one hand it may denote someone who is depressed and lacking the energy to set new goals. Her sights are on easily attainable aims, to ensure that she won't fail. She may be afraid of branching out and risking the possibility of failure. On the other hand, it is possible that the writer has recently achieved a goal and is resting on her laurels for a while. The surrounding handwriting will tell you which is true.

A t crossed higher than what copybook demands indicates someone with high goals. The writer seizes opportunities to advance herself and is willing to work long and hard to get what she wants out of life.

Some t bars fly high above the stem into the graphological stratosphere. If it's just a few of them it is the sign of the visionary who looks ahead and sees the possibilities of tomorrow. Otherwise, the writer is out of touch with reality. It is important to balance out those "visionary t's" with others that stay in touch with the stem.

t Bar Length

The t bar length reveals how much will power the writer puts into attaining her goals. Copybook has a rather short bar, which shows a conventional, conservative attitude. The writer pursues her goals with a practical outlook and, with other supporting signs in her writing, can be counted on to finish what she starts.

The very short t bar is made by the insecure person whose will power is only so-so. She sticks to what she knows and does her best not to annoy anyone by pursuing her goals too heartily.

A long t bar is a sign of a dynamic will. The left-right thrust distinguishes the writer as someone who knows what she wants and is not afraid to push herself forward to get it. With other supporting signs in her writing, she is forceful and able to direct other people. Her enthusiasm and excitement help get things moving.

An extremely long t bar that crosses entire words is not necessarily a good thing. It usually betokens someone who is extremely controlling and forceful in applying her will power. She tends to bully others into doing things her way.

Fine Points

The trait-stroke method defines the t-bar as "self-confidence." The theory is that the longer the bar, the greater the writer's confidence. When the length is excessive, however, it becomes a defense mechanism.

t Bar Pressure

The pressure exerted on the bar as it moves from left to right is a very important indicator of stamina. It tells whether the writer has the sustained energy to meet his objectives.

Strong pressure throughout the t bar indicates that the writer has the stamina and vitality to withstand pressure in the pursuit of his goals. A weak-pressured t bar is made by one who runs out of steam and gives up too easily.

Pressure that starts out strong and fades away before the end of the effort symbolizes the same behavior in reality. The writer starts out strong but his energy peters out before he completes the job.

Various t Bars

The form of the cross bar has to do with ideas, attitudes, and theories, since it is in the upper zone. t bars come in an amazing variety. Here are just a few:

A *t bar that slants downward,* especially when heavy pressured, is called the "domineering t." That pretty well describes the writer's behavior. He wants to dominate others and boss them around. He can be quite a tyrant.

When the *t bar points upward,* it's a sign of optimism, ambition, and hopefulness. The writer is looking forward with excitement to moving ahead and succeeding.

The *concave t bar* bows inward, as if someone were pressing down on it. The writer is easily persuaded to change course and often allows others to take advantage of him.

The opposite, or *convex t bar,* is an arcade, which says "self-protection." The writer stands on her own two feet and repudiates the help of anyone else. She isn't about to open herself up and make herself vulnerable by accepting a helping hand.

When the *t bar connects to the next letter,* or is *connected to its own stem,* it is a sign of quick intellect. The writer makes easy mental connections and is resourceful when it comes to dealing with problems.

Lasso-like t bars that swing to the left before returning to the right are found in the writings of people who suffer guilt feelings. They return to the past frequently in their minds, trying to figure out why they didn't handle things better. In numerous cases I've found this form where a violent death (murder or suicide) occurred close to the writer.

Chicken Scratch

The most bizarre and strange forms of t crossings are found in the handwritings of prison inmates. These are idiosyncratic thinkers who see the world different from the way others see it. They make their own rules and disregard the standard, normal ways of behaving in favor of their own selfish aims.

Uncrossed t's demonstrate procrastination. The writer has a hard time crossing through the t, so you can imagine what it's like for her to make a decision and follow through on it!

A t crossed to the right of the stem shows enthusiasm and excitement. The writer is so anxious to get going on a new project that she can hardly wait.

A *t made in one stroke at the end of a word,* with the bar coming up from the baseline in an arcade movement is called an "initiative t." It is made by someone who doesn't wait to be told what to do. He jumps right in and gets started without needing a blueprint or instructions.

Pointed t bars have been dubbed "sarcastic t's." The sharp point on the end of the bar is used like a dagger to cut others down to size. The writer uses sarcasm to ridicule and make others feel "less than." He uses cruel and cutting remarks as a defense against his own sense of insecurity.

Occasionally, you'll find a *t crossed twice.* This is a form of compulsive behavior. The writer is insecure and anxious—the type who goes back into the house several times to make sure she turned off the gas. This sign can take on a sinister cast when combined with other negative indicators, such as very heavy pressure.

Although a moderate variety is normal and acceptable, when one handwriting contains a wide variety of t forms, it suggests that the writer is uncertain about where she wants to go and what she wants to do. Look for balance.

The next two figures illustrate various letter t's.

Various types of t bars.

Copybook

Connected

Sharp point

Slants down

Slants up

Lasso

Concave

Convex

Tales from the Quill

The father of a young teenager who was hospitalized in a behavioral program crossed his t's twice, and used extremely heavy pressure and slashing strokes. The father was accused of tormenting the teenager with some rather shocking punishments. One of the milder ones was forcing her to go to school in her pajamas when she overslept. I probably wouldn't be allowed to relate some of his more "creative" efforts, which qualified as torture.

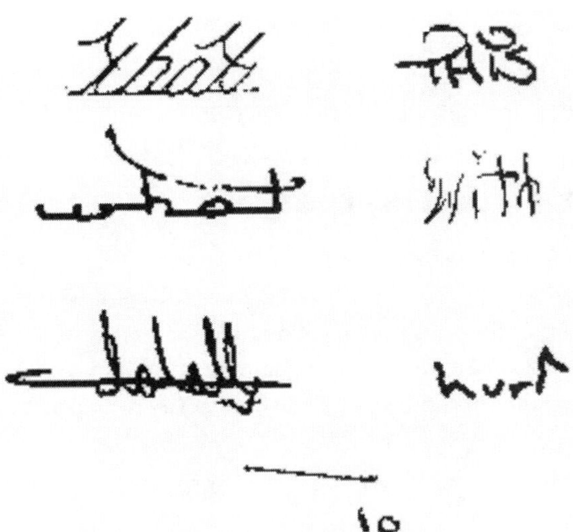

Unusual forms of t bars.

Seeing i to i

Handwriting analyst Anita Beckenstein laughingly, points out that the only difference between an i dot and an idiot is i. The small letter "i" may look insignificant, but it has its place in handwriting analysis. The style and placement of the i dot provide some valuable information to add to your database of knowledge about the writer.

The careful, precise, round dot that is placed close to the stem is said to mean that the writer is loyal. Okay, I guess that makes sense—loyally sticks by the stem. A dot flying high and to the right is made by an impatient, adventurous person who is interested in the future.

A circular dot is generally made by one who has not yet reached maturity, usually a teenager. The writer of the circle i dot is usually gullible and naive. He presents a paradox: On the one hand he wants to stand out from the crowd, but on the other hand needs their acceptance.

When the i dot takes the form of a heavy slash, brutality is often the cause. It may be that writer has a mean mouth, or worse.

If i dots are formed like a dash or a comma, they may signify an ironic sense of humor. When there's also a little hook, this is a sign of irritability.

Fine Points

The trait-stroke method uses the i dot to determine the writer's attention to details. The closer to the stem and the rounder the dot, the greater attention the writer pays to details.

Tales from the Quill

A notable exception to the "immaturity" definition of the circular i dot is Walt Disney, whose i dot is a very large circle. The story goes that it was his art department who created Disney's distinctive signature, and that he really hated writing it! In fact, many of the signatures shown in print weren't made by Disney himself. The way he writes his own name looks rather like a locomotive—another of those symbolic signatures (see an example in Chapter 18).

Missing i dots are probably an indication of a poor memory and/or a tendency to procrastinate. In some cases it is an act of rebellion; "I'm not going to do what I'm supposed to do!" The next figure illustrates some ways to dot the letter i.

Ways to dot your i.

Comma

Dash

Round

Circle

Chicken Scratch

The letter f that is sharply pointed on the bottom, like other angular forms, is a sign of aggression. Because the angle is hidden in the lower zone, the aggression may take the form of subtle displays of hostility that are hard to put your finger on.

Let's Get Organized

The letter f is the only tri-zonal letter. That means it passes through all three zones. The top and bottom of the f are, theoretically, supposed to be the same length and width. In other words, the top and bottom loops should mirror each other.

The f is used as a gauge for the writer's sense of organization. If the top and bottom loops are the same height and width, the writer is said to be well-organized. If the emphasis is on the upper loop, she plans better than she executes. If the emphasis is on the lower loop, she is more interested in doing than planning.

A fluid f is made in one smooth stroke, and signifies efficiency and effortless movement. Louise Rice (remember her from Chapter 1—the newspaperwoman who brought graphology to the U.S.) felt it typified altruism, possibly because of its graceful rightward movement.

The f with a large knot around the stem is supposed to mean pride in one's family—perhaps because "f" stands for family? Well, it stands for lots of other things, too, like "food." Some graphologists believe that an inflated lower loop on the f is an indicator of a particular love for food. Maybe we should ask to see the handwritings of people who really love food and check out their f's.

The letter f also stands for "father." Shirl Solomon, who wrote a wonderful book called, *Knowing Your Children Through Their Handwriting and Drawings* (Crown Publishers, 1978), believes that the lower loop of the letter f represents father, even though it is in the lower zone (area of "mother") because it is where the letter ends up (Remember, in graphology, everything starts with mother, ends with father). So, the shape of the lower loop of the f may tell you how the writer feels about her father.

Of course, the letter f stands for other words, too, but this is a "g" rated book, so we'll leave it at that.

The x-Files: The Small x

The letter "x" has an important place in history. Those who couldn't write their name could make their mark, their "x" to sign a legal document.

To analyze the x, determine whether the cross bars are straight or bowed, and whether the pressure is heavier on one side or the other. Even its placement in the check box on a form will reveal information about the writer. Is it on the left side of the box or the right side? That tells you something about how the writer feels about the past and the future. If he makes only one diagonal line without a cross-bar, consider it carelessness. You can also check the pressure. For such a simple structure there are an amazing number of forms of the letter x.

Tales from the Quill

Richard Kokochak, who specializes in jury screening using handwriting analysis, has turned analyzing the letter x into a science on its own merits. Richard analyzes the direction the cross bars are made, where they are placed on the jury questionnaire, the pressure, style, and several other aspects of this deceptively simple letter. He helped select more than 50 juries in just over two years using handwriting analysis.

The Letter k Is Okay

The downstroke of the small letter "k" symbolizes a person. The cross-bars of the k are like the arms, and that opens up several possibilities.

A warm, affectionate person who loves to hug and hold his partner close frequently wraps the arms of the cross bar around the stem in a loop. One whose cross bars don't touch the stem is not so comfortable with physical contact.

The k with cross bars that slash *through* the stem suggests some hostility, which may be directed at the self, since the movement is toward the left. Then, there's the k that has a "buckle" instead of a cross bar, which is actually closer to copybook style. The atomistic school of graphology calls a large buckled k the "defiant k" or the "rebellious k," presumably because it bursts out above the middle zone and makes its presence known.

There is a rather unusual form of the letter k that appears in enough handwritings to deserve a mention. Rather than forming a buckle or a cross bar, the downstroke pops outward into a wiggly line (see the illustration). Other graphologists I polled on this one agreed that the writer behaves erratically, or at least out of character at times, and tends to be manipulative.

Letter k forms.

Large nuke

Pops out lucky

Slashes peek

Separate ark

Loops desk

mmm mmm Good

The m's and n's are used by the trait school to determine the writer's thinking style. The theory is that rounded tops on these letters signify "cumulative" thinking. Since the rounded top is an arcade form, it follows that cumulative in this context means successively building one idea on top of another. So, a "cumulative thinker" would be one who remembers and uses what he has learned in the past. He "accumulates" ideas.

According to the trait method, writing the m and n with sharply pointed tops is a sign of the "investigative" thinker who wants to know the reasons why for everything.

The m and n with sharply pointed bottoms are made by the "analytical thinker." Analytical means to analyze, so the pointed m and n writer digs for facts and then carefully examines them.

The m and n with a thready, wavy top is called the "superficial" thinker. Her mind skims along the surface, picking up what it needs along the way and discarding the rest.

You'll probably find an assortment of m's and n's in most handwritings because we use all the different types of thinking for different purposes. However, one will probably be dominant.

Fine Points

Here's an intriguing bit of information: The copybook "m" has three humps, which signify (from left to right) me, you, and the world at large. If the first hump is the higher, the writer is self-confident and relies on her own opinions. If the second or third hump is higher, other people's opinions are more important than her own.

Pointed top/bottom

Pointed bottom

Thready

Arcade

Garland

Letter m and n forms.

Mind Your p's and q's

Well, never mind the q's, but the letter p has some interesting messages attached to it. As a mostly lower-zone letter, the p is often referred to as the "physical p." Thus, a long loop on the p would show an interest in physical activity. However, in my experience, the reverse is not necessarily true. You might note that someone makes short p's and say "you don't care for physical activity," only to discover that the writer is the captain of the women's volleyball team.

The rounded top p is called the "peaceful p." Actually, this applies to any letter that is rounded because the writer who shies away from angles is more of a peace lover.

There's also the "argumentative p." This is the copybook form of p, which requires a tall, straight stroke that moves high into the upper zone. The person who makes the argumentative p invariably loves to engage others in a debate, if not a downright argument.

The p with a large lower loop is known as the "bluffing p." It is often used by very flirtatious women who don't back up their implicit sexual promises. It may also appear in the handwritings of sales people. Some of these are illustrated in the next figure.

Small letter p.

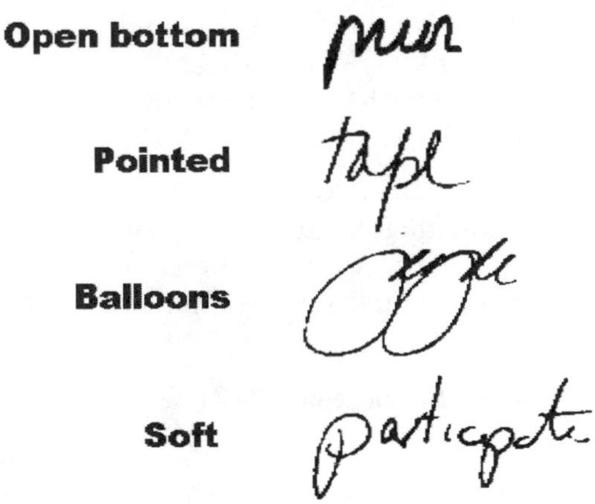

Open bottom

Pointed

Balloons

Soft

r You Still with Me?

Don't ask why, but the small letter 'r' has been connected to the writer's dress sense. An r that looks like a backwards 3 is said to be a sign of the natty dresser, someone who pays a lot of attention to her appearance and the image she projects. Maybe it's because it takes more time and effort to make this letter form.

Fine Points

My original graphology instructor, Charlie Cole, used to say that people who make loops on top of their r's like to sing in the shower. Check it out—it's true!

The flat-topped r is made by those who work well with their hands and enjoy using tools. I'm guessing that the theory behind this interpretation is that the flat top represents an arcade, which is favored by people who are interested in building.

The "needle point" r has a sharp top and is used by those who live by their intellect. They're very sharp-minded and curious about learning new facts. The rounded top r is a sign of someone who is more accepting and doesn't put a lot of energy into seeking new information.

The printed r or any printed letter in a generally cursive writing is often a sign of creativity. The printed r is also called the "parochial r," because it is taught in Catholic schools. These r's are illustrated in the next figure.

Small letter r.

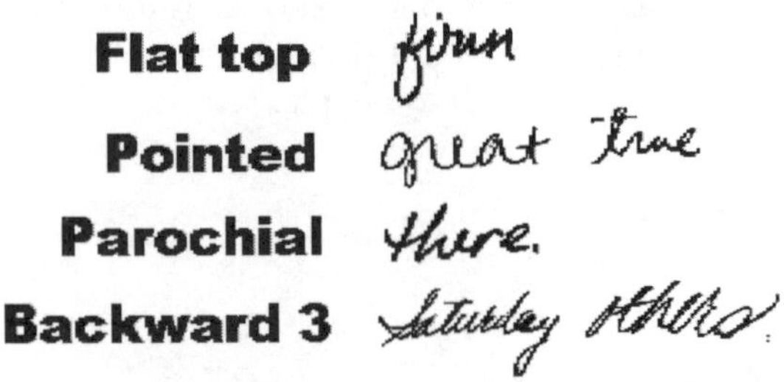

Flat top

Pointed

Parochial

Backward 3

Oh, My Dear! Signs of Culture

The so-called "signs of culture" in handwriting include the Greek E. Even though this is actually a capital letter, it is sometimes found used in the lower case. The trait school defines it as someone who has an interest in literature and likes to read.

The "lyrical d," another Greek letter, is also supposed to indicate cultural leanings. Some graphologists believe it is mostly adopted by poets. Interestingly, you won't find it in the writings of Dickinson, Milay, or Whitman, though I have seen it in Prince Charles' writing (Appendix E).

Finally, the figure-eight g is considered a sign of literary talent. It is made in one smooth, fluid stroke that presumes a quick, facile mind. Add to that a philosophical bent and a sense of humor, according to Huntington Hartford in *You Are What You Write* (Macmillan, 1973). You'll find these forms in the next figure.

Greek g

Greek d

Greek e

Greek letters.

Tales from the Quill

The trait-stroke schools like to talk about "cultural letters," but it's a fascinating fact that many highly cultured people, including brilliant scholars and literary giants make no "cultural letters" in their scripts at all. Moreover, the Greek E is seen fairly frequently in the handwritings of prison inmates!

L.A. Confidential: The Communication Letters

The middle zone, as the area of daily life and relationships, is where we communicate. Therefore, the middle zone letters are where we look to find out *how* the writer communicates. The round letters, o and a, lend themselves especially well for the purpose.

Think of o's and a's as little mouths. How many of those little mouths are open and how many are closed? If all the o's and a's are closed, it suggests someone who is closed-mouthed and careful in what she reveals. It doesn't necessarily mean she doesn't like to talk. Maybe she talks a lot without saying much. Look for a balance of open and closed forms. You'd have to look at the whole picture to discover whether the writer is a talker. If the writing is crowded, with lots of words covering the paper, you can bet that the writer is quite chatty. When the o's and a's are wide open at the top, he has loose lips. Gossip is his favorite sport.

The lowercase a that looks like a typographical letter a, with a covering stroke over the top, is often made by those who have something they'd rather not discuss. In many cases there is child sexual abuse in their background. However, please note that this is a creative form of the letter a, and many artistic types use it. Don't accuse everyone who makes this form of having been abused as a child.

The type of a or o for which the writer makes a full circle before actually forming the letter is a sign of "talking around" a subject. For instance, in one family where several members use this form, they never directly address family problems. They talk all around the situation without ever getting to the point.

Intrusions

Clear communication calls for direct, simple speech. Those who proliferate an overabundance of technical jargon or multifarious, meandering discourse end up only obfuscating the essential underlying connotation. See what I mean?

Chicken Scratch

Intruded ovals often are made by victims of sexual abuse. When hooks, loops, or black marks appear inside middle-zone letters, check for other signs of abuse.

Anything beyond the plain facts is fluff or intent to distract and distort the information. Extra strokes in communication letters effectively tamper with clear communication. One way to interfere with the free flow of information in handwriting is to add extra loops to the o's and a's.

Extra loops are the equivalent of zipping your mouth shut and locking it. A loop on the left side of the letter, since the left side represents the self, suggests a form of denial or, in effect, keeping secrets from yourself. When the loop is on the right side, the secrets are kept from others. Some writers make loops on both sides of the letter. That can mean a real Sneaky Pete. But he's probably only fooling himself.

Secrets and Lies

Tiny loops that hang down inside o's and a's are a fairly uncommon phenomenon, but they show up often enough to mention. Loops are containers for emotion, so extra loops inside the o's and a's indicate unreleased emotion about some experience or

Double loop

Covering stroke

Circled

Clear

Single loop

Communication letters.

event. We don't know what it was, but it usually stands for something unpleasant. The writer might desperately want to talk about what's troubling her, but just can't get the words out.

Hooks inside o's and a's are not a good sign. Some graphologists call them "stingers," as they represent sneaky, nasty ways of communicating. Others say it is the sign of someone who "speaks with a forked tongue." One graphologist goes so far as to call it the indisputable sign of a pathological liar. That may or may not be true, but just make sure to check on the facts before believing anything this writer tells you.

e Is for Ear

Part of communication is listening, as well as speaking. The trait school uses the small letter "e" to determine whether a writer is a good listener or not. Think of the e as an ear. If the letter e is wide open it would signify someone who listens well. If the letter e is squeezed shut, the writer has his hands over his ears. He isn't a good listener. I'm sure this could be extrapolated to include other letters, too.

Tales from the Quill

In a lecture at a graphology convention in 1991, the handwriting of one of the children involved in the McMartin preschool scandal was presented to the audience. The McMartin school was closed and its owners sent to prison for seven years before they were proclaimed innocent at trial. One of the parents, who later committed suicide, had accused teachers and other school officials of horribly sexually abusing the children (as well as murdering babies and animals). The child whose handwriting was shown at the conference used the typographical form of the letter a in her handwriting. Whatever this child's background was, there was something in it that she did not want uncovered.

I'll Believe Anything You Say

When left open wide, the small letter b is akin to a mouth naively hanging open with the writer ready to believe anything you tell him. Innocent or just plain clueless? The overall writing will reveal the writer's level of maturity.

The Least You Need to Know

- Some individual letter forms can help you interpret personality. Use them judiciously and not without an understanding of the whole picture.
- The small t relates to goals. Check the stem height, cross bar length and placement, and overall pressure. Beware of bizarre style t crosses.
- Communication letters are like little mouths. Check to see if they're open, closed, or have forked tongue!
- Extra loops, hooks, or other intrusions into the oval letters are known as "contaminated ovals," and usually mean problems in communication.
- Greek letters are viewed by some people as a sign of culture.

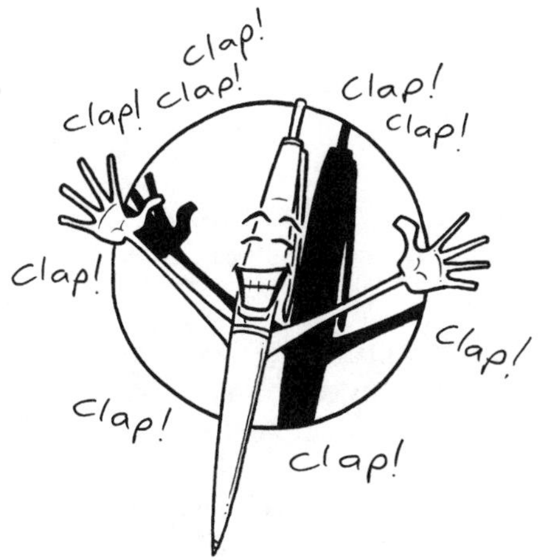

Chapter 21

Writing in Public

In This Chapter

- Handwriting on forms can be fun to analyze
- Don't forget to check: check writing
- You can analyze numbers, too!
- The envelope: dressing up the message
- Doodling is scribbles that speak

Have you applied for a job lately? How about a credit card or Ed McMahon's Sweepstakes? Have you written a check for a purchase, or signed for a registered letter? Computers may be gaining ground in taking over for the pen in some instances, but many of life's situations still require that we write.

We know that, in general, writing reveals who we really are, but what about writing specifically done for other people to see? Do the same principles apply? Of course they do, but keep in mind that when we know someone else is going to read what we write, it may have some effect on what we produce; at least, it will for those who are more conscious about what others think of them.

There are many circumstances where we are called on to fill out forms of one type of another. Writing a letter usually means addressing an envelope. We may write a check in the grocery store. Could it be that interpreting "public writing" is different in some ways from other types of writing?

Form over Substance

When it comes to filling out forms, usually we are instructed to "print clearly." Some people are more comfortable with printing. I, for one, find myself rapidly lapsing into an untidy mélange of print and script when forced to write in those tiny little boxes. I just can't seem to sustain the effort it takes to keep printing over the entire page. For those of us who are uncomfortable using a printed style, the effects on our handwriting can be disastrous.

Fine Points

For the simple reason that it may not be the writer's natural style, it's probably best not to accept a hand-printed application form as a sample for analysis unless the employer also supplies an essay-type sample to go with it. As a new graphologist, don't do an analysis without an adequate sample.

What about a carefully hand-printed form, where all the letters line up, neatly printed inside the appropriate boxes? You can bet the writer is a meticulous, detail-oriented person who wants to be clearly understood. If the words slurp over into adjoining boxes with little regard for the boundaries, that's the way the writer approaches other areas of his life, too.

Numbers are often an essential part of the information to be provided. The way the writer approaches them is especially telling, as we'll see in the next section.

Checks and Balances

What you are writing can have an effect on how you write it. When I make out a check to the IRS, I know my handwriting doesn't exude the same warm fuzzies it does on a Valentine's card to my husband. Every word, every number I write is an effort. It's like ripping my fingernails out, one by one. I don't want to part with that money and it shows. I'm convinced that the agent who stamps "received" on my quarterly payments can feel the hostility dripping from my pen.

If you are called on to analyze handwriting on a check, be aware that the writing of the payee's name may tell you something about how the writer feels about their relationship. Capital letters written taller than normal suggest respect (or maybe it's fear) for the person whose name they represent. If they are written smaller than normal it's likely there are some unpleasant or unresolved feelings toward that person.

Ambiguous or crossed-out numbers convey a sense that the writer is trying to hide something. Maybe the check writer knows she doesn't have the funds in the bank to cover the amount she's spending. Quite often in such a case, the writing becomes thready and unclear. It's like equivocating in conversation, as if the writer is saying, "If I don't write the numbers clearly, they aren't real. I can defend myself later when I'm in trouble and claim that I wrote something different than what it looks like."

Your Number's Up!

Filthy lucre it may be, but the almighty buck pays the rent. For some that's enough. Others, however, devote their whole lives to the pursuit of mammon. The way we write numbers imparts important information about the writer's view of money and other material values.

Someone who writes numbers with careless indifference indicates that money means little to him. Or, he may simply want others to *think* he doesn't care about money. It may be difficult for the writer to handle money; perhaps he is even embarrassed by it.

Those who make the effort to write numbers clearly give money a healthy respect. They understand where it belongs in their life. They take it seriously, but don't allow financial concerns to consume them.

Chicken Scratch

The way you write checks can mean the difference between giving a forger the go-ahead to steal from you and protecting yourself. The more clearly and consistently you write the numerals and sign your name, the less likely you are to become the victim of a forger.

Numbers that are written small and precisely are a sign of someone who focuses keenly on financial matters. In some cases the writer may be a bit of a miser. When the number 2 is written like a checkmark, it's a sign of someone who is good with numbers, like an accountant or mathematician.

When numbers are written too large, and especially with heavy pressure, the writer loves money and puts a financial value on everything. She wants to look like a big spender. Greed is also a strong possibility. In either case, the writer tends to be unrealistic about money and doesn't understand its relative value.

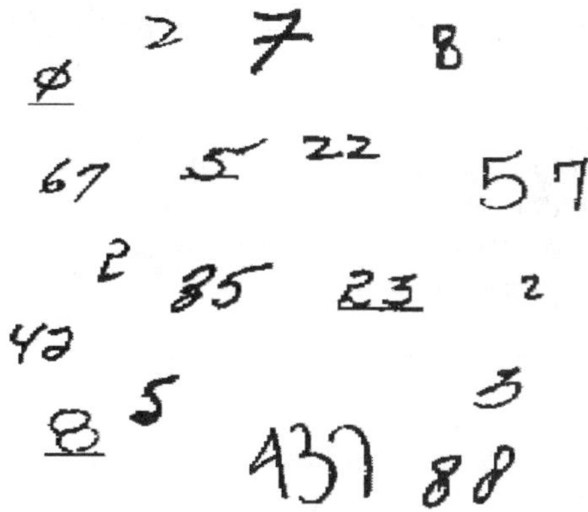

Various styles of numbers.

Fine Points

"The Three Column Figure Test" in *Test Your Personality* (Freund Publishing House Ltd, 1995) by Israeli graphologist Rudi Danor provides personality interpretations for the way the subject writes three columns of numbers. Fascinating!

Bizarre-looking numbers that are made into doodles or symbols imply that the writer doesn't understand the concept of money. For her, numbers are useful only for their aesthetic value. She has no concept of propriety or protocol when it comes to using her assets.

Numbers are a prominent part of the address when we send someone a letter. The placement of the address is yet another revealing piece of information about the writer.

Pushing the Envelope

The envelope is the writer's emissary. It precedes him and delivers the all-important message inside. Yet, addressing an envelope is a little different than writing what goes into it. The writing on the envelope is meant to be seen by others: the people at the post office who sort the mail, the carrier who brings it to the addressee, the company mail clerk, and the person for whom it was intended.

Pulver likened the envelope to the clothes that cover the body (the message). It tells us how the writer likes to dress. Is he neat and well-groomed, or did his lunchtime hotdog dribble mustard on his shirt and he didn't bother to wipe it off? Or, at the other end of the spectrum, did she spend an inordinate amount of time on her grooming, making sure every hair was in place, lipstick just the right color, with accessories to match?

Translating this idea into envelope writing, what's most important is whether the writing is at least legible, if not particularly neat. An illegible address may not get the mail to the proper place at the proper time, and maybe that's the subconscious message the writer wants to get across. Perhaps she has mixed feelings about the person on the receiving end; feels ambivalent about writing the message; or would rather not be sending it at all.

Moreover, if the writing on the envelope is symbolic of how the writer wants to be seen in the eyes of others, the person who doesn't bother to make it legible is unlikely to care about good manners in social situations. Personal obligations mean little to him. He is inconsiderate and refuses to adapt, expecting everyone else to cater to his whims.

Which Way Did He Go?

As we discussed in Chapter 18, the capital letters in handwriting represent the ideal self, while the lower case letters represent the real self. The same is true when it comes to the envelope and the text inside. The envelope symbolizes the ideal self, while the message inside is a metaphor for the real self.

Does the address appear balanced on the envelope? If not, what is causing the imbalance? Like the arrangement of handwriting on the page, the arrangement of

Tales from the Quill

I once knew someone who refused to use a clean envelope or paper. When I received her letters they were invariably enclosed in an envelope that had once contained a bill, an advertisement, or something else. In fact, she'd write on the back of flyers, stick a label over the original address and tape up the flap. At first I took it personally, but then I learned it was standard practice for this individual. Whether she was ecologically inclined, penny-pinching, or just plain eccentric is up for debate.

the envelope clues us in about how the writer views the world. A carefully written address emphasizes caution. The writer is circumspect, guarded. She takes care in what she allows the world to see about her.

An envelope written with a great deal more ornamentation than is found in the message reveals the person who puts on a show of formality. She stands on ceremony with strangers, wanting to impress on them that she is something more than she really is. Unfortunately, her unnatural behavior tends to make her come across as nothing more than showy and pretentious.

In the next illustration, the art of a prison inmate decorates the outside of an envelope.

Chicken Scratch

Some prison inmates, frequently Latino gang members, cover their envelopes with tattoo-like drawings. The drawing is often a man and a woman in an embrace, and may be accompanied by symbols such as hearts and stars. Envelopes like these are works of art.

Gang writing on an envelope.

The upper right-hand segment of the envelope is out of bounds. That's reserved for the stamp. If the person writing the address is so hurried and careless that the writing takes over the area designated for postage, it means he has placed the writing too high up on the envelope. Chances are he's a dreamer who lacks a clear understanding of what is appropriate in a given situation. This is the maverick type who often tends to find himself in trouble with authority. He is unrealistic and just doesn't seem to know where things belong. Check the writing for immaturity.

An address placed low down on the envelope says that the writer is earthbound. Her spirit never soars with enthusiasm. Pessimism and discouragement or out-and-out depression may be the cause. If the address is placed low and also far to the left of where it belongs, it signifies someone who is afraid of getting involved in life. Profoundly introverted, she pulls in her horns and hides in her shell (apologies for the mixed metaphors!).

The writer who clings to the left side of the envelope demonstrates psychological damage caused by past experiences. His behavior is passive and anxious. He staunchly sticks with what and whom he knows, rather than being willing to make new friends or try different activities.

Writing that moves to the extreme right side of the envelope expresses extroversion and excitement for life. The writer longs for social contact and pursues new friendships somewhat indiscriminately, so that she won't have to be alone. When it is also placed low on the envelope, there is a drive for physical activity and interest in material pursuits.

In and Out

When possible, it's interesting to compare the writing on the envelope with the text inside. If both are alike, the person can be judged genuine and natural. If not, the envelope becomes a mask behind which she hides. So we ask ourselves, why? Is she simply trying to protect herself, or does she deliberately intend to fool us in some way? Or, it may simply be that the writer wants to make sure the envelope arrives safely at its destination! The answers may be found in the text.

When the writing on the envelope is much larger than that of the message inside, Pulver said it is like someone who, when he isn't getting across to the other person, speaks louder. The trouble is, he doesn't speak any clearer.

Writing that is smaller on the outside than the inside text suggests someone who doesn't want others to know that she feels good about herself. She assumes a posture of false modesty, leading everyone to believe she's just a humble, unassuming little ol' person, when really, she's not at all.

Please Come Again

If the envelope doesn't have a printed return address, the polite thing to do is write one in so the recipient will immediately know where the letter originated. When I receive an envelope in the mail with no return address, I wonder what the person has to hide. Perhaps he doesn't want to be connected with what's inside the envelope. That's what anonymous note writers do, because obviously they don't want to be associated with what they've written.

Tales from the Quill

Anonymous letters often contain some shockingly obscene and threatening drawings, handwriting, or other material, yet in many cases the writer turns out to be the recipient. Huh? Yep, the person writes a nasty note to himself, then sets off a hue and cry to get some attention. Pretty embarrassing when the handwriting expert digs out the truth, wouldn't you think? And the police don't take kindly to false alarms.

Now we're about to head into the Land of Doodles. For this section, we have a guest contributor, artist and graphologist Lena Rivkin. Lena is on the Art faculty at Mount St. Mary's College in Brentwood, California.

How Do You Doodle?

The art of *doodling* is a symbolic language and should not be disregarded. It can be a creative and powerful tool to reveal the unconscious mind.

Write Words

Doodle means to draw or scribble aimlessly, absent-mindedly, or while preoccupied.

I am a prolific "phonepad doodler." I rarely communicate over the phone without a pen or drawing tool in my hand. In fact, friends can always hear my pencil sharpener buzzing through the phone! Doodling helps me think, concentrate, and relax. The telephone exchange seems complete only when I am making these unconscious designs.

Since childhood, I've found myself making marks with a pen that did not seem to make any logical sense. I would be concentrating on something else, but at the same time, something compelled me to take a writing or drawing tool and move my hand. Although I later became an artist, I have since learned that many people who have no artistic ability at all doodle just as much as those who do.

Some people who doodle have a need to release excess pent-up energy. And some doodles accompany a fantasy or daydream. Some are executed deliberately, with a concentrated effort to experiment with forms, lines, and shapes.

The subconscious act of doodling is similar to a dream state. It can release such emotions as inner contentment, complacency, calmness, and excitement, as well as stress, frustration, restlessness, uneasiness, and anger. The pen is on automatic pilot. Without any effort or direction on your part, it just takes off. Often, people are totally unaware that they are doodling. The very effortlessness of the act may be an element of letting go.

Because a doodle is a symbolic language it's not easy to pin down a definite interpretation. However, you can learn the meaning of various visual symbols by applying the same principles we use to analyze handwriting: the visual form and placement on the page, scale, pressure, fluidity of line, rhythm, and movement.

Pressure in handwriting communicates the inner climate and intensity of the writer, and the same approach is applied when observing a doodle. Perhaps the doodler was having a heated telephone conversation. Heavy lines and dark shading might be applied—a visual translation of one's inner mood. In contrast, positive, joyous thoughts are communicated in a more lyrical way with lighter pressure and curved lines, visually demonstrating an elevated mood.

Tales from the Quill

André Breton, founder of the Surrealist group in Paris in 1924, developed the idea of creating artwork by means of a direct method of tapping the subconscious/unconscious called "automatic writing." In "automatic writing" he used free association, using words and ideas that avoided conscious editing. This process caught fire subsequently with other Surrealists, not only with writers but also with visual artists such as Jóan Miro, and others.

Doodles as Safety Valve

There are many kinds of doodles. The markings may be visually complex or more simplified. However, none are meaningless. The unconscious has a specific range of visual formations. Like an individual's signature, one's doodles are recognizable. If you were to see all of my doodles, you would know they are mine.

I have observed the "corporate doodler," for whom doodling may be a saving grace at many a meeting! When meetings become tiresome and laborious, doodling can keep a person on track and focused. Emotions are not often welcome on the surface at a business meeting, but the act of doodling can be a container for one's reactions. And since no one can read others' doodles, they can be a special code that only the doodler can decipher.

The "notebook doodler" often ornaments words he's already written in the notebook. He may decorate some of the elements of the notebook, such as doodling around the holes punched in the paper. He sometimes embroiders the pages with intersecting lines and shapes, often filling up entire pages with a variety of forms.

"Napkin doodles" from restaurants can be worth collecting. Some of these doodles may be especially creative, particularly after a few drinks! The napkin doodle is often created around the restaurant's imprinted logo, using the logo as a starting point. Sometimes the paper napkin absorbs the ink and can create an interesting visual bleeding effect.

"Sand doodles" are etched into the sand on the beach by the writer's fingers and toes or a stick. The texture of the sand feels good to the touch, and while there are numerous distractions (talking, eating, watching events such as sports and children splashing, and throwing Frisbees), the interest in a spontaneous sand engraving is addictive to many. In sand doodling, one must not get too attached to one's creation!

"Dilemma doodling" is the doodling done by someone who is working through a quandary or needs time to think through an idea. Doodling can be a catalyst to aid in the thought process without judgment or criticism from the conscious mind. Unconscious thoughts are able to surface through this process. Many people who doodle at these times may not realize the significance doodling has played when the light goes on for them and the solution to their problem just seems to "appear."

"Restaurant doodles" often happen when a paper tablecloth and crayons are features of a restaurant. While waiting to order a meal, the hungry doodler can converse with companions while projecting her inner self on the table. Many a masterpiece has been lost under the spaghetti Bolognese.

The doodles of children are widely used in psychiatric work as a therapeutic tool. The images a child produces may reflect specific physical illness and point to family stress, accidents, difficult sibling relationships, and other trauma. Questions that seem unanswerable on the basis of physical data alone may be answered through evaluation of a child's spontaneous doodle.

Chicken Scratch

Children who draw themselves in one corner of the page, with all the other family members in another corner demonstrate feelings of separation and loneliness. If the father figure is drawn much larger than the others, perhaps with jagged teeth and large hands, this indicates that he is someone the child fears.

But What Do They Mean?

The meanings of visual symbols can sometimes be quite obvious, and many doodles can have a universal, as well as a personal meaning. It is fitting together the parts of the puzzle and evaluating the gestalt that reveals much about the inner self. Doodles can be the key to creative breakthroughs. The following are a few of an almost unlimited range of ideas for interpreting doodles.

People doodles often stimulate conscious feelings regarding bodily image and self-concept, both physically and psychologically. For example, small-scale drawings with weakly drawn arms could indicate feelings of inadequacy. Some people enhance their doodles of people to arouse feelings of projected importance or power.

Doodles of houses represent a place where nurturing and security are sought. Chimneys emitting smoke can communicate feelings of warmth and affection. Houses without windows and/or doors can represent withdrawing into the self and not allowing others to see in. An open door allows intimacy, but on the other hand, a long pathway leading to the door decreases access.

Animal doodles suggest a love of animals and an interest in helping others. Since many animals are dependent, this type of doodle may be drawn by someone who is sensitive to others' needs. Interest in the outdoors, freedom of movement, and a playful attitude may also be indicated.

Boxes denote someone who is most comfortable with order and structure. He uses a linear thinking style to put ideas in their proper order. This is also someone who compartmentalizes various areas of his life. Sometimes there is a closed-in predictability about the delineation of a box that thwarts spontaneity.

Abstract imagery with angular edges (triangular forms, zigzag forms, diamonds, stars) denote sharp, critical-thinking skills. If done with pressure they symbolize determination, decisiveness, intensity, clear boundaries, definite ideas, and seriousness. Abstract imagery with round forms conveys a soft side, flexibility, sensitivity, vulnerability, playfulness, gracefulness, and compassion.

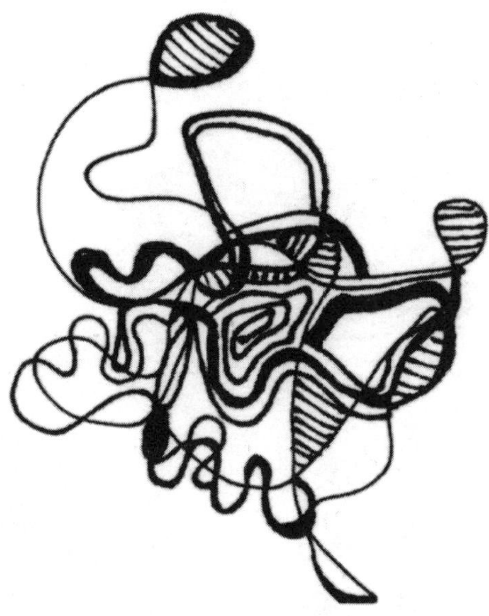

Hearts suggest the importance of affection, human contact, emotions, and love. Flowers represent an attitude of growth and development. A dead flower might indicate disappointment, depression, uneasiness, or inner tension. A bright, living flower conveys enthusiasm, hopefulness, a love of beauty, or a fantasy of what the doodler would like to have in her life.

Doodles done on a small scale may express someone who concentrates well, is detail-oriented, meticulous, focused, and introspective; but she also may be constricted and emotionally reserved. The small movements indicate well-developed, fine-motor skills.

Large-scale doodles exemplify someone who enjoys recognition, is ambitious, outgoing, emotionally expressive, and spontaneous. Well-developed gross motor control allows the wide arm movements needed for this type of doodle.

If You Want to Learn More

Here are some books that I've found helpful and that are available through the Internet at **http://www.Amazon.com**.

Chicken Scratch

Be careful where you doodle! When your mind is wandering, make sure no important documents are nearby, or they might end up decorated with messages from your subconscious. I've doodled all over an original handwriting sample that had to be returned to the client—embarrassing, at best.

- *Advances in Art Therapy* by Harriet Wadeson (John Wiley & Sons, 1989)
- *Approaches to Art Therapy* by Judith Aron Rubin (Brunner/Mazel, 1987)
- *Art & Soul: Reflections on an Artistic Psychology* by Bruce L. Moon (Charles C Thomas Pub. Ltd., 1996)
- *Artful Scribbles* by Howard Gardner, (Basic Books, 1989)
- *Art Therapy with Children* by Edith Kramer (Magnolia Street Pub., 2nd edition, 1993).
- *Depth Psychology of Art* by Shaun McNiff (Charles C Thomas Pub. Ltd., 1989)
- *Visual Thinking* by Rudolph Arnheim (University California Press, 1989)
- *Freud & Cezanne: Psychotherapy as Modern Art* by Alexander Jasnow (Ablex Pub Corp., 1993)

The Least You Need to Know

- It's unwise to analyze forms or other materials that may not be done in the writer's natural style.
- How someone writes numbers can reveal a great deal about their view of money.
- The writing on envelopes should not be overlooked as a potential source of information about the writer and his perspective on the world.
- Doodles are a rich resource for clues about the doodler's unconscious mind.

Chapter 22

Waving the Red Flag: Danger Signs

In This Chapter

- The problem of honesty
- The red flags of dishonesty
- The red flags of violence
- Mixing drugs and handwriting

No one is all bad, or all good, either. I believe the saying is true: There's a little bit of larceny in us all. In fact, the human animal is a conglomeration of attributes, mannerisms, and characteristics that run the gamut from almost totally, 100 percent honest to dirty rotten scoundrel. Conscience is buffered by many shades of gray on the honesty/dishonesty yardstick.

What one person views as lacking integrity or honesty may be perfectly acceptable to another. How about someone who makes personal photocopies on the company copy machine? Or long-distance phone calls? Or stamping personal letters at the boss' expense?

For the scrupulously honest individual, taking even a paperclip home is unthinkable. Someone else might feel justified in handling her personal business on company time, with an attitude that says, "the company can afford it," or "they owe me!" And few people, if they hit the jackpot at the corner phone booth would walk away and leave the pile of change for the next guy. Yet, that money obviously belongs to the phone company.

Please note: There is no such thing as a "criminal handwriting." When identifying signs of potential for dishonesty or violence in handwriting, the important word is

Fine Points

One red flag appearing a few times shows a tendency. When present consistently, the behavior is part of the overall personality pattern.

"potential." Each of the subjects in this chapter deserves an entire book, but for our purposes, we'll stick to an introduction of the more noticeable and significant red flags.

In every chapter so far, we've covered the positive and negative aspects of each element of handwriting, using "natural and spontaneous" as a benchmark. Now, however, we're going to go beyond plain old negative behavior, and move into the realm of pathology. We'll consider the question of potential dishonesty, the possibility of violent behavior, and the effects of substance abuse on handwriting.

One True Thing: Honesty and Integrity

There are two basic problems in determining dishonesty and *integrity* in handwriting: First, *honesty* is somewhat subjective and the writer's view of dishonesty will affect how it appears in his writing. Even when someone's behavior positively stinks it may not clearly show up in his handwriting if he doesn't feel guilty about it.

Second, handwriting reveals only attitudes and potential. Since we don't have a crystal ball, we can't predict whether the writer will act on his potential or not. Thus, one whose handwriting is filled with signs of dishonesty may or may not act on his potential for bad behavior. That doesn't make it any less useful to know that the potential is present.

There are numerous types of dishonesty, from deliberate lying to concealing information, to "bending the truth" slightly to save someone's feelings. Yes, even those little white lies are a form of dishonesty that some people feel are necessary and important in our society.

Graphologists generally look for groups of four or more graphological red flags before reaching a conclusion of probable dishonesty, but the overall pattern is, as always, the most important clue. Nevertheless, there are some individual red flags that, when combined, can provide some important evidence of potential for undesirable behavior.

Write Words

Honesty, the way I see it, is never deceiving, stealing, or taking advantage of the trust of others, and **integrity** means staying true to your own set of principles and beliefs.

Dishonest acts can be either spontaneous or premeditated. Some people suffer no qualms about stealing, lying, or cheating on a daily basis. Then there are those who, in normal circumstances, would be horrified at the thought of committing a dishonest act. Under pressure, however, when opportunity presents itself they might cave in and behave in a manner that is out of character. Is the impoverished parent who sneaks a carton of milk to feed her baby in the same category as the teenager who shoplifts the latest music video?

Both stole, but with very different psychological motivations. The signs in handwriting will be different for both types. Again, it's the overall pattern that counts. And, as Pulver points out, it's not our job to judge, but to interpret.

Read the Road Signs

Some of the following red flags for dishonest behavior have been covered in previous chapters because they are part of the range of normal behaviors. However, outside the context of their "normal" meaning, and when combined with other negative traits, they take on a more menacing significance.

- *Cover Stroke.* Whether an upstroke or a downstroke, it literally covers over and looks like a single line (see the next example). To produce a cover stroke the writer makes a sudden change of direction.

  A change of direction in handwriting symbolizes a change of direction in the writer's thinking. She has second thoughts about revealing something. When the coverstroke is in the lower zone, which is less common, the writer may have something embarrassing to hide about her sex life (see Chapter 10).

  A cover stroke on a circular letter in the middle zone, such as a or o, is more difficult to execute than on a straight letter. It often indicates avoidance or denial of the truth. Again, embarrassment may be a factor.

Fine Points

Spontaneous, natural writing is far less likely to contain red flags than slow, artificial writing. On the other hand, very fast, thready writing may signal a problem.

Cover Strokes.

- *Slow arcade.* The slow arcade is made by someone who is highly conscious of the way things look. She is image-conscious and has a "do as I say, not as I do" outlook. The hypocrite often writes with a slow arcade. When the arcade is at the end of a word and curls back to the left, it suggests someone who deliberately conceals the truth, perhaps by evasion. It may not be an overt lie, but a sin of omission (see Chapter 15).

- *Secondary thread.* The writer is evasiveness personified. He is determined to avoid taking sides or committing to any specific course of action. He is opportunistic, and manipulates and exploits every situation he can to suit his own needs. In the worst cases, the writer is a con artist who gets by, using all kinds of chicanery and deception. He bends the truth the way he bends the middle zone. By remaining ambiguous, he is able to dodge responsibility. If he can't be pinned down to a particular statement, he can't be blamed for the outcome (see Chapter 15).
- *Extremely wavy baseline.* This is less a sign of direct dishonesty than one of plain old unreliability. The writer may tell you'll she'll do something, but it never gets done. She'll say she's going to be somewhere, but never shows up. Her passive-aggressive behavior keeps on edge anyone who is counting on her. You'll never know whether she'll follow through or not. Chances are, she won't. The problems depicted by this sign are intensified by the addition of thready writing (see Chapter 8).
- *Counter strokes.* These are strokes that turn in the direction opposite to what is normal and expected. One example is an ending stroke that should move to the right, but instead returns to the left (see Chapter 11).

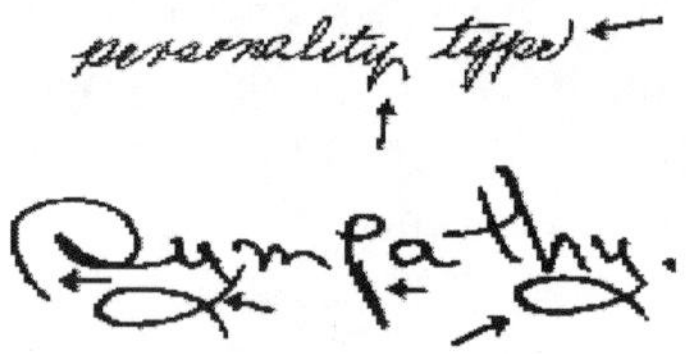

Counter strokes.

- *Fragmented strokes.* Bent, or broken and patched up, or *soldered* strokes suggest the writer wants to make herself look better than she is.
- *Coiled forms.* Strokes that curl into shapes like a snail's shell are a sign of extreme self-centeredness (see the next figure). The coiled stroke goes into the center in a leftward motion, bringing everything back to the self. This is a form of elaboration that suggests vanity and a need to protect the ego. The writer draws attention to herself, but when things go wrong she makes excuses and will say anything to make herself look good.

Tales from the Quill

The encircled oval is often made by adult children of alcoholics who have been taught to deny their feelings. They may talk all around their emotions, never quite coming to the point. In *Change Your Handwriting, Change Your Life,* graphologist Vimala Rodgers calls this the "Cleopatra stroke," because "Cleopatra was the Queen of DeNile...." This form is also called the "double-joined oval" in the British schools of graphology.

Coiled Forms.

- *Excessively complicated strokes.* These strokes reduce clarity and can come from a need to cover up information with excessive secrecy or draw your attention away from the truth. When the complications involve many circular strokes it suggests a trap that the writer uses to lure and ensnare the unwary; a graphological Roach Motel, with the roach on the outside.
- *Exaggerations.* Exaggerations of any sort draw the eye and obstruct the simple truth. You can expect self-aggrandizement, trickery, and bluffing from this writer. His need to push himself forward through these outlandish forms is a sign of insincerity and misrepresentation.
- *Double-looped ovals.* When made inside the communication letters (a, o, and other middle-zone letters), these slow things down and render clear communication impossible. The extra loops are, in effect, like trying to hear someone over the phone when her hand is covering the mouthpiece. The message comes through muffled at best (see Chapter 20). Although some systems of handwriting analysis have named this trait "deceit," there are many cases where the person simply cannot get the words out of her mouth, even

Write Words

Strokes are **soldered**, or patched up, by laying one stroke over the other. The difference between soldering and covering is that cover strokes are made in one movement, while soldered strokes are made separately.

Chicken Scratch

Oval letters that open at the bottom are a major red flag. Although usually called "embezzler's ovals," those who write them commit the most heinous of crimes and are unredeemably bad. See cannibalistic serial killer Jeffrey Dahmer's handwriting in Appendix E.

when she would like to. The emotions are locked in her throat.

- *Letters are omitted.* In a slow handwriting where some letters are omitted, we conclude that the writer deliberately leaves out important information. Certain facts that might be detrimental to him if known, are conveniently eliminated or swept under the rug. The same is true when ending strokes are suspended in mid air, rather than returning to the baseline. Information is dropped; the writer's not telling the whole truth.
- *Letters are made to look like other letters.* Similar to omitted letters, these represent a deliberate attempt to distort a situation and make it appear other than it is. The small letters o and a are sometimes used interchangeably by someone who distorts or evades.
- *Signature does not match the text.* This tells us that the writer is not totally what she seems. The form of the text tells the truth (see Chapter 18).

Felon's Claw or Cat's Paw

The so-called "felon's claw" (also known as "cat's paw") is included here because of its name. It has, however, little to do with felons, and nothing at all to do with cats. The felon's claw is a counter stroke, made claw-shaped by its cramped arcade form, and located in the middle and lower zones.

The person who chooses the claw-shape has been made to feel guilty all his life. As an adult he repeatedly sets himself up for punishment by creating situations that result in the familiar feelings of shame. Deep down, the felon's-claw writer believes he is worthless and engages in behavior that validates that belief.

In the lower zone the claw form is especially associated with guilt of a sexual nature. In most cases, the writer experienced sexual abuse in childhood and feels guilty about it, blaming himself, rather than the perpetrator.

The felon's-claw writer of the next example confronted her parents about the incest she suffered at the hands of her older brother, only to be accused of lying. Consequently, even though she knew intellectually that what her brother had done was wrong, she felt burdened with the guilt of her parents' anger with her for admitting to their dirty family secret.

Felon's Claw.

Like a hook, the claw keeps the writer holding on to frustration, embarrassment, and past grievances. Her defensive attitude makes it hard for others to deal with her, as she is constantly concerned with protecting her ego. Some graphologists have reported that felon's claws appearing in the middle zone, combined with contaminated oval letters (ovals with double loops or hooks inside them), is a sign of the thief!

No Evil "d" Goes Unpunished

Some specific letter forms seem to lend themselves especially well to interpretations of nasty behavior. One is called the "maniac d." In a handwriting that is moving along normally, the small letter "d" (actually, it can be any upper zone letter) suddenly flops over to the far right. You can see an example in the infamous Zodiac Killer's writing in Appendix E. It signifies sudden uncontrolled explosive behavior in someone who otherwise may appear as mild-mannered as a mouse. After he has acted out his rage, the writer returns to his normal behavior.

Mack the Knife

The "shark's tooth," so-named for its resemblance to the eating apparatus of the Great White, is a particularly unpleasant handwriting feature. It combines a counter stroke with a curved form and is easiest to see in the small letters r, s, w, m, and n. The final stroke of these letters either bows opposite the direction it was intended to go, or curves exaggeratedly in the proper direction. Either way, it ends up looking like a shark's tooth.

This letter form (illustrated along with some other red flag forms) exposes a cunning person who acts loyal and pats you on the back with a knife in his other hand. The writer tells you what he thinks you want to hear while secretly furthering his own interests. When a straight answer is called for he'll sweet-talk you into thinking you know what he's saying, but you really don't, because he talks his way over, around, under and…well, you get the picture.

Tales from the Quill

Joanna, whose handwriting contained many felon's claws often gossiped about her friend Sandy in a way that ensured the talk would get back to Sandy. Naturally, Sandy would feel hurt and angrily confront Joanna. By putting herself in a negative light through her bad behavior, Joanna gets to feel guilty, which is what she unconsciously needs. Psychologists call this kind of behavior a "secondary gain."

Unloving Spoonful

Graphologists seem to like giving silly names to oddly shaped strokes. This one is called the "spoon-e." Evidently, whoever came up with that appellation thought it looked like a spoon. Since I haven't come up with anything more clever, we'll go with it. The spoon-e, which is a fairly uncommon structure, is a combination curve/angle where an angle doesn't belong, and is another example of a counter stroke.

The standard lower case letter "e" begins at the center and makes a smooth outward motion that ends to the right. A spoon-e, on the other hand, starts with a straight stroke that is hidden by the curve. The movement requires a stop-and-turn motion, which puts a brake on the forward motion and results in the counter stroke.

The spoon-e signifies someone whose behavior is calculating and cautious under the guise of correctness. Strong self-control is indicated, not necessarily in the positive sense, but as in premeditated behavior. That is, he doesn't show how he really feels, but acts in a way that he believes will produce the desired results. The writer is evasive, hiding his true motives behind a pleasant face. Like an owl that swoops down on the unsuspecting rabbit, the spoon-e writer's behavior is cagey and shrewd. When he strikes, the other person never sees it coming. The following figure shows an example of the shark's tooth and a spoon-e along with an elliptical g, which we'll learn about next.

Spoon-e (left), shark's tooth (right) elliptical g (below).

Spoon e

Shark's tooth r

Elliptical g

The Awful Oval

As we run the gamut of unpleasant behavior, the elliptical g deserves a mention. The middle zone portion of the letter, rather than being a smooth, round form, is squeezed into an ovoid shape diagonal to the baseline. The downstroke, which is supposed to go straight down, below the baseline instead, moves upward before descending with a rightward curve that looks like a backward C.

The writer is sly and devious, hiding her true intentions, which are to deceive and mislead. Those she deals with may not be able to quite put their finger on what's wrong because "she seems so nice!" They know only that they don't quite trust her. Her motivations are self-centered, and she works to get what she wants, even at others' expense. She may be a braggart who boasts and puffs herself up. She wants to give the impression that she is far more than what she really is.

Stabbing strokes in the middle of ovals indicate communication problems. One high-profile graphologist calls this the sign of the pathological liar.

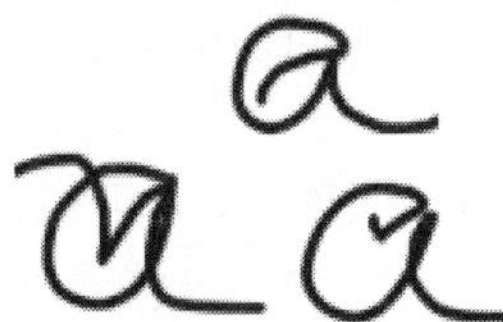

Stabbed ovals.

Tales from the Quill

Ellen worked as a secretary for MediMart Pharmaceuticals for seven years, smiling on the outside, but hating every moment of her job. One day she quit without notice. Before she left, Ellen secretly sabotaged the computer system, programming complicated passwords into the most important files and deleting dozens of others that were needed on a daily basis. She also left realistic-looking plastic bugs in the desk drawers of her former boss. Her otherwise copybook handwriting featured the elliptical g.

Downhill Racer: Signs of Violence

Strong variability in slant, baseline, size, and other aspects of the handwriting always adds to the negative interpretation of the red flags. Although the big picture is always more important than the small details, don't ignore the fine points. If you see any of the following red flags in a handwriting, pay close attention.

- *Extremely heavy pressure.* The writer is suffering from a buildup of excess frustration. He doesn't appropriately release his strong feelings, and may resort to drugs and alcohol which, in turn, may lead to violent behavior (see Chapter 12).
- *Variable pressure.* The writer of variable pressure is unpredictable, unreliable, and inconsistent. He blows hot and cold, and you never know when he'll fly into a rage. Variable pressure is often seen in the handwritings of criminals (see Chapter 12).
- *Muddiness.* Muddy writing is made by unrelieved pressure and exposes extreme tension. Plain, unvarnished lying is a characteristic of this writer. He doesn't have the intellect or the interest in trying to finesse his way through a situation. He simply blurts out whatever comes to mind, regardless of how unlikely the story. In combination with other negative traits, such as dot-grinding (we'll discuss this in a minute), the writer may be sadistic (see Chapter 12).
- *Extreme right slant.* When combined with extremely heavy pressure, this is a dangerous combination—Molotov-cocktail kind of dangerous. When this writer erupts, everyone in the immediate vicinity had better duck for cover. He goes ballistic (see Chapter 16).
- *Bizarre t-crosses.* Often seen in the handwritings of criminals, these strange forms signify the writer's willingness to go to whatever ends are necessary to achieve his goals. The behavior is usually of the most grossly violent type and may include torture (see Chapter 20 for an illustration).
- *Club strokes.* When pressure suddenly thickens on the ends of letters or words, it signifies an outburst of emotion. If the thickened pressure looks like a club in the middle zone, you can be sure that the writer uses his words to bludgeon. If the club appears in the lower zone, stay away from the writer when he's carrying a baseball bat. The next figure illustrates the club stroke.

Club strokes.

never tath t them

- *Stabbing or slashing strokes.* Here's the opposite of the club stroke. This stroke starts out heavy on the left side and thins to a nasty-looking point that is made in a downward, slashing motion. The writer has a bad temper and a cruel tongue that slashes his victims. He may like sharp knives.
- *Dot grinding.* Punctuation is extremely heavy and actually ground into the paper. Kathy Urbiha, a registered nurse and graphologist who works with prison inmates, reports that she frequently sees dot grinding, particularly with compulsive-type sexual offenders. Dot grinding reveals inner tension and a habit of

ruminating on or reliving the offending behavior (see Chapter 19). Another form of this characteristic is the "black spot." Klara Roman identified it in people who suffer from guilt. The black spot symbolically covers up information they want to keep from you. Some examples appear in the next illustration.

Black spots.

- *Harpoons.* These are extremely long, hooked strokes coming from below the baseline. These initial strokes, as seen in serial-killer Ted Bundy's handwriting, expose hidden aggressive behavior that is compulsively acted out. (see Appendix E).
- *Extreme angularity.* Handwriting in which the angle is the dominant connective form shows aggression. When combined with narrow forms and heavy pressure, the antisocial personality is usually behind the writing. The writer needs to dominate in all his relationships (see Chapter 15).

Fine Points

Club strokes and stabbing strokes are seen most often in t crossings, i dots, and other horizontal movement.

- *Disturbed rhythm.* Roda Wieser, a German graphologist, found that criminals' handwritings lacked the elastic, swinging rhythm of noncriminals' writings. The criminals' rhythm was either extremely brittle or extremely slack. In either case, their inner personalities lack harmony and their outer behaviors show it. The writer of brittle rhythm snaps at the least provocation. The writer of slack writing gives in to every impulse (see Chapter 11).
- *Jump-up letters.* These are letters that pop up out of the middle zone and jump into the upper zone where they don't belong. They are a red flag when combined with other negative indicators. By themselves they signify someone who is normally calm and passive, but occasionally rears up over others and asserts herself.
- *Capitals in cursive.* When capital letters appear mid-word in cursive writing this is a sign of inappropriate behavior. The writer does things to get attention, like blurting out rude remarks or just generally acting like a jerk.

Chicken Scratch

When you detect what looks like a red flag in someone's handwriting, make sure it isn't the result of illness, writing conditions, or a bad pen before you decide that the writer's behavior is pathological.

- *Changing styles.* Writing that changes from cursive to printing, or to some other style in a relatively short period of time (from one paragraph to the next, for example) is an indication of someone who is unpredictable. You never know how she's going to act.

Don't Drink and Write: Drugs and Alcohol

Substance abuse is a very complex subject which, like the previous discussion, really merits an entire volume to cover it fully. However, we'll look at some general indicators for the addictive personality, just to open up some of the possibilities.

Substance abuse involves physiological, as well as psychological changes. The handwriting indicators in the early stages of drug or alcohol abuse may be somewhat different from those found later.

Research shows that a low level of alcohol in the blood has relatively little effect on handwriting. The writing tends to become slightly more irregular and may increase in size.

Once the writer is inebriated, his coordination is affected and motor disturbances appear in the handwriting. The letters grow in size, breaks between letters increase, and legibility is reduced. Finally, when the blood alcohol level rises to around .3, the person becomes incapable of writing at all, and will probably lose consciousness.

Fine Points

The so-called addictive personality encompasses far more than just problem drinking and drug addiction. For a more in-depth discussion of this personality type, I have written a monograph on the subject, *The Addictive Personality and Its Handwriting.* (You can order a copy by calling (661) 259-8979.)

Even with short-term alcohol use, motor activities can become impaired. If you've ever been with someone who had "one too many," you probably couldn't help but notice her slurred speech, unsteady walk, and clumsy movements. The motor system was impacted by the alcohol and it shows in the handwriting.

Hallucinogens, such as marijuana and LSD, affect the liver, spleen, gall-bladder, lungs, and nerve centers of the brain. Used over a period of time, some types of recreational-drug use can result in tremor that carries over to handwriting. Tremor shows up as a very shaky-looking writing line. LSD use is characterized by bizarre forms of letters.

Tales from the Quill

Some years ago, around the holidays, Smirnoff Vodka had a billboard displaying five lines of handwriting. The first line was written by a sober volunteer. It said, "I can drink and drive," after which he was given an alcoholic beverage. After the drink he wrote the same sentence again. The exercise was repeated five times; each writing becoming less controlled. The last sentence was a totally illegible, garbled line. The message was, "If you can't even control a pen, how are you going to control a car?"

To Your Good Health!

The brain sends messages through the pen about some areas in the body where there may be physiological problems, but it does so only in a very general way. Before beginning any discussion of health issues in handwriting, I have to say, loud and clear: Do not diagnose illness unless you have a medical license!

Unfortunately, studies of health and its effects on handwriting have been far too few. One particularly successful research project was conducted over more than 30 years by graphologist Alfred Kanfer. His research that successfully predicted cancer from handwriting, including his own, two years before his death. His work is described in detail in *You Are What You Write* (Macmillan, 1973), by Huntington Hartford.

San Diego, California graphologist William Knowles has been working with physicians to validate Kanfer's work with some success. Other people in the field, such as Rose Toomey, have also performed research with medical doctors and self-published their findings, which are available through graphology booksellers (see Chapter 4).

As shown in the following illustration, we can use the lower-case letter f as a symbol for the human body. The top of the upper loop represents the head and the bottom of the lower loop represents the feet. You can figure out where everything else belongs.

Letter f as the human figure.

Tales from the Quill

A graphologist noted many unnecessary dots of ink on a page of writing she was analyzing. Considered in the overall picture, she felt that the dots might signify a health problem, and suggested her client seek medical attention. The client later reported that when she saw the doctor he immediately scheduled her for a hysterectomy, stating that had she waited any longer she probably would not have lived.

Some health problems evident in handwriting are temporary and some are permanent. You'll probably need a magnifying glass to see them. A headache, sore throat, or toothache may show up as a tiny dot, sometimes referred to as a bleb, at the top of an upper zone loop. An ulcer or other stomach problem might appear as a dot in the middle zone. Problems with the feet often occur as a dot in the lower loops. Broken bones are sometimes revealed as a slight break in the loop. A blow to some part of the body may show up under magnification as a slight wavy line.

Diseases that affect gross motor functions, such as Parkinson's, may be seen in tremor over the entire writing. Heart disease sometimes produces unnecessary dots of ink on various parts of the paper.

Examining the handwritings of people with a diagnosed illness can be very interesting. You can do your own research and see if you can find where the disease shows up. Please, please, please, just don't tell someone, "Oh! Your handwriting shows you have gallbladder problems," or "Looks like you're going to have a heart attack!" If you see something that looks like a potential problem, tactfully suggest that it might be time for a checkup.

The next chapter helps synthesize everything you've learned so far so you can write a coherent report. After all, isn't that what it's really all about?

The Least You Need to Know

- "Honesty" is largely subjective, which makes it hard to determine for certain in handwriting.
- There are some definite red flags that can help you determine the level of potential for bad behavior.
- The red flags signify potential only. We do not know whether the writer will act on that potential.
- Drugs and alcohol impair handwriting.

Part 6
The Last Word

Before wrapping up your study of handwriting analysis, you'll need to know how to report what you've found. That's what we'll do in this part. We'll also deal with some practical matters, such as how to turn all this knowledge into a paying business, and how to keep yourself and your clients out of court.

You'll also find some interesting samples of the famous and the infamous, which you can use to test what you've learned.

Is graphology the career for you? Whether you decide to go forward full-bore or use what you've learned just for your own personal enlightenment, you'll now have a good foundation for understanding yourself and others in a way you never thought possible.

Chapter 23

Writing the Analysis

In This Chapter

- What do you do, now that you know what you know?
- Putting it in the blender
- The mini analysis
- Going more in-depth

Now that you've got all this wonderful knowledge about handwriting, what do you do with it? As you've discovered, no one particular element of the writing can be interpreted out of context. Knowing that the writing is right-slanted might tell you that the writer is moderately emotional, but you need more information to get a good 'fix' on the personality. For instance, along with the slant, the pressure will reveal how long the emotions stay with the writer. Then you need to add information about the margins to know whether the writer's emotions are holding her back; and all the other pieces of the puzzle that play a part in making the writer who she really is.

This chapter will help you put all those discrete pieces together into a coherent whole. You'll learn how to synthesize your findings and make the whole greater than the sum of its parts—that's the gestalt.

Putting It All Together: The First Impression

When you first look at a handwriting sample it can seem like a jigsaw puzzle of a thousand pieces, all in the same color. Even though you've learned the basic principles

Fine Points

Some teachers ask the students to start writing reports from the very beginning, but I suggest you don't try to write up your results too soon. Make sure you really understand the writing before you attempt to report on it.

of handwriting analysis, you may not yet have achieved that "Aha!" flash of insight that gives you the key to understanding the essence of the writer's personality.

Some graphologists seem to instantly "know" what a handwriting reveals about the writer. Others stumble around, trying to add up the bits and pieces, but they just don't get it, even after years of serious study. What's the difference? One has learned how to synthesize the various elements of the writing, while the other simply develops a list of unrelated personality traits.

Making up a 'laundry list' of traits is easy. Anyone can pick out "resentment strokes," "yieldingness strokes," "vanity strokes," as some schools teach their students to do. But how does a list of traits help your client? It doesn't. A report that speaks to the writer's heart takes more than just a superficial dusting on the surface of his or her personality. A meaningful report means having a thorough understanding of the writer's motivations and needs.

Don't be discouraged; there are no tricks and you don't have to be psychic. The ability to look at a handwriting and quickly grasp the core personality can be learned. Using some specific techniques that will help you synthesize and fit together all those things you know, you'll master it before you can say graphogobbledgook.

Finding the Guiding Image

In handwriting analysis, synthesis means making a series of deductions to arrive at the desired end—an accurate picture of the writer's personality. There are several methods of synthesis that apply graphological theories or principles. Trial and error will tell what works best for you.

Write Words

Guiding image is the writer's core personality. It's the underlying character of the writer, which you can find in the two major opposing forces in the handwriting you are examining.

One method I particularly like is finding the *"guiding image."* Everyone has personality conflicts or contradictions of some type, and the guiding image is made up of the two major opposing forces in the personality. For instance, let's say the writing has a strong right slant, showing a need to move out toward others, but at the same time, the spaces between the words are very wide, which indicates a need for the writer to separate himself from others.

He needs to move toward others and also has a need for space? Sounds like a contradiction, doesn't it? These are the opposing forces or the basic conflict in the writer's personality. Examining the surrounding factors in the writing will explain the apparent inconsistency. Perhaps the writer *wants* to reach out to others but is afraid to (that's what a narrow middle zone would show).

Once you are able to identify the opposing forces, you'll have a basis for writing the analysis. The following checklist will help to get you started by giving you some specific traits to look for in the writing. I've included some hints in parentheses so you'll know where to look in the writing.

Handwriting Analysis Checklist

__ Emotionally responsive (right slant)

__ Emotionally reserved (upright slant)

__ Retains past emotional experiences (strong pressure)

__ Quickly forgets emotional experiences (light pressure)

__ Detail-oriented (careful i dots and t crosses)

__ Prefers the big picture more than small details (i dots and t crosses high and to the right)

__ Sensitive to criticism (big loops)

__ Criticism has little effect (no loops)

__ Enjoys verbal communication (large middle zone)

__ Tends to be secretive (small middle zone)

__ Relies on intuition to make decisions (smooth breaks)

__ Logical thinker (strong connectedness)

__ Enjoys physical activity (large lower zone)

__ Sedentary type (small lower zone)

__ Well organized (balanced overall arrangement)

__ Needs help getting organized (messy overall arrangement)

Using statements from the checklist, write on a new sheet of paper a couple of sentences describing the writer's personality. For instance, take "logical thinker," you could say something like this: "John is a logical thinker. That means he is more comfortable having all the facts and figures before making a decision, and is less likely to listen to his intuition."

Tales from the Quill

You are welcome to copy the handwriting checklist and make it into a trait chart to give friends when you're practicing your skills, or you can make your own. Just leave out the notes in parentheses and check off the items that apply to their handwriting. With practically no effort at all, you've given them a mini analysis! Believe me, they'll be impressed!

See how easy that is? Do that for each item and you'll quickly have a one-page analysis. Once you're comfortable with doing these quickie profiles, you'll be ready to go on to a more detailed analysis.

How Do You Do? Asking the Writing Questions

Asking the writing questions helps you get deeper into the writer's personality. Just be ready to listen to the answers. How can you ask a writing question? Will it answer you? Following are some examples and clues on how to find the answers in the writing:

1. Is the writer reactive or proactive?

   Reactive: The writer is affected by her environment and feels good about herself only when others are treating her well.

   Variable slant, baseline, middle zone height; small or poorly formed capital letters.

   Proactive: The writer responds to the environment, but makes her own choices based on an internal set of values.

   Good rhythm, direction, speed; zonal balance.

2. Is the writer resilient or not?

   Resilient: She bounces back when obstacles arise to block her progress or keep her from achieving her goals.

   Strong left to right movement, fluidity, rhythm.

   Not Resilient: The writer is easily distracted or frustrated.

   Variable baseline, dished t bars, slack ductus.

3. Does the writer have initiative or not?

   Has initiative: The writer acts on his own without being prompted.

   Simplification, lack of beginning strokes, speed, stick PPI.

   Lacks initiative: He waits to be told what to do.

   Long beginning strokes, slowness, school type, elaboration.

4. *Learns from mistakes:* Does the writer acknowledge her mistakes and learn from them or not?

   Zonal balance, upper zone not too tall, lower zone returns to baseline.

   Justifies and rationalizes mistakes: Does she blame others or make excuses?

   Upper zone too tall and narrow, copybook style, complicated ovals.

5. Does the writer keep her feelings to herself or act them out?

   Inhibits feelings: poorly formed lower zone, narrowness, wide right margin, narrow left margin, sharp ductus.

   Acts out feelings: right slant, elaborate capitals, moderate to large size, heavy pressure, pastosity.

6. *Reliability:* Does the writer keep commitments?

   Good rhythm, left to right movement, balance, harmony, clear middle zone, clear line spacing, no zonal interference.

7. *Goal-setting:* Does the writer use his imagination and will power for goal setting?

   Well formed upper zone, strong horizontal movement, good pressure.

8. *Sense of Security:* Does the writer feel secure within himself?

   Good rhythm, well-formed capitals (especially the PPI), good pressure.

9. *Perspective:* Does the writer have a clear perspective on life?

   Good zonal balance, clear line spacing, good margins.

10. *Integrity:* Does the writer make and keep commitments to herself and others? A function of self-discipline and will power.

    Good rhythm, simplification of form, fluidity, moderate pressure, clear ovals, balance.

11. *Goal-directed:* Does the writer have goals, a mission in life?

    Strong left to right movement, pressure, balanced margins, moderately straight baseline.

12. *Impulsive:* Is he propelled by the impulse of the moment?

    Wavy baseline, variable pressure, slackness, muddiness.

13. What motivates the writer?

    Approval: The writer's need for approval leads to emotional dependence and vulnerability to the moods and behaviors of others. It results in a lack of power.

    Rounded writing, strong garlands, long lead-in strokes, bowed t-bars, variable baseline.

    Money and material possessions: If the writer is driven by a need for material things, anything that threatens her economic security leaves her vulnerable. She is restricted to what she accomplishes through her financial worth.

    Heavy pressure, overblown lower zone, pastosity.

    Pleasure and comfort: The writer bases decisions on the pleasure they bring. Decisions are based on how the outcome will affect him; he wants only what feels good at the moment. He sees the world in terms of what's in it for him.

    Large middle and lower zones, pastosity, loose rhythm; ending strokes return to the left, extra large capitals, narrow right margin, narrow line spacing.

    Recognition: The writer's self-image is identified with her work and her accomplishments that bring personal acclaim.

    Moderately strong pressure, large capitals, good rhythm.

Other Questions You Could Ask

You might not want to use these in the analysis, but it helps to imagine the writer in different life situations. Ask yourself how the writer would:

- React in a traffic jam?
- Handle an irate customer?
- Deal with a child having a tantrum in public?
- Act at a party?
- Perform in bed?
- Ask the boss for a raise?
- Break off a bad relationship?

Trying It Both Ways

As we discussed in Chapter 1, there are two main ways of analyzing handwriting, the French atomistic method and the German gestalt method. We'll analyze the handwriting in the next figure from the point of view of both methods.

The writer of the following sample is a 28-year-old, right-handed woman who was raised as an army brat. A computer freak and avid reader of science fiction, she spends much of her time playing computer games.

Once again I find myself writing you a
letter! But this time I'll be standing
over your shoulder to make sure you
get it analized.
Already I have run out of things to say,
What I do for excitement on the weekends!
Yesterday we had a great time shopping
at Montclair Plaza. Rick bought me
6 books. That's because I got him
GFA Basic 3.07 with compiler. He
has a 600 hundred page manual
to read, so he needed to get me
something to do While he reads it.
End of this letter!

Heidi

Handwriting sample.

The Gestalt Method

Here's one way to view the handwriting from the gestalt, or holistic approach. We start with how the writing looks overall:

- *General impression:* There is a lot of activity in the writing. It is well-organized with no extremes to disrupt the overall unity. However, there are some minor disturbances in the rhythm.
- *Form level (form level is a combination of many factors, but it basically means "does the writing look well-balanced and harmonious or not"):* Moderately high. The writing is simplified and spontaneous with dynamic left-to-right movement. The signature is congruent with the body of writing.
- *Space/form/movement:* In the overall picture of space, form, and movement, the movement dominates.
- *Picture of Space:* Moderately good distribution of space between words, lines, letters, and fairly well-balanced margins.
- *Picture of Form:* Simplified, original forms with some irregularity.
- *Picture of Movement:* Rapid progression from left to right with moderate rhythmical pressure. Movement into the lower zone is stunted, with emphasis on the upper zone. Rhythm is interrupted by tension.

Chicken Scratch

Be very careful how you word negative information in a report. It's very easy to misconstrue the tone in writing, and once you hand over the analysis it literally is out of your hands. Worse, the client probably won't tell you how your words hurt him.

What is the conclusion? This is an original writing with a medium-size middle zone, largely connected, with interesting letter combinations. Garlands and arcades predominate with a mixture of curved and linear forms that are disproportionately short in the lower zone. Secondary expansion is stronger than primary.

The Synthesis

In putting our overall impressions together, it helps to give them a context. Let's break them up into four areas: intellect, social skills, drives, and controls.

- *Intellect:* Original, rhythmic, quick, simplified, connected. She's a quick thinker who doesn't rely on tried and true methods, but can formulate new ways of doing things. The writer may have some difficulty concentrating due to interference by emotions. May be impulsive, acting before thinking.
- *Social skills:* Strong movement, right slant, good pressure pattern, stunted lower zone, irregularity. She is sensitive and understands complex people problems, but does not always have the patience to deal with them. The result is some inconsistency in her social behavior.
- *Drives:* Good pressure, stunted lower zone, irregularity. She's an intellectually lively, active individual whose enthusiasm is quickly aroused and discharged. Physical activity may give way to mental activity.

- *Controls:* Tension, irregularity, connectedness, good organization. She is spontaneous and impulsive at times, but with generally good self-discipline. She is flexible and adapts well on a surface level, but is unlikely to change her value system, even under pressure.
- *Self-image*: Large PPI and other capitals, medium-size middle zone, strong left-to–right, upper-zone movement, stunted lower zone. The writer is independent, with the ability to project her needs onto the world. She's not afraid to reach out for what she wants on the surface, but she may neglect her deeper needs.

Fine Points

There is a big difference between the genuine French (atomistic) method of graphology and the trait-stroke offshoot that is taught in some U.S. schools of graphology. The French method considers groups of signs, rather than individual ones, as the trait-stroke method does.

The Empirical Strikes Back: The French Method

With the French or atomistic method we also get a first impression. Then we look at the various elements of handwriting without making any interpretation.

- *First impression:* The writing of an intelligent, moderately emotional young woman.
- *Size:* Very uneven, ranging from above–normal, to less-than–average, middle-zone height (shifting self-image, self-doubt, sense of inadequacy vies with attempts at self-assertion).
- *Speed:* Uneven, fast, leaning forward but also retracing (quick reactions but conscious control, except when emotions run high).
- *Pressure:* Moderate, but uneven, with some blurred edges along the stroke (moral standards may be slack). Light stroke with fast speed suggests fluctuating health and vitality.
- *Direction:* Rising baseline, some variability (struggles with depression).
- *Continuity:* Strong, connectedness (logic, sequence of ideas), figure 8 g's, simplifications (resourceful solutions to problems).
- *Form:* Uneven but simplified style. Garlands, arcades, and thread combine (versatile, adaptable person who wants to get along with others). The arcades show a need to maintain a low profile. Threaded forms show good intuition.
- *Organization:* Overall good, indicating general ability to organize her life and time. However, the right margin tends to pull leftward, which shows a tendency to back off due to a fear of failure.

If the atomistic graphologist is well-trained, he will reach a conclusion about the writer's personality similar to the conclusion reached by the gestalt graphologist. It's more a question of competency than method.

Typecasting: Using Typologies

Using typologies can help speed up the process of analysis by as much as 75 percent. Typologies categorize personality types into groups and are used by many psychologists. The Myers-Briggs Temperament Indicator, based on Jung's two attitudes and four functions, is widely used.

Jung described two attitudes—extrovert and introvert—and four ways of functioning—thinking, feeling, sensing, and intuiting. Although one function is used primarily, everyone uses all the functions to some degree or another.

Fine Points

There are numerous books in print on the Jungian types, such as *Please Understand Me*, by Kiersey & Bates (Prometheus Nemesis Book Company, 1984), and *Type Talk*, by Kroeger & Thuesen (Dell Publishing, 1988). Several handwriting analysts (including yours truly) have also written monographs applying Jung's and other types to handwriting.

Think of how much information you would already have if you could look at a handwriting sample and immediately decide whether the writer was an introvert or an extrovert. That's pretty easy, isn't it? Identifying thinking or feeling, sensing or intuiting, is nearly as easy and supplies a tremendous amount of information about the person. You can apply what you know about the general type, and personalize it to fit the writing you are analyzing.

Besides Jung's, some of the other typologies I've found helpful include Freud's neurotic types: Depressive, Schizoid, Obsessional, and Histrionic types; Fromm's Receptive, Exploitive, Hoarding, Marketing types; Adler's Comfort, Pleasing, Superiority, and Control types; Maslow's hierarchy of needs; and the Enneagram with its nine types.

My favorite book on Freud's types is *The Art of Psychotherapy* (Methuen, 1979, 1980) by Anthony Storr. If you're interested in learning about the Enneagram, try *The Enneagram Made Easy* (HarperCollins, 1994) by Elizabeth Wagele and Renee Baron. Felix Klein wrote monographs describing Fromm's, Maslow's, and Adler's types and their handwriting equivalents. You can order them from Janice Klein (her address is in Appendix B.)

Saying What You See—Writing the Report

The report you provide speaks for you. Always edit your work carefully. Typographical errors, misspellings, and poor grammar detract from the message. Long, run-on sentences tend to be confusing and obfuscate the meaning. Try to figure out what this analyst is trying to say:

> "The writer has a desire to distinguish himself from others, at the same time enjoying the approval of others, although he is self-reliant and at ease with people, evaluating and appraising others in a critical, fault-finding way."

Huh? This sentence was taken from an actual analysis that someone paid good money for. Let's try rearranging and rewording it:

> "While the writer enjoys the approval of other people, he wants to distinguish himself from the crowd. Once he becomes comfortable in a group, however, he tends to be critical and fault-finding."

Some sentences should be short and to the point, connected by slightly longer, explanatory ones. Read the analysis out loud. If anything sounds blurred or confusing to you, it certainly won't be clear to the client. Rewrite or cut out any sentence that doesn't read well.

Use easily understood language, not graphological or psychological terms. And don't make psychological or medical diagnoses unless you are legally qualified to do so.

The Mechanics

Make sure you know what question needs to be answered by the analysis. Is it a profile that needs only to cover the high points of the personality? Or a comprehensive analysis that will discuss the more in-depth issues, such as childhood development? Or, is the report meant to determine whether the writer's personality is suitable for a job?

The profile analysis is usually about 350 to 700 words long. That's one to two typed pages. It should be an overview of the writer's strengths and weaknesses, and isn't the place to discuss early childhood trauma. A comprehensive report is usually several pages long and is often accompanied by various charts or graphs. This is where it's appropriate to thoroughly discuss all aspects of the writer's background and show how it helped to mold his temperament.

Fine Points

Keep a style and grammar manual handy. Strunk & White's *The Elements of Style* and *The Elements of Grammar* (Allyn & Bacon, 1995) are excellent, but *Woe is I* (G.P. Putnam's Sons, 1996) by Patricia T. O'Connor is also a lot of fun to read. A computer grammar checking program is a good idea, and your favorite dictionary is a big help, too.

There are three parts common to all analyses—a beginning, a middle, and an end. The important thing is to make everything in each of those parts accurate and beneficial to the client. An introductory paragraph or two outlining what handwriting analysis is and what the client can expect isn't a bad idea. Then, make a statement about the purpose of the analysis.

Chicken Scratch

Put yourself in the reader's place. Would you appreciate reading, "Joe, your handwriting shows you are suicidal and were sexually abused as a child"? Instead, it probably would be more useful to say something like this: "I can see that you've endured some very painful and difficult experiences in your life."

Be upbeat. You have the power to wound with your words, and no one is all bad. Even the lowest form-level (worst-looking!) writing has something you can comment on positively. Analyses should always begin and end on a positive note. You want to provide self-knowledge, not a reason for self-immolation. Dealing with someone's psyche is a tremendous responsibility, and your analysis can have a very favorable effect if you present it well. Any negatives should be sandwiched somewhere in the middle and discussed diplomatically, in terms of the writer's coping mechanisms.

End the analysis on an encouraging note that will leave the client feeling hopeful and eager to improve his life with the information you have provided. A call to some type of action leaves the client feeling that he has benefited from the report. You might offer some suggestions for graphotherapy (we'll discuss that in the next chapter) or psychotherapy, if called for. If you feel that the client needs a referral to a psychologist, you could offer to refer him to one if you know a good counselor. Sometimes the client will be limited by what his insurance provider allows, so the referral may have to come from the provider.

The handwriting itself will tell you how to approach the client. If the style is highly simplified, stripped of any extra strokes, you can be more direct and candid, and "tell it like it is." If a writing has many loops and garlands, then you'd know the client is very sensitive and needs kid-glove handling.

Don't Try This At Home: Analysis Do's and Don'ts

There are some do's and don'ts to consider when you write your analyses:

Do's:

- Answer any questions directly and accurately.
- Be sure you can back up every statement in your report.
- Couch negative comments in diplomatic language.
- Make suggestions for developing weak areas.
- Allow the client room to disagree. You may be wrong. Or you may be right and she just isn't ready to accept it right now.

Don'ts:

- Diagnose physical or mental illness without a license.
- Forget what it's like to be the person who is being analyzed. Remember how vulnerable you felt when it was your writing under the magnifying glass.

Tales from the Quill

A graphologist was asked to analyze the writing of a man the client had met through the Internet. Was he honest? Did he have integrity? The writing was feminine looking and school type with no negative indicators. After making her report, the graphologist learned that the writer was a convicted con artist and rapist. The devastated analyst was convinced that the supposed writer had conned a female friend into writing the sample for him.

- Be dogmatic.
- Be too hard on yourself if you miss something important or are just plain wrong. Every graphologist has a humiliating story to share.

Professional Is as Professional Does

You must be able to coherently report your findings or you will have wasted your time and your client's. Some analysts provide verbal reports, while others (like me) are more comfortable in writing. One advantage to a verbal report is being able to explain what you mean on the spot (sometimes a reader misunderstands what the writer meant). On the other hand, when the client has the report in hand, he can re-read and review the material easily. If writing isn't your forte, consider taking a creative or business writing course.

A poorly prepared report that is full of grammatical and typographical errors detracts from the message and reflects poorly on graphology as a profession. If you do your part to present a professional image, we all benefit.

The Least You Need to Know

- The analysis should be a synthesis of all the writing elements, not just a list of traits.
- A checklist will help you get started writing the analysis.
- Ask the writing questions about specific situations to help you get deeper into the personality.
- Choosing a typology will help you get lots of extra information about the writer.

Chapter 24

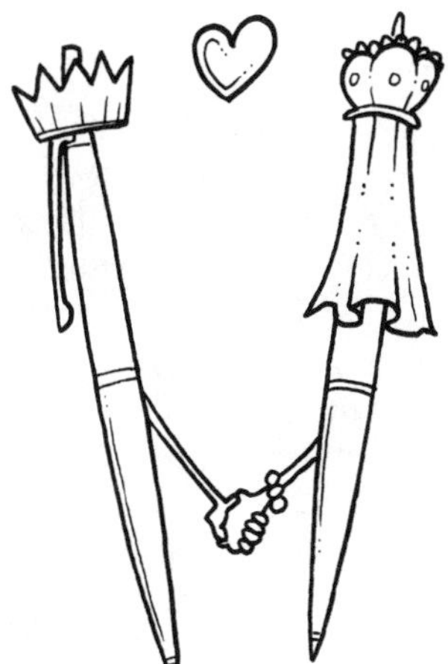

And They Lived Happily Ever After

In This Chapter

- Compatibility isn't enough
- Essential ingredients
- Similar drives help
- Relationship nightmares

Have you ever begun a relationship that looked as if it was going to be absolutely wonderful, only to have it turn out perfectly awful? That guy you just knew was Mr. Right couldn't have been more wrong? Or the woman you adored suddenly transmuted into a totally alien screaming meemie?

It's easy to be on our best behavior on the first date when everything about the new guy or gal is electrifying, sensational, and all those other superlatives that rarely survive the first blush of romance. But once the humdrum rhythm of daily life sets in and the shiny newness begins to wear off, those annoying little foibles start showing up.

Handwriting provides much of the information you need to bring out the best and understand the worst in a relationship. Appreciating your partner's motivations and needs *before* entering the relationship could help you avoid a lot of needless heartache.

Of course, other important factors also enter into the equation, such as chemistry and goodwill. Handwriting analysis isn't going to fix up a bad match or stop you from falling into a victim role, if that's what you do. What it will do, however, is equip you to recognize negative patterns that you may be guilty of perpetuating so you can begin to break out of them.

Chicken Scratch

Some people ask for a compatibility analysis, but when the results turn out negative, they ignore it and plunge ahead anyway. After the relationship falls apart and they call to tell you "I wish I had listened to the analysis," it's not nice to say, "I told you so"!

Goodwill Hunting

So you've met this guy. He's got everything on your list: He's tall, dark and handsome, has a great personality, a good job, a nice car, and his own home. And he's not married. What more could a girl ask for? Try goodwill. Without it, a relationship is doomed. What is goodwill? It's an attitude that overrides circumstances that might otherwise cause the relationship to fail. Goodwill implies willingness to overlook the other partner's imperfections and weaknesses, and to show unconditional love. I couldn't say it any better than the Bible: *Love believes all things, hopes all things, endures all things. Love never fails.*

This isn't to suggest either party should become a pushover, a doormat, or accept abuse. The goodwill has to flow in both directions. If only one person is showing goodwill toward the other, the relationship becomes like a car with a flat tire. It may limp along for a while, but eventually, the tire will fall off the wheel, with major damage resulting.

It would be great if goodwill was something we could see in handwriting. But it's intangible. All we as graphologists can do is point out areas of strength that the couple can build on, and those nasty old potential trouble spots that need work.

The Happy Couple

What makes for a happy couple still? Two people may have everything it takes for a compatible relationship, but it doesn't work out. On the other side of the coin, a couple may seem so different that they are totally incompatible, but if both want to make the relationship work, it will. Chemistry is the magic ingredient. Like goodwill, chemistry is not something you can find in handwriting. So, we'll have to start with what we *can* find and leave the chemistry to the couple.

I asked the members of the Vanguard Forum Online (an e-mail handwriting analysis discussion group) what they felt were the most important elements of a good relationship. Sex was cited only a couple of times. The top three, mentioned by nearly all who responded, were:

- Good communicator
- Sense of humor
- Sensitivity

I've made a series of tables summarizing the 25 qualities that the members of the online group said they look for in a personal relationship. And, because this is a book about

Tales from the Quill

I especially liked Alice Konkel's response to "what do you look for in a mate?" She said, "I would look for someone who can really get their arms around life, easy to laugh, especially at himself, cries from the soul and smiles big and with his eyes. He needs to be smart enough to be interesting. He needs to have enough passion to take a stand on important things, but they don't need to be my things."

handwriting, I've also included clusters of handwriting characteristics to look for. (The handwriting characteristics don't have a 1-1 relationship with the personality traits.)

Elements of a Good Relationship

Values	Handwriting Features
Spiritual	Well-developed upper zone (not too tall or narrow)
Strong belief system	Light to moderate pressure
Honest but diplomatic	Good rhythm
Integrity	Moderately simplified
Commitment	No middle zone complications
Responsibility	Steady baseline
	Good overall organization and alignment

Important Personal Traits in a Good Relationship

Attitude Toward Self	Handwriting Features
Self-esteem	Good rhythm
Self-respect	Originality
Self-confidence	Well-developed capitals; horizontal width (low narrowness)
Sense of humor	Clear signature
Likes who they are	Moderately strong pressure
	Low rigidity

General Qualities Needed for a Good Relationship

Inner Qualities	Handwriting Features
Intelligence	Simplification
Sensitivity	Originality
Caring	Some thread mixed with garland
Flexibility	Moderate to few angles
Tolerance	Low narrowness
Loving	Fluid forms
Gentle	Light to moderate pressure
Generous	Good overall spatial arrangement (not too crowded)
Cooperative	

Important Attitudes Toward Others

Attitude Toward Others	Handwriting Features
People-oriented	Medium to large size
Good communicator	Well-developed lower zone; pastosity
Varied interests	Medium word spacing Balanced margins (narrow right margin)

Important Sexual Elements

Sexuality	Handwriting Features
Sensual	Well-developed lower zone
Intimacy	Pastosity Moderate to close word spacing

Although opposites attract in some ways, there are a couple of areas where it is probably important for both parties to be at least in the same ballpark. Physical drive is one of them, intelligence is the other.

Driving Miss Daisy Crazy

There are times when life can be so filled with problems that sex is the only fun thing you've got going for you. A partner who shares the same drives and intimate interests can make everything look a little brighter; but for a couple whose drives are very different, a rough road may lie ahead.

After all, if you have low energy, it's not very pleasant to be browbeaten by your high-energy partner into visiting friends after a long day of work, when all you want to do is curl up in bed with a whodunit. Neither does it feel good to the energetic person if he's forced into being a couch potato, just because his low-energy mate doesn't feel like going out. It doesn't take a lot of brains to figure out that couples with similar physical drives are likely to be more content with each other than couples whose drives are very different.

Fine Points

Remember, the lower zone is where the "biological urges" reside. That means the length, width, and shape of the lower zone are clues to how much the writer needs food, sex, and various creature comforts. We may not be able to differentiate which is more important to him, but we can determine how strong his drive is.

Like everything else in handwriting, it takes a combination of factors to determine drive. Look at the whole writing sample: Is it "moving"? Or is it stagnant, sitting rooted to the page, going nowhere? That's the first clue. Pressure and pastosity are also important factors. Thicker, heavier-pressured writing, while not an indicator of physical strength, does reveal stronger drives.

Check the length and width of the lower loops. The longer and wider they are, the greater the drive, but only to a point. Extreme length and width, however, may be interpreted quite differently (we'll discuss that a bit later).

Low drive

- Writing looks static, with little rightward movement
- Light pressure
- Short, cramped lower zone
- Sharp ductus

Moderate drive

- Moderate movement to the right
- Medium pressure
- Lower zone is copybook length and width
- Medium ductus

Fine Points

Check the edges of the stroke to see whether they are more blurred (pastose) or sharp and clean. The thickness of the writing line (ductus) is best seen under magnification.

Strong drive

- Strong left-to-right overall movement
- Medium to heavy pressure
- Moderately long and full lower zone
- Pastose ductus

Excessive drive

- ➤ Extreme rightward movement
- ➤ Very heavy pressure
- ➤ Extremely long and/or full lower zone
- ➤ Muddy ductus

Strong and weak sex drive.

The Complete Idiot's
Handwriting Analysis
an excellent additio
already spectacular

Fine Points

"I.Q." can be accurately determined from handwriting. There's a formula that scores five characteristics (Organization, Simplification, Expressiveness, Rhythm, and Originality) in handwriting. The resulting score is usually within about five points of the Stanford-Binet test score.

Intelligence

The other factor that should be fairly equal is intelligence. It's easier to share your mate's interests when you understand them. That doesn't mean you have to play golf or go to the opera if you hate it, but at least you can relate on some level to what the other person enjoys.

Divorce Court

It's a fascinating fact that what first attracts one person to another frequently is the same thing that ends up turning them off. The man who enjoys his girlfriend's independence and ability to be self-supporting may end up resenting the fact that she doesn't need him to take care of her. Or, the woman who is attracted to a man because he is sensitive to her feelings may later become angry with him for being a wimp.

Every relationship has its good and bad points. To fall back on a tired old cliche, it takes two to tango. No one is 100 percent at fault for what goes wrong. We choose each other for a reason; it's just that sometimes one person outgrows that reason and it may be time to move on. Plus, some relationships were never meant to be.

Relationships from Hell

In this section we discuss some general types of relationships that you will probably want to avoid. On the other hand, if you are looking to be neglected, criticized, or outright abused, there's someone for everyone! The following types apply to both sexes:

Just remember, when you are looking at handwriting, not all the elements may be present. Look for a preponderance of characteristics.

Tales from the Quill

Sally's husband, Mark starting working the graveyard shift (11 p.m. to 7 a.m.). When he arrived at home in the morning, Sally was getting out of bed and getting ready for her day. They hardly had time for a quick kiss hello and goodbye, let alone sex. Most days, Sally didn't want to give up the morning to stay in bed with Mark and he resented it. However, a handwriting analysis revealed more basic problems than the sexual frustration caused by their work schedules.

Romancing the Stone

Outgoing Ellen saw Bruce as the strong, silent type, which she thought meant he was powerful and protective. But shortly after the wedding, when he sat silent in front of the television night after night, rebuffing her attempts at conversation, she felt she had hit a stone wall.

The Stone Wall doesn't relate well to others, except in the early stages of courtship, when he's pretending to be someone else. He doesn't need or want much social interaction. In fact, he's much happier on his own or with someone who will leave him alone in his own world.

He may actually hold conversations in his head and act as if they had spoken been aloud. Then, when you don't know what he's talking about, he gets angry. And when he gets angry, he cuts you off and acts as if you don't exist. He's a withholding and emotionally cold type who doesn't understand personal relationships, so he expends his energy developing his intellectual side instead.

The Stone Wall

- ➤ Very wide overall spacing, particularly word spacing, and very wide right margin
- ➤ Very small size
- ➤ Extremely simplified forms
- ➤ Cramped lower zone
- ➤ Sharp, pointed strokes
- ➤ Linear, not curved style

The Stone Wall type.

Flirt Alert

The Flirt is a social butterfly who's happiest when she's center stage. This is not someone who sits on the sidelines, waiting to be introduced. She claims the spotlight. She seeks intense, passionate relationships, but don't count on her for long-term commitment. She doesn't want to deal with anything unpleasant, and if you get sad or sick, she won't be around for long.

Chicken Scratch

Don't expect to see *all* the signs of any particular type in one handwriting. Remember, no one is a "pure" type. Several elements in a handwriting sample are enough to tell you that the writer has aspects of that type in his personality.

The Flirt demands unlimited attention, affection, and approval. Without it, she'll soon be in the arms of someone else. In fact, even with it, she won't stay satisfied for long.

If you want fun and excitement with no strings attached, the Flirt may be what you are looking for. But if what you seek is a nurturing partner, you'll be in for a rocky ride.

The Flirt

- ➤ Loose rhythm
- ➤ Showy, elaborate capitals

- Elaborate writing with swirls and decorations
- Lots of rightward movement
- Narrow right margin
- Wavy baseline
- Large lower zone

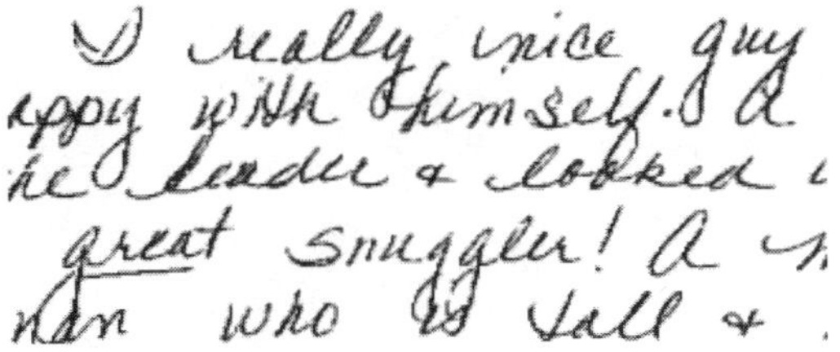

The Flirt type.

Mission Impossible

Those who feel compelled to brag about their sexual prowess frequently don't perform when it comes down to the nitty-gritty. There are several possibilities. Extreme width in the lower zone suggests someone who spends a lot more time fantasizing about his sex life than acting on it. Someone who is sexually frustrated, perhaps due to impotence, may make a downstroke that ends in a tic instead of a loop. Whether the impotence is physically or emotionally based is for a doctor to decide.

Extremely long loops are another sign of frustration. The energy stays in the lower zone, unreleased. Some individuals with extremely long lower zones use sex more as a tranquilizer than as a means of emotional, as well as physical, intimacy. They flit from partner to partner, seeking as much sex as they can get, yet never feeling satisfied. The sexual addict would fall under this category.

Women Who Love Men Who Walk All Over Them

Some people call her the Earth Mother, others, the Caretaker. And then there are those who tell it like it is: She's the professional Doormat.

Loving someone means treating that person kindly and caring about his needs. This type of person goes far beyond that. She lives to help others, and will put her own needs last, if she considers them at all. Her biggest fear is of not being seen as loving and helpful. It's easy to take advantage of this type. She won't say "no" even when it's in her best interests.

Write Words

The **victim-rescuer-abuser triad** is a common occurrence in unhealthy relationships. Eventually, both partners take turns playing all of the roles.

Frequently, the Doormat type is attracted to bad boys: drug addicts, alcoholics, criminals, or just plain creeps. She is sure she can rescue them, but what usually happens to rescuers is that they eventually resent it that their efforts at "helping" are not appreciated. There's a shift into the abuser role as they begin nagging, "after all I've done for you...." This losing *victim-rescuer-abuser triad* reminds me of Alice's tea party with the Mad Hatter, where everyone would periodically get up and move around to the next seat.

The Doormat

- ➤ Small overall size
- ➤ Rounded writing
- ➤ PPI is especially curved on the downstroke
- ➤ Bowed t-bars
- ➤ Light pressure
- ➤ Slight downhill slant to the baseline
- ➤ Close word spacing

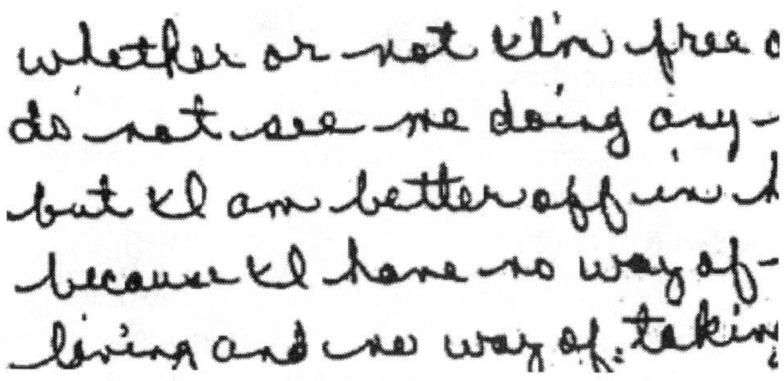

The Doormat type.

Men Who Love Women Who Let Them Walk All Over Them

The Doormat usually gets walked on by the type of partner I think of as a Raptor (You know—those creatures in *Jurassic Park* that viciously attacked everything in sight). He is angry and aggressive, critical and perfectionistic. He knows everything and you are nothing in his eyes. Everything must be done his way, or else.

The "or else" may include yelling, name calling, or even physical violence. The Raptor is a batterer, physically, emotionally, or both.

The Raptor

- ➤ Very heavy pressure
- ➤ Either muddy or very sharp writing
- ➤ Strong right slant
- ➤ Compressed, narrow writing

First, I have several contacts in ,
contacts to identify opportunities. Sec
and that will help me to secure

The Raptor type.

Call Me Irresponsible

Loving a Peter Pan type may be fun for some, but it can also be emotionally draining. You never know whether he will show up on time, or even show up at all. Is he telling the truth or not? It's anyone's guess. The boy who never grew up doesn't stick to social conventions. He makes up his own rules as he goes along.

This type is a con artist who will say or do whatever it takes to get him what he wants.

The Peter Pan

- Secondary thread forms combined with angle forms
- Light pressure
- Complications in the middle zone
- Large overall size
- Very loose, disturbed rhythm
- Strong right slant

Fine Points

The main difference between the handwriting of a compliant victim and that of an ordinary "nice" person is the rhythm (see Chapter 11). The victim type's rhythm is droopy and slack, while the just-plain-nice person's rhythm looks stronger, more elastic.

material here is very
reflection on the society
think. So I'm amazed

The Peter Pan type.

Attila and His Hun

The Attila is an extreme personality type, but one that is insidious enough and found frequently enough to mention. Former FBI profiler Roy Hazelwood interviewed a group of women who had all had relationships with men who, it turned out, were sexual sadists.

These women (Hazelwood calls them the Compliant Victim types) were not poor, innocent young girls who were ignorant about men and relationships. In fact, Hazelwood described them as well-groomed, articulate, and intelligent. They ranged across a wide spectrum of education and careers, from a fire systems engineer, to an insurance broker, secretary, nurse, and loan officer. Yet, they shared several personality traits:

- ➤ Low self-esteem
- ➤ An all-encompassing fear of abandonment
- ➤ Inability to deal with criticism
- ➤ Distrust of others
- ➤ Difficulty making decisions
- ➤ Fear of emotional withdrawal by their partner
- ➤ Inability to show their emotions

Every woman said that the man she became involved with was charming and that nothing stood out about him as unusual or threatening. Eventually though, the abuser revealed that he was extremely possessive. He set up rules for behavior and refused to allow his partner even to go to the store alone or without permission. He isolated his victim from friends and family, until she was entirely dependent upon him for everything. He cut her off from everything she used to care about as an individual. The sample of Nicole Brown Simpson's handwriting in the next illustration is a good example of all the traits Hazelwood found.

Dear O.J.
I'd like to see you, to talk to you in
person. But I know you can't do that.
I've been attending these meetings - to
help me turn negatives into positives - to
help me get rid of my anger .... I've
learned to "let things go" (the most
powerful, helpful thing I've ever learned)
I've learned that all things that upset

Nicole Brown Simpson

Sadistic men have a strong need to be in control, and often have friendships where they dominate the other person. They usually have stable jobs. Because their schtick involves dominating an unwilling partner, they tend to prey on conventional, loving women.

The Attila Type.

- ➤ Long, heavy t-bars
- ➤ Extremely heavy punctuation
- ➤ Very heavy pressure
- ➤ Muddy ductus
- ➤ Strong degree of narrowness, retracing
- ➤ Extremely long, narrow lower zone
- ➤ Very rigid overall

Chicken Scratch

One major red flag for the sadistic type is extremely heavy pressure, which shows unrelenting frustration and anger. When combined with a strong right slant or large, block-printed writing and very dark punctuation, and pressure so strong that it leaves deep ridges on the other side of the paper, these are warning signals that should not be ignored.

The Attila type.

The Compliant Victim

- ➤ Excessive roundedness
- ➤ Large overall size
- ➤ Crowded spacing
- ➤ Personal pronoun I rounded and lying on it's back

Freudian Slip or Victoria's Secret?

In Chapter 9, we discussed the lower zone and a few of the many distinctive and unusual shapes chosen by some writers. Keeping in mind that the "normal" way to make a lower loop is to plunge straight down into the lower zone, make a turn to the left, then release the tension on the way back up to the baseline, any departure from that course suggests a digression in the flow of energy.

In most, if not all, cases of *unusual lower zones*, something occurred in the writer's early life to affect his view of sex. Even one instance of molestation can be enough to make a child aware of sexual activity in a different way.

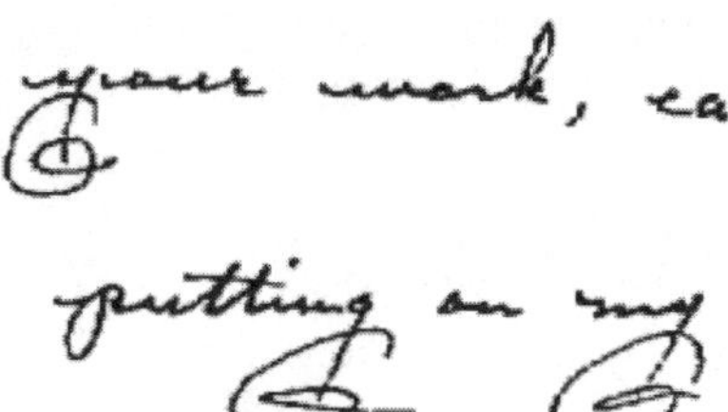

Unusual lower zone.

Write Words

An **unusual lower zone** includes twists, ties, angles, tics, extreme width, and extreme length.

People react to the same experiences in different ways. One abuse victim might become promiscuous while another might become sexually withholding. Personal sensitivity, environment, and background, all play a part. But one thing is certain, the lower zone of handwriting hides many secrets, and when there is a sexual issue, the lower zone is usually affected.

Dump That Chump

You may know an abuser whose handwriting doesn't fall into one of these categories. Please understand, the ones listed here are very general types, intended to give you an idea of what to look for. If the abuser has no remorse, his or her handwriting may not show some of the characteristics that would otherwise appear. More importantly, if someone mistreats you, regardless of what his handwriting shows, do something about it. Get help from a therapist, support group, or minister. Don't allow yourself to be abused. It almost certainly won't get better.

Handwriting analysis should not be the sole deciding factor in whether someone should or shouldn't marry his or her Significant Other, but it can arm them with what they need to know about each other's temperament, needs, and motivations. By identifying potential problem areas and learning how to build on strengths, their chances of a happy, satisfying relationship will be greatly improved.

The Least You Need to Know

- ➤ It's not the graphologist's responsibility to determine whether a couple is compatible, but only to show areas of strength and potential problems.
- ➤ Relationships are often happier when both partners have matching physical drives.
- ➤ Couples with similar intellectual development and interests can develop a deeper level of sharing.
- ➤ Handwriting usually gives clues to abusive behavior, but they may be so subtle that you won't recognize them. Pay attention to the behavior.

Chapter 25

Making Handwriting Analysis Pay

In This Chapter

- You *can* make money as a graphologist!
- What does a successful entrepreneur look like?
- Creating a clear vision
- Marketing your services
- The many uses of handwriting analysis

How much money would you like to make working as a handwriting analyst? Twenty thousand dollars a year? Fifty? One-hundred thousand dollars? More? I have a friend who always says, "You can't make a living at graphology." That's because she sits in her house and waits for assignments to fall in her lap. The good news is, there *are* graphologists who are making a living—a very good living—doing what they love, and you can, too.

When I began my full-time graphology practice in 1989, I had been analyzing handwriting, first as a hobby, then as a sideline for more than 20 years. In 1989 I thought I was doing quite well, having prepared some 300 handwriting analysis reports. Five years later I was writing more than 1,000 reports a year. That's an average of five a day, every day, which is more handwriting than I ever expected or wanted to analyze!

The point is, you *can* become a successful handwriting professional, if you have the keys to unlock the door to success in the field. Like any entrepreneurial business, starting a handwriting consulting practice takes commitment, hard work, and, unless you're independently wealthy, a leap of faith. But in this field there's one more challenge.

Most professionals don't have to explain what their work is to the people they are hoping to turn into clients. Handwriting analysis, on the other hand, often meets with skepticism because many people have never heard of it, and some believe it's akin to fortune telling. So, along with selling our services, we sometimes have to educate prospective clients.

Tales from the Quill

In 1989 I suddenly lost my job as assistant administrator in a medical office. I was already deeply in debt and the single mother of three teenagers. The day after I was fired, my 12-year-old car bit the dust. Totally. What more perfect time to start my home-based business! Temp work paid the bills while I pursued clients. I discovered that once I saw myself as what I wanted to be, I could become it.

I Should Have Been Committed

After burning much midnight oil writing marketing letters that first year; after overloading the post office with flyers I mailed to human resource departments; after lecturing to countless civic groups, and after landing some radio and print interviews, I wondered why the clients weren't pouring in as fast as they should.

My very wise friend, Bob Joseph, made me look at myself in the mirror of truth when he told me, "You really aren't committed to making a success of this business." I sputtered and stuttered an angry retort. After all, look at all I'd done! But when I honestly considered my attitude, I knew he was right. *I hadn't expected to be successful,* so I wasn't.

The first step to success is setting a goal. It takes a sincere desire and a commitment to that goal, along with a workable plan to accomplish it. If you've got someone to support you and pay the rent while you're building the business, you're way ahead of the game. If you don't, there are some serious questions to ask yourself. Start with, "Is this what I really want?" If the answer is yes, it's time to consider the sacrifices that must be made in starting any new business. For example:

- Are you willing to give up time with your family?
- Are you willing to work long hours?
- Are you willing to cut some of the fun things out of the budget so the money will be available for the business?

Only you can decide whether you have what it takes to create a successful handwriting analysis business:

- A real love of handwriting
- A desire to help others, not just build your own ego
- The wherewithal to either get out and market yourself or get someone else to do it for you

Knowing your limits and your capacity to achieve will be part of the answer. And what's the best way to do a reality check? Have your handwriting analyzed, of course!

Unlocking the Door to a Successful Practice

An entrepreneur is someone who creates a business at his own financial risk. That takes guts, which is one of the characteristics identified in a study of entrepreneur's handwritings published in *Perceptual and Motor Skills,* an academic periodical. Well, okay, they called it "risk-taking," but I think "guts" is much more descriptive.

Fine Points

A study was undertaken by three handwriting analysts, Arlyn Imberman, Roger Rubin, and Felix Klein, to identify the characteristics of an entrepreneur. Their findings, which had a very strong correlation with two psychologist's results, were published in the periodical *Perceptual and Motor Skills.*

The following list describes the personality traits of the successful entrepreneur and the handwriting indicators that match those traits. Do you have what it takes?

Personality Traits of the Successful Entrepreneur and Their Handwriting Indicators

Personality Trait	Handwriting Indicator
Independent (free from the influence of others)	Stick PPI Missing initial strokes Firm final strokes Simplification Initial emphasis
Risk taker (willing to expose oneself to possible loss)	Originality Good rhythm Flexibility Pressure moderate to strong Rightward movement Moderate angles Strong upper zone

continues

continued

Personality Trait	Handwriting Indicator
Innovator (makes changes, introduces new practices)	Originality Simplification Some primary thread, garlands Strong capitals Good zonal balance High diacritics
Visionary (imagines how things can be, regardless of the current reality)	Originality Rhythm Combination forms Spatial arrangement open Strong upper-zone dynamics Creative arcades
Need to achieve (wants to attain a high standard of performance)	Strong pressure Rightward movement Narrowing right margin Large capitals Regularity Some angles
Internal locus of control (inner-motivated)	Originality Congruent signature Speed Moderate to heavy pressure Good arrangement
Uses talents/sets own agenda (strong sense of purpose)	Strong picture of space Good organization Moderate to strong pressure
Tries and tries again (sticks with it when the going is rough)	Firm baseline Blunt final strokes Lower zone follow-through Good middle-zone width
Desires to run own business (need for independent action)	Strong picture of movement Horizontal expansion Strong middle-zone forms Right trend
Failures increase determination (persists when obstacles arise)	Tied forms Lower-zone follow-through Zonal balance Firm, slightly rising baseline Flexibility
Thrives on applause but tolerates disapproval (good self-esteem)	Large capitals Moderate middle-zone size Flexibility Good rhythm

Personality Trait	Handwriting Indicator
Trusts gut instincts (intuition)	Primary thread Smooth breaks or strong connectedness Airy spatial arrangement
Always ready to act (responsive)	Short or missing initial strokes Simplification Fast speed Moderate right slant Initial emphasis Originality

The entrepreneur wears many hats.

In the *Perceptual and Motor Skills* study, the one item the graphologists identified that was considered a hindrance is fear of failure. The handwriting indicators for fear of failure are:

- Retracing
- Narrowness

- Tight spacing
- Narrow margins
- High copybook form
- Strong contraction
- Small capitals
- Strong left trend
- Slow speed
- Extremes, crossed out signature

Seeing Clearly

Successful people have something in common: They all knew well in advance what their future looked like. If you are going to be a successful handwriting professional, you must start seeing yourself as one now. Close your eyes. Yes, right now (well, after you finish reading the instructions).

In your mind's eye, *see* your dream office. This is a mental exercise, so you can afford to be extravagant. What style furniture is there? What color is the carpet? How many windows and what type of window treatment? What does the wallcovering look like? Is it wood paneling? Textured wallpaper? Plain paint with some good framed artwork? Okay, you can open your eyes now.

Give your office a good computer with a fast modem, a fax, scanner, photocopier, and of course, that most important of all business machines, a telephone. You'll need to order a business line, which is probably less expensive than you think. Business lines come with a free listing in the yellow pages, and you can expand your listing to sound like an advertisement.

Fine Points

Handwriting examiner Jacqueline Joseph maximized her yellow pages listing by calling her business "Accurate Document Examiners." Alphabetically, that also placed her ahead of her competition.

Business calls are billed at a higher rate than residential ones. To save money, if your office is at home, make outgoing calls on your residential line. If you have small children or grandchildren at home, don't allow them to answer your business calls. Why advertise the fact that you aren't as big as Microsoft (yet)? You might want to buy some computer software that will answer your calls for you. Your computer can put people on hold, just like the big guys.

Your office can be as plain or as fancy as you like, but you can do it for under $5,000, which can't be said of too many businesses.

Don't Miss the Train

It may seem obvious, but before you hang out your shingle, get good training. Make sure you have a firm foundation in graphological principles. Of course, if you've read and studied this book you have an excellent start. Beyond that, you may want to take a correspondence course (you'll find a list in Appendix B). Do lots and lots of handwriting analyses, and ask for feedback, so you'll know how accurate you are.

The well-educated graphologist knows that knowledge of handwriting is not enough by itself. A basic understanding of personality development and abnormal psychology are just as important, if not more so. And, if you are going into the personnel screening field, you'll also need to know about EEOC laws. A good book on organizational behavior would help, too.

Putting Words in Your Mouth

Having buckets of wonderful knowledge is great, but if you can't express it to your clients so they understand what you want to tell them, it won't mean a hill of beans. Chapter 23 gave you some clues about writing the analysis. Even if you prefer to give oral analyses, you should know how to organize your thoughts, and writing them down is good practice. A manual of style and grammar is helpful, as is a good thesaurus.

Pay Your Dues

Paying your dues goes far beyond belonging to an organization. As you study and learn graphology, begin to think about giving something back. You can contribute to the field by participating in research projects, writing articles or analyses for a newsletter, and volunteering to do analyses for charity auctions or other events. There's a double benefit in volunteering. Not only are you helping the field, you are also gaining experience and can list your activities on your professional curriculum vitae.

Tales from the Quill

Graphologist Pauline Clapp's handwriting study group volunteered to do demonstration analyses for an alcohol treatment center and donate the proceeds to the center. The response was gratifying. They analyzed dozens of people's handwritings, which made them feel good for volunteering; the people they analyzed felt good, too, and the center was very happy to receive the donation.

Clothes Make the (Wo)Man

In creating a business, presenting a professional image is part of what makes prospective clients believe in you. When you're going out on sales calls, don't show up for a meeting in a tank top and shorts. If funds are limited, you don't have to buy an expensive wardrobe, but it's a good idea to invest in one or two really good suits and accessories. If you look successful you'll command greater respect (read that: money!).

The materials you use are just as important as your personal appearance. If you are proficient in desktop publishing you may want to prepare brochures and business cards yourself. If not, have them done by a reputable printing company who can help you choose or design a logo that represents what you want to project.

Money Talks

The fees you charge will depend largely on what the market will reasonably bear in your geographical area and your level of expertise. It's a good idea to have a range of analyses so you can give the client a choice. Someone who can't afford to pay $95 for a regular personality profile may be willing to part with $45 for a short summary analysis.

Our primary goal is to help people. There may be times when you decide to discount your services if you feel the person is really in need. Keep in mind, however, that if you are too quick to cut your fees, it gives the impression that you were charging too much in the first place, or that you aren't worth what you ask.

By the way, I don't recommend offering free analyses as a trial. You'll end up doing lots of freebies, and get lots of compliments, but usually they don't bring in the business. What I do is offer a guarantee—if they don't find the analysis accurate and helpful, they don't have to pay the bill. I've never had a bill returned unpaid.

Target the Right Market

Marketing consulting services (and especially graphology services) is a challenge to begin with, so it helps to at least know the field you are going to market to. Successful graphologists have told me that it's best to choose a specific type of industry in which to do your marketing, preferably one you are familiar with. Or, pick one that interests you and find out as much about it as possible. In bygone days I've worked in a real estate office, medical office, and retail stores; and I've done a lot of work for temp agencies.

Those are the markets I feel most comfortable marketing to because I know the environment. I know what types of challenges workers face, and I know how to speak their language. Of course, if someone from a different industry pops up and wants to drop business in your lap, I don't recommend you refuse it!

Referrals seem to be the best way to get clients in this business. Ask everyone you know if they have a friend or associate in business whose name they will share. Asking for an executive by name is much more likely to get you through to her. One successful graphologist contacts people whose names she sees in the newspaper if they have made some accomplishment, and sends a letter of congratulations with information about her services.

Newspaper ads have not worked for any analyst I've ever asked, even those who have spent thousands of dollars on them; but direct mail has been a fairly good source of business. I send out a few letters at a time to a carefully targeted audience and follow them up with phone calls.

Fine Points

Each industry has its own catch phrases, and if you know them, you'll have an edge when marketing your services. For instance, in real estate, a FSBO ("fisbo") is the acronym for a house that's "for sale by owner."

Don't Be Invisible

You have to let your market know you are there. It's one thing to put an ad in the yellow pages, but unless someone is looking for you, he won't know you exist. One way to make yourself visible is to contact local business and civic groups (you can find them in the yellow pages, at the library, or on the Internet) and let them know you are available for lectures.

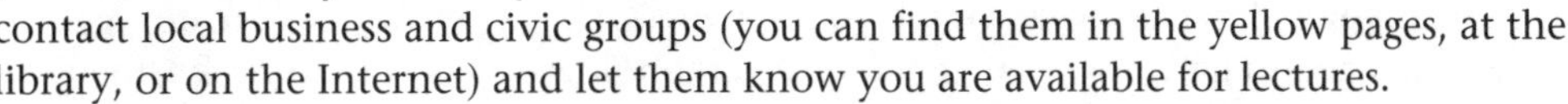

You won't get paid by the Lion's or the Kiwanis or Rotary Clubs, but giving a 20 minute lecture is good experience. When you go to these meetings, collect as many business cards as you can, and also distribute your own cards to everyone there. I used to get cards by holding a drawing for a free analysis (this is one exception to my "no free analyses" rule), then follow up later with a letter.

Press releases are an important way to get exposure. You can use any number of excuses to send them out. If you start teaching a class, give a lecture, donate an analysis at a charity auction, or appear on a television or radio show, it's a good reason for a press release. There are plenty of books about marketing that can tell you how it's done.

Persistence, Persistence, Persistence

When you've chosen your target market and have sent out literature, always follow up with phone calls. It's said that it takes eight calls before you'll actually get to talk to the person you're trying to reach. If you give up at one or two calls, you'll never make it.

If you don't want to keeping phoning, write letters, mail the prospective client articles that you see in newspapers or magazines that pertain to their field—you're doing them a real service. Or, make up a newsletter about your services. The idea is to keep your name in front of the prospect's face. A postcard is a very effective way of getting through to someone because the message is right in front of her. She doesn't even have to open an envelope.

Being persistent is really tough for some of us because we don't want to make an annoying pest of ourselves. But books on selling claim that 80 percent of the total sales force gives up too soon. So, 80 percent of the business goes to 20 percent of the sales force.

Tales from the Quill

I once contacted a prospective client about using handwriting analysis. He said, "We're not interested, but you can keep us in your tickler file if you want to try again in a few months." After calling back time and time again, I finally got an appointment with the guy. When I walked into his office, the first thing he said was, "I'm so glad you kept after me!"

Raising the Standard

Every individual has a personal set of ethics and standards and no one has the right to tell anyone else what to do or not to do. Unless, that is, what they are doing is outright unethical and harmful to their clients or graphology. This is a serious business. We are dealing with people's lives and need to be responsible for the way we present ourselves as handwriting analysts. I invite you to review the Graphologist's Code of Ethics in Appendix C.

What about doing quickie analyses at parties? Many analysts feel fine doing them, because they introduce graphology to people who otherwise might never have heard of it. My good friend Marlene Vallen is especially talented at getting a "quick fix" on a writer. We've dubbed her the Queen of Quickies.

Personally I don't care to do them (though I have in the past, to bolster my income) I'm more comfortable doing the analysis in writing. Also, I feel they project the kind of image that makes it hard for graphology to be viewed as a serious profession. I've never attended a party where a lawyer or a psychologist was hired as the entertainment.

I don't have a problem with doing basically the same thing at a trade show, but calling them "demonstration analyses." It's a fine difference, but a trade show or convention is a business atmosphere, not like fortune telling at a party.

Chicken Scratch

Inflating one's credentials is unethical. When a handwriting analyst is called upon to testify in court and is unable to substantiate his claims about supposed degrees and courses (which has happened), he ends up looking very foolish.

The Resume Tells the "Did Do," Handwriting Tells the "Can Do"

Security magazine reported that in 1995, the cost of workplace violence was near $36 billion a year. That cost included homicides, physical attacks, rapes, assaults, threats and intimidation, loss of productivity due to employee distraction, investigations, and attorney fees. Around the same time, a national retail security survey revealed that employee theft, administrative error, and vendor fraud accounted for more than $25 billion, or 1.83 percent of total annual sales. And, The Zalud Report claimed that 33 percent of all employees have stolen money or merchandise on the job at least once.

Who steals from their employer? The cleaning crew? The mail clerk? You might be surprised to learn that losses caused by company executives were 16 times higher than those of other employees.

Faced with these alarming statistics, employers are seeking ways to protect themselves. Handwriting analysis is one tool of choice rapidly gaining in popularity. Many companies use it to help prepare for second interviews, using information in the report to draw out a candidate about questionable areas. Some use it as a counseling tool, to more effectively place employees in positions where they have the greatest potential for success.

Thousands of businesses throughout the world find that handwriting analysis helps them reduce turnover, improve employee morale, and reduce security risks. Progressive decision-makers find that a handwriting analysis report, provided by a competent professional, gives them a complete, detailed, objective behavioral profile of issues that may not be forthcoming in an interview.

Writing What's Wrong

A specialized branch of graphology sometimes referred to as "graphotherapy" is actually a form of handwriting remediation. It makes sense that if handwriting is a true reflection of one's psyche and the result of accumulated experiences, that changes made deliberately to handwriting can help one change uncomfortable personality traits.

Of course, we write the way we do for a reason. Psychologists tell us that we create a variety of defenses to help us deal with difficult emotions. Handwriting manifests some of the defenses we use.

Some systems of graphotherapy require the client to make changes to bits and pieces of their handwriting. For instance, the client might be instructed to change his writing slant, raise his t-bars, or adjust his lower loops. While changing one's t-crossings might not be a big deal, meddling with the lower zone is.

In effect, making changes directly to the handwriting is like ripping away the client's defenses without replacing them with something more

Fine Points

Neurophysiologist Marta Oakley used biofeedback to test handwriting movement patterns. She explains, "Producing those patterns caused a highly significant increase in beta waves in both parietal lobes in all students. This area, known for its 'selective attending,' is essential in learning."

positive. This kind of graphotherapy can be very damaging, and that's why I don't recommend making *major* changes directly to someone's handwriting. Altering the writing *patterns,* rather than individual writing elements, makes more sense, because the client is working on a subliminal level.

Using a series of *writing movement patterns* such as the ones in the next illustration can help the writer make changes from the inside out, rather than the band-aid effect of changing bits and pieces of handwriting. Some amazing results have been reported by graphologists working with clients to change what they view as undesirable traits.

In Tucson, Ron Laufer has received media attention for his work with anorexic and bulimic clients. These young women had tried numerous other treatments without success, but the graphotherapy exercises seemed to make the difference.

Denver handwriting remediation specialist Jeanette Farmer has created a program that is being used in some school systems to help at-risk children improve their behavior through handwriting exercises. Her system includes a plastic template and music. The children use the template to form the specific movements that develop the neural pathways to help them develop self-discipline.

In more than 10 years of researching the psychological/physiological link of handwriting in the brain, Jeanette has found that stimulating the left brain through handwriting exercises helps activate its sequential processing skills necessary for reading, spelling, and math. Children and adults with attention deficit disorder (ADD) or attention deficit hyperactivity disorder (ADHD), learning disabilities, and special needs (Down syndrome, brain injured) have been helped through this innovative tool.

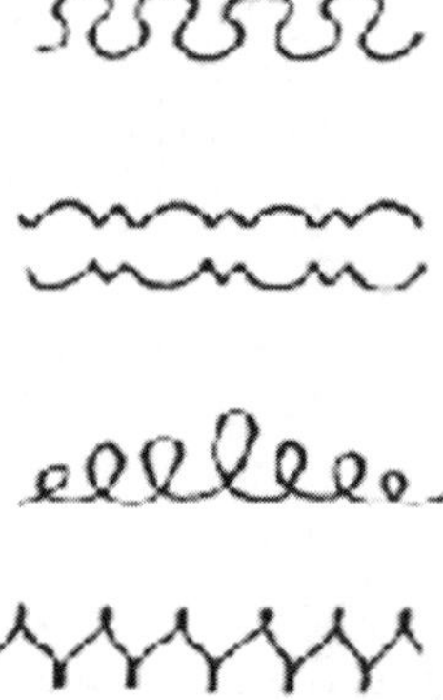

Handwriting exercises to change movement patterns.

You don't have to have a major problem to be helped by graphotherapy. Small, annoying habits can be helped, too. Want to get more organized? Need to learn how to relax? Graphotherapy may be the answer for you. The exercises are very simple and take only 10 minutes twice a day.

Tales from the Quill

Little Shelby was having trouble learning her ABCs. The teacher told Shelby's mother she would have to help, but that was a battle that often ended in tears for both. When the school began using Jeanette Farmer's handwriting remediation program in January, Shelby was in danger of being held back. But by the end of the school year, the teacher couldn't believe her improvement. She gave all the credit to Farmer's program. Shelby is now sailing through school, saved from being labeled "learning disordered."

To see results, consistency is vital. The exercises have to be performed at about the same time each day over a period of several weeks. The handwriting and the behavior will change naturally, without any outside interference. The exercises depicted are balancing ones. They'll help you get mentally organized. The rounded forms are best done at night, because they are more relaxing. The ones with angles should be done in the morning, to help wake up your intellect.

The Least You Need to Know

- The business of handwriting analysis can be lucrative, but there are important steps to follow along the path to success.
- You have to decide what sacrifices you are willing to make in order to be in business for yourself.
- To create a successful business, you can't just be a good graphologist—you also have to be good at sales and marketing.
- There are many different applications for graphology. Working with human resource managers is the most popular.
- If you want to change your personality, you can do it through handwriting remediation exercises.

Chapter 26

Computers and Graphology—Strange Bedfellows?

In This Chapter

- When PCs were new
- I don't do Windows
- Graphs and graphology
- How it works

One warm spring day in 1978, my husband came home from his first computer show, jumping up and down with excitement. He greeted me with the news that we were going to sell my Ford Pinto and buy a computer. I loved that car and, for a long time after that, I hated computers!

Way back then, there were no commercial computer programs on the market. No Word Perfect or Microsoft Word. No video games yet (not even Pong!). Windows wasn't even a twinkle in Bill Gates's eye.

In fact, when you flipped the computer's "on" switch, nothing happened. You had to load BASIC, the programming language, before the *$%#$@#$ thing would do anything at all. BASIC was fed in by magnetic tape from a cassette player. That took at least 10 minutes, and if there was a speck of dirt on the tape, it would crash and you had to start all over again. A far cry from the 500 mhz Pentium III that I'm using to write these words.

One of the first computer geeks, my husband bought the thing in the ugly bright orange metal box to play math games. He soon began trying to win me over by extolling the virtues of some wonderful new thing the computer could do called "word processing." I didn't even want to hear about it. My old Remington typewriter was just fine, thanks. What did I need with a computer?

My thinking began to change when my husband offered to show off his programming skills and write a handwriting analysis program for me. By then I had been studying handwriting for about 10 years, and the idea of automating the process, at least to some degree, was intriguing. I came up with a list of important characteristics and definitions, and he wrote the program.

We called it Bionetix. The idea was to link the human element (bio) with the machine (netix). Now it sounds more like the name of a science fiction movie. The Bionetix program was pretty limited in what it could do, but the people who ordered analyses seemed to like the novel dot-matrix-printed output. Well, we later divorced, and my ex got custody of the computer. It was nearly 20 years before I seriously considered getting into the software business again.

Fine Points

The computer can't see the fine nuances in handwriting that a well-trained analyst can. Yet, while software can never replace the human analyst, it's a great help in speeding up the analysis process and writing the report.

Meantime, I had several offers to computerize handwriting analysis over the years, but the people making the suggestions didn't impress me as knowing what they were doing. As you can see from this book, handwriting analysis is very complex. I've always believed—and still do—that the best analysis needs the human touch. I didn't think a computer could do handwriting analysis justice—that is, until a couple of years ago.

Once Upon a Time

One day I got a phone call from someone who said he'd seen an article about me in the Los Angeles *Times* a couple of months before. He was with RI Software, a computer development company interested in graphology. They were researching the possibility of creating a computer program to analyze handwriting. He had interviewed some other graphologists, but hadn't yet found a good fit for the project.

Thanks to my early introduction to computers and a stint doing word processing for temp agencies when I had three kids to feed, I was very comfortable at the keyboard. I had even used desktop publishing software for eight years while editing *AHAF Journal* for the American Handwriting Analysis Foundation. Then, of course, there were was the thousand or so handwriting analyses I did each year. The computer was now my friend.

But, computer literacy notwithstanding, I gave the gentleman on the phone my standard response: "There are just too many variables for a computer to be able to give an accurate analysis, and I wouldn't want to be associated with something that comes out looking like a canned report."

Tales from the Quill

One of several computer programmers who contacted me to work with him on developing handwriting analysis software made me an offer I could easily refuse. He thought that I would be delighted to work with his company for however long it took to produce a program, and all for the privilege of being listed as an author. No money, just my name on the software. It wasn't too difficult to make a decision on that one!

Mr. Computer Guy was undeterred. "I don't care how many variables there are," he told me firmly. "If they can be defined, we can computerize them." Oh, did I mention that he and his partners at RI Software are at the top of their field, and consult to companies like Microsoft?

He must have been prepared for an argument, because he immediately had a couple of persuasive selling points ready: The software would have my name on it, and I would have full control over what went into it. More importantly, if it worked well, it could help validate graphology as a science. As RI's head programmer pointed out, something has to be replicated to be deemed scientific. In other words, it must mean the same thing, every time. If the software did what it was intended to do, the results would be replicable.

Under those terms, I reluctantly agreed to become involved in the project. RI promptly gave me carte blanche to include anything I felt was important. The only thing they promised that turned out not to be true was, "You won't have to do too much. It'll take you only a couple of weeks to input everything." Uh huh. Right. Try a couple of *years!* (Good thing I have an understanding husband.) Of course, I asked for their handwriting first. We made a good team.

Chicken Scratch

This chapter's discussion of *Sheila Lowe's Handwriting Analyzer* program is not intended as an advertisement, but is meant to provide information. Of course, if you wanted to order it, we wouldn't turn you down....

Do I Really Want to Do This?

After wading through page after page of research material, I finally decided on 4,000 handwriting characteristics. These would be the variables. I assigned each one a personality attribute and a value (score). Then, I wrote nearly 200 pages of text for the reports. Finally, I scanned and edited more than 400 samples of handwriting for the illustrations.

RI Software was responsible for designing the "look," and the extremely complicated programming to make the whole thing work properly. They called it, *Sheila Lowe's Handwriting Analyzer (SLHA)*. Original, huh? Well, it's descriptive anyway.

Passing the Bar (Graph)

Besides offering various types of reports, we decided to use bar graphs as a visual aid. The graphs would show a list of personality traits weighted on a scale of five, from low to extreme. Next, we added a pie chart and called it the Lowe Interest Indicator, which is rather like Klara Roman's Psychogram (see Chapter 4).

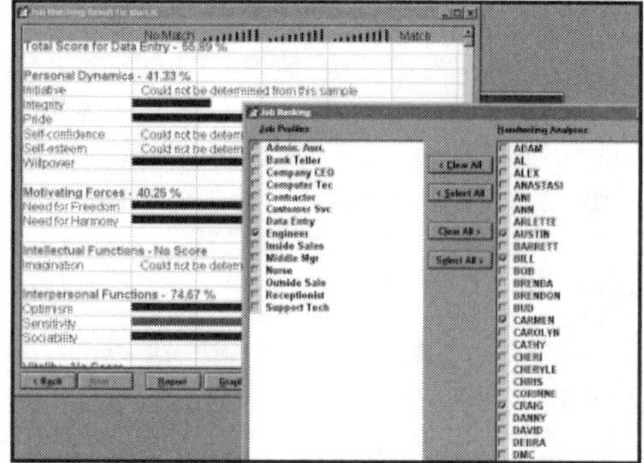

Personality Bar Graph.

The Interest Indicator, as depicted in the next illustration, graphically demonstrates how the writer's energy is distributed in various areas of personality functioning. Finally, we delivered the coup de grâce—the Job Profile Manager and Job Ranking Graph.

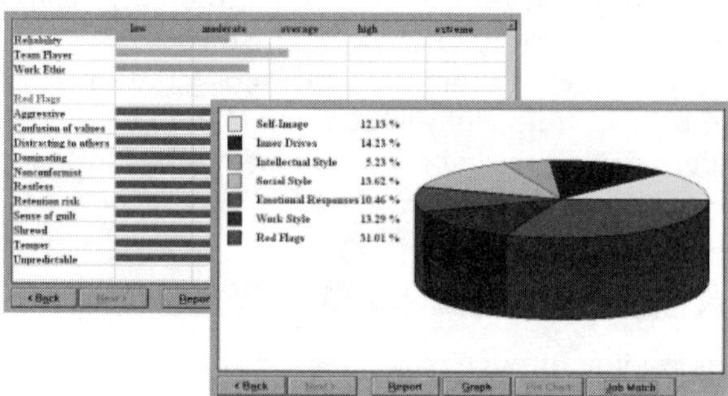

Lowe Interest Indicator.

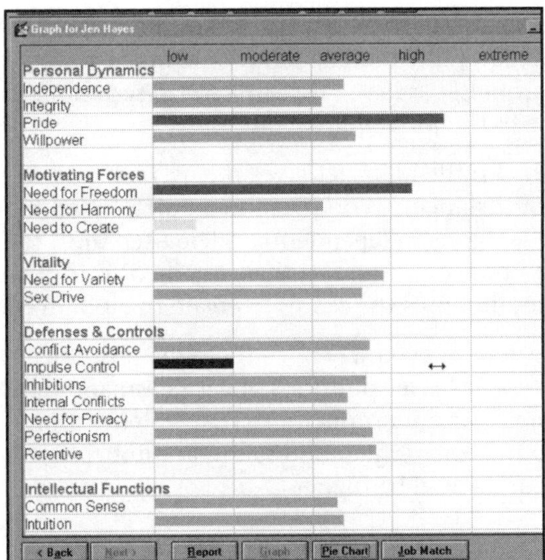

Job Profile Graph.

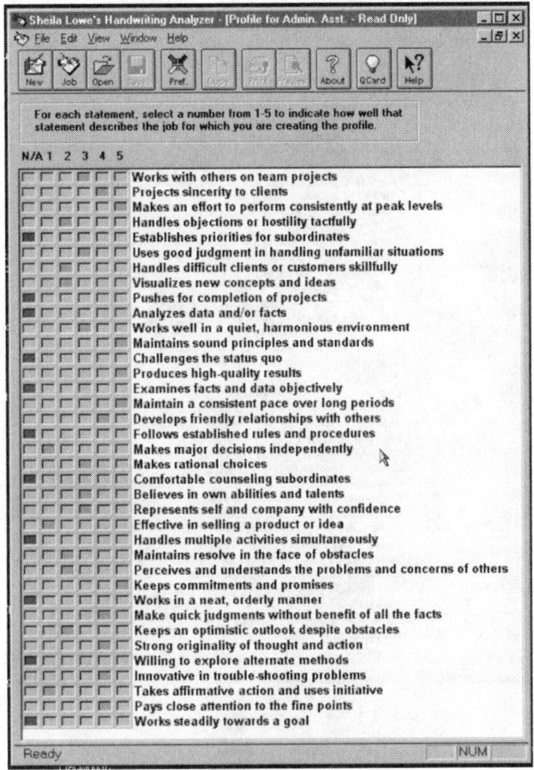

Job Ranking.

Although the *Handwriting Analyzer* ships with 14 generic job profiles, every company has its own individual needs and requirements. The Job Profile Manager allows the business user to create her own profiles, based on a specific job description, so she can most closely match the candidate to the job requirements.

To create a new job profile, the Job Profile Manager gives the user a list of about 40 general statements about jobs. For instance, "Works well in a quiet, harmonious environment," or "Makes major decisions independently." The user ranks each statement on a scale of five, in relation to how important that statement is to the particular job under consideration. The computer uses the scores to create the job profile.

All jobs are not created equal, sometimes even when it's the same position. For instance, there are many different types of sales positions. A car salesman might not be required to work in a quiet, harmonious environment, so that statement on the job profile manager would receive a low score. A diamond salesman probably would, so the job profile score in that category would be higher.

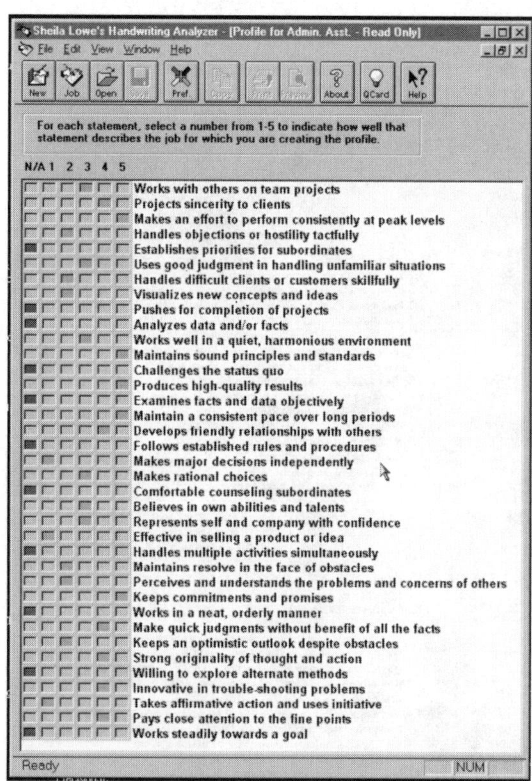

Job Profile Manager.

After you've selected a job profile, the computer compares the scores from the handwriting analysis you've already done (more on that in a minute), to the scores required for the job. The resulting graph shows how close the candidate comes to a perfect match.

For the narrative report, you can choose up to 11 categories, including Social Styles, Intellectual Preferences, and Management Styles, depending on what you need to know. The reports range from one to three pages, depending on how many categories are selected. If you don't want to spend a lot of time reading, you can choose the Key Phrases report, which is a bulleted list of statements, rather than a narrative; or the Success Potential Indicator, a short version of the bar graph.

Fine Points

There are two versions of the *Handwriting Analyzer*. One is for business reports and the other for personal reports. The Professional Analyzer includes both business and personal versions; or the Personal version is available as a stand-alone.

Job Ranking was added in version 4.0. It allows you to compare multiple candidates, side-by-side, to determine whose scores come closest to the job requirements in each category.

The Personal version of the *Handwriting Analyzer* is not licensed for business applications, because some of the more personal material covered would not be appropriate in a business report. Also, the Personal version doesn't have the charts and graphs that the Professional version has. Another popular feature of the Professional version is its ability to export the report to any word processor for editing.

We have had many inquiries about making the software Mac compatible. RI Software tells me it's too big a programming headache to create a Mac version. However, many users have reported that they can successfully run the program on the newer Macs and those that can run Windows emulation software (such as SoftWindows).

How'd They Do That?

Probably the question I am most often asked about the *Handwriting Analyzer* is, "Do I need a scanner?" The answer is, no. It's possible that sometime in the future we'll work on the ability to scan a sample. However, even then, the computer will be able to handle only the measurable aspects of handwriting. The rest of the analysis will still require human input.

The second question is, "Then how does it work?"

Easy. It's a matter of comparing the sample you want to analyze to on-screen illustrations. Once you enter the *Analyzer,* you'll find a list of 48 categories of handwriting elements, such as "Organization," "Writing Style," "Rhythm," and so on. You know—the stuff you've read about in this book.

Each category shows a series of pictures of handwriting on the screen. Let's say you selected the category, "Slant." Seven types of slant are illustrated, from "Upright" to "Variable." All you do is click your mouse on the picture where the slant looks most like the handwriting sample you are analyzing (descriptions on the illustrations and "QCards" tell you what to look for). After you've matched up the handwriting in at least 10 categories as you want, you can generate a report, simply by clicking on the "Report" button.

Left margin.

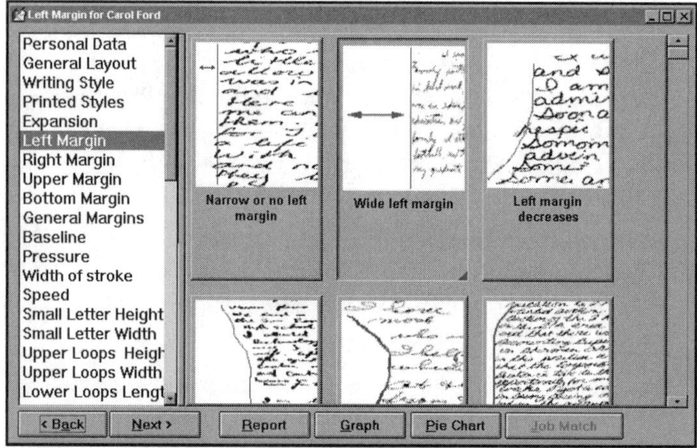

Chicken Scratch

No report or graph is available before at least 10 choices have been made. We've even marked the most important categories, to make it easy for you. The more categories you choose from, the greater the accuracy of the report.

Even those who are using the software but are not trained graphologists have reported accuracy ratings between 89 to 99 percent. That's because the scores assigned to each of those 4,000+ variables are carefully weighted, with the most important handwriting characteristics (gestalt aspects of space, form, movement) having greater weight than the lesser ones (individual letters or strokes). The computer performs a series of checks and balances and algorithms to generate the final analysis.

If you're a visual person, this explanation is probably about as clear as mud, even with the illustrations. RI Software and I would like to invite you to try out the *Handwriting Analyzer* for yourself. You are welcome to download a free demo copy from our Web site at: **http:/www.writinganalysis.com** and let us know what you think of it. It works in any Windows environment and on the newer Macs. You won't be able to save or print the report you do, but you can read it on-screen, and you'll get a good idea of how easy it is to use.

To give you an idea of what to expect from a Handwriting Analyzer report, the following is an excerpt using the handwriting of Bill Clinton:

> *Personal Dynamics*
>
> There may be times when he will bend his ethics to some degree when he feels it would be the best choice, but it is not an easy choice for him to make. Mr.

Clinton is not the type to push too hard for his rights, unless doing nothing would substantially interfere with his comfort. He prefers not to have to assert himself when a more cooperative spirit works for him. He does not need a great deal of admiration and recognition from others to feel good about himself, but it doesn't hurt!

His ability to make necessary adjustments in a variety of circumstances indicates a certain amount of independence and autonomy. He has the capacity to act in cooperation with others or independently, depending on the situation. He is aware of his own value and goes under the assumption that others are, too. A sense of self-belief allows him to readily accept new responsibilities. He has learned to believe in himself by developing his potentials over time, so that if threatened by major opposition, he may question his adequacy momentarily, but come out more successful than before.

His willpower is not always as steady as he would like it to be, and it requires some effort on his part to stay on target. From time to time, and despite his best efforts, he vacillates between following the path he has chosen for himself and going off on a more interesting or challenging tangent.

Motivating Forces

Mr. Clinton does his best to maintain equilibrium and build a consensus, avoiding fights and arguments whenever possible. However, when his values or principles are called into question, you can expect him to come up with a sharp response. By and large he accepts things the way they were done in the past. He probably will not expend very much energy on creating brand new methods of operating. He can make a commitment to a course of action or a relationship, but the arrangement must also include some freedom of action.

But Won't It Put Me Out of Business?

Some graphologists have been very vocal in their fear that the *Handwriting Analyzer* software will take business away from them. In fact, the opposite is true. So far, desktop publishing hasn't put any print shops out of business. And I don't think the medical books on CD-ROM have hurt any doctor's practice.

Just like the word processor made typing much easier and faster, software can take much of the drudgery out of analyzing handwriting. People who aren't comfortable with their grammar or writing skills can relax, because the computer writes the report for them. Many who have bought the software have developed such an interest in graphology that they have gone on to study it for themselves. The truth is, the more people know about handwriting analysis, the more popular and credible it will become.

On the eve of the 21st century, computers have become as ubiquitous as the telephone—an integral part of our daily lives. Change doesn't come easy, I know. I was one of those who was dragged, kicking and screaming, from DOS to Windows. But even I will admit, albeit grudgingly, that my computing life is easier for making that change. Once those reluctant graphologists give the software a try, I believe they'll see the benefits.

Who Uses It?

Besides handwriting professionals, police departments, psychologists, human resource managers, and just plain folks are among the thousands of people around the world who have tried the *Handwriting Analyzer* software. Businesses using it include every type and size you can imagine, from insurance companies, home developers, marketing and computer companies, and even a race track!

Tales from the Quill

Most of the top graphologists in the U.S. have bought the *Handwriting Analyzer.* One of the busiest handwriting analysts in the country, Sharon Johnson, said that her business has tripled since she started using the *SLHA* when it was first released. She is able to do so many more analyses because the process is so quick and easy. Her clients have told her that they really enjoy the graphs, too. Sharon employs other analysts around the country to help her with her company's 500+ active clients.

Some small companies would like to use graphology to help them select employees, but don't feel they can afford to pay for several analyses, which could run into hundreds of dollars. Rather than forego the analysis entirely, they do the report themselves, using the software, and get the answers they need.

Individuals who are interested in analyzing handwriting only for themselves and their family, not as a career, often order the Personal version. They might never order an analysis from a human graphologist, but enjoy using the software themselves.

Study Guide

The software can be a helpful teaching tool for people studying graphology. Students prepare an analysis and compare their results to the computer's. They test themselves by trying to find where in the handwriting the various statements come from in the computer-generated report.

By the way, I don't mean to brag (yeah, right), but *Sheila Lowe's Handwriting Analyzer* won the Ziff-Davis Five Star Editor's Pick Award, and has been featured in *Entrepreneur* magazine, *PC World,* and other prestigious places.

Is *SLHA* Alone out There?

It was bound to happen. *Sheila Lowe's Handwriting Analyzer* is no longer the only Windows-based handwriting analysis software on the market, but it is still the most sophisticated. There's a link to a page describing the various other programs on our Web site at **http://www.writinganalysis.com**.

Tales from the Quill

The first commercially available DOS program for handwriting analysis, called The Handwriting Analyst, came out in the 1980s. Unlike Windows-based software, it was a menu-driven program and was accompanied by a book of illustrations of samples that the user could use as a reference. One of the founding members of the American Handwriting Analysis Foundation and a highly respected graphologist, Dorothy Hodos, was the handwriting analyst on this project.

Speeding on the Information Superhighway

I heard a news item on the radio yesterday, that fully 50 percent of homes in the United States have computers. Many of those 100,000,000 computers are connected to the Internet, and lots of them are searching for graphology. What do you think they find?

A search on "graphology" through the **http://www.Altavista.digital.com** *search engine* yielded references to 3,214 graphology Web pages. Using the words "handwriting analysis," the number jumped to 3,424 pages. These pages are owned and maintained by graphologists from many different countries around the world.

In viewing some of them I had to cringe, because they project precisely the sort of "fortune-telling" image that handwriting professionals are trying so hard to shed. But many others provide valuable information and interesting graphics.

Grapho Lists

Write Words

A **search engine** helps you sort through the gazillions of pages of information available on the World Wide Web, to find what you are looking for. Yahoo, Altavista, Lycos, Excite, and InfoSeek are just a few examples of commonly used search engines.

Several graphology e-mail discussion groups exist on the Internet. RI Software operates, and I (loosely) moderate, The Vanguard Forum Online (VFO). Its international membership is comprised of people interested in handwriting on many different levels. We discuss various aspects of handwriting and human behavior, and the only rule is that there are to be no personal attacks on other members (this has been a problem in some groups). For information about the VFO, you can e-mail RI Software at *write@writinganalysis.com,* or me at *WriteChoice@prodigy.net.*

Gary Brown in Oregon started the first graphology e-mail list as a result of a round table discussion at a handwriting analysis conference in 1992. The idea was to unify different groups of graphologists by bringing them together through the Internet. Members discuss various aspects of handwriting analysis. For information e-mail Gary at *GBrown0007@aol.com.*

Jyera Low Toong Jye in Singapore, manages an Internet mailing list of nearly 400 members. The stated purpose of this list is to:

- Contribute questions and/or answers to the Grapho *FAQ*
- Surf the World Wide Web to look for new information to be added to FAQ or GCLUB library
- Talk about books and exchange book reviews
- Discuss handwriting analysis issues
- Initiate or participate in experimental projects
- Learn about graphology/handwriting analysis from each other
- Find someone to chat with via e-mail

Write Words

FAQ stands for "frequently asked questions." Most Web pages include a FAQ list.

To request membership, e-mail *tjlow@singnet.com.sg.*

Some handwriting analysis organizations now have their own Web sites to provide information, handwriting samples, and analyses for visitors to read. You can find some of them listed in Appendix A.

The International Graphoanalysis Society, a handwriting analysis proprietary vocational school, is at: **http://www.igas.com**. As far as I can tell, IGAS provides services for their students, only.

What's Next?

The latest release of *Sheila Lowe's Handwriting Analyzer* (5.0) has a relationship compatibility module for the Personal version. It is similar to the Job Manager, and you can compare the handwritings of two people to discover their strengths and weaknesses as a couple. *SLHA* 5.0 now gives the user the choice of producing a report written in the first-person voice or one in the second-person, depending on who the client is and how formal you need to be. We've also added lots of new illustrations to choose from.

In the not-too-distant future, we plan to work with a psychologist to create a special module for mental-health professionals. It is based on the *Diagnostic and Statistical Manual IV* and will feature some of the major personality disorders that can be identified in handwriting. After that, we plan on developing the Criminal Profiling module for law enforcement and other investigators.

On a related note, my newsletter, *The Vanguard,* is now available by e-mail, as well as "snail mail." Subscribers who received the first issue through cyberspace were thrilled at how easy it was and that they could print it out in color!

The possibilities are practically endless. See you in cyberspace!

The Least You Need to Know

- Computers are here to stay.
- Professional software is available to accurately analyze handwriting.
- The Internet has lots of information available about graphology. All you need is a basic computer system and you can surf the World Wide Web.

Chapter 27

Order in the Court

In This Chapter

- What's legal and what's not
- Invading their privacy?
- Avoiding accusations of defamation
- Protecting yourself and your client

Well, we've been through a lot together—about two years' worth of material if you were studying handwriting analysis in a classroom setting. Now we have to look at some important legal and ethical concerns to make sure that your practice of handwriting analysis maintains the highest possible standards.

Our discussion in this chapter focuses mainly on handwriting analysis in the employment field, but the principles apply to all applications of graphology. Whether you are doing analyses for a corporation or an individual, please don't skip these very important considerations. Knowing and following them will help to protect you in your practice.

Is It Legal?

Over the last few years, employers have begun to recognize handwriting analysis as an important tool in personnel selection and employee management. At the same time, they want to protect themselves from lawsuit-happy applicants and employees, and are concerned about the legality of using someone's handwriting this way.

Chicken Scratch

Handwriting practitioners who blatantly ignore employment laws and professional ethics put the entire field at risk. A lack of governmental regulations doesn't excuse poor professional practices. What one graphologist does affects all the rest.

Here's where I should probably insert some legal mumbo jumbo, telling you that what follows should not be construed as legal advice and that state laws vary, so you should check with your attorney. The information in this chapter applies generally to all handwriting professionals practicing in the United States. Okay, that said, let's move on.

Is It an Invasion of Privacy?

One of the biggest concerns employers raise is whether a handwriting analysis invades applicants' privacy. Some people do feel that their handwriting is private and shouldn't be used to tell anything about them.

In cases related to other personal matters, such as your likeness, the courts have decided that you have no right to privacy. Just ask the paparazzi! The same is true of your voice. Barring illegal wiretaps, if someone records your voice, it's not an invasion of privacy. That is, unless the situation where you were recorded was intended to be private.

Did you know that if you have a large bay window in the front of your house and you leave the curtains open, that you have no expectation of privacy if someone looks in? You'd have to pull the drapes and the peeper would have to go to extreme measures to see in before your right to privacy would be violated. Makes you want to draw the shades, doesn't it!

The law says that if a person doesn't take "reasonable steps" to protect his privacy, there is no expectation of privacy. We can apply this principle to handwriting analysis. When the applicant fills out the employment application form in his handwriting, he knows the employer and others are going to read it; therefore, there is no expectation of privacy.

Here's where a potential problem may arise. Let's say that Mr. Jones at XYZ Company, a small manufacturing business, hires a handwriting analyst to prepare a report on an applicant he is considering hiring for the sales manager position. The analyst prepares the report and blithely faxes it over to the office, assuming that Mr. Jones or his secretary will be there to receive the fax.

Instead, the receptionist picks up the fax, reads the report, and is interested in some comments that could be taken as negative about the applicant. In water cooler conversation, she repeats what she read to her friend, coloring it slightly with her own viewpoint. Her friend repeats the remark to someone in the receiving room, coloring it a bit more with her own viewpoint, and so on, and so on.... You get the picture.

The applicant's privacy may have been invaded, because even though he may have known a handwriting analyst would prepare a report about him, he did not expect that report to be distributed beyond those with a need to know. For the handwriting

Tales from the Quill

A high-profile handwriting professional received a telephone call informing her she was being sued. Why? The person bringing the lawsuit had been refused employment at a company who used handwriting analysis in the employment screening process, and she claimed she had not given permission for the handwriting analysis, so it was an invasion her privacy. At the trial, the handwriting analyst was able to show that the applicant had indeed signed a waiver, giving permission for her handwriting to be analyzed. The case was dismissed.

analyst to protect himself is a simple matter. Just call ahead and ask that Mr. Jones or someone he designates stand by the fax machine while the report is transmitting. That way, no one else will see what is said, and privacy is maintained.

Alternatively, you might mail the report and mark the envelope "Personal and Confidential." Or, some handwriting analysts prefer to give only oral reports.

You Have Defamed Me, Sir!

If an employer makes the handwriting analysis available to an applicant and the applicant feels it defames her, she might threaten a suit. Would she have grounds? Let's look at what constitutes *defamation*.

Defamation means spreading information, which is not true or which the person doing the spreading has no reasonable grounds to believe is true, to a "significant and important audience." When the graphologist writes a report, she is providing her opinion based on her background and knowledge of handwriting. Someone's opinion can't be wrong. However, if the case went to court and the graphologist had to defend her opinion, she had better be prepared to show exactly where and how she formed that opinion. Believe me, you don't want to face a Marcia Clark-type attorney unprepared!

Write Words

Defamation means the dissemination of information, which is not true or for which there is no reasonable grounds for the person making the representation to believe it to be true, to a significant and important audience.

The problem for the handwriting analysis community is, there's a real scarcity of recent research to back up our claims. We have to go back to the 1930s and 1940s for the best studies. It's very important to be aware of what has been done in research. You can download a copy of my *Annotated Bibliography of Research in the United States Since 1970* from my Web site at **http://www.writinganalysis.com**, or e-mail me at *writechoice@prodigy.net* for a copy.

Waivering the White Flag

One very good way to protect yourself is to ask the client to sign a waiver, releasing you from responsibility. The legal term is, "holding harmless." This means that if an applicant or employee decides to sue, he'll have to go after the employer, not you.

You can also supply a form for the applicant to sign, which says "You will not be denied employment based solely on the findings of the handwriting analyst." And this brings up another important point: Always make it clear to the employer that she should *not* base her opinion solely on your findings! The handwriting analysis should be one part of a bigger puzzle, which includes reference and background checks, skill testing, and anything else the employer can legally dream up.

To reiterate the earlier part of this discussion, the handwriting analysis report should be given only to those who have a direct need to know. That would probably be the prospective employee's supervisor or the human resources manager.

Sex, Drugs, and Rock 'n' Roll

Well, maybe not rock 'n' roll, but let's consider the issue of reporting on sexuality and substance abuse. The real question is, what should or should not be included in the handwriting analysis report?

To be safe and smart, the report you hand to your client should be prepared with a specific question in mind. For instance, "Does this person have the personality requirements for the job?" or "Why am I having problems keeping a relationship?" or "What is a good field for me to look for work?"

Fine Points

In the case of an applicant seeking a position as a schoolteacher or healthcare worker where red flags for inappropriate sexual behavior appear, the graphologist would be justified in discussing them with the client.

Once you know the question, your report should address the answer, directly and specifically. That means, unless the applicant's sexual functioning has some direct effect on the job, it is inappropriate to talk about. The applicant's sexual preferences or sex drive is not the employer's or your business.

To know what is appropriate and fair game for discussion, you'll need a good job description. Besides knowing the type of duties the employee will be handling, you'll need to know what type of environment she'll be working in. For instance, will she be in a private office on her own, with employees reporting to her? Or does the job require interaction with a team? Will her duties keep her tied to a desk, or will she be driving around in her car much of the time? Whom will she report to?

With the answers to these questions, you'll be much better equipped to provide a report that will be helpful to your client, the employer. Without them, all you can give is a mish-mash of personality traits, kind of like vegetable soup—good, unless you wanted navy bean. You have to know what they're looking for.

The job description will provide clues about whether the successful candidate needs to be more independent or more subordinate; whether she needs to handle many routine tasks or is required to make quick changes; whether the job calls for a more sedentary or a more active person; whether an outgoing personality is important, and numerous other items that the employer wants to know about.

Anyway, back to the original point. Don't discuss personal aspects that have no bearing on the job. There is one caveat to that rule: If you see danger signs—red flags—you are obligated to report them to your client. But do so in person or over the phone; don't put such warnings in writing. This would include signs of possible substance abuse, such as those outlined in Chapter 22.

Point of Impact

The Equal Employment Opportunity Commission (EEOC) deals with, among other things, job application testing procedures. They want to know whether a test discriminates against a prospective employee. If the answer is yes, the test violates Title 7 of the Civil Rights Act. It's called *Disparate Impact.*

A test would be discriminatory if it centered on race, age, gender, ethnicity, or religious affiliation. Add to that the Americans With Disabilities Act (ADA), which forbids discrimination against persons with mental or physical disabilities.

Handwriting analysis does not conclusively reveal age, gender, race, or religion, and the analyst usually does not meet or even see the applicant. Thus, it is one of the most non-discriminatory tests available. People who have contacted the EEOC to find out whether there was any reason why an employer shouldn't use handwriting analysis were told that "we are not aware of any evidence or cases which suggest that graphology has an adverse impact on a protected class."

Write Words

Disparate Impact occurs when an employment policy indirectly discriminates against one or more protected classes of individuals, or similar standards have different consequences. Protected classes include gender, race, age, religion, and national origin.

Sample Questions

When you instruct your client on how to obtain a legally sound handwriting sample, you may want to suggest he ask the applicant to write answers to questions such as the following:

- What would you like to accomplish over the next year?
- What special qualities do you have that will help you achieve your goals?
- What other qualities would you like to develop further?
- What interests you most about this position?
- What motivates you to do your best in a job?
- What is the biggest mistake you've made and what have you done about it?

Telling It Like It Is: Ethics and the Handwriting Analyst

Don't make hiring recommendations, that's not your job. The employer is the one who has all the facts and is responsible for deciding whether to hire an applicant or not. All you have is one piece of the puzzle, the handwriting, and you are not equipped to tell the employer that he should or should not hire someone. What you *can* do is provide an objective analysis of the applicant's personality based on the requirements for the job.

What if danger signs appear in the writing (see Chapter 22), such as potential for violence or evidence of substance abuse? The wise handwriting professional doesn't put such an opinion on writing, but discusses his or her concerns in person (or over the phone) with the client. Most importantly, make it clear to the client that handwriting is an indicator of past behavior and reveals only potential for future actions. You don't have a crystal ball and you aren't God (and isn't *that* relief!). It's not possible to predict whether the applicant will act on his potential, either for good or for bad.

Nobody's Perfect

Just as someone's personality may change over time, so can handwriting. According to the writer's reaction to various external factors such as physical or emotional trauma—a death in the family, divorce, health problems, or a job change—her handwriting may undergo some alteration.

Some medications, as well as alcohol and "recreational" drugs, may also have either a temporary or a lasting effect on the handwriting, and may potentially affect the handwriting analysis results somewhat. A tremendous range of variation exists in the human, and no method of personality assessment is perfect—even handwriting analysis!

What They Don't Know Can Hurt Them

As a handwriting professional, you'll need to train your clients in what you expect from them, as well as tell them what they can expect from you. Prepare an information sheet instructing them on what you will provide them, how much it will cost, and what kinds of information they can expect from it.

Also let the client know how to avoid any potential problems from lawsuits over handwriting analyses. Rita Risser's book, *Stay Out Of Court,* boils it down to three essential points:

- Request a handwriting sample of all applicants, whether their handwriting is to be analyzed or not.
- The analysis should keep the results of the handwriting analysis focused strictly on personality characteristics necessary for successful job performance.
- The handwriting analysis should be supplied only to those with a direct need to know the results (hiring committee, employer, supervisor).

It's best to examine original samples at least one page in length (this might be a good time to review Chapter 3 on what constitutes a good sample). When an inadequate sample (such as a photocopy, fax copy, or just a few lines) is supplied, the handwriting analyst's findings are considered qualified and subject to verification by examination of the original.

Ask Not What Your Client Can Do for You

The client/employer should be able to expect certain things from you, the handwriting analyst. Let's call it the Client's Bill of Rights:

- The Client has the right to expect competent services.
- The Client has the right to receive timely results.
- The Client has the right to expect an accurate analysis.
- The Client has the right to have his questions answered about the applicant's personality.

A prospective client may not know how to select a competent handwriting analyst. The most important thing for them to know is that any handwriting analyst engaged in preparing handwriting analysis reports for money should be certified by a reputable organization. Barring personal references from a happy user, he would be wise to contact one of the non-profit organizations, such as the American Handwriting Analysis Foundation (AHAF) or the American Association of Handwriting Analysts (AAHA). I'll tell you a bit more about them in a moment.

Tales from the Quill

A business owner who wanted to use handwriting analysis to hire a new receptionist saw a newspaper article featuring a graphologist in her town. The article claimed this woman was the "top graphologist in the country," and the business owner decided to contact her. On close questioning, the "top graphologist" admitted that her training was only a book claiming to make her a handwriting analyst in 10 minutes and "lots of analyses for her friends and relatives."

Once the client gets the referral and contacts the handwriting analyst he can ask to see references or testimonial letters. On the other side of this coin, if you are starting your professional practice as a handwriting analyst, you should begin requesting testimonial letters from the people you analyze and putting the letters into a portfolio. After all, when you select a doctor, a real estate agent, or an accountant, you probably want to know something about her background and training, and who her clients are, don't you? If not, you should! And so should your clients.

The client isn't the only one with rights. You have rights, too. So here's my Analyst's Bill of Rights:

- The Analyst has the right to expect an adequate handwriting sample for analysis.
- The Analyst has the right to qualify his or her opinion when the sample is less than adequate.
- The Analyst has the right to expect fees for services at the going rate, paid in a timely manner.
- The Analyst has the right to refuse to analyze a handwriting sample if the client does not offer proof of a reasonable "need to know," such as for employment.

When You Really Need to Know

As things stand at the beginning of the 21st century, anyone is free to call themselves a graphologist. While other human services fields have regulations and licensing to control what their practitioners can and can't do, there are no regulations governing handwriting analysts in the United States.

Even hairdressers must qualify for a license before they legally may touch your head. When it comes to handwriting analysis, which deals with the human psyche, the only limitations are those that the conscientious graphologist places upon herself. Without licensing or some type of state certification, the irresponsible practice of handwriting analysis runs wild. And, unfortunately, there are plenty of charlatans who take advantage of the unsuspecting public.

So, how's a prospective client supposed to know whether the person advertising handwriting analysis services is a professional who has devoted years to building a solid foundation of knowledge and honorable practice, or some jerk who thinks handwriting analysis is all about how you cross your t's and dot your i's?

Fine Points

A controversy over whether licensing would help has raged for years. At a cost of around $50,000 just to start the process on a state level, the point is moot. The organizations don't have the funds.

The good news is, there are several not-for-profit graphology organizations, as well as proprietary schools, which have instituted their own certification programs. Philosophical differences aside, they all seem to support a common goal—to elevate the status of graphology and re-invent it as a viable career option.

Becoming Certified: Just What Does It Mean?

In reality, under the present circumstances, only those who wish to be regulated are. If graphology is ever to achieve serious recognition as a profession, ethical practitioners must shoulder the responsibility of policing themselves—at least, until there's a graphologist's union.

Each graphology organization has its own unique certification process. Rumors are, efforts are being made toward reciprocation, so that, regardless of affiliation, members approved by one certifying board eventually will be recognized by the others.

In most cases, the certification examinations are done at home, open book. Sound easy? Not as easy as you'd think. Although you could answer all the questions based on theory by looking them up, there is more to the exams. Each one requires the applicant to prepare different types of handwriting analysis reports, justifying their findings. There's no way you can copy that from a book!

Not-for-profit groups, such as the American Handwriting Analysis Foundation (AHAF) based on the West Coast, and American Association of Handwriting Analysts (AAHA) in the Midwest, are educational organizations with members across a broad spectrum of interest in graphology.

Anyone can become a member of these groups, whether newly interested, hobbyist, or professional. Neither AHAF nor AAHA sponsors courses of their own, but they do provide lists of approved instructors and books for those who are interested in learning about handwriting. AHAF has chapters around the country that meet regularly, and AAHA has regional seminars in the spring and fall.

The National Society for Graphology on the East Coast, is another handwriting organization. It sponsors courses by Felix Klein, taught by his widow, Janice Klein. Members are not required to be students to join the organization, but may attend monthly meetings in New York City.

The contact information for these organizations is listed in Appendix B.

The other proprietary schools, such as INSYTE, Academy of Handwriting Sciences, the Step-By-Step System of Handwriting Analysis, and the Institute of Graphology offer their own certifications. You must graduate their courses to be certified by them. All are courses on my recommended list.

Finally, specifically for the handwriting professional, there is the Vanguard Network. The Vanguard is not a formal organization, but is a network of ethical handwriting professionals and serious students actively pursuing a career in the field. Members of the network are committed to high professional standards and enriching the body of knowledge currently available.

Chicken Scratch

Beware of any school or organization that warns you against associating with members of other groups—and there are some. Such attempts to protect the school's or organization's own membership seriously limit knowledge and understanding.

A professional-level certification examination has recently been put in place, with examinations held on-site at the Vanguard Conferences. Only practicing professionals with a solid background and experience are qualified to take the test. There is an additional test for those who specialize in employment profiling.

If you are a newer graphologist and want to know how well you are doing, there is a "benchmark test" and the possibility of entering an internship program. Interns are matched up with mentors who check their work and help them prepare for the professional examination. A free syllabus is available which details the requirements for the Vanguard Certification Program.

The Vanguard is actually an outgrowth of my own professional practice. Members enjoy the loose arrangement, which leaves no room for the political posturing sometimes seen in more conventional organizational structures. Besides the certification program, we offer seminars, conferences, an online e-mail discussion group, and a quarterly newsletter among the benefits available to members. You'll find information on joining the network in Appendix B.

The Last Word—Really!

It looks like our journey of discovery is about to come to a close. Feeling brain-dead? Don't worry, overload is a common condition right about this time. The best advice I can give you is to just relax and let it all simmer. Then, one day soon, you'll look at a handwriting sample and all of a sudden, you'll realize that you know what it means. Everything will come together and you'll get that big Aha! The personality behind the handwriting will become clear.

One very important lesson that I hope has come across in these pages is that nothing in handwriting means anything by itself. You must always look at the whole picture and consider any particular sign or feature in the context in which it appears.

By this time you should be able to answer some basic questions about personality from handwriting. Test yourself with these questions:

- Is the writing balanced and organized? (Chapters 5 and 6)
- Is the writer open and adaptable or full or fears? (Chapters 7 and 10)
- How does the writer behave socially? (Chapters 14, 15, and 16)
- How does the writer behave sexually? (Chapters 9 and 12)
- Where is the writer's main focus—mental, physical, emotional? (Chapter 9)
- How well-balanced is the writer's personality? (Chapters 5, 6, and 11)
- How is the writer's self-image? (Chapters 17, 18, and 19)
- What is the writer's energy level? (Chapters 8, 12, and 13)
- Are there danger signs? (Chapter 22)

Just remember, handwriting can't tell you everything about the writer—people are just too complex for that. But it can give you some important clues to help you understand how people function within their environment.

To learn how to analyze handwriting well, keep looking at handwritings and do lots of analyses. But no matter how many handwritings you study, and no matter how many analyses you do, never forget: Behind every handwriting is a human being, just like you. As the great graphologist and human being Felix Klein reminded fellow graphologists in a letter shortly before his death in 1994, *"Be kind. Everyone is fighting a hard battle."*

Happy Analyzing!

Fine Points

In my experience teaching graphology over the years, I've found that students learn more when they see a large number of handwriting samples to illustrate the various elements they are studying. Trying to comprehend all the possibilities from just a few samples can stunt your graphological growth.

The Least You Need to Know

- Handwriting analysis is legal, but should be used only within certain guidelines.
- Some opinions should not be committed to paper.
- Don't use psychological or medical jargon unless you have the proper credentials.
- Becoming certified is an important step for graphologists who care about their clients.

Appendix A

Glossary

airstroke The movement of the pen as it is raised from the paper and continues in the same direction in the air.

angular forms Sharp, straight strokes that are made by stopping the pen and changing direction before continuing.

arcade forms Forms that look like arches, rounded on the top and open at the bottom. Fast arcades have a more positive connotation than slow arcades.

baseline The invisible line upon which writing "rests."

connectedness The degree to which one letter attaches to another.

connective forms The shape of the connections between letters. The primary connective forms are garland, arcade, angular, and thread.

copybook The standard of handwriting instruction taught in a particular school. The most common copybook standards in the United States are D'Nealian and Palmer.

covering stroke A stroke that unnecessarily covers over another stroke in a concealing action.

cursive writing Writing in which one letter is joined to the next.

double curve An indefinite connective form that combines the arcade and the garland. Also called a "double s link," due to its resemblance to the letter s.

downstroke The movement of the pen toward the writer. The backbone of handwriting, without which the writing becomes completely illegible.

figure and ground The dark space (ink) and white space (paper). In the handwriting gestalt, it refers to the balance between the ink and the paper.

final The ending stroke on a letter when it is at the end of a word.

form The writer's chosen writing style. The way the writing looks, whether it is copybook, elaborated, simplified, or printed.

fullness The width of letters compared to their height. The ratio of height to width in the copybook model is 1:1 in the middle zone and 1:.5 in the upper and lower zones. Full writing is wider than copybook.

garland forms A cup-like connective form that is open at the top and rounded on the bottom.

gestalt The German word that means "complete" or "whole." A good gestalt needs nothing added or taken away to make it "look right." Also a school of handwriting analysis that looks at handwriting as a whole picture.

initial An added stroke at the beginning of a letter as it moves into the word.

knots Extra loops that appear as if tied in a knot.

letter space The amount of space left between letters.

ligature The connections that tie one letter to another.

line direction Movement of the baseline. May slant up, down, or straight across the page.

line space The amount of space left between lines.

margins The amount of space left around the writing on all four sides.

movement Writing in four dimensions: across the page, up and down as it goes from left to right, into the paper, and above the paper (airstroke).

narrowness The width of upper- and lower-zone letters is less than half the middle-zone height (see, also, **fullness**).

natural handwriting The writing of someone who has reached graphic maturity and no longer needs to stop and consciously think about what he is writing.

pen hold The place where the writer grasps the barrel of the pen and the angle at which he holds it.

personal pronoun I The capital letter I, the one single letter in the English language that represents the writer.

pressure There are several types of pressure: Grip pressure refers to how tightly the writer holds the pen; Primary pressure is the degree to which the pen digs into the paper; Secondary pressure is the rhythm of light/dark strokes produced by movement on the paper.

printed writing Disconnected writing.

printscript A creative combination of printing and cursive writing.

Psychogram A circular graph devised by Dr. Klara Roman in the 1930s to provide a visual measurement of personality.

rhythm Periodicity, alternation of movement.

school model Same as copybook—the style of writing taught in school.

simplification Eliminating extra or superfluous strokes from the copybook model.

size May refer to the overall size of the writing or the proportions between zones.

slant The angle between the up- and downstrokes in relation to the baseline.

space The overall pattern of spatial arrangement on the paper. Includes the width of margins, and letter, word, and line spacing.

speed The personal pace at which the writer's pen moves across the paper.

supported strokes Upstrokes partially covering the previous downstrokes. Originally taught in European schools.

tension The degree of force exerted on the pen compared to the degree of relaxation.

thready forms An indefinite connective form that looks flat and wavy.

trait stroke A school of handwriting analysis that assigns personality trait names to individual writing strokes.

tremor Shakiness along the writing stroke produced by poor physical health, anxiety, or external causes.

upstroke Movement of the pen away from the writer.

variability The degree to which the writing varies from the copybook model.

word space The amount of space left between words.

writing impulse The result of the pen touching down on the paper and moving across the page, until it is raised from the paper.

writing zones The three distinct areas of writing: upper, middle, and lower zones. Each represents a specific area of personality functioning, but all work together to produce the whole person.

Appendix B

Recommended Handwriting Analysis Organizations and Schools

Recommended Organizations

The Vanguard Network for Handwriting Professionals and Serious Students

The Vanguard is not a formal organization. It is a network of ethical handwriting professionals and serious students actively pursuing a career in handwriting analysis. Members of the network are committed to maintaining ethical professional standards and cultivating their analytical abilities and competency.

The Vanguard offers the first advanced testing specifically designed for those engaged in the professional practice of graphology. The program is authored and administered by a team of highly skilled, dedicated handwriting and mental health professionals. Vanguard is committed to offering examinations that challenge applicants to demonstrate mastery of the academic fundamentals demanded by their discipline. The examinations provide a benchmark by which to gauge the applicant's competence on various levels of expertise.

The Vanguard offers a quarterly periodical, seminars, and conferences. Information about events, a certification syllabus, and a free copy of the Vanguard newsletter are available for downloading from **http://www.writinganalysis.com**. You may contact me directly by phone at (661) 259-8979 or e-mail at *writechoice@prodigy.net.*

Nonprofit Handwriting Analysis Organizations in the United States

There are several handwriting analysis organizations in the United States. If you are interested in joining a formal organization, I recommend contacting the following ones. They are all not-for-profit educational groups that welcome anyone who is interested in handwriting. Most offer newsletters, conferences, and certification testing.

American Handwriting Analysis Foundation
P.O. Box
San Jose, CA 95150
Phone: (800) 826-7774
e-mail: *ahaf@tucson.com*
Web site: **http://www.tucson.com/handwriting**

American Association of Handwriting Analysts
P O Box 3087
Southfield, MI 48037-3087
Phone: (248) 746-0740
e-mail: *AAHAOffice@aol.com*

National Society for Graphology
250 W. 57th St., Suite 1228A
New York, NY 10108
Phone: (212) 265-1148

American Society of Professional Graphologists
2025 Kings Highway
Brooklyn, NY 11229
Phone: (718) 339-6868

Handwriting Analysis Research Library
Robert E. Backman, Curator
91 Washington St.
Greenfield, MA 01301-3411
Phone: (413) 774-4667

Overseas Handwriting Analysis Organizations

UNITED KINGDOM

The British Academy of Graphology
Administrative Centre
11 Roundacre
London SW19 6DB
United Kingdom
Phone: (181) 876 5338
Web site: **http://www.graphology.co.uk**

British Institute of Graphology
24–26 High Street
Hampton Hill, Middx TW12 1PD
Web site: **www.BritishGraphology.org**

International Graphology Association
Stonedge, Dunkerton, Bath BA28AS
England
e-mail: *ljw@graphology.ork.uk*

BELGIUM

Belgian Graphologists' Association
67, rue de la allee
1050 Brussels
Belgium
Phone: (2) 653-0611

THE NETHERLANDS

Dutch Graphological Society
Postbus 918
3160 AC Rhoon
The Netherlands
Phone: (10) 501-6119
e-mail: *maresi.de.monchy@wxs.nl*

FRANCE

Groupement des Graphologues Conseils de France
c/o Monique Riley
49, rue Ste. Radegonde
78100 St. Germain-en-Laye
France
Phone: (1) 39-73-12-16

SPAIN

Maria-Victoria Sen Samaranch
Paseo Bonanova 17
08022 Barcelona
Spain
Phone: (93) 418-0223

GERMANY

Helmut Ploog
Rossinistreet 9
D-85598 Baldham Near Munich
Germany
Phone: 81-06-83-05
e-mail: *dr.ploog@t-online.de*

CANADA

Graziella Pettinati
3330 Chemin Ste. Foy
Ste. Foy, QC
Canada GIX 1Z8
Phone: (418) 659-7254
e-mail: *graffiti@acica.com*

ITALY

Fausto Brugnatelli
Milan, Italy
e-mail: *brgcons@tiscalinet.it*

Recommended Schools of Handwriting Analysis

Numerous correspondence courses are available in handwriting analysis, and I am pleased to recommend several of which I have personal knowledge and experience. They are all distance learning programs that you can do in your own time, in your own home.

Felix Klein's Courses

The Felix Klein gestalt graphology courses, now taught by Janice Klein, consist of three levels: Elementary, Intermediate, and Advanced. Each level has 10 lessons and may be paid for on a lesson-by-lesson basis (no contract to sign). The Elementary course includes trend, connections, slant, pressure, style evaluation, and so forth.

The Intermediate level covers the "pictures" of movement, form, and space; printed writing; insincerity and dishonesty, and so on, and requires the student to write analyses for the samples that accompany each lesson.

The Advanced level includes personnel selection and vocational guidance; lessons on the psychological theories of Freud, Jung, Adler, Fromm, and Wittlich, and how those theories can be seen in handwriting. Additionally, New York area students have the option of learning in private sessions. Students who successfully complete all three courses may apply for professional certification by the National Society of Graphology. Contact: Janice Klein, 250 W. 57th St., Suite 1228A, New York, NY 10108. Phone: (212)-265-1148.

The Insyte Challenge

This course, taught by Sister June Canoles, combines holistic and trait-stroke methods. Students must EVALUATE from day one in lesson one. It includes 20 lessons of approximately 26 pages each with practice exercises in each lesson, final tests, super sheets, flash cards, scrapbook work, and enrichment cassettes. Comprehensive exams are given after every five lessons to indicate what each student knows and can use to do an analysis.

The main emphasis is on the holistic approach toward analysis. Their aim is to turn out analysts who can write a professional, concise report. Students are free to call for further information if they do not understand any part of the course. A short, individualized cassette tape addressing the student's concerns is included with each corrected chapter. Sister June is working toward California State Certification.

Contact: June Canoles, Insyte, Inc., 10351 S. Blaney Ave., Cupertino, CA, 95014-3122. e-mail: *J96Write@aol.com.*

Step-by-Step System of Handwriting Analysis

The SSS course is a very comprehensive course taught by Erika Karohs, for the serious student who wants to become a truly professional analyst. Prior knowledge of handwriting analysis is desirable but not a prerequisite. The course starts from the very beginning. With the course you will also receive a free four-volume set of "Measurements in Handwriting with Interpretations for All Measurements."

The Basic Course is trait-stroke oriented and covers 100 personality traits with many illustrations and comprehensive illustrations. It provides a worksheet that can be used as a guide for writing the analysis, and self-tests with model answers for each lesson. In essence, you get all the information for which other handwriting analysis schools charge hundreds (thousands!) of dollars.

The Basic II Course is trait-stroke oriented and covers both basic (review) and evaluated traits. It is thoroughly illustrated and features comprehensive trait descriptions. It provides a worksheet that can be used as a guide for writing the analysis and 18 self-tests with model answers for each lesson.

The Intermediate Course of Handwriting Analysis is an integrated course that combines both trait strokes and a holistic approach.

The student receives full e-mail support throughout the courses. Please write for a brochure or go to **http://members.tripod.com/~Margarete/Intermediate_Graphology_Course.html**.

Contact: Erika Karohs; 4080 Sunset Lane, Pebble Beach, CA. 93953. Phone: (408)-624-8151. e-mail: *karohs@juno.com.*

Handwriting Analysis: A Fundamental Course

This course is recommended for the student who is new to graphology or one who desires a review of the essential teachings of handwriting analysis. The director of education of the American Association of Handwriting Analysts writes: "This course lives up to its name. Its contents are concise yet comprehensive; challenging yet uncomplicated."

There are three levels with emphasis on a progression from Basic to Advanced material. The student may enroll for the entire course, but is encouraged to divide the material into three separate learning experiences, and pay as he goes. While the suggested study time is a minimum of 12 months, the pace may be adjusted according to the needs of the individual student. Comprehension and application skills are assessed through a series of self-study questions and a final exam for each level. Certificates of Completion are awarded to the graduates of each level.

Contact: Kate Wright, P.O. Box 3087 Southfield, MI 48037-3087. Phone: (248) 746-0719. Fax: (248) 746-0756. e-mail: *hwateacher@aol.com.*

Academy of Handwriting Sciences

The Academy maintains a faculty of 12 teachers and offers a long-distance learning program which includes four courses. The course may be taken through correspondence or on-site with a satellite teacher in selected areas around the U.S.

The four courses include beginning, intermediate, advanced and vocational studies. The comprehensive training includes step-by-step lessons, hundreds of handwriting illustrations, flash cards, review questions, examinations, complex charts, extensive report writing, recommended reading, and more. The Academy provides a personalized and thorough review of the student's lessons and questions. A certificate of achievement is awarded at the satisfactory completion of each course.

The courses are designed to build on the knowledge of the previous lesson material and enable the student to gain a holistic concept of handwriting analysis. The emphasis on report writing teaches the student how to prepare a professional, legally sound report. The courses are self-paced and lessons can be submitted via mail, fax, or e-mail. Enrollment with the Academy also entitles the student to a free subscription to the quarterly newsletter *Penline*. Courses can be purchased separately and payment terms can be arranged on a case-by-case basis.

Contact: Heidi H. Harralson, Director of Teaching, P.O. Box 65095, Tucson, AZ 85728. Phone: (520) 529-8531. e-mail: *Hapiwriter@aol.com.*

Institute of Graphological Sciences

The first Texas State-licensed school in the United States, the tIGS courses combine the trait stroke with the holistic approach. This bimodal approach draws on the merits and capabilities of all aspects of graphology. Course work couples the traits with the gestalt method, emphasizing space, form and movement.

Students learn to create an in-depth psychological profile through a thorough understanding of every graphological factor presented. Complete cassette tape programs accompany all course texts, and many supplemental books are available. Professional graders grade the course exams. Instruction is available by correspondence or in the classroom.

Contact: Pat Johnson, PO Box 793743, Dallas TX 75379. Phone: (800) 960-1034 or (214) 351-3668.

Appendix C

Bibliography

Jacoby, Hans J. *Analysis of Handwriting*. London: George Allen & Unwin Ltd, 1938.

Pulver, Max. *The Symbolism of Handwriting*. London: Scriptor Books, 1994 (translated from the German original 1931 edition).

Roman, Klara. *Encyclopedia of the Written Word*. New York: Frederick Ungar, 1968.

Roman, Klara. *Personality in Handwriting*. New York: Pantheon Books, 1952.

Saudek, Robert. *Experiments in Handwriting*. London: George Allen & Unwin, 1929; reprint edition, Books for Professionals, 1978.

———. *The Psychology of Handwriting*. London: George Allen & Unwin, 1926; reprint edition, Books for Professionals, 1978.

Sonnemann, Ulrich. *The Psychology of Handwriting*. New York: Grune & Stratton, 1950.

Victor, Frank. *Handwriting, A Personality Projection*. Charles C. Thomas, Publisher, Springfield, Illinois, 1952; reprint edition, Fern Ridge Press, Eugene, Oregon, 1989.

Wolff, Werner. *Diagrams of the Unconscious*. New York: Grune & Stratton, 1948.

Appendix D

Code of Ethics for Graphologists Practicing in the United States

The following Code of Ethics was developed by a board of handwriting professionals as a result of the 1995 Vanguard Conference at Los Angeles, California. The code is not attached to any group or organization, but was adopted as a globally applicable first step toward standardizing the profession of handwriting analysis.

Preamble*

Graphology is the study of writing as it relates to personality. A graphologist is a person trained over a period of at least two years of intensive study in the field of handwriting analysis/graphology.

Graphologists work to develop a valid and reliable body of scientifically acceptable knowledge based on research. They may apply that knowledge to human behavior as it is manifested via handwriting. In doing so, they perform many roles, such as researcher, educator, diagnostician, supervisor, consultant, and expert witness. Their goal is to broaden knowledge of behavior and, where appropriate, to apply it pragmatically, to improve the condition of both the individual and society.

Graphologists respect the central importance of freedom of inquiry and expression in research, teaching, and publication. They also strive to help the public in developing informed judgments and choices concerning human behavior. This Code of Ethics provides a common set of values upon which graphologists build their professional and scientific work.

---

*The preamble was adapted from the code of ethics of the American Psychological Association.

This Code is intended to provide both the general principles and the decision rules to cover most situations encountered by graphologists. It has as its primary goal the welfare and protection of the individuals and groups with whom graphologists work. It is the individual responsibility of each graphologist to aspire to the highest standards of conduct. Graphologists respect and protect human and civil rights, and do not knowingly participate in or condone unfair discriminatory practice.

The development of a dynamic, meaningful code of ethics for a graphologist's work-related conduct requires a personal commitment to a lifelong effort to act ethically; to encourage ethical behavior by students, supervisees, employees, and colleagues, as appropriate; and to consult with others, as needed, concerning ethics of the profession. Each graphologist supplements, but does not violate, the Code's value and rules on the basis of guidance drawn from personal values, culture, and experience.

Recognizing the different titles the profession of handwriting analysis has had in the United States, for the purposes of this Code, the title GRAPHOLOGIST is used. "Graphologist" shall include therefore, the other known titles, such as analyst, handwriting analyst, handwriting examiner, handwriting professional, and graphoanalyst. The choice of graphologist as the name of the professional in no way reflects negatively on the other titles; however, since the profession is known around the world by its generic name, "graphology," we have decided to use this name only.

Code of Ethics

1. The object of this Code of Ethics is to define the rights and responsibilities of graphologists wishing to exercise their profession in accordance with acceptable professional standards and the respective laws of the state in which the graphologist practices.
2. The graphologist is expected to maintain and develop his or her specialized skills by obtaining appropriate professional training. This may be accomplished through such venues as academic seminars, technical training, workshops, or the like. The graphologist is to follow developments in the profession and be aware of the literature relevant to the practice of graphology.
3. The graphologist studies the personality of the writer by examining an original sample of writing. When examining a facsimile or a photocopy of the original sample, the graphologist should have accompanying information regarding the pressure. It is further recommended that when giving a report on a fax or a photocopied sample, a disclaimer be included to indicate that the opinion rendered is qualified until such time as an original is made available.
4. The graphologist shall practice only within his or her area of competence or expertise. Consistent with the laws in the state where the graphologist practices, no diagnosis regarding physical or mental health problems will be given unless the graphologist is a psychologist or a physician.

5. The work undertaken by the graphologist concerning the human person imposes the respect of moral and professional values. The graphologist must safeguard at all times their own independence, integrity and sense of humanity. The practice of graphology must be free of racial, gender, religious or political biases.
6. The graphologist, as with other professionals, shall not use the information obtained from the handwriting to harm the writer, even if the writer is not the client, but a third party. Furthermore, in conveying their findings, the graphologist should specify that the information contained therein is confidential and should be used for professional purposes only. Graphologists who perform third-party analyses shall request of the client to inform the writer that their handwriting sample is subject to examination by a professional graphologist.
7. The graphologist shall adhere to the highest levels of confidentiality and shall not disclose any information regarding the client. In accordance with the laws of confidentiality, the report produced by the graphologist shall be provided only to the client supplying the sample. A disclaimer in the report is desirable, stating that, should the legal owner of the report choose to disseminate said written reports further, it would be at the sole discretion and responsibility of the owner of such reports.
8. The graphologist shall not disseminate or publish texts or analyses without the written agreement of the interested party or the owner of the document. However, handwriting samples may be used as long as the graphologist respects the anonymity and protects the identity of the writers.
9. Being the sole judge of the worth of the documents submitted to him/her, the graphologist shall reserve the right to refuse to provide an analysis without having to give any reason for doing so. The graphologist shall refuse to express an opinion on a document they know or suspect to be stolen, obtained in violation of any state or federal law, or under other questionable circumstances.
10. Each association, or grouping of graphologists, having signed this Code of Ethics, shall undertake to ensure that it is respected and applied by all their qualified members. Each respective association of graphologists signatory to this Code shall establish and maintain a Board of Ethics. The responsibilities of such Board shall be to investigate the complaints made to the Board regarding questionable behavior of the graphologist; meet with the graphologist in question and render a decision on whether or not any rules of the Code of Ethics have been violated. Such a decision shall be made public by listing the name of the graphologist in the publication of said association, to the local association of attorneys, and to the National Board of Ethics of Graphology.

In cases of flagrant misconduct, the certifying body of the offending graphologist should consider suspension or revocation of certification and membership. Flagrant cases would include, but are not limited to breach of confidentiality, misrepresentation, fraudulent claims of education, and overstatement of credentials.

Should the state where the offending graphologist practices adopt certification or licensing laws of graphologists, the Board of Ethics, upon finding the Code has been violated, shall relate such findings to the Regulatory authorities of the state.

__________________________________ ______________

Signature Date

If you wish to participate in this Code of Ethics, please sign and return the original document to:

The Vanguard
25746 Leticia Dr.
Valencia CA 91355-2263

Keep a copy for your records.

Appendix E

Example #1

Example #2

The Good, the Bad, and the Ugly

This appendix contains handwritings of some famous and some infamous people. The samples are here for your enjoyment and to help you practice your new-found graphology skills.

Founding Fathers and Presidents

tice has been allowed, will be a source
of much discontent; and of course
calls for very correct proceedings
in the execution of the Treaties, and
Laws respecting the case. —
Mount Vernon 22 July
1796.
G. Washington

George Washington

either with them. He is acquainted that
we have full Powers to treat & conclude;
and that the Congress promise in our Commission to ratify and confirm, &c. — I am
ever, Yours most affectionately
April 14. 1782 B Franklin

Benjamin Franklin

John Hancock

John Hancock

Abraham Lincoln

under God, shall have a new birth of freedom and that government of the people, by the people, for the people, shall not perish from the earth.

Abraham Lincoln

Theodore Roosevelt

We stand for enforcement of the law and for obedience to the law; our government is a government of orderly liberty equally alien to tyranny and to anarchy; and its foundation stone is the observance of the law, alike by the people and by their public servants. We hold ever before us as the all-important end of policy and administration the reign of peace at home and throughout the world; of peace, which comes only by doing justice.

Theodore Roosevelt

Woodrow Wilson

deal of inconvenience. The fact is, I've been rushed beyond all precedent; was obliged at last, to revise it on a (violently vibrating) Bay Line boat, and now send it off while I am en route at this place. Pray forgive me.—

In haste, with much regard

Sincerely Yours,

Woodrow Wilson

Harry Truman

Discussing plans for the campaign of 1944, and many other things of interest to the President and the new nominee for Vice President.

This was in July 1944.

H.S.T.

Dwight D. Eisenhower

Darling:

This is the briefest kind of a note; it merely represents my final chance in 1942 to tell you I love you and that you mean everything to me. Before the New Year can become the old I hope to see you, in person, to tell you these things much more explicitly than I can on cold paper. But whether I see you soon or not — I want you to know, and to remember, that my eventual return to you fills the nicest dreams and most comforting thoughts I have. In my time I've been entangled momentarily — I've never been in love with anyone but you! I never will,

John F. Kennedy

for your country – my fellow
citizen of the world – ask not
what America or others will do for you –
but rather what you can do
for freedom. Rather ask of us –

Lyndon B. Johnson

Lyndon B. Johnson

Richard Milhouse Nixon

the show up to an
earlier hour. It is too
good to be wasted on
inebriated night owls
who get bored. The
Johnny Carson –
With warm regards
RN

Gerald R. Ford

We hope you and your
family have a wonderful Holiday
Season.
Warmest regards,
Jerry Ford

Jimmy Carter

This is the approach we're taking at our Center -
J Carter

Ronald Reagan

Well Here's everything you wish yourself for Christmas
Ronald Reagan

George Bush

Thanks so very much for the hospitality; but, even more, thanks for all you and the teachers there are doing to help all those great kids. Sincerely. George Bush

William Jefferson Clinton

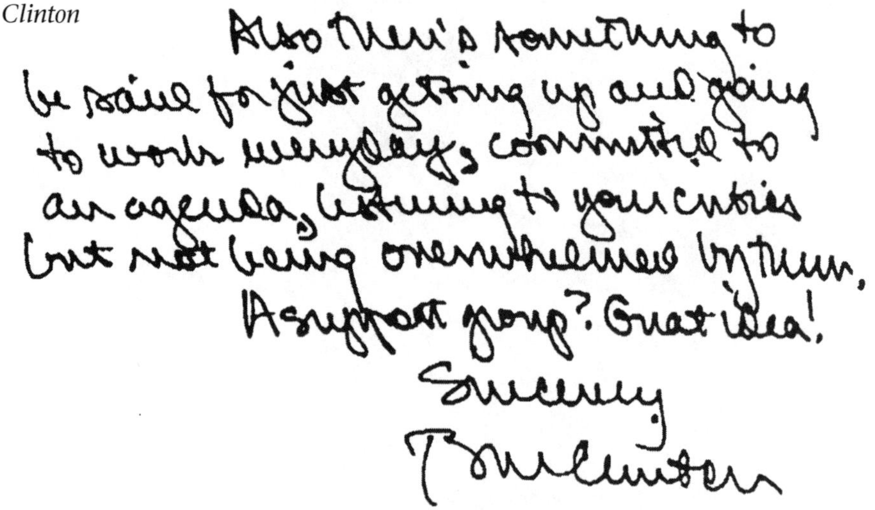

Also there's something to be said for just getting up and going to work everyday, committed to an agenda, listening to your critics but not being overwhelmed by them. A support group? Great idea!

Sincerely

Bill Clinton

American Heroes

Charles Lindbergh

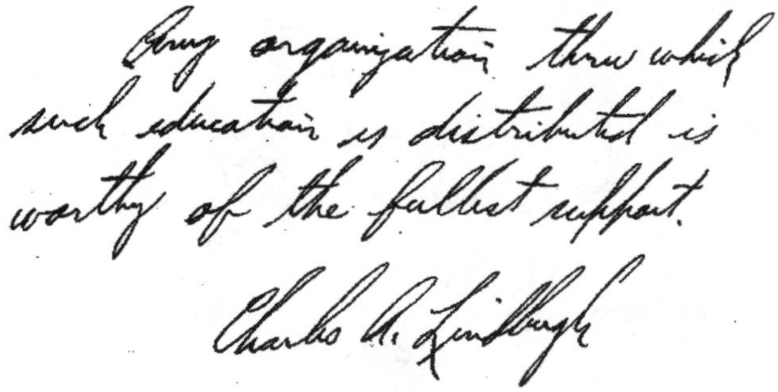

Any organization thru which such education is distributed is worthy of the fullest support.

Charles A. Lindbergh

John Glenn

Warmest regards from John H. Glenn Jr.

time
When we got home safe to
the fire I felt as though I
had been years away - and
would an ocean voyage
And it seemed to me that it
is terrifying how nearly one

Anne Morrow Lindbergh

Perhaps we can consider
an idea or two that
should be tested to
see if it may be of
some value —
All good wishes,
Jonas Salk
9 Feb. 1987

Jonas Salk

Colin Powell

The Clinton Affair

Hillary Rodham Clinton

Thanks for your encouragement and support. With your help and support, we'll have a great victory on November 3rd.
Best wishes —
Hillary

Gennifer Flowers

Bill, I've tried to explain my financial situation to you and how badly I need a job. Enclosed, is some correspondence that will be of interest to you. Unfortunately, it looks like I will have to persue the law suit to, hopefully, get some money to live on, until I can get employment.
Please, be in touch.

Gennifer

Kathleen Willey

Kathleen Willey

Dear Mr. President,
What a wonderful week you have had! Congratulation on all of your well deserved successes.
I would very much like to have a few minutes of your time to discuss something of importance to me.
I will wait to hear from you —
Fondly, Kathleen

November 22, 1993

Monica Lewinksy

Maybe the next time we come to eat here you can join us. I would like that a lot.

Have fun with your class at Nathan's next week.

All the best,
Monica Lewinsky

Linda Tripp

Linda R. Tripp

Kenneth Starr

Date: July 28, 1998 Kenneth W. Starr
KENNETH W. STARR
Independent Counsel

Paula Jones

Paula Jones
PAULA JONES

Entertainers

Paula Cole

I have my compositional tool (my piano) my cat friends and my habits (I've nearly forgotten them while touring over a year now – madness). I can see myself and my music gestating at home over many cups of tea and nights awake.

Kurt Cobain

...nsitive, unappreciati...
a goddess of a wife who sweats ambition and empath...
much of what I used to be. full of love and Joy, 19...
...yone is good and wil do her no harm. And that terrifies m...
...ction. I cant stand the thought of Frances becoming t...
...er that I've become. I have It Good. Very Good.
...of seven I've become hateful towards all humans in genera...
...people to get along and have empathy. Empathy! Onl...
...ople too much I guess. Thank you all from th...
...letters and concern during the past years. Fr...

Christian Slater

football game at Richard
Marcio's house. I will
call when I get there
Love you
C

Jimmy Smits

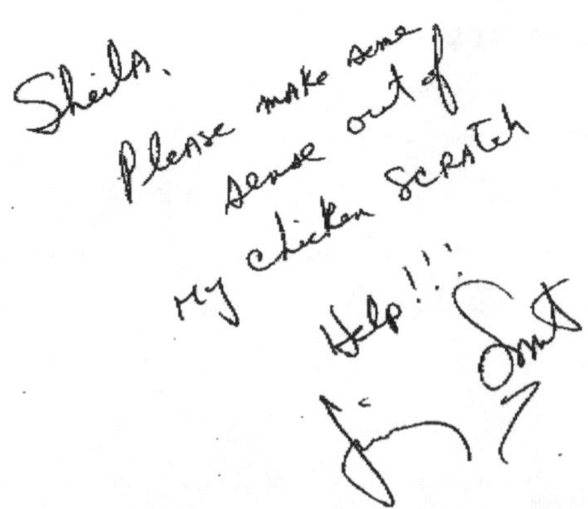

Sheila.
Please make some
sense out of
my chicken SCRATCH
Help!!!
Jimmy Smits

Dubious Characters

Jack the Ripper

police officers just for jolly wouldnt
you. Keep this letter back till I
do a bit more work, then give
it out straight. My knife's so nice
and sharp I want to get to work
right away if I get a chance.
Good luck.

Yours truly
Jack the Ripper

Dont mind me giving the trade name.

Richard Ramirez

I've been incarcerated
for 10 years. you might of heard
about me. I'm presently awaiting
trial in San Francisco. I can't
use the phone here. But when I
go to San Francisco jail I could
call you if you'd like. I'm 6'1"
175 lbs have black hair and
I'm 35 years old. I'm hoping
you'll write back.

Take Care,
Richard

here's my address:
Richard Ramirez E370[illegible]
San Quentin Prison
San Quentin CA
94974

Ted Bundy

Thank you for your October 2 letter and the card you sent October 27. You heard the news about Graham signing another death warrant against me. I'm doing fine. This is the third warrant (a record) that I've gone through in nine months. I've grown somewhat accustomed to living with such a threat.

There's a good chance that the courts will block the November 18 execution. If they do, I'll write again and some of the things you raised in your letter about doing

the system checks out from
one end to the other in my
tests. What you do not know
is whether the death machine
is at the sight or whether
it is being stored in my
basement for future use.
I think you do not have the
man power to stop this one
by continually searching the
road sides looking for this
thing. & it wont do to re route
& re schedule the bus as bec
ause the bomb can be adapted
to new conditions.
Have fun !! By the way
it could be rather messy
if you try to bluff me.

PS. Be shure to
print the part I
marked out on
page 3 or I shall
do my thing

JonBenet Ramsey ransom letter

Mr. Ramsey,

Listen carefully! We are a group of individuals that represent a small foreign faction. We respect your bussiness but not the country that it serves. At this time we have your daughter in our posession. She is safe and unharmed and if you want her to see 1997, you must follow our instructions to the letter.

You will withdraw $118,000.00 from your account. $100,000 will be in $100 bills and the remaining $18,000 in $20 bills. Make sure that you bring an adequate size attache to the bank. When you get home you will put the money in a brown paper bag. I will call you between 8 and 10 am tomorrow to instruct you on delivery. The delivery will be exhausting so I advise you to be rested. If we monitor you getting the money early, we might call you early to arrange an earlier delivery of the

Jeffrey Dahmer

During my stay at CCC, I have had a chance to look at my life from an angle that was never presented to me before. What I did was deplorable. The world has enough misery in it without my adding more to it. Sir, I can assure you that it will never happen again. This is why, Judge Gardner, I am requesting from you a sentence modification. So that I may be allowed to continue my life as a productive member of our society.

Respectfully Yours,
Jeff Dahmer

Adolph Hitler

Das zweite Kriegsjahr [illegible]

1939 – Auf den Polenfeldzug –

1940 – Nach Norwegen
Belgien
Holland
Frankreich
und England.

[illegible]

Rückblick:
1923.

im W.H. aufgeben. Mit der Gauleitung Baden bitte
ich eine offizielle Propaganda für diese Schrift
zu verbieten. Anempfehlung an den badischen Orts-
gruppen, aber keine [illegible].

Viele Grüße
Ihr H. Himmler

Henrich Himmler

Lyle Menendez

I'd be glad to correspond.
My time is limited now but
we can try. I have everything
I need but thanks for the

Eric Menendez

I'M SORRY THAT IT HAS
TAKEN ME SO LONG TO GET BACK
TO YOU. I'VE JUST BEEN SO BUSY
I HOPE YOU ARTWORK IS STILL
GOING WELL! I KNOW HOW MUCH
FUN THAT IS.
I'LL HEAR FROM YOU SOON
Erik

British Royalty

Princess Diana

the last few days — I can't imagine what you must be going through, the pain & total devastation. Diana

Prince Charles

BUCKINGHAM PALACE

4th October, 1988

Thank you so much for your very kind message on Saturday. It was enormously appreciated and obviously brought me luck for at least I completed the course!

Charles

Index

A

E

F

G

H

I

J

K

L

M

N

O

P

Q

R

S

T

U

V

W

X-Z